THE BLUE

The Niinnion Tablet from Eleusis

BLUE GUIDE

ATHENS

AND ENVIRONS

Robin Barber

*Maps, plans and atlas drawn by
John Flower*

A & C Black
London

W W Norton
New York

Third edition 1992

Published by A & C Black (Publishers) Limited
35 Bedford Row, London WC1R 4JH

© A & C Black (Publishers) Limited

ISBN   0–7136–3506–1

A CIP catalogue record for this book
is available from the British Library

Published in the United States of America by
WW Norton & Company, Incorporated
500 Fifth Avenue, New York NY 10110

Published simultaneously in Canada by
Penguin Books Canada Limited
2801 John Street, Markham, Ontario L3R 1B4

ISBN   0–393–30838–3

Robin Barber was born in Chapel en le Frith, Derbyshire, in 1940. At
present Senior Lecturer in Classics at Edinburgh University, he is an
M.A. (Classics) and Ph.D. of St. Andrews University and holds the
Oxford Diploma in Classical Archaeology. He has travelled in Greece
for over 25 years, five of which were spent there, first as Greek State
Scholar (for research in Aegean archaeology), then as Assistant
Director of the British School at Athens. He has done fieldwork in
Crete and the Cyclades and published numerous articles on Greek art
and archaeology. His book *The Cyclades in the Bronze Age* appeared
in 1987. He is also author of *Blue Guide Greece*. Amongst particular
Greek enthusiasms, he would count the poems of G. Seferis, the
rebetika songs of Sotiria Bellou and walking in the countryside.

Typeset by CRB Typesetting Services, Ely, Cambs.
Printed and bound in Great Britain by
Butler & Tanner Ltd, Frome and London

PREFACE

The first edition of the Blue Guide to Athens and Environs was produced by Stuart Rossiter in 1962 in advance of the Blue Guide to Greece, on which he was working at the time. A second edition appeared in 1981.

This third edition takes account of archaeological and other developments in the city since 1981 and provides, in addition, a revised and expanded section of Practical Information.

My renewed thanks are due to many of those mentioned in the preface to the fifth edition of the Blue Guide to Greece whose contributions were relevant to Athens and Attica. In the preparation of this volume I have been helped particularly by Ann Thomas, John Camp, Olga Hadjianastasiou and Guy Sanders. I am greatly indebted to Karin Skawran for compiling, at very short notice, the part of the introductory article which covers Early Christian and Byzantine antiquities and to Peter Lock for his advice on post-Byzantine material

John Flower's contribution in the form of new or revised maps and plans has been, as always, fundamental, as has the ready and good humoured assistance of Gemma Davies and Judy Tither at A & C Black.

The problems of contemporary Athenian life are not unknown to the outside world. They are however not so very different from those of any other modern city and the visitor will find ample compensation in the extensive survivals of the city's rich and fascinating history, in the quaint corners and chance encounters in which Athens abounds, and in seeking out the gentler delights of rural Attica. Athens too has more to offer than ancient remains. There is much fine 19 and 20C architecture; the city has a flourishing community of artists and Greece's rich musical tradition (as well as the exciting work of contemporary composers) is well represented in the capital. Amongst more modest pleasures of Athenian life taverna-hunting has always been a preoccupation of habitués. Whether this leads you to the slopes of Hymettos, Piraeus, the coast or countryside of Attica, or the courtyard (avli) or interior (according to season) of a traditional city taverna, a little courage in tackling the unknown is likely to be well rewarded in terms of informal local colour and good, if unpretentious, food and wine.

A NOTE ON BLUE GUIDES

The Blue Guides series began in 1918 when Muirhead Guide-Books Limited published 'Blue Guide London and its Environs'. Finlay and James Muirhead already had extensive experience of guide-book publishing: before the First World War they had been the editors of the English editions of the German Baedekers, and by 1915 they had acquired the copyright of most of the famous 'Red' handbooks from John Murray.

An agreement made with the French publishing house Hachette et Cie in 1917 led to the translation of Muirhead's London Guide, which became the first 'Guide Bleu'—Hachette had previously published the blue-covered 'Guides Joanne'. Subsequently, Hachette's 'Guide Bleu Paris et ses Environs' was adapted and published in London by Muirhead. The collaboration between the two publishing houses continued until 1933.

In 1931 Ernest Benn took over the Blue Guides, appointing Russell Muirhead, Finlay Muirhead's son, editor in 1934. The Muirheads' connection with Blue Guides ended in 1963 when Stuart Rossiter, who had been working on the Guides since 1954, became house editor, revising and compiling several of the books himself.

The Blue Guides are now published by A & C Black, who acquired Ernest Benn in 1984, so continuing the tradition of guide-book publishing which began in 1826 with 'Black's Economical Tourist of Scotland'. The Blue Guide series continues to grow: there are now more than 40 titles in print with revised editions appearing regularly and many new Blue Guides in preparation.

'Blue Guides' is a registered trade mark.

CONTENTS

Maps and Plans

EXPLANATIONS

The arrangement of this guide by routes conforms in every way to the past traditions of the series without innovations.

TYPE. The main routes are described in large type. Smaller type is used for branch-routes and excursions, for historical and preliminary paragraphs, and (generally speaking) for descriptions of minor importance.

DISTANCES (placed in front of the place-name) are given cumulatively from the starting-point of the route or sub-route in kilometres and miles; on diversions from a route (placed *after* the place-name), they are specific to that place from the point of divergence from the route. Road distances have been calculated where possible from the km posts on the roads themselves, otherwise from measurement on official maps; constant realignments make it certain that these distances will vary slightly from those measured by motorists on their milometers. A Greek asked a walking distance will always give the answer as a walking *time*. Archaeologists, however, invariably use metres and the site plans are accordingly scaled in metres.

ASTERISKS indicate points of special interest or excellence.

ABBREVIATIONS. In addition to generally accepted and self-explanatory abbreviations, the following occur in the Guide:

A', B' tou Protou (i.e. 'the first'), the second, etc.
A.J.A. American Journal of Archaeology
Akr. Akroterion (i.e. Cape)
Ay. Ayios, Ayia, etc. (Saint or Saints)
B.C.H. Bulletin de Correspondence Hellénique
B.S.A. Annual of the British School At Athens
c circa
C century
dr(s) drachmas(s)
fl. floruit
Hdt. Herodotus
Hesp. Hesperia
J.H.S. Journal of Hellenic Studies
Leof. Leoforos (Avenue)
N.T.O. see below)
Od. Odhos (Street)
Plat. Plateia (Square)
R. rooms
Rest. restaurant
Rte route
Thuc. Thucydides

EOT (NTO) Ελληνικός Οργανισμός Τουρισμού (National Tourist Organisation).
KTEA (KTEL) Κοινόν Ταμείον Εισπράξεων Λεωφορείων (Joint Pool of Bus Owners).
O.T.E. Οργανισμός Τηλεπικοινωνιών Ελλάδος (Greek Telecommunications Organisation).

PRACTICAL INFORMATION

General

Sources of Information—Abroad. Information about any matter to do with visiting Greece may be obtained from the NATIONAL TOUR-IST ORGANISATION OF GREECE (in Greek EOT) which has offices in London (4 Conduit St W1R 0DJ), New York (645 Fifth Avenue), Los Angeles (611 West Sixth Street), Chicago (168 North Michigan Avenue). There are also branches in Canada (1300 Bay Street Toronto, and 1233 Rue de la Montagne, Montreal) and Australia (51–57 Pitt Street, Sydney), as well as other countries. Leaflets about Athens, street plans and the regularly revised 'General Information about Greece' are available.

Two excellent English-language monthlies (published in Athens but available in Britain (from BAS Overseas Publications Ltd, Unit 1C, 159 Mortlake Road, Kew, Surrey, TW9 4AW) are invaluable for planning travel both to and within Greece, since they contain an extremely wide range of information. They are *Greek Travel Pages* (price in Athens c £6.50 1991) and the *Key Travel Guide* (£2.50). These publications give details of air, rail and bus travel, hotel information (not below C category) and much other useful matter (customs, shop hours, etc). The English magazine *Time Out* is useful for cut-rate travel, including buses.

For accommodation, the detailed and comprehensive *Guide to the Greek Hotels*, published annually in mid-March by the Hellenic Chamber of Hotels and available through EOT (price in Athens, £6.00, 1991) gives information about hotels of all categories, with prices.

For other background information, see bibliography (below).

Sources of Information—in Athens *Information Bureaux. National Tourist Office*, 2 Karayeóryi Servías, Síntagma Sq (within National Bank of Greece); 1 Ermoú, Síntagma Sq (within General Bank, usually less crowded than the preceding); 4 Stadhíou; in booking hall of Omonia Underground Stn; and at the Airport. *Royal National Foundation*, 9 Filellínon.

Telephone Information. Excellent general services dealing with any query are provided by the *Tourist Police* (tel. 171) and *ELPA*, the Motoring Organisation (tel. 174). English is spoken.

Leaflets, Newspapers, Magazines. The National Tourist Organisation (see above) publishes (weekly, free) 'The Week in Athens' in English and French. The 'Athens News' is published daily in English, and 'Greek News' weekly, also in English. 'The Athenian', a well-produced monthly magazine in English, has articles on various aspects of Greek life and culture and useful information about entertainment, restaurants and basic services in the capital. The weekly 'Athinórama' (Αθηνόραμα; Thursdays, in Greek) has comprehensive information about all forms of entertainment (including gastronomic) in Athens, for those with some knowledge of Greek.

Travel Agents. *Trans Hellenic*, 36 Voúlis; *Alfa*, 12 Vas. Sofías; *Ghiolman and Hellas*, 7 and 14 Filellínon; *American Express*, 2 Ermoú; *Wagons-lits/Cook*, 2 Kar. Servías; *Hermes en Grèce* and *CHAT* 4 Stadhíou; and many others. One small and helpful is Astoria, Aiólou 104 (7th. floor). The *Periyitikí Léskhi*, 12 Polytekhníou, organises excursions to many places difficult of access by public transport.

Shipping Offices, mostly in Piraeus (Rte 12), except *Hellenic Mediterranean Lines* at 28 Amalías, *Strintzis Lines*, 48 Amalías.

Airline Offices. *British Airways*, 10 Othonos (Sindagma); *Olympic Airways*, 6 Othonos (all bookings); 96 Singroú (coach terminal); *TWA*, 8 Xenofóndos: *PAN AM*, 4 Othonos; *Air France* and *Lufthansa*, 4 Karayeóryi Servías; *Qantas*, 5 Mitropóleos.

Street plans of central Athens are available from the National Tourist Organisation and from booksellers and kiosks in Athens. The Greek motoring organisation (ELPA, see below) produces a useful book of street plans of the city and suburbs, with index, and there are other similar publications (e.g. by K. Daravingas).

Prices. These change and relative values alter so frequently in accordance with fluctuations in the exchange rate that prices are rarely quoted in the following pages, though some general estimates of the relative costs in comparison with those prevailing in the UK are given. At present (1991) the exchange rate is favourable to visitors from western Europe and the USA and Greece, on the whole, seems cheap.

Season. Climatically the best months to visit Greece are April to mid-June and September–October. In July and August the average maximum temperature is 32° C, minimum 22°). During the not infrequent 'heat-waves', shade temperatures may surpass 38° in Athens. March and November and later often have surprisingly warm days with long hours of sunshine, but in the earlier part of the year the sea is rarely warm enough for bathing. Equally it can be rainy with chilly evenings until well into April. In winter Athens is subject to very changeable weather, bitter winds and squally rain alternating with dazzling sunny intervals, so that a heavy overcoat and sunglasses may be needed together; but snow (though commonly visible on the surrounding hills) rarely settles in the city.

Since the best way of seeing Athens is on foot and at quieter times, Sundays (especially in July and August, when many people are away) and holiday periods (e.g. between Christmas and the New Year) can be good from this point of view, though it is necessary to check carefully the opening days and hours of museums, sites, galleries etc.

Public Holidays and Religious Festivals. Official public holidays in Greece are: New Year's Day; 6 January (Epiphany: *Blessing of the Waters* in Plateía Dhexamení, Kolonáki); Katharí Dheftéra ('Clean Monday'), the Orthodox Shrove Day; 25 March (Independence Day); Orthodox Good Friday; Easter Monday; 1 May; Ascension Day; 15 August (Assumption); 12 October (*Anniversary of 1944 Liberation*) hoisting of national flag on Acropolis; 28 October, 'Okhi' day (rejection of Italian ultimatum in 1940); Christmas Day; and 26 December (St. Stephen). In addition Athens celebrates the feast of her patron saint, St. Dionysios the Areopagite (3 October). Easter is marked by a candlelight procession on Lykabettos.

Health. Climate and unfamiliar food may cause problems. Elementary precautions are obvious: avoidance of over-exposure to the sun (which burns even when a breeze makes it seem cool), and of too much oily food. It is advisable to carry one or two patent remedies. Rice and lemon juice are good for upset stomachs. Chemists can advise on other medicines. Dog bites need immediate treatment by a doctor.

Equipment. Most people require sunglasses in Greece, even in winter. Suntan lotion, a sunhat, and initial caution in exposing oneself to the sun are important in the summer. A pocket compass can be useful, since many directional indications in the Guide are given by compass-points. Those travelling informally should consider taking a small camping stove for hotel-room breakfasts, etc. It is a good idea to carry washing powder, a few clothes pegs and a strong piece of string for a temporary clothes line. An electric torch is useful. Some form of mosquito repellant should be carried (though it may not be needed): small electrical devices are available from all chemists.

Weights and Measures. The French metric system of weights and measures adopted in Greece in 1958, is used with the terms substantially unaltered. Thus μέτρο, χιλιόμετρο (khiliómetro), etc. Some liquids are measured by weight (κιλό, kiló), not in litres. The standard unit of land measurement, the *stremma*, is equal to ¼ acre.

Foreign newspapers are obtainable at central kiosks in Athens late on the day of publication at about three times the home price.

Travel to Athens

Air. This is the quickest and most convenient method of getting to Greece and can be relatively cheap. Scheduled flights are operated by British Airways (from London and, less frequently, Manchester) and Olympic Airways (London only), with several flights a day in summer, including some direct services to Salonika, Corfu, Rhodes, and Crete. The cheapest fares usually apply to trips of not more than one month's duration, where the ticket is booked well in advance and no change at all is permitted to the dates or times. As there are frequent changes in fare structures, current information should be sought from the airlines. Summer fares are usually higher than winter, and travel at weekends more expensive than on weekdays. CHARTER FLIGHTS operate from many regional airports (as well as from London). While these are mainly intended for buyers of complete package holidays at rates which include accommodation, it is also possible to use them for travel only (with a nominal charge for accommodation). These flights are not necessarily very much cheaper than the cheapest fares on scheduled flights and may involve travelling at inconvenient times. On the other hand, they may allow direct travel from a local airport and, especially out of season, seats are often sold at discount prices when booked close to the departure date. Other European and American airlines also operate regular scheduled services to Athens.

Airport at *Ellinikó*, 9.5km SE on the coast, for both international and internal flights (two terminals, separately approached: all foreign airlines use the East Terminal, while Olympic Airways operate from the West Terminal). Bus between East and West terminals. Direct bus from East Airport (**18**, yellow) to Leof. Amalías, frequent 6.00 a.m. to midnight; also **121** to Leof. Olgas. Direct bus of Olympic Airways from West Airport to Leof. Amalías; also **122** to Leof. Olgas; see further, suburban services below. To Piraeus (Dhimotikó Théatro): from East Airport **19**, yellow, also **101**; from West Airport **107** or **109**, the latter starting from Voula. Yellow buses are express.

Rail. Rail travel is no longer cheap and, unless the cost is further inflated by the purchase of sleepers, not very comfortable. The cost of rail travel can be reduced with the InterRail pass for the under 26s or the InterRail Plus 26 pass (for those over 26) valid either for 15 days or a month. The direct routes are from North European ports via France and Italy, or via Belgium/Holland and Germany and Austria into Yugoslavia. Couchettes or sleepers, if required, should be booked well in advance. Those who dislike the antiseptic nature of air travel may well consider taking the train to an Italian port followed by a boat crossing to Greece (see below). Timetable and other information about rail travel is available from British Rail International, International Rail Centre, Victoria Station, London SW1V 1JY (tel. 071-834 2345) or from any British Rail Travel Centre (best at the larger stations).

Railway Station International. *Lárissa* (2, *1*), in the NW of the city, for the standard-gauge line to Thebes, Larissa, Salonika, and Idhoméni (connecting via Gevgelija and Belgrade with the European trunk lines). (The *Peloponnísou* station (2, *1*), adjoining Larissa to the SW, serves only Corinth and the Peloponnese). Booking offices at station or, in town, 1 Karólou, 6 Sína (Panepistemíou), 17 Filellínon. Access to Larissa station by bus **405** from Leof. Alexándras, trolley **1** from Leof. Amalías or Panepistomíou.

Sea. There is no regular direct passenger line from Britain to Greece, which would in any case require a good deal of time. There are however a substantial number (less frequent out of season) of passenger/car ferry services from Adriatic ports (Brindisi, Bari, Ancona and, less frequently, Venice) to Patras (often via Corfu and/ or Igoumenitsa), with onward bus connections to Athens, or direct to Piraeus through the Corinth canal. There are some services too from Marseilles and Genoa. The Brindisi–Patras route takes about 20 hours, via Corfu and Igoumenitsa; the others correspondingly longer. Amongst the companies providing these services are Fragline (Brindisi), Adriatica (Brindisi, Venice), Ventouris (Bari), Karageorghis (Ancona), Minoan Lines (Ancona), Hellenic Mediterranean Lines (H.M.L.) (Brindisi), Libra Maritime (Brindisi) and Anco Ferries (Brindisi). Some routes continue to Turkey, Cyprus, the Levant or Egypt.

   Port at Piraeus (see Rte 12); Athens may be reached in 25 minutes by the Electric Railway, by bus, or taxi (approx. 10 × bus fare).

Road. The shortest overland route from Britain is c 3150km (1950 miles), via southern Germany, Austria and Yugoslavia and takes an absolute minimum of four days. For the trip to be enjoyable a more leisurely drive is preferable, perhaps following the Adriatic coast through Yugoslavia (considerably longer). Alternatively, car ferries may be used from one of the Italian ports mentioned above (the Brindisi route is the fastest, but not necessarily the most pleasant). Motorail services from a Channel port or Paris to southern France or Italy (Milan best) reduce the strain of driving. The services (including route and customs information, and bookings) provided by the AA and RAC are essential. For the Greek motoring organisation (ELPA), see below.

BUS. This is the cheapest (and least comfortable) method of getting to Greece. Vehicles travel either direct from a Channel port, or via one of the Adriatic ferries. There may or may not be night stops *en route*. The apparent economy may not be real when the cost of the food and accommodation is taken into account. Travellers should be certain to choose a reliable operator. Information may be obtained from the Victoria Coach Station in London, student travel agencies, or newspaper advertisements (see above). The journey takes about 3–4 days.

Travelling Formalities
Passports (British Visitors' Passports are valid) are the only travel documents necessary for British nationals to travel in Greece. Application forms are available from any Post Office. Full passport requests may take some time to process and several weeks should be allowed. Those wishing to stay in Greece for longer than three months must apply (Aliens' Bureau, 173 Leofóros Alexándras), at the end of that period and not before, for a *permis de séjour* (άδεια παραμονής, adhia paramonís). They may be required to submit proof of financial self-sufficiency.

Customs. Normal EEC regulations on import/export of goods, alcohol, tobacco, etc. apply. Valuable items (especially electronic equipment) may be entered in the passport and re-export required (or else payment of import tax) at the end of the period of stay. This restriction always applies to private cars. Those wishing to keep a foreign-registered car in Greece for more than six months must apply for a permit from the appropriate customs department (14 Od. Frantzí, Athens 117 42) when an extension of up to 9 months may be granted according to circumstances.

Currency. Drs 100,000 in Greek currency may be imported by foreign nationals but the amount of travellers' cheques etc, is not limited. Foreign banknotes of more than 1000 US dollars must be declared on arrival. Any foreign currency, in whatever form, whose re-export may be desired on departure, must be declared on arrival. Declaration is also necessary if you wish to deposit foreign currency in a foreign exchange account in Greece belonging either to yourself or to a third party. The export limits are Drs. 20,000 for foreign visitors; foreign currency up to $1000, unless provision has been made on arrival (see above).

Travel Within Athens

Public Transport, Tickets. Buses, some trolley routes and the electric railway serve the capital between about 5.00 a.m. and midnight, with some all-night routes. Though frequent, services are often very crowded. There is a flat fare over a large area of the centre of Athens and suburbs, at present (1991) 50 drs. Tickets (usable on both electric railway and buses, except express airport services) must be bought in advance—from bus company kiosks near main bus stops, many ordinary kiosks (periptera), shops (often newsagents) bearing the sign (ΠΩΛΟΥΝΤΑΙ ΕΙΣΙΤΗΡΙΑ), machines and ticket offices at electric railway stations. The traveller is responsible for cancelling the ticket by inserting it in one of the orange machines on board buses or at railway station barriers. Failure to do this results in an instant fine, at present Drs. 1000. Supplements are charged on night bus services.

City and Suburban Buses, Yellow Trolleys. A route map of central Athens, showing stops and bus numbers is available from bus kiosks near the main stops. Owing to the one-way traffic system, outward routes through the city seldom coincide with the return journey; between the Omonia area and Sindagma Sq., traffic goes N by Leof. Venizelou (Panepistimiou), S by either Akadhimias or Stadhiou. The most important stops in central Athens are either side of the University and Academy (3, 6), in Akadhimias and Panepistimiou (Venizelou) respectively. As an approximate guide, the first digit of the bus number indicates its general destination, as follows: **0**, Central Athens; **1**, coastal suburbs S towards Vouliagmeni; **2**, S suburbs on slopes of Hymettos; **3** and **4**, SE and E to central and eastern Attica; **5**, Kifissia and N suburbs; **6** and **7**, NW and **8**, W towards Dhafni; **9**, SW to Piraeus. (For other routes in the vicinity of Athens, see below.)

Among the most useful routes are:

(a) *Within the city*. **2/11/12** (trolleys). *Pangrati–Sindagma–Patissia* (for National Archaeological Museum and Mavromateon bus termini); **022**. *Marasleion–Gennadhion Library–Kolonaki Sq.–University–Patission–Kipseli;* **023**. *Kipseli–University–Likavittos;* **026**. *Votanikos–Assomaton–Monastiraki–Sindagma–Ippokratous;* **040** (green bus). *Piraeus–Sindagma* (Od. Filellinon); **049**. *Piraeus* (Dhimotiko Theatro)–*Omonia* (Od. Athinas); **051**. *Od. Veranzerou–Akadhimia Platonos* (Plato's Academy); **230**. *Od. Ippokratous–Akadhimias–Akropolis–Thission*

(b) *Suburban and Attica*. **115**. *Leof. Olgas Varliza*, **118**. *Olgas Vouliagmeni;* **121**. *Olgas–Ay. Nikolaos Glifadha;* **122**. *Olgas–Ano Voula;* **224**. *University–Kaisariani;* **421**. *Od. Vasileos Irakleiou Museum–Palaia Pendeli;* **503**. *Pl. Kaningos–Varibobi;* **538/589**. *Pl. Kaningos–Kitissia;* **603**. *University–Psikhiko.* From Piraeus, **109**. *Piraeus–Glifadha–Voula.*

To *Sounion* (via coast or inland route), *Lavrion, Porto Rafti, Markopoulo/Vravrona, Kalamos/Amphiaraion, Oropos,* and places in E Attica, from 14 Od. Mavromateon (3, 1). To *Marathon, Rafina, Ayia Marina/Rhamnous,* from 29 Od. Mavromateon/Leof. Alexandras (3, 1). (To central and SE Attica, also from Thissíon.)

To *Megara* from Thissíon (6, 3).

To *Eleusis* from Plat. Koumoundhoúrou (Eleftherías; 2, 6).

Electric Railway. Frequent metropolitan service from *Kifissia* via *Omonia* to *Piraeus* in 40 min. Intermediate halts (S of Omonia): Monastírion (2, **8**), Thissíon, (2, **8**), Petrálona, El. Venizélos/Távros, Kallithéa, Moskháton, New Pháleron; N of Omonia: Victoría, Attikí, Ayios Nikólaos, Káto Patíssia, Ayios Eleftheírios, Patíssia, Perissós, Pevkákia, Néa Ionía, Iráklion, Iríni (for Olympic Stadium), Maroússi, KAT (Accident Hospital).

Taxis (metered) are numerous and cheap in the towns. Charges are modest (minimum fare drs 280). Tip by rounding up to the nearest

50 drs; a little more if a long journey. Surcharges operate from a public transport terminal (Drs. 200 Airport, Drs. 60 Bus or Rly Station), during night hours (rural tarrif) and at holiday periods (a flat Drs. 70 on top of the fare). Outside the city boundary, a higher tariff applies (at present Drs. 82 per km).

There are now several firms operating radio-taxis. These are generally reliable and the supplement is modest (Drs. 300), though the telephone lines can be very busy. Amongst them are *Ikaros* 3214058; *Radio Taxi* 5132316; *Omonia* 5021131, 2921910.

At busy times and with (or sometimes without) the permission of the original hirer, the driver may pick up other passengers going in roughly the same direction. Enquiry is made by shouting one's destination through the window. A deduction should be made for such passengers when they reach their destination, since the fare shown on the meter will be that from the original point of hire. This may not always be easy to negotiate but, at peak hours, it is probably worth ignoring the relatively small mark-up.

In country areas, meters are not often found but there is a standard tariff which may or may not be publicly displayed or adhered to, and an agreement as to the fare should always be made in advance. If in doubt, enquire the price from several drivers. Travellers are advised to make good use of taxis which, judiciously employed, can enable one to see far more than might otherwise be possible in the time, where public transport is lacking, and at relatively modest cost. They can, in certain circumstances, work out cheaper than a hired car. For not-too-distant excursions, an arrangement can be made for the driver to return later, at a specified time, at a total fare less than that for two single journeys.

Car Hire (self-drive). There are numerous car hire companies in Greece (lists in the main Sources of Information and from the National Tourist Organisation). Major firms include *Hertz*, 12 Singroú; *Avis*, 48 Amalías; *Hellascars*, 7 Stadhíou; *Budget*, 90 Singroú; etc. Several airports have representatives of the larger companies.

Hire in Greece is relatively expensive (in 1991, about £260–£280 per week for a small car, with unlimited mileage and inclusive of all taxes, in the high season). In Athens itself, a car can only be an embarassment; outside the city however, the advantages to be gained in terms of extra mobility and access to remoter areas often make it an attractive option, particularly if costs can be shared. The cheapest rate is achieved by taking a full week's hire, with unlimited mileage. Three-day unlimited mileage rates are also available; otherwise the cost is calculated by adding a charge per kilometre to a modest daily rate. It is probably advantageous (though in no way essential) to arrange hire before leaving home. This is easy with international companies. Some travel firms offer inclusive 'packages' with flight, and car on arrival; others provide the option of car hire at a reduced rate. On the spot, reductions can sometimes be negotiated at quieter periods or from smaller companies. When calculating rates from hire company leaflets, potential customers should be sure to include taxes (usually high—about 20 per cent) and any charges for additional insurance cover which may be desired.

Motoring. Driving (on the right) is conducted in a competitive spirit which can be alarming to the visitor and accords Greece the dubious distinction of having the highest accident rate in Europe. Private motorists can get road maps, information etc. from the GREEK MOTORING ORGANISATION (ELPA: ΕΛΠΑ). The Athens head-quarters is at the Athens Tower, 2 Odhós Mesoyeíon. The roadside assistance and rescue service (dial 104, in Athens) is extremely efficient and has reciprocal arrangements with other European motoring organisations. A similar service (EXPRESS) is also very efficient and can be joined by monthly subscription.

Walking, although the best way of getting around Athens, is not without its hazards. Pavements are often narrow and uneven and the irregular phasing of traffic lights makes it unwise to rely on the green pedestrian sign to ensure a safe crossing of the street. Some of the longer boulevards can be tiring in hot weather or crowds. In the countryside outside Athens (e.g. on the slopes of Parnes) it can be a great pleasure, partly for the natural surroundings; partly for the seemingly endless supply of friendly, helpful and hospitable people that the pedestrian is likely to encounter. It is virtually impossible to plan walks in any detail, since large scale maps showing footpaths are not generally available. Directions may be sought locally (for useful words, see below on finding Archaeological Sites).

Accommodation and Food

Hotels (Ξενοδοχεῖα: Xenodhokhía). Lists of hotels can be found in the various Sources of Information (see above). The most comprehensive is the 'Guide to the Greek Hotels'. Other publications tend not to list hotels in categories below 'C'.

There are six official categories: L, and **A–E**. The de Luxe hotels compare favourably with their counterparts in other countries, almost all have restaurants; their rooms all have private bathrooms and air-conditioning. In all hotels of Class **A**, most of Class **B**, many of Class **C** (especially in Athens) and some of Class **D** a proportion of rooms (sometimes all) are equipped with private bath or shower. Class **C**, at present the most numerous, is the least easy to appraise. Many Greek hotels do not have restaurants. Hotels classed **D** or **E** have no public rooms and sometimes only cold water, though their standard of cleanliness and service may well be adequate for a short stay. (**F–A** = Furnished Apartments.)

Charges are fixed annually by the Government. Hoteliers may not exceed the maximum permitted figure; the charge appropriate to each room, quoted with service and taxes included, is entered in a notice fixed usually to the inside of the door. Central heating or air conditioning is always extra. Considerable reductions can be obtained in November–March.

Despite the official categorisation, hotels can still vary widely. The independent traveller will realise that here as elsewhere, many hotels are geared to package tours and coach groups rather than to the unexpected overnight guest. Furthermore some hotels can legally insist on demi-pension terms, thus tying the visitor to their usually unimaginative restaurants. It is difficult to get single rooms; single occupation of a double room is usually charged at 80 per cent of double price.

Charges vary considerably within each category, so that a cheap B-class hotel can be less expensive than a dearer C. It is thus worth investigating establishments which seem at first sight likely to be too expensive. In 1991 (also applicable winter (1991/2)), a twin room in a good middle-range C class hotel, with private bath, cost about £25 (accommodation only). It is advisable to inspect the accommodation before making a definite agreement. Hoteliers are always willing to show rooms and respect an adverse decision.

Athens has numerous hotels in every class. Several of the higher class hotels are located in the area of Sindagma Sq., more modest round Omonia. The following are a select list of hotels in central Athens (not below Class C). Other areas provided with hotels which visitors may consider are the West coast of Attica (Glifádha, Vouliagméni, Várkiza, Soúnion) and centres such as Néa Mákri on the East; also Kifissiá and vicinity. The more distant (see Rtes 13, 15) are on the whole more pleasant but communications with places other than Athens itself are likely to be inadequate: C Afrodhíti, 21 Apóllonos (Centre); Akhíllion, 32 Ayíou Konstandínou (Omónia); B Aléxandros, 8 Timoléontos Vássou (Ambelókipoi); B (P) Athenian Inn, 22 Kháritos (Kolonáki); C Cápitol, 11 Maríkas Kotopoúli (Omónia); C Caprí, 6 Psaromilíngou (Plateía Koumoundhoúrou (Eleftherías)); L Chandris, 385 Singroú; A Electra Palace, 18 Nikodhímou (Plaka); C Erechtheíon, 8 Flamaríou/Ayías Marínis (Thissíon); A Espéria Palace, 22 Stadhíou (Centre); C Evripídhis, 79 Evripídhou (Plateía Koumoundhoúrou (Eleftherías)); C Exarkhíon, 55 Themistokléous (Centre); L Hilton, 46 Vassilíssis Sofías; L Intercontinental, 89–93 Singroú; C Jason, 3–5 Nikifórou (Omónia); L Ledra-Marriot, 115 Singroú; C Lycabette, 6 Valaorítou (Centre); L Megále Vrettanía (Grande Bretagne), 1 Vassiléos Yeoryíou (Síndagma); C Marína, 13 Voúlgari (Omónia); C Mouseíon, 16 Bouboulínas/Tósitsa (Centre); B (P) Myrtó House, 40 Níkis (Síndagma); B Pan, 1 Mitropóleos (Síndagma); C Phíllipos, 3 Mitséon (S of Akropolis); B Pláka, 7 Kapnikaréas (Plaka); A President, 43 Kifissías (Ambelókipoi); L St George Lycabettus, 2 Kleoménous (Kolonáki); B Stádhion, 38 Vassiléos Konstantínou (Stadium); B Stanley, 1 Odhisséos (Plateía Karaiskáki); C Thissíon, 2 Ayías Marínis (Thissíon); B Titánia, 52 Panepistemíou (Centre).

Furnished Flats: B Aléxandros, 8 Timoléontos Vássou (Ambelókipoi); B Ava, 9 Lissikrátous (Plaka); A Embassy, 15 Timoléontos Vássou (Ambelókipoi); A Perlí, 4 Arnis (Ilíssia).

Booking. The Hellenic Chamber of Hotels (publisher of the Guide to Greek Hotels), 24 Stadhíou (Tel 3236962) offers a postal booking service. Their desk next to the EOT information counter in the National Bank of Greece in Síndagma (2 Karayeóryi Servías; Tel 3237193) offers an on-the-spot service.

Youth Hostels. The Greek Youth Hostel Association (4 Odhós Dhragatsaníou) is affiliated to the International Youth Hostels Federation. Its hostels may be used by members of any affiliated association. Accommodation is usually simple and members are obliged to keep early hours; stay is generally limited to 5 days. There are hostels at 1 Ayíou Meletíou (170 beds; open always); 2 Alexándras (220 beds; July–Sept only); 20 Ioulianoú (82 beds); 5 Kipsélis (180 beds); 4 Patissíon. —In Athens also are the YWCA (11 Odhós Ameríkis) and the YMCA (28 Odhós Omírou), maximum stay 10 days, meals extra. In July and August the Polytechnic School in Athens also accommodates groups of students.

Car-Camping Sites are run or licensed by the NTOG (modest charges). An up-to-date list may be obtained from the Athens Office.

There are also some private camping sites. NTOG-run or licensed sites closest to central Athens (*=open all year, remainder April or June to October) are—AKROPOLIS (B) at Néa Kifissiá, 15km N of Athens on the Athens–Lamia National Highway; ATHENS CAMPING* (C) at 198 Leofóros Athinón, Peristéri (11km, Rte 16, to Corinth); DAFNI CAMPING* (A) (11km, Dhafní, Rte 16); DIONISSIOTIS CAMPING* (A) at Néa Kifissiá, 8km on Lamia road; NEA KIFISSIA at Kifissiá; VOULA NTOG CAMPING* (A), 2 Odhós Alkyonídhon, Voúla, Attica (19km, Rte 13 to Sounion).

Food and Drink

Cafés (Kafeneía) are numerous, serving coffee, soft, and a limited range of alcoholic drinks. Those in or near the main squares and avenues cater for tourists. The traditional Greek **Café** (Καφενείον) is an austere establishment usually thronged with male patrons for whom it is both local club and political forum. Coffee (καφέ) is always served in the "Turkish" fashion with the grounds. It may be drunk heavily sweetened (variglikó), medium (métrio) or without sugar (skhétto). Cafés displaying the sign ΚΑΦΕΝΕΙΟΝ–ΜΠΑΡ (Café-Bar) also serve drinks.

Zakharoplasteía, properly speaking, are confectioners selling a wide range of traditional and modern cakes and sweets. Often now they also have the function of a superior type of café or tea-room, serving alcoholic drinks too, and the largest also substantial hot and cold dishes. Among the best known are Au Délicieux, 17 Kanári/Sólonos (Kolonáki); Delice, 3 Vassiléos Alexándrou/13 Vrasídha (Hilton); Flóca, 118 Leofóros Kifissías; 4 Koraí, and elsewhere; Mondial, 31 Patriarkhou Ioakeim (Kolonaki); Miké, 8 D. Soútsou/Dorylaíou (Ambelókipoi); Vársos, 5 Kassavéti (Kifissiá); Zonar, 9 Panepistemíou (Centre).

The simplest kind of meal, consisting of milk, coffee, bread, butter, honey, etc., can be had in a *Galaktopoleion*, or dairy. Such establishments are now very rare in Athens, while others of a more western type (tea-rooms, fast-food canteens) are increasingly common.

The **Ouzerí** serves mezédhes (often including seafood such as octopus and shrimps), traditionally with ouzo but most offer also wine, beer and soft drinks: Andréas, 32 Themistokléous (Centre); Apótsos, 10 Stadhíou (Centre); Petrinó, 32 Themistokléous/Akadhimías (Centre).

Restaurants (Εστιατόρια: Estiatória) and **Tavernas** (Ταβέρνες: Tavérnes). In Athens lunch is usually taken between 13.00 and 15.00 (earlier on Sunday) and dinner (generally the more important) between 20.00 and 23.00 (summer 21.00 and 01.00), though hotels catering particularly for foreigners conform more nearly to Western times. Estiatória display at the entrance a bill of fare, showing their category (L, A–D) and the prices of each dish, both basic and with tax and service included. There are usually translations into English. Fixed-price and table d'hôte meals are rare. A service charge is added by law so that any small gratuity to the waiter (on the plate) is a recognition of personal service. The wine boy (mikrós), however, receives only what is left for him on the *table* (c 5 per cent).

The distinction between a restaurant proper and a taverna is nowadays not clearly definable, but in general the **Tavérna** is less formal, patronised for a convivial evening rather than for luncheon, and partly at least out of doors; its fare is uncompromisingly Greek.

Tavernas (some open evenings only, 20.30 or 21.00 to 01.00 or later) offer excellent food and entertainment of a characteristically Greek kind. They are crowded and convivial; a table once occupied is often kept for the evening. The menu may be in Greek only, but it is not unusual to choose dishes at the kitchen.

An *Exokhikón kéndron* (EOXIKON KENTPON) ('rural centre') combines the functions of café and taverna in a country or seaside setting.

Restaurants (lunch usually between 12.30 and 15.00; dinner between 20.30 and 24.00). International food and décor (not cheap) at **L** class hotels. Otherwise, for up-to-date guidance consult current periodicals, e.g. *The Athenian, Athinorama* (see Practical Information).

Tavernas are ubiquitous. Many in Plaka cater for tourists; a more local atmosphere may be sought e.g. behind the Hilton or on the slopes of Lykabettus. In summer Athenians tend to dine farther out in Attica.

Most of the establishments contained in this list are of traditional Greek type. Even those marked '+' as being more expensive than the average are modestly priced, at least by British standards. Luxury hotels and restaurants serving non-Greek food are listed in the various Sources of Information. 'L' signifies that the establishment is best for lunch and may not be open in the evenings; the reverse is true of the remainder, though many tavernas now open at lunchtime, especially in the tourist season. Many establishments close on Sundays, others on one day early in the week. Since arrangements vary with the season, telephone numbers are given to facilitate enquiry: Anna, 10 Grigoríou, Néa Filothéi suburb (6928435); Bakalariákia, 41 Kidhathenaíon (Plaka) (3225084); Balkóni tou Imittoú, 9–11 P. Melá (Karéa—suburb) (7640240); +Bálthazar, 27 Tsókha /Vournázou (Leofóros Alexándras N) (6441215); L Corfú, 6 Kriezótou (Centre) (3613011); Dhelfí, 13 Níkis (Síndagma) (3234869); +Dourambéis, 29 Ath. Dhilavéri (Piraeus) fish (4122092); Éden, 3 Fléssa (Plaka)—vegetarian (3248858); +Fátsio, 5 Evfroníou (Hilton) (7216390); L Fílippou, 19 Xenokrátous (Kolonáki) (7216390); Fóndas, 6 Arrianítou (Exárkheia) (3633502); Kalýva, 60 Vassiléos Pávlou (Kastélla, Piraeus) (4122593); Karavítis, Arktínou/Pavsaníou (Pangráti) (7215155); L Kentrikón, 3 Kolokotróni Síndagma (3232482); Kostís, 18 Kidhathenaíon (Plaka) (3229636); Kostoyiánnis, 37 Zaími (Museum) (8212496); Mánessis, 3 Márkou Moussoúrou (Metz) (9227684); Megarítis, 2 Ferekídhou/Arátou (Pangráti) (7012155); +Myrtiá, 32–34 Trivonianoú (Metz) (9023633); +Papákia, 40 Póndou (Hilton–Ilíssia) (7793072); Pithári, 17 Dhaskaloyiánni (Lycabettus peripherique) (6440530); L Plátanos, 4 Dhiogénous (Plaka) (3220666); Rodhiá, 44 Aristíppou (Lycabettus) (7229883); Roúga, 7 Kapsáli (Kolonáki Square) (7227934); Skalákia, 32 Aiginítou (Ilíssia) (7229290); Sintriváni, 5 Filellínon Síntagma (3238862); Théspis, 18 Thespídhos (Plaka) (3238242); Tría Adhélfia, 7 Elpídhos (8229322) (Plateía Viktorías); Tsékouras, 2 Epikhármou (Plaka) (3233710); Vassílaina, 72 Aitolikoú (Ayía Sofía, Piraeus)—multi-course, fixed menu (4612457); Virínis, 11 Arkhimídhous (Pankráti) (7012021); Tís Xanthís, 5 Irínis Athenaías (Lófos tou Stréfi, Exárkheia) (8820780); Xínou, 4 Angélou Yéronda (Pláka) (3221065); +Yerofínakas, 10 Pindhárou (Centre) (3622719).

Every neighbourhood has a range of tavernas and searching them out is a recreation in itself. Outside central Athens, there are pleasant tavernas in Kifissiá and lining the road to the N (Dhrosiá etc; Rte 22), also between Paianía and Koropí, and Voúla and Vári (Rte 17A, B). There are many tavernas in coastal resorts.

The fish tavernas of Mikró Limáni (Tourkolímano) (Piraeus) are famous and the setting attractive but they can be very expensive and the service obtrusive.

Dining Out. In the larger centres a few restaurants and de luxe hotels achieve an international standard of cuisine. Well-prepared Greek dishes, however, are greatly to be preferred to feeble attempts at emulating alien styles. The basic ingredients are usually excellent and, since all Greeks eat out frequently, there is a wide choice of places (see above). Travellers are well advised always to choose establishments crowded with locals, where the food will be better (and cheaper) and the atmosphere livelier.

Restaurant and taverna meals of comparable standard are considerably cheaper than in Britain. The pattern of meals is also less stereotyped, the sharing of portions being quite usual; it is essential to order each course separately as several dishes ordered together may arrive together. In tavernas it is usual to visit the kitchens to choose one's dishes, and in waterside tavernas it is customary to choose one's fish from the ice; this will then be weighed, the price appearing on the menu per kilo. The oily content of most Greek food is too exuberant for some tastes, and, though the local wine is a good counteragent, travellers will be well advised to take care until they become used to it. Frozen foods (still rare in Greece) must be indicated by law on the menu with the letters KAT.

Good table wines (unresinated, *arretsínoto*), both red and white, are obtainable in bottles everywhere and some of the better-known have a nation-wide distribution. Retsína, the resinated white wine characteristic particularly of Attica and the Peloponnese, has lost some of its former popularity in proportion as other wines have improved. It can always be obtained in bottles, but the traditional can or jug from the barrel is to be preferred, when available. This can still be more refreshing and less soporific in the heat of the day with an al fresco meal. Beer (of Bavarian type) is brewed in Greece and other lagers are brewed under licence or imported. The ordinary water of Athens (as generally in Greece) is safe, but mineral waters from spas such as Loutraki are readily available.

Food and Wine. The favourite Greek apéritif is *oúzo*, a strong colourless drink made from grape-stems and flavoured with aniseed; it is served with *Mezé*, snacks consisting of anything from a simple slice of cheese or tomato or an olive to pieces of smoked eel or fried octopus. As in Italy the Greek meal may begin with a foundation course of rice, such as *piláfi sáltsa*, or of pasta (*makarónia*), perhaps baked with minced meat (*pastítsio*) or with *tirópita* (cheese pie). Alternatives are soup or hors d'oeuvre, the latter being particularly good. *Taramosaláta* is a paste made from the roe of grey mullet and olive oil. *Tzatzíki* is composed of chopped cucumber in yoghourt heavily flavoured with garlic. The main course may be meat (κρέας, kréas), or fish or a dish on a vegetable base, baked (του φούρνου, too foúrnu), boiled (βραστό, vrastó), fried (τηγανιτό, tiganitó), roast (ψητό, psitó), or grilled (σχάρας, skháras). The chef's suggestions will be found under ΠΙΑΤΑ ΤΗΣ ΗΜΕΡΑΣ (piáta tis iméras; dishes of the day). *Moussaká* consists of layers of aubergines, minced beef, and cheese, with butter and spices, baked in the oven. Many foreign dishes may appear in transliteration, e.g.: Εσκαλόπ (escalope),

Σνίτσελ Χολσταϊν (Schnitzel Holstein), Μπιντόκ αλα ρους (Bintok á la Russe), Κρέμ Καραμελέ (créme caramelle), Σαλάτ ντέ φρουλί (salade de fruits). Many sweets have Turkish names, and 'shish kebab' is frequently used as a synonym for *souvlákia*, pieces of meat grilled on a skewer. Also cooked in this fashion is *kokorétsi*, which consists of alternate pieces of lamb's liver, kidney, sweetbreads, and heart, wrapped in intestines. When not grilled, meat is often stewed with oil in unappetising chunks. Greek cheeses tend to monotony; the ubiquitous *féta* is better eaten—peasant-fashion—with black pepper, oil and rígani (oregano) than on its own. Sweets, however, are elaborate and varied, though more often partaken separately than as a course of a meal. Among the most popular are *baklavás*, composed of layered pastry filled with honey and nuts; *kataïf*, wheat shredded and filled with sweetened nuts; and *galaktoboúreko*, pastry filled with vanilla custard.

WINE (κρασί) in Greece is generally of good quality and has greater strength than the wines of France. Wines may be divided into two categories: resinated and unresinated. *Retsína,* flavoured with resin from pine trees, is most characteristic of the south, and to the trained palate varies as much in taste and quality as do unresinated wines. Although a great amount is bottled, retsína is better drunk young from cask. Rosé varieties (κοκκινέλλι), are locally much sought after. There is a large variety of wines, white (άσπρο, áspro), red (μαύρο, mávro, literally 'black'), or rosé (κόκκινο, kókkino, literally 'red'). There are good draught red wines from Nemea, Rhodes and Corfu. It is invidious to recommend bottled wines from the vast range available but some of the following may be sampled: Hymettus (red and white), Santa Elena (white), Pallíni (white), Vílitsa (white), Zítsa (white, semi-sparkling), Sámaina (white), Castel Daniélis (red), Tsántali (white, rosé), Chevalier de Rhodes (red), Náoussa (red), Robólla (white). The latter three are rather more expensive but no Greek wine is costly by British standards. The champagne of Rhodes is pleasant. The wines of the Carras estate are also good.

The MENU which follows contains a large number of the simpler dishes to be met with:

OPEKTIKA (orektiká), Hors d'oeuvre

Διάφορα ορεκτικά (dhiáfora orektiká), Hors d'oeuvre variés
Ταραμοσαλάτα (taramosaláta), see above
Ντολμάδες Γιαλαντζή (dolmádhes Yalantzí), Stuffed vine leaves served hot with egg-lemon sauce
Ντολμαδάκια (dolmadhákia), Cold stuffed vine leaves
'Ελιές (elliés), Olives

ΣΟΥΠΕΣ (soupes), Soups

Σούπα αυγολέμονο (soúpa avgholémono), Egg and lemon soup
Σούπα απο χόρτα (soúpa apo hórta), Vegetable soup
Μαγειρίτσα (mayirítsa), Tripe soup generally with rice (Easter speciality)
Ψαρόσουπα (psarósoupa), Fish soup

ZYMAPIKA (Zimárika), Pasta and Rice dishes

Πιλάφι σάλτσα (piláfi sáltsa), Pilaf
Σπαγέτο σάλτσα μέ τυρί (spagéto sáltsa me tirí), Spaghetti
Μακαρόνια (makarónia), Macaroni

ΨΑΡΙΑ (psária), Fish

Στρείδια (strídhia), Oysters
Συναγρίδα (sinagrídha), Sea bream
Μπαρμπούνια (barboúnia), Red mullet
Μαρίδες (marídhes), Whitebait
Αστακός (astakós), Lobster

Γαρίδες (garídhes), Scampi (Dublin Bay prawns)
Καλαμαράκια (kalamarákia), Baby squids
Κταπόδι (ktapódhi), Octopus
Λιθρίνια (lithrínia), Bass

ΛΑΔΕΡΑ (ladherá), Vegetables or ΧΟΡΤΑ (khórta), Greens

Πατάτες τηγανιτές (patátes tiganités), Fried potatoes
Φασολάκια φρ. βουτ (fasolákia fr. voútiro), Beans in butter
Μπιζέλια (biséllia), Peas
Ντομάτες γεμιστές ρύζι (domátes yemistés rízi), Stuffed tomatoes

ΑΥΓΑ (avgá) Eggs

Ομελέτα Ζαμπόν (Omelétta Zambón), Ham omelette
Αυγά Μπρουγέ (avgá 'brouillé'), Scrambled eggs
Αυγά α λά Ρούς (avqá 'à la Russe'), Eggs with Russian salad

ΕΝΤΡΑΔΕΣ (entrádhes), Entrées

Αρνάκι φασολάκια (arnáki fasolákia), Lamb with beans
Μοσχάρι (moskhári), Veal
Σηκοτάκια (sikotákia), Liver
Κοτόπουλο (kotópoulo), Chicken
Χήνα (khina), Goose
Παπί (papí), Duck
Τζουτζουκάκια (tsoutsoukákia), Meat balls in tomato sauce
Κοτολέτες Χοιρινές (kotoléttes khirinés), Pork cutlets

ΣΧΑΡΑΣ (skháras), Grills

Σουβλάκια απω φιλέτο (souvláltia apo filóto), Shish Kebab (see above)
Μπριζόλες μοσχ. (brizóles moskh.), Veal chops
Κεφτέδες σχάρας (keftédhes skháras), Grilled meat balls
Γουρουνόπουλο ψητό (gourounópoulo psitó) Roast sucking-pig
Παϊδάκια Χοιρινά (païdhákia khiriná), Pork chops

ΣΑΛΑΤΕΣ (salátes), Salads

Ντομάτα σαλάτα (domáta saláta), Tomato salad
Μαρούλι (Maroúli), Lettuce
Ραδίκια (radhikia), Radishes
Κολοκυθάκια (kolokithákia), Courgettes
Αγγουράκι (angouráki), Cucumber
Αγκινάρες (ankináres), Artichokes
Μελιτζάνες (melizánes), Aubergines (eggplants)
Πιπεριές (piperiés), Green peppers
Ρωσσική (Russikí), Russian

ΤΥΡΙΑ (tiriá), Cheeses

Φέτα (féta), Soft white cheese of goat's milk
Κασέρι (kasséri), Hard yellow cheese
Γραβιέρα (graviéra), Greek gruyère
Ροκφόρ ('Roquefort'), Blue cheeses generally

ΓΛΥΚΑ (gliká), Sweets

Χαλβά (halvá), Sweet made from sesame
Μπακλαβά (baklavá) see above
Καταϊφι (kataïfi) see above
Γαλακτομπούρεκο (galaktoboúreko) see above
Ρυζόγαλο (rizógalo), Rice pudding
Γιαούρτι (yiaoúrti), Yoghourt

ΦΡΟΥΤΑ (froúta), Fruits

Μήλο (mílo), Apple
Μπανάνα (banána), Banana
Αχλάδι (akhládhi), Pear
Πορτοκάλι (portokáli), Orange
Κεράσια (Kerásia), Cherries
Φράουλες (fráoules), Strawberries
Δαμάσκηνα (dhamáskina), Plums
Ροδάκινα (rodhákina), Peaches
Βερύκοκα (veríkoka), Apricots
Πεπόνι (pepóni), Melon
Καρπούζι (karpoúzi), Water-melon

MISCELLANEOUS

Ψωμί (psomí), Bread
Βούτυρο (voútiro), Butter
Αλάτι (aláti), Salt
Πιπέρι (pipéri), Pepper
Μουστάρδα (moustárdha), Mustard
Λάδι (ládhi), Oil
Ξίδι (Xídhi), Vinegar
Γάλα (ghála), Milk
Ζάχαρι (zákhari), Sugar
Νερό (neró), Water
Παγωμένο (pagoméno), Iced
Παγωτό (paghotó), Ice Cream

Services and Facilities

Police (Emergency) Tel. 100; *Traffic Police* 523-0111.

Embassies, Legations, and Consulates. *British*, 1 Ploutárkhou (4, *8*); *United States*, Leof. Vas. Sofías (5, *6*) and (visas) 9 Leof. Venizélou (Panepistemíou); *Australia*, 15 Mesogeíon; *Canada*, 4 Yennadhíou, *Yugoslavia*, (visas) 25 Evrou (late mornings only).

Churches, CHURCH OF ENGLAND (7, *5*; St Paul's), Od. Filellínon: services on Sun at 8.00, 9.00 and 10.00; special times on Saints' days; AMERICAN CHURCH (4, *5*; *St Andrew's*), 66 Sína; ROMAN CATHOLIC CHURCH (4, *7*; *St Denis*), Leof. Venizélou (Panepistemíou).

Banks. Head Offices: *Bank of Greece*, 21 Venizélou (Panepistemíou); *National Bank of Greece*, 86 Aiólou; *Commercial Bank of Greece*, 11 Sofokléous; *Ionian and Popular Bank of Greece*, Pesmazóglou/Venizélou (Panepistemíou), etc. Normal hours, 8.00–14.00 (13.30, Friday), Monday–Friday.—Of many branches with exchange facilities, several near Síndagma Sq. are open additional hours: *National*, 2 Karayeóryi Servías (Monday–Friday 14.00–21.00, Saturday and Sunday, 8.00–20.00); *Ionian and Popular*, 2 Mitropóleos (Monday–Friday 14.00–17.30, Saturday 9.00–12.30); *General*, 1 Ermoú (0.800–20.00 daily); *Commercial*, 11 Venizélou (Panepistemíou) (Monday–Saturday 14.00–15.30, Sunday 9.00–12.00).

Changing money etc. In addition to the numerous banks, *Bureaux de Change* are operated by some travel agents and hotels will often change money, though it is advisable to ensure that the proper rate is being offered and that commission charges are not excessive. Post Offices may also be used (see below). Travellers' cheques are undoubtedly the easiest way of carrying funds. Major credit cards are accepted by a fair number of establishments but are sometimes regarded with suspicion.

Postal Services. The main Post Office (Ταχυδρομείον: Takhidhromíon; yellow signs) in Athens is in Od. Eólou (just off Omonia Sq.). Amongst useful branches are those in Síndagma Sq. (NW corner) and the Omonia underground station. Present opening hours are 07.00 or 07.30 to 20.30., Monday to Friday; 07.00 to 14.00 or 15.00, Saturday and 09.00 to 13.30., Sunday (Síndagma office only). Minor post offices close at 14.00 and do not open at weekends. Apart from their usual services, Post Offices now change travellers' cheques. Letter boxes (ΓΡΑΜΜΑΤΟΚΙΒΩΤΙΑ) are painted yellow and may be marked ΕΣΩΤΕΡΙΚΟΥ (Inland), ΕΞΩΤΕΡΙΚΟΥ (Abroad), or ΕΠΕΙΓΟΝΤΑ (Express). Postage stamps are obtainable at some kiosks and shops as well as post offices (10 per cent surcharge). A transit period of 4–5 days to the United Kingdom is normal but there are often considerable delays to post (especially postcards) in the summer season and internal mail is not exempt from problems.The charge for Express letters is reasonable and usually ensures delivery in the UK two days after posting. A registered letter is ένα συστημένο γράμμα (éna sistiméno grámma). Correspondence marked 'POSTE RESTANTE' (to be called for) may be sent to any post office and collected by the addressée on proof of identity (passport preferable). A small fee may be charged. The surname of the addressée should be clearly written, and no 'Esq.' added. PARCELS are not delivered in Greece. They must be collected from the Post Office, where they are subject to handling fees, full customs charges, and often to delay.

Telephones. The Greek telephone and telegraph services are run by a public corporation, the Οργανισμός Τηλεπικοινωνιών Ελλάδος (OTE; always referred to by its acronym—'ό, té'), which is quite separate from the postal authority. Major offices have a 24-hour service.

OTE CENTRES: 85 Patission, (open 24 hrs); also 15 Stadhíou; 53 Sólonos; 7 Kratínou (these 07.00 or 08.00 to 22.00 or midnight).

Long-distance calls can also be made from most hotels, many kiosks and any other establishment which has a metre (μετρητή: metríti) attached to the telephone. The meter records the number of units and payment is made accordingly. The availability of metered phones means that it is not usually necessary to visit an OTE centre to make a long-distance call (either domestic or international). The charge per unit is fixed—lowest at OTE, slightly more expensive at kiosks and shops; highest in hotels. The cheap rate periods are 15.00 to 17.00 and 20.00 to 08.00. International calls are, at present charges and exchange rates, about 25 per cent higher than in the UK. There is international direct dialling. Otherwise, for Greek long-distance calls, dial 132: international 161; telegrams: domestic 155, international 165. Police 100. Time 141 (in Greek).

Local calls can be made from many kiosks, shops, etc., usually from a red phone with a coin slot taking, at present, a 10-drachma piece. There are also public coin boxes, which are frequently out of order.

Shops. Shopping hours in Athens are not settled at present. Most open from c 09.00 to c 20.00, closing in the middle of the day and not opening on Saturday evening. Supermarkets open from 08.00 to 20.00 (1500 on Saturdays). The PERIPTERO (Περίπτερον), or kiosk, developed from a French model, is a characteristic feature of Greek life. Selling newspapers, reading matter, postcards, cigarettes, chocolate, toilet articles, roll film, postage stamps, etc., some kiosks are open for about 18 hours a day.

Duty chemists are listed in daily newspapers, 'The Week in Athens', or may be discovered by dialling 173 on the telephone.

Booksellers. *Eleftheroudhakis*, 4 Níkis; *Kaufmann*, 28 Stadhíou, also 11 Voukourestíou; *Pantelidhis*, 9 Ameríkis; *Andromeda*, 46–50 Mavromikhaíli (excellent specialist Classics and Archaeology); *Dhodhóni*, 3 Asklipíou (Greek); *Foliá tou Vivlíou* (mostly Greek),

25/29 Panepistimíou (in arcade); *Protoporía* 3–5 Gravías (Greek); second-hand shops at lower end of Ippokrátous.

Learned Institutions. *British School at Athens*, 52 Souidhías; *British Council*, 17 Kolonáki Sq., with good library; *American School of Classical Studies*, and *Gennadhion Library*, 54 and 61 Souidhías; American Library at *Hellenic-American Union*, 22 Massalías; *Greek Archaeological Society*, 20 Venizélou (Panepistemíou); *Direction of Antiquities Services*, 4 Aristídhou; *École Française d'Athènes*, 6 Dhidhótou; *Institut Français d'Athènes*, 29 Sína; *Deutsches Archäologisches Institut*, 1 Fidhíou; *National Library* see Rte 10; *Municipal Library*, Od. Kleisthénous; *Parliament Library*, Parliament Building; *Benakios Library*, 2 Anthímou Gazí; *National Research Institute* (Byzantine and Modern Greek studies), 4 Leof. Vas. Konstandínou; *College of Music*, 35 Piraiós; *Foreign Press Service*, 3 Zalokósta.

Entertainment and Sport

For up–to–date information on entertainment the newspapers and periodicals suggested in **Sources of Information** (above) should be consulted. *Athinórama* is particularly useful for entertainments and venues, with addresses and telephone numbers.

Art Galleries are numerous and the works shown are often interesting and of a high standard. Two of the best known are *Ora 7*, Xenofóntos and *Zígos* 33, Iofóntos. A Guide to Galleries and Exhibitions is published by the Gallery *Odhigós*. It is available from some peripterons in central Athens or from Gallery Odhigós, 46 Fokianoú, Athens 116 35. *Athinórama* also carries a full list.

Theatres. WINTER SEASON (October–May): *Ethnikón* (National Theatre Company), 22 Ay. Konstandínou; *Olympía* (Lirikí Skiní), 59 Leof. Akadhimías, opera and operetta; *Tékhnis* (Arts), 44 Odhós Stadhíou and others; SUMMER SEASON (June–September) in the Odeion of Herodes Atticus (Athens Festival) and other outside venues (including Lycabettus and Piraeus). Bus excursions are also organised to productions in the ancient theatre at Epidauros (c 3hrs travel, each way). Information and tickets for Festival and some other performances (including Epidauros) from the Athens Festival Office at 4 Stadhíou (in arcade). *Folk Dancing* (Dora Stratou company) in the Dora Stratou theatre below the Philopappos monument. *Son et lumière* centred on the Acropolis viewed from seating on the Pnyx (access path past chapel of Ayios Dhimítrios Loumbardhiáris, at the beginning of the Mouseion avenue, end of Rte 1).

Cinemas are numerous and cheap all over Athens. The principal houses (many with films in English) are in Stadhíou and Venizélou (Panepistemíou).

Concerts. Athens State Orchestra (Monday) in winter at Pallas, 1 Vourkourestíou, in summer at the Odeion; recitals at Parnassos Hall (Od. Chr. Ladhá). The Hall of the Friends of Music (Rte 10) will provide an important new venue.

Popular Music. Apart from public concerts, in *Boites*. There is normally no entrance charge but drinks are more expensive, to compensate: *Zoom*, 37 Kidhathenaíon, Plaka; *Zígos*, 22 Kidha-thenaíon; *Kíttaro*, 48 Ipírou/Akharnón; also at expensive night-clubs along the coast towards Glifádha. *Rembétika*, the traditional music of the dispossessed (comparable in content to the American blues) is enjoying a new popularity. The most famous old–timers still singing are Sotiría Bellou (at the Club Khárama, Kaisarianí and Mikhaílis Dhaskalákis at Pikermi, Attica (22km from Athens, on the road to Rafina, Rte 21). The same system of payment applies as at boites, though charges are rather higher. Programmes at these traditional establishments do not begin until c 2300 and the main singer rarely appears before 00.30. Similar music can be heard from contemporary groups in a boite setting at such centres as *Rembetikí Istoría*, 181 Ippokrátous. Other establishments offer music in the ordinary folk tradition, each usually performing works from one area of Greece: *To Armenáki*, 1 Patriárkhou Ioakeím, Távros (islands), *Kríti*, Ay. Thomá, Ambelókipi (Crete).

Sport. *Tennis* at Athens Tennis Club, 2 Leof. Olgas, also squash; *Panellínios*, 26 Od. Mavromatéon; Attikí, Filothei; all-weather in the beach complex at Voúla. *Swimming*, open-air pool Leof. Olgas, indoor pool, 277 Patissíon, also in many high class hotels (including the Hilton), open to non–residents on payment of a fee. *Golf* at Varibóbi; also at Glifádha. *Sailing* (Wednesday and Saturday after-noon and Sunday) in Phaleron Bay. *Horse Riding* at Riding Club Attica, Varibóbi; Riding Club of Greece, Parádhissos, Maroússi, and others. *Horse Racing* at Phaleron Delta (bottom of Leofóros Singroú); information in daily papers. *Motor Racing*, the Acropolis Rally (late May) for touring cars starts and ends in Athens; Autumn Rally in November. *Football* is popular in Greece. Matches are mainly on Sunday afternoons. The most important clubs in the Athens area are *Panathenaikós* or *PAOK* (ground near the N end of Leofóros Alex-ándras); *Athlitikí Enosis Konstantinoupóleos*, known as *AEK* (Néa Filadhélfia) and Olimpiakós (Piraeus, Karaïskáki Stadium, by Neon Fáliron electric railway station).

Festivals. *Athens Festival of Music and Drama*, June–August. — *Wine Festival* at Daphni (Rte 16) in September.

Museums, Archaeological Sites, Churches etc

Ancient remains of any significance are usually signposted and the sites enclosed. An admission charge is normally made, the amount varying with the importance of the place concerned. Students are allowed reduced prices on production of a valid identity card. *Bona fide* foreign students of any branch of classical studies can obtain a free pass through their institutions. Opening hours of sites and museums vary in accordance with the season, the importance of the antiquities and local conditions. Museums (but not sites) are closed on Mondays—except for the Benaki Museum in Athens which closes on Tuesday. For smaller sites/museums, it is advisable to reckon on opening hours of 8.30–13.00, for absolute safety. In fact the closing time is usually about 15.00 and, at the more important centres, as late as 17.00 for museums and 19.00 for sites. The National Tourist Organisation in Athens provides an information sheet on opening hours, as do the travel guides. Museums not belonging to the state do not conform to these arrangements. Both sites and museums are closed on 1 January, 25 March, Good Friday morning, Easter Day and Christmas Day. Hours are restricted on Christmas Eve, New Year's Eve, 2 January, 5 January, the last Saturday of Carnival, Thursday in Holy Week, Easter Tuesday. At major sites, where the number of visitors can detract considerably from one's pleasure in the tourist season, it is highly desirable to begin one's visit at opening time in the morning, before the large parties arrive. The antiquities can then be inspected at reasonable leisure and the surroundings enjoyed.

In general photography (hand cameras) is free on archaeological sites, and may be indulged freely (save where unpublished material is on display) in museums on purchase of a second ticket for the camera. ΑΠΑΓΟΡΕΥΕΤΑΙ (apagorévetai) means forbidden. Set fees (not cheap) are charged for using tripods, etc.

The Greek Antiquities Service treats its visitors' safety as their own responsibility. Travellers should, perhaps, be warned that holes are not always fenced, nor heights guarded by railings; the very nature of archaeological remains ensures the maximum number of objects that can be tripped over. It is particularly dangerous to move about while reading or sighting a camera.

Assistance beyond that given in the text can usually be canvassed on the spot with the use of the following vocabulary: *yiá* (towards) *ta arkhaía* ('ancient things'), *to kástro* (any fortified height), *tis anaskafés* (excavations), *to froúrio* (medieval castle). Licensed guides are available in Athens, and on some major sites; casual offers of guidance are better politely declined in Athens and Piraeus, but can be disinterested and invaluable elsewhere.

Orthodox churches (sometimes open) may be visited at any reasonable hour; when they are closed inquiry should be made for the key. Women are not permitted to enter the sanctuary.

Antiquities. The regulations to protect Greece's heritage are strictly enforced. Importation of antiquities and works of art is free, but such articles should be declared on entry so that they can be re-exported. Except with special permission, it is forbidden to export antiquities and works of art (dated before 1830) which have been obtained in any way in Greece. If a traveller's luggage contains antiquities not covered by an export permit, the articles are liable to be confiscated and prosecution may follow. Note that the use of metal detectors is strictly forbidden in Greece and it is an offence to remove any object, however seemingly insignificant, from an archaeological site.

Diving and underwater photography are not permitted in most parts of Greece.

Language

The Greek alphabet now as in later classical times comprises 24 letters:

Α α, Β β, Γ γ, Δ δ, Ε ε, Ζ ζ, Η η, Θ θ, Ι ι, Κ κ, Λ λ, Μ μ, Ν ν, Ξ ξ, Ο ο, Π π, Ρ ϱ, Σ σ ς, Τ τ, Υ υ, Φ φ, Χ χ, Ψ ψ, Ω ω.

VOWELS. There are five basic vowel sounds in Greek to which even combinations written as diphthongs conform: α is pronounced very short; ε and αι as e in egg (when accented more open, as in the first e in there); η, ι, υ, ει, οι, υι have the sound of ea in eat; ο, ω as the o in dot; ου as English oo in pool. The combinations αυ and ευ are pronounced av and ev when followed by loud consonants (af and ef before mute consonants).

CONSONANTS are pronounced roughly as their English equivalents with the following exceptions: β = v; γ is hard and guttural, before a and o like the English g in hag, before other vowels approaching the y in your; γγ and γκ are usually equivalent to ng; δ = th as in this; θ as th in think; before an i sound λ resembles the lli sound in million; ξ has its full value always, as in ex-king; ρ is always rolled; σ (ς) is a sibilant as in oasis; τ is pronounced half way between t and d; φ = ph or f; χ akin to the Scottish ch, a guttural h; ψ = ps as in lips. The English sound b is represented in Greek by the double consonant μπ, d by ντ. All Greek words of two syllables or more have one accent which serves to show the stressed syllable. The classical breathing marks are still sometimes written but have no significance in speech. In the termination ον, the n sound tends to disappear in speech and the ν is often omitted in writing.

Manners and Customs. *Calendar and Time:* Greece abandoned the Julian calendar only in 1923 so that even 20C dates can be in Old or New Style. All moveable festivals are governed by the fixing of Easter according to the Orthodox calendar. Greece uses Eastern European Time (2 hours ahead of GMT); πμ—am and μμ—pm. When making an appointment it is advisable to confirm that it is an 'English rendezvous', i.e. one to be kept at the hour stated. The siesta hours after lunch (often late) should not be disturbed by calling or telephoning.

Attention should be paid by travellers to the more formal conventions of Greeks. The handshake the health taken seriously. The correct reply to Καλώς ωρίσατε (kalós orísate: welcome) is Καλώς σας βρήκαμε (kalós sas ply to Καλώς ωρίσατε (kalós orísate: welcome) is Καλώς σας βρήκαμε (kalós sas vríkame: glad to see you). To the inquiry Τί κάνετε, (tí kánete; how do you do?) or πώς είσθε; (pos íste; how are you?) the reply should be καλά, ευχαριστώ, και σείς (kalá efkharistó, ke sis): well, thank you—and you?—or έτσι καί έτσι (etsi ke etsi) so-so. General greetings are χαίρετε (khérete; greetings, hello); Γειάσας (yásas; hello, goodbye—literally your health) and Στό καλό (sto kaló; keep well), both useful for greeting strangers on the road. Περαστικά (perastiká is a useful word of comfort in time of sickness or misfortune meaning 'may things improve'. Except in the centre of Athens it is still customary to greet shopkeepers, the company in cafés, etc., with καλημέρα (kaliméra: good day) or καλησπέρα (kalispéra: good evening). Σας παρακαλώ (sas parakaló: please) is used when asking for a favour or information, but not when ordering something which is to be paid for, when Θά ήθελα (tha íthela: I should like) is more appropriate. The Greek for yes is ναί (né), or more formally μάλιστα (málista); for no, όχι (ókhi). Αντίο (addío), goodbye, so long, in Greek has none of the finality of its Italian origin.

In direct contrast to English custom, personal questions showing interest in a stranger's life, politics, and money are the basis of conversation in Greece, and travellers must not be offended at being asked in the most direct way about their movements, family, occupation, salary, and politics, though they will usually find discussion of the last singularly inconclusive.

By Greek custom the bill for an evening out is invariably paid by the host; the common foreign habit of sharing out payment round the table is looked upon as mean and unconvivial, and visitors valuing their 'face' will do it discreetly elsewhere. A stranger is rarely allowed to play host to a native.

It is not good manners to fill a wine-glass, nor to drain a glass of wine poured for one, the custom being to pour it half full and keep it 'topped up'. Glasses are often touched with the toast εις υγείαν σας, your health (generally shortened in speech to the familiar yásas or yámas or, to a single individual, yásou); they are then raised to the light, the bouquet savoured, and the wine sipped before drinking (thus all five senses have been employed in the pleasure).

Entering a Greek house one may formally be offered preserves with coffee and water; this must never be refused. Strictly to conform to custom the water should be drunk first, the preserves eaten and the spoon placed in the glass, and the coffee drunk at leisure. Payment must, of course, never be offered for any service of hospitality. An acceptable way of reducing an obligation is by making a present to a child of the house. Equally hospitality should not be abused; those offering it nearly always have less resources than their foreign guests—even the proverbially poor student.

The 'Volta', or evening parade, universal throughout provincial Greece, has no fixed venue in Athens. Fasting is taken seriously in Lent.

Carnival after three weeks' festivities reaches its peak on the Sunday before Clean Monday with processions and student revels. Its manifestations are strong in Patras, Naoussa, and in Athens are centred on Plaka. Procession of shrouded bier on *Good Friday* (Epitáfios); 'Christos anésti' (Christ is risen) celebration, with ceremonial lighting of the Paschal candle and release of doves, in front of churches at midnight preceding *Easter Sunday*, followed by candlelight processions and 'open house'. Roasting of Paschal lambs and cracking of Easter eggs on morning of Easter Day. These ceremonies are performed with pomp in the capital—*Okhi Day* commemorating the Greek 'no' (Οχι) to the Italian ultimatum of 1940, is celebrated with remembrance services and military processions, especially in Salonika.

Transliteration. Regarding Greek place-names, Col. Leake wrote 150 years ago 'It is impossible in any manner to avoid inconsistency'. Many recent writers on Greece have tried to make a virtue of 'the avoidance of pedantry', but even pedantry is preferable to chaos, and some measure of consistency must be attempted, even if doomed to incomplete success. Modern Greek is not the same language as ancient Greek, and in any case many modern places in Greece have names derived from Albanian, Turkish, or 'Frankish' roots. The most acceptable compromise is gained by using one set of rules for modern place names, and another for those of ancient times.

Names of modern localities have been transliterated in accordance with the phonetic system codified by the Permanent Committee on Geographical Names (E. Gleichen and J.H. Reynolds, *Alphabets of Foreign Languages*, P.C.G.N. for British Official Use, London 1951, pp 52–56), used alike by NATO and by professional and archaeological journals. Though this results sometimes in visual ugliness, and for those with a knowledge of Greek increasing irritation (disguising the familiar apparently unnecessarily: thus Khlóï), it has three merits: a great measure of alphabetical consistency for indexing; easy cross-reference to most official maps and to original excavation reports; and the possibility for non-Greek-speakers of producing a recognisable approximate pronunciation. Where the result has seemed too *outré* to be born and where there is a recognised and familiar English version (e.g. Rhodes), this has been used at least in all subsidiary references.

Ancient names have been given in the traditional English form used by classical scholars and archaeologists, preferring the purely English form where this exists (e.g. Aristotle, Homer), and the Latin form where this has become accepted everyday English usage: e.g. Boeotia, not Boiotia; Plato, not Platon. In other instances the form nearest to the ancient Greek has generally been preferred (with k for χ, rather than the misleading c), and (e.g.) Sounion rather than Sunium.

This duality, though producing inconsistencies between ancient and modern (e.g. respectively ch and kh for χ), highlights the pitfall that the modern place bearing the equivalent of a Classical name is not necessarily in the location of its ancient counterpart. Where they are coincident, some reconciliation may have to be affected: it is well for Christians to remember the Beroea of St. Paul, but advisable when journeying there to think of the modern town as Vérria.

It should be pointed out that, until the recent designation of demotic Greek as opposed to katharevousa (formal Greek) as the state language, place names had often both a katharevousa and a demotic form (αι Αθήναι, η Αθήνα for Athens). Formal versions of place names may occasionally linger on old signs. The final -v of neuter names, sometimes retained in our texts, is often omitted in practice. Neither modern form is necessarily the ancient form: thus Thorikos, anciently ή Θόρικος has become ό Θορικός. In addition *all* place-names, like other nouns, decline; this often produces a change of stress as well as of inflexion. Some places have their more familiar spoken form in the accusative (given, where thought desirable, in the text), though they appear on maps in the nominative; places ending in -on often drop the 'n' in speech, sometimes the whole syllable. Street names are in the genitive when called after a person, e.g. Ermou (of Hermes), also in the genitive when leading to a place, e.g., Patission (to Patissia). As in English, a church may be spoken of by the name of its saint in the nominative or genitive. In the vexing instance where the Greek name is in itself a transliteration from Roman characters, each example has been treated on its apparent merits. Thus Βεραντζέρου (which in Greek pronunciation bears little resemblance to the Fr. *Béranger*) has been rendered Veranzérou; Βύρωνος similarly has been rendered Víronos by sound since Lord Byron properly appears in Greek literary criticism as Μπάυρον. Names of modern Greeks have been rendered where possible as their owners transliterated them or as arbitrary custom has demanded.

No consistency can be attempted in the language or spelling of hotel names, since they are often chosen quite arbitrarily themselves. What is displayed on the building is likely not to correspond with the name listed in the hotel guide—only experience can help in the realisation that (e.g.) Ilios, Helios, and Soleil designate the same hotel (Ηλιος), or that Mont Blanc and Lefkon Oros are one and the same.

In this book, at its first mention, a place-name is given also in lower case Greek, where the difference from English may make this an aid to reading maps and road signs. On main roads signposts are printed in Greek and Roman characters (but inevitably not in a consistent transliteration). In the Guide, accents have been put on transliterated place names at their main entry, since they show pronunciation stress. For the sake of economy they have sometimes been omitted elsewhere, though an attempt has been made normally to accent words which travellers may need to use for asking directions; the names in the index are fully accented. Ancient names, if accented, have been given their modern stress, where this may be a help in asking directions. Breathings are not normally given. Accents on initial vowels are not given, in accordance with modern practice.

Books About Athens and Attica

K. Andrews, *Athens* (Methuen Cities of the World Series, 1967), not easy to obtain but one of the best books ever written about Greece: a sensitive and finely written appreciation of Athens and its people; K. Andrews, *Athens alive* (Athens, 1979), excerpts from writers about Athens between A.D. 7 and 1940; C. Bouras et al., *Churches of Attica* (Athens, 1970); M. Chatzidakis, *Byzantine Athens* (Athens, n. d.); Commercial Bank of Greece, *Neoclassical buildings in Greece* (Athens, 1967 and reprint); W. W. Davenport et al., *Athens* (Time-Life Books, 1978); L. D. Loukopoulou, *Attika* (National Bank of Greece, Athens, 1973); L. Mikhelí, *Unknown Athens* (Athens, 1990); also other works on Athens, Monastiraki, Plaka, Piraeus; Greek Ministry of Culture, *Athens from the end of the ancient era to Greek independence* (Athens, 1985), Greek and English parallel text with illustrations; Greek Ministry of Culture, *Historical map of Athens* (Athens, 1985); Pausanias (tr. P. Levi), *Guide to Greece* Vol. 1, (Penguin, 1971); TAPA (Greek Archaeological Receipts Fund), *Athens Capital City* (Athens, 1985), in French or Greek; J. Travlos, *Pictorial dictionary of ancient Athens*, (New York, 1971); J. Travlos, *Bildlexicon zur Topographie des antiken Attika* (Tübingen, 1988); R.E. Wycherley, *The stones of Athens* (Princeton U.P., 1978).

Other Books on Ancient Art, Archaeology and History

Prehistory: Sinclair Hood, *The arts in prehistoric Greece* (Pelican History of Art, 1978). **History**: A.R. Burn, *A traveller's history of Greece: the Pelican history of Greece* (Pelican, 13th rev. ed., 1982); W. Miller, *The Latins in the Levant* (J. Murray, 1908); J. Campbell and P. Sherrard, *A history of modern Greece* (Cambridge University Press, 1968). **Art and archaeology**: C.M. Robertson, *A shorter history of Greek art* (Cambridge University Press, 1981); A.W. Lawrence, *Greek architecture* (Pelican History of Art, 1968); D.E. Strong, *Roman art* (Pelican History of Art, 1976); F. Sear, *Roman architecture* (Batsford, 1982); D. Talbot Rice, *Art of the Byzantine era* (Thames and Hudson, 1963); R. Krautheimer, *Early Christian and Byzantine architecture* (Pelican History of Art, 1975); British School at Athens/ Society for the Promotion of Hellenic Studies, *Archaeological Reports*, an annual, and somewhat technical, survey of recent discoveries in Greece and its ancient colonies. The best source of up-to-date information. Enquiries to the Secretary, Hellenic Society, 31–4 Gordon Square, London WC1H 0PY. **Other**: A Huxley and W. Taylor, *Flowers of Greece and the Aegean* (Chatto and Windus, 1977).

Ministry of Culture and TAPA publications are mostly available from the bookshop in the National Archaeological Museum; Bank publications from 12 Thoukidhídhou (Plaka) or 2 Karyeóryí Servóas (Síndagma) (National Bank of Greece) or 45 Mitropoleos (Commercial Bank).

ART AND ARCHITECTURE IN ATHENS—AN INTRODUCTION

by *R.L.N. Barber* and *K.M. Skawran*

PREHISTORIC AND CLASSICAL

Most visitors to Athens are attracted by the monuments of her Classical past, of which ample remains survive on archaeological sites and in museums. The city and surrounding area also have important Byzantine churches and collections; and some fine examples of Folk Art. This brief account is intended to provide a background against which the buildings and objects to be seen in Athens and its vicinity can be understood. For a fuller description, which also covers the rest of Greece, see the introductory articles in 'Blue Guide Greece'.

The earliest archaeological discoveries in Athens go back to the Neolithic and Early Bronze Age phases (c 6000–c 3500 BC, Agora Museum) but are limited in extent and interest. In the time of the first Minoan palaces in Crete (c 2200–c 1700 BC), the Greek mainland was still a cultural backwater but with the advent of the Mycenaean period (c 1550 BC) monumental architecture and a much richer material culture appear in continental Greece. The remarkable finds from the Shaft Graves at Mycenae, including objects imported from Crete and elsewhere, which are the first major witness to the wealth of Mycenaean society, can be seen in the NAM in Athens; the tholos tombs—in the suburb of Menidhi, at Marathon and Thorikos—are examples of the Mycenaean architectural achievement. Parts of the massive fortifications can still be seen on the Athenian acropolis, though nothing now survives of the palace which once stood there. In spite of the destruction of the Mycenaean palaces, possibly as the result of internal conflicts, about 1200 BC, Mycenaean civilisation continued to flourish (finds from Perati, Brauron Museum) until a terminal decline set in c 1100 BC. Greece then entered a Dark Age of depopulation and material decline, for which the main evidence is pottery (SubMycenaean and ProtoGeometric, Kerameikos Museum).

Although the Protogeometric period (c 1025–c 900 BC) shows clear artistic revival in more precise pottery forms and decoration, as well as in some other aspects of material culture, it is convenient to set the end of the Dark Ages in a historical sense at about 800 BC (the Late Geometric period), when there are more substantial and widespread signs of recovery and development (e.g. numerous dedications and the building of some temples in major sanctuaries). From this point the history of Greek material culture can be discussed in terms of its principal forms of expression.

Pottery is frequently used by archaeologists purely as a tool for dating—hence what often seems an obsessive attention to classification and typology. But much of it is of greater interest for its aesthetic qualities and/or its iconography.

Each stage (Early, Middle, Late) of the Geometric period (c 900–c 725 BC) has its own distinctive features but, in general, Geometric pottery is characterised by precision of shape and decoration and a careful attention to suiting the motifs to the structure and form of the vessel, in the best examples creating a visual harmony unsurpassed in the history of vase-painting. In the Late Geometric period, figured scenes, themselves geometricised, become more popular, some of them perhaps representing incidents from the poems of Homer, which were particularly influential at this time. The larger vases are enormous and were used as grave markers, a function which is reflected in the scenes of funerary ritual with which they are decorated (NAM, Kerameikos Museum).

Towards 725 BC the orderliness of the Geometric style began to break down under the influence of new motifs and stylistic features derived from the East Mediterranean, inaugurating the so-called Orientalising phase (c 725–c 625 BC) which is symbolic of this newly expansionist stage of Greek cultural development. Most Athenian Orientalising vases (the style is called Protoattic) are decorated with large figured scenes, often with animals or exotic creatures (sirens etc.). Athenian vase-painters used an outline style with painted interior detail, while Corinthian artists (Protocorinthian) quickly developed a 'black-figure' technique, where the figure is painted in black silhouette, sometimes with other colours added on top, and the details are incised. Corinthian vases, often very small and with a correspondingly precise 'miniaturist' style of decoration, dominated the market at this period and were frequently exported to other Greek states (including Athens) and abroad. Towards 600 BC Athenian artists took over the Corinthian black-figure technique but used it for their own large-scale narrative scenes—subjects drawn from the Trojan War or other mythological cycles (e.g. the Labours of Herakles). In the hands of its masters (Exekias, the Amasis Painter 550–530 BC; NAM etc.), the Attic black-figure style is notable for a magnificent stately elegance with exquisite detail. From c 530 this technique was gradually superceded by that of red-figure in which the background was painted black and the figures left 'reserved' in the natural colour of the clay, the interior detail being painted in with brush or goat's hair. Although less imposing than black-figure the new technique allowed a more natural representation of figures and encouraged the depiction of many scenes from everyday life (athletics, parties etc.) in addition to those of traditional mythology. Some 5C red-figure vases show the influence of contemporary wall painting (e.g. in the use of variable ground-lines, ill suited to vase painting) of which nothing else has survived. Towards 400 BC the style became more florid and ornate (added white paint, gilding) and the subject matter often rather trivial (boudoir scenes). During the 4C vase-painting virtually died out in Athens, though it continued to flourish in the Greek colonies of the West (S Italy, Sicily). In the Hellenistic period (c 330–c 50 BC) pottery, when decorated, is usually made in moulds with ornament in relief (Megarian bowls, Agora Museum).

A striking and attractive group of 5C Athenian vases (NAM) which does not fall into any of the above categories is decorated in the 'white-ground' technique which was particularly applied to the tall *lekythos* shape used especially for funerary rituals and often decorated with appropriate scenes (offerings at the tomb). The ground of the vase is coated white, the figures and other elements drawn in outline and broad washes of colour are applied for hair, garments etc.

Sculpture was made in large and small scale, in the round and in relief and in a range of materials (stone, terracotta, metal, even wood—though little of the latter has survived). Until the end of the Classical period most sculpture served religious functions and it was only in Hellenistic times that the erection of statues of famous mortals became common practice.

Down to c 650 BC all surviving figures are small, though there may have been larger pieces in wood which have not survived. They are usually offerings from sanctuaries. Human figures may represent the deity to whom they were dedicated or be symbolic worshippers; animals probably indicate the desire of the donor to provide the deity with a valuable gift. From c 650 BC we see the development of monumental stone (then bronze) sculpture, the most familiar Archaic types being the male *kouros* (NAM) and the female *kore* (Akropolis Museum). The forms are relatively static over a long period (to c 480 BC), the kouros usually standing rigidly, one foot advanced, the hands by the sides; the kore also upright but often holding out an offering (fruit or a small animal or bird), sometimes clutching her garment and pulling it tight over the legs. The artistic interest of the naked kouros is concentrated on the anatomy, of the kore in the careful treatment of the drapery, frequently with added colour. Formal patterning of both anatomy and drapery gradually gives way to greater naturalism, though the development is unlikely to have been as regular as is often implied. These figures were sometimes cult statues (the Piraeus kouros, Piraeus Museum, which is also one of very few bronzes to have survived), more often offerings in sanctuaries where they may have been symbolic servants or worshippers. Many stood in cemeteries as grave markers. Some of the male figures are gigantic (Sounion kouros, NAM). By the early 5C, some figures (Kritian Boy, Akropolis Museum) show a much more naturalistic pose and treatment of hair and musculature. The earliest phase of classical sculpture, often termed the 'Severe Style', is represented by the ambitious but slightly awkward bronze Poseidon (or Zeus) in the NAM. The spectacular achievements which quickly followed can be exemplified by the figures from the Parthenon pediments (Akropolis Museum; British Museum, London; casts in Centre for Acropolis Studies) where complex poses, realistic anatomy and spectacular drapery effects are achieved at will. It is noteworthy however that classical sculptors made little effort to show feeling through facial expression and the features of the figures remain calm and idealised, in whatever action they are engaged (copy of Diadoumenos of Polykleitos, NAM). Although some features of Hellenistic sculpture have their roots in developments of the 4C (greater expression of feeling and physical character), it is only then that we find full-blown efforts at emotional realism, including portraiture, and a willingness to tackle non-idealised everyday subjects (Horse and Jockey, NAM; bronze portrait from Delos, NAM). The diversity of Hellenistic work includes many pieces directly derivative from the Classical tradition, though the subjects can be rather frivolous and fussy (Pan and Aphrodite, NAM) or else presented with a baroque extravagance (Lykosoura figures by Damophon, NAM). Roman sculpture is largely derived from Hellenistic prototypes (though note also the Archaising reliefs in Piraeus Museum) but strongly influenced by its use for imperial propaganda (emperors in military dress, official portraits) and the use of commemorative figures in funerary ritual.

Most of the works so far mentioned have been in the round. Relief sculpture follows the same general course as far as stylistic development is concerned but some examples and formats are worthy of particular mention. Greek temples were often decorated with sculpture (see below, Architecture). The Acropolis Museum contains a fine series of early pedimental sculptures showing experiments, not only in the representation of form, but also in solving the difficult problem of filling the triangular field in a satisfactory way. The Archaic three-bodied monster is colourful, its fishy tail filling the declining height of the pediment; the Introduction of Herakles is static and highly Archaic; the Athena and fallen giants of the late 5C Gigantomachy much more compositionally successful. The frieze and metopes of the Parthenon (Acropolis Museum; British Museum, London) show the mature classical style in other formats. The peak and edges of pediments were often decorated with free-standing sculptures (acroteria) (Nike from Stoa of Zeus, Agora Museum colonnade).

Much of the relief sculpture to be seen in Athens is in the form of tombstones (Kerameikos Museum, NAM) and votive or record reliefs (NAM, Brauron Museum, Eleusis Museum etc.). Archaic tombstones are tall, narrow and have one (or two) figures only. Later stones are lower and broader and can accomodate more figures. The depth of relief is very low in the Archaic period but can be so deep in the 4C that the figures are virtually in the round. Later examples were often contained in a temple-like frame. The most familiar motif on classical gravestones is of the dead bidding farewell to the living with a handshake. Record reliefs commemorated (and sanctified) treaties between states and other formal agreements. Votives were set up in sanctuaries as offerings to deities and often depict the deities themselves (Apollo, Artemis and Leto, Brauron Museum) or scenes of ritual (Sacrifices to Asklepios, NAM; to Artemis, Brauron). Asklepios is sometimes depicted in the act of healing (Piraeus Museum).

Parts of Greek Temple

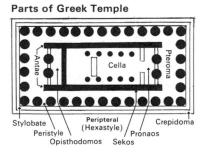

Stylobate · Peristyle · Opisthodomos · Peripteral (Hexastyle) · Sekos · Pronaos · Crepidoma · Antae · Cella · Pteroma

Athens and Attica have some fine examples of Classical *Architecture*. The two main orders of Greek architecture are the Doric (baseless columns, two-part capitals, plain architrave, metope and triglyph frieze) and Ionic (moulded column bases, volute capitals, three-stepped architrave, continuous frieze, also frequent use of subsidiary mouldings). The Corinthian order, which was particularly popular in the Roman period, is essentially the same as Ionic, though the capital is formed of acanthus leaves. The most common form of the classical temple (Hephaisteion or Theseion, Athenian agora) was rectangular with a surrounding colonnade of 6 columns on the front and 13 on the sides (the corner columns are counted each time). Earlier temples tended to be longer and narrower. The interior consisted of a porch, cella (the main room where the cult statue stood, the position of the base being often still visible) and a back room or *opisthodomos*, which balanced the porch but did not communicate with the cella. There are however numerous variations in plan, in proportions and in the application of sculptured decoration. This

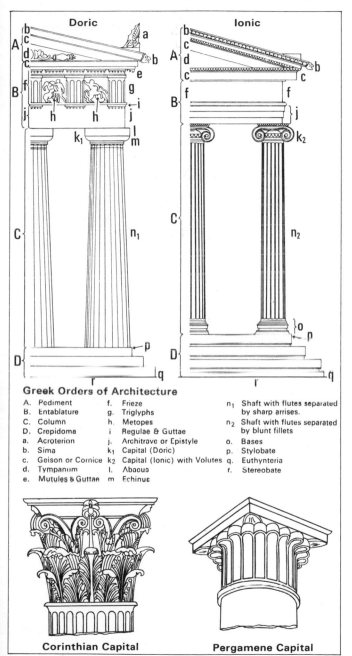

Greek Orders of Architecture

A. Pediment
B. Entablature
C. Column
D. Crepidoma
a. Acroterion
b. Sima
c. Geison or Cornice
d. Tympanum
e. Mutules & Guttae

f. Frieze
g. Triglyphs
h. Metopes
i. Regulae & Guttae
j. Architrave or Epistyle
k_1 Capital (Doric)
k_2 Capital (Ionic) with Volutes
l. Abacus
m. Echinus

n_1 Shaft with flutes separated by sharp arrises.
n_2 Shaft with flutes separated by blunt fillets
o. Bases
p. Stylobate
q. Euthynteria
r. Stereobate

Corinthian Capital

Pergamene Capital

latter might be found in some or all of the metopes of Doric buildings, on the frieze of Ionic and in the pediments of both. In addition there were often *acroteria* (see above). The Parthenon (Doric) is large (8 x 17 columns) and has an unusual Ionic-type continuous frieze, peculiarly set within the colonnade; the Temple of Athena Nike (Ionic) is minute, has only one room and no external colonnade (columns only at the front and rear) and a sculptured frieze; the Erechtheion (Ionic) is a most unusual shape (see description) but its style is clearly Ionic and a continuous sculptured frieze (white marble figures on a background of darker stone) united the disparate elements of the structure. The construction of the Parthenon was carried out with the aid of numerous sophisticated technical refinements which helped to produce a subtle visual effect.

Most of the buildings of which substantial remains survive are temples but the Propylaia to the Athenian acropolis was an elaborate entrance system, which also incorporated ritual dining rooms. Although its facades were Doric, use was made of Ionic columns in the interior and elaborate ceiling decoration (coffers). The stoa was a common element of both City and Sanctuary architecture. In its simplest form a plain rectangular structure with a frontal colonnade (earliest form of the Royal Stoa, Athenian Agora), it sometimes had wings (Royal Stoa, later form; Stoa of Zeus, Athenian Agora). There might be a second, internal row of columns and rooms at the back. The stoa in the Sanctuary of Artemis at Brauron was shaped in the form of the Greek letter Π and had ritual dining rooms behind. The Hellenistic Stoa of Attalos (Athenian Agora) was two-storeyed and had Doric and Ionic, as well as Pergamene features. Other unique building types were the Telesterion (Ritual Hall) at Eleusis and the Tholos and Prison in the Athenian Agora.

Although much Roman building used monumental masonry similar to earlier Greek, a distinctively Roman technique can be recognised at many sites where there are remains of this period. An interior mass of concreted rubble is faced with courses of thin brick. The strength and flexibility of this type of masonry allowed much more ambitious architectural forms than had been possible with the traditional 'post and lintel' system. The bath-buildings with their high vaulted ceilings are a case in point.

EARLY CHRISTIAN AND BYZANTINE

Christian art in Athens and its surroundings developed from the 5C AD. The empress Eudocia, wife of Theodosius II (408–450), was an Athenian and saw to it that many buildings destroyed by the barbarians (e.g. Hadrian's Library) were restored.

By the middle of the 5C Christianity was established. It was a period of great building activity in which churches were erected and temples, like the Parthenon, converted into churches. Fragments of 12C frescoes from the Panayia Athiniotissa can still be seen today on either side of the entrance to the Parthenon (from the 10 to 12C the church served as the Metropolis of Athens). The Asclepion was transformed into the church of Ay. Anargyroi, while the Theseion later became the monastery of Ay. Georgios. Fresco fragments assigned to the 11C have survived, as well as an inscription.

Typical of this early period are the large three-aisled wood-roofed basilicas. Most of the surviving examples are in Salonica. The fine Theotokos church of Skripou in Boeotia is another. Near the Temple of Olympian Zeus in Athens are the remains of two three-aisled basilicas and the foundations of another are situated between the modern sports ground and the swimming pool. The basilica of the Ilissos was lavishly decorated and fragments of its beautiful mosaic floor can be seen in the Byzantine Museum.

Variants of the basilican type can be found throughout Attica. Simple one- or two-aisled chapels occur in Koropi (Ay. Petros, Ay. Athanasios and Ay. Georgios); in Markopoulo (the *Deeisis* church, Ay. Athanasios); in Kouvaras (Ay. Georgios); and in Liopesi (Ay. Paraskevi). Domed basilicas were also common: in Khalidhou (Ay. Nikolaos); in Koropi (Ay. Angeloi) and, further afield, in Megara (Panayia Kyparissiotika in the Monastery of Ay. Hierotheos).

Not much has survived from the 7–9C, a period often referred to as the 'Dark Ages'. Attacked from the north and south, the Greek population suffered also pestilence and earthquakes. Crete was conquered by the Arabs in 823, while Athens lost its geographical importance. Thebes became the administrative and economic centre of Greece.

Between 726 and 843 the Byzantine Empire was further torn by the bitter conflict over the cult of icons (the Iconoclast Controversy). Figural imagery was banned and much existing church decoration was destroyed.

Under the Macedonian Dynasty (867–1056) the situation improved. In 961 Crete was freed from the Arabs and in 1018 Basil II reconquered the Balkans from the Bulqars. The record of church building during the 9C attests the progress of ecclesiastical rehabilitation to which the final restoration of icons had given new impetus.

From the 10–12C a number of well-known bishops, like Michael Choniatis (in Athens between 1182–1204), contributed significantly to the flowering of art in Athens. From early travellers' accounts we know that Athens and its surroundings boasted some three hundred churches. Many of these were demolished when, after 1832, the city expanded and when, in their search for antiquities, archaeologists excavated many sites in Athens.

By the 9C the domed-inscribed-cross type of groundplan, typical of the Middle Byzantine period, had been established. A square hall, usually of modest size, was covered by a small central dome carried on four piers or, ideally, columns, abutted by four radiating barrel or cross vaults (or small domes) over the corner bays, the whole preceded by a *narthex* or vestibule at the west, and screened on the east from the tripartite sanctuary. This comprised the central *bema* with the altar, flanked by the *prothesis* (north) and the *diakonikon* (south).

From the second half of the 10C builders made use of the *cloisonné* technique in which individual squared stones were enclosed with tile-like bricks in both horizontal and vertical joints. This kind of masonry was usually found in the upper courses of the facade, in the dome and around the windows. It frequently comprised simple geometric patterning and pseudo-cufic ornamentation.

Although the form of the domed-inscribed-cross type of church remained remarkably constant, minor variations of the type can be found in and around Athens.

The oldest of the Athenian churches based on the centralised plan is Ay. Apostoloi (c 1000 AD) below the Acropolis. Built over a nymphaeum of the 2C BC, it is characterised by its four large and four half-domes, which create a feeling of lightness and spaciousness in the interior. The skilful application of the *cloissoné* technique on the facade attests the sophistication of the builders.

The Monastery of Sotira Lykodemou (the present Russian church), built before 1030 AD, is of the large dome type better known in the Monastery of Daphni (c 1080). The dome here covers the whole span of the square *naos*, the corners of which are bridged by squinches to form the octagonal base of the large dome.

The Kapnikarea (c 1050) is characterised by its harmonious and elegant proportions which are particularly evident on the eastern front, where the *cloisonné* style is effectively used to break the verticality and flatness of the facade.

The church of Ay. Theodoroi in the centre of Athens (c 1070) is of heavier proportions. Its exterior decoration includes terracotta slabs with pseudo-cufic ornamentation.

Belonging to the 12C is the Gorgoepikoös church (the Little Metropolis or Ay. Eleutherios) which is best known for its sculptural ornamentation and plastic simplicity. Here the tile articulation of the facade has been replaced by marble slabs with a variety of relief images.

The once famous Monastery of Kaisariani on Mt Hymettos has a large unadorned facade and a tall, narrow dome supported by four columns. This type of groundplan is widely represented in Attica outside Athens (the Monastery of Asteri; the Monastery of St John Kynigos on Mt Hymettos and the Omorfi Ekklesia); also in Megara (Ay. Nikolaos, Ay. Sotiras and Ay. Athanasios); in Menidi (Ay. Nikolaos) and in Markopoulo Oropou (the Zoödochos Piyi). In the Metamorphosis tou Sotiras church in Koropi (which has exceptional frescoes of the late 10 or early 11C), the dome is supported in the west by two square piers and in the east by the dividing walls of the sanctuary.

One of the major developments following the overthrow of the Iconoclasts was the establishment of a standard programme for the distribution of religious images in church decoration.

No complete cycle of frescoes or mosaics has survived, but the mosaics in the Monastery of Daphni are an indication of church decoration at the height of the Middle Byzantine period.

The most sacred areas, the dome and higher vaults and the sanctuary, were reserved for the holiest personages. The bust of Christ *Pantocrator* (Christ the Judge) was the most favoured image for the summit of the dome. His presence formed the centre, formally and spiritually, around which the rest of the images in the church were arranged in a strictly hierarchical manner. He is accompanied in the zone below by a celestial host, while the prophets feature between the windows of the drum and the Evangelists commonly in the pendentives (in Daphni scenes from Christ's life are represented here). The *narthex* usually had its own heavenly zone.

Almost invariably the conch of the apse was reserved for the Virgin, either enthroned with the Child on her lap (Daphni) or standing with the child on her arm, or alone with arms upraised.

The communion of the Apostles was usually depicted on the wall below the conch of the apse, with the bishops of the church shown in the lowest register of the apse wall. Deacons appeared just outside the sanctuary. The Ascension normally fills the bema vault, while the rest of the scenes of Christ's life—usually limited to twelve major episodes of the Festival Cycle, appeared on the vaults and upper surfaces of the walls.

Subordinate cycles of Christ's Passion, the infancy of Christ, Christ's miracles, the life of the Virgin or a favoured saint, were sometimes added to the decorative programme of the church.

Holy physicians were usually admitted to the sanctuary, while holy monks, female martyrs and canonised Emperors were commonly relegated to the *narthex*. Sacred warriors and martyrs figured in the nave in relatively high positions where such were available, while half-figures and busts of saints in medallions decorated the soffits of arches.

This hierarchical system of images had to be suitably adjusted to the basilican type of church (Sicily). No such examples have survived in Athens or its vicinity.

POST-BYZANTINE

Although Greece has many fine buildings of the Frankish (especially castles) and Ottoman periods, they are not well exemplified in the area of Athens. The period of Frankish domination here (c 1204–1460) is chiefly represented by the remains of towers. One such on the Acropolis was demolished in 1874, though it can be seen in earlier illustrations; another at Eleusis met a similar fate (1960). There is a surviving example on the road from Markopoulo to Brauron and evidence of others at Kaisariani, Varnavas, Marathon and Panakton. The Cistercian cloister at Dafni is a rare piece of ecclesiastical architecture of this period, although many earlier buildings (the Parthenon, Erechtheion and Theseion) were reused as churches. From the Ottoman period (1460–1830) a little outside our area at Chalkis in Euboea is the Karababa fortress, while in Athens are the Tsidharaki mosque at Monastiraki and, nearby in Plaka, the Fetiche mosque and the medresse gateway.

As an architectural postscript some attention should be paid to the undeservedly neglected modern architecture of Athens. Fine Neo-classical buildings of the 19C and early 20C can be seen in many parts of Athens (see description of Odd. Panepistemiou, Stadhiou, below; index under Kaftanzoglou, Kleanthes, Ziller), many of their architectural features directly inspired by the classical, but some also making use of Byzantine (St. Denis Roman Catholic Church). Outside the centre private houses of the same period and style are more modest but can be very charming. Public buildings and blocks of flats of the early to mid 20C show the declining influence of classicism and a new simple elegance (Arsakeion extension), as well as sometimes period styles (Rex cinema).

As regards non-architectural post-Classical material, the Byzantine Museum (also to some extent the Benaki) contains a good selection of objects of that period—pottery, metalwork, church plate and furniture, as well as icons and wall paintings. Frankish and Ottoman material culture is much less well represented (Benaki Museum, Agora Museum).

The folk culture of Greece has attracted increasing interest in recent years and there are excellent collections in Athens (Museum of Greek Folk Art; Benaki Museum) which are of particular interest for their attractive textiles, embroideries and garments which demonstrate different regional traditions. Woodwork, metalwork etc. is also represented.

For contemporary art, see section on *Art Galleries* under Practical Information and the entries on the Ethnike Pinakotheke, the Vorres Museum (Paiania) and the Pieridhes Gallery (Glifadha) in the main text.

(Note: *NAM* = National Archaeological Museum)

HISTORY AND TOPOGRAPHY

Ancient History. The slopes of the Acropolis have been occupied since Neolithic times. As the early migrations had least effect in Attica, there may be some truth in the classical Athenian claim to be autochthonous. Athens first attained the status of a town in the Middle Helladic period, when the worship of Athena was established on the Acropolis in addition to that of Poseidon Erechtheus; this bears out the traditional date assigned to Kekrops (1581 BC), mythical founder of the royal line. The fabled union (synoecism) of several cities into one state under Theseus (1300 BC) is doubtful, but an Achaean–Ionian kingdom of Mycenaean type does seem to have been based on Athens.

The Dorian invasions are followed by an obscure period, characterised by Geometric pottery, during which the Phoenician alphabet was adopted (? late 8C) to express Greek in writing. Athens begins to emerge for the first time as an artistic centre of Greece; this probably coincides with a historical unification of Attica under Athens (8C BC). The 7C is marked by the vigorous 'Protoattic' style of pottery, though sculpture is comparatively little developed. An attempt by Kylon in 632 BC to seize power was thwarted; the archon Megakles and the whole Alkmaeonid family in perpetuity were banished for allowing the murder of Kylon while in sanctuary, which led to an unsuccessful war with Megara, his father-in-law's city. At the beginning of the 6C, when the 'Archaic' style of sculpture was already passing from the Cyclades to Athens, Solon reorganised Athenian agriculture and encouraged commerce with more distant parts. He inspired the conquest of Salamis from Megara soon after 570 BC by Peisistratos, whose triumph enabled him later to seize power. After ten years' exile in Thrace Peisistratos defeated his opponents at Pallene c 545. By the acquisition of the Thracian Chersonese and the colonising of the Hellespont, he and his sons laid the foundations of the Athenian empire. His edition of Homer made Athens the literary centre of Greece, while he instituted the Great Dionysia of the City, the festival from which Attic drama was born. He began the architectural embellishment of the city, and in his reform of the Panathenaic festival (566 BC) he gave it a prestige equal to that of the gatherings at Olympia and Delphi. Under Peisistratid autocracy Athenian mature black-figure pottery ousted its Corinthian rival by its masterful technique and art, with an export to Syria and Spain. The reign of Hippias, elder son of Peisistratos, became oppressive after the murder of his brother Hipparchos during the conspiracy of Harmodios and Aristogeiton (514 BC). His overthrow was engineered by the Alkmaeonids with the assistance of Kleomenes, king of Sparta. Liberty was thus regained only at the expense of joining the Peloponnesian League, and Hippias retired to plot at the court of Darius, king of Persia . The Athenians aided Plataea against Thebes, and in 506 defeated Chalkis; an expedition against them the same year by Kleomenes failed.

When Aristagoras of Miletus, originator of the Ionian revolt against Darius, appealed for help in 498 BC only Athens and Eretria responded. Twenty Athenian ships took part in the burning of Sardis. In revenge Darius dispatched a huge army and fleet, accompanied by the aged Hippias, to sack Eretria. Heading for Athens, the Persian army was met at Marathon (August or September 490) by 9000 Athenians and 1000 Plataeans under Miltiades and decisively defeated. An unsuccessful war against Aegina, at this time supreme at sea, helped to wake Athens to her maritime danger before the Persian storm again broke in 480, when Xerxes came to avenge his father's defeat. The heroism of the Spartans under Leonidas at Thermopylae retarded but did not stop his advance.   Members of the Delian League at first contributed ships to a common fleet, an arrangement commuted later to a money tribute to Athens, after which the treasury of the league was moved (454 BC) from Delos to the Athenian acropolis. Under Pericles the Athenians put much of the profit towards the aggrandisement of their city, and having defeated Aegina and Corinth, abandoned an unprofitable rivalry on the land with Sparta and Thebes for commercial expansion at sea signing a thirty years' truce in 445. The Periclean vision of a pan-Hellenic congress was nullified by Sparta's refusal to co-operate. The circle of Pericles included some of the greatest names in Athenian arts and letters. Stimulated by Zeno and Anaxagoras, he extended his patronage to the visiting Herodotus; inspired Thucydides; encouraged Attic drama, which attained in his day its completest development in the art of Sophocles (495–406 BC); and gave free scope to the genius of Pheidias in the design of the Parthenon. In the foundation of Aegean cleruchies Pericles anticipated the Roman Colonial system.

The Peloponnesian War (431–404 BC) was the inevitable outcome of rivalry between Sparta and Athens. With the death of Pericles in 429, the now fully-developed democracy lost its most capable leader. The ill-fated Sicilian Expedition (415–414 BC), urged on by Alcibiades, was the prelude to the disaster of Aegospotami in 405. The humiliating conditions of peace forced on Athens in 404 included the destruction of her enceinte. For a brief time even democracy was eclipsed in the *coup d'état* of the Thirty Tyrants, until Thrasyboulos restored the constitution in 403, marring its record by the execution of Socrates (399). The comedies of Aristophanes (fl. 427–387) span these troubled times.

The recovery of Athens was swift. Against Sparta Konon won his great victory at Cnidos in 394 BC; and assisted by Thebes Athens re-established her naval hegemony with the Second Maritime League, organised in 378. Art and literature declined but little, and philosophy and oratory reached their apotheosis in the 4C. It was the age of Plato (428–347), Xenophon (c 430–354), and Isocrates (436–338). A new danger now arose in the person of Philip of Macedon, who conquered Amphipolis in 357, Potidaea in 356, and Methone in 353. Spurred on by the oratory of Demosthenes (383–322), Athens took up the role of champion of Greek liberty, but was finally vanquished at Chaeronea in 388.

The subject city was treated with favour by Alexander the Great, whose Macedonian tutor, Aristotle, taught in the Lyceum. An unsuccessful bid for independence on Alexander's death (323 BC) led to the imposition by the usurper Kassander of a collaborating governor, Demetrios of Phaleron (318–307). A brief liberation by Demetrios Poliorketes, claimant to the Macedonian throne, was followed by a period of alternate freedom and subjection to Macedonia; after a defeat by Antigonus Gonatas in the Chremonidean War (266–263), Athens suffered a garrison until 229, although her democratic institutions were respected. Supremacy in science had now passed to Alexandria, but Athens still led in philosophy; in Menander (342–291) comedy reached a new peak. The fall of Perseus in 168 BC substituted the Roman for the Macedonian rule, but the city of

Athens continued to flourish, retaining many privileges when the province of Achaia was formed out of S Greece after 146. Having espoused the cause of Mithridates in 86 BC, it was captured by Sulla, when its fortifications were razed, its treasures looted, and its privileges curtailed. It nevertheless received a free pardon from Julius Caesar for siding with Pompey and from Antony and Augustus after supporting Brutus, who removed here after the Ides of March. Athens continued to be the fashionable seat of learning in the ancient world, attracting the sons of rich Romans, including Cicero and Horace.

St. Paul preached 'in the midst of Mars' hill' (Acts, xvii, 22) in AD 54. Hadrian (120–128), under whom Plutarch was procurator of Achaia, frequently lived in the city and adorned it with imperial buildings. His example was followed by Herodes Atticus in the time of the Antonines, when the city was visited by Pausanias; and Athens remained the centre of Greek education until the Edict of Justinian in AD 529 closed the schools of philosophy.

Later History. The agora suffered in the first Gothic (Herulian) raid of 267, but Alaric's capture of the city in 396 seems to have caused less damage to its monuments. In the reign of Justinian, or earlier, many temples were consecrated to Christian use and modified. Under Byzantine rule Athens dwindled to an unimportant small town. It was sacked c 580 by the Slavs. Constans II wintered in the city in 662 on his way to Sicily, and Theodore of Tarsus studied here before becoming Archbishop of Canterbury (669–690). Basil II, the Bulgar-slayer, celebrated his victories of 1018 in the Parthenon.

After the fall of Constantinople in 1204, the Greek provinces N of the Isthmus of Corinth fell to the share of Boniface III, Marquis of Montferrat, with the title of King of Thessalonica. Boniface granted Attica and Boeotia to Otho de la Roche, a Burgundian knight, with the title of Grand Seigneur (Megas Kyr; i.e. Μέγας Κύριος) of Athens and Thebes. A century of pacific and prosperous 'Frankish' rule brought some amelioration to the condition of the Athenians but no part in affairs; trading privileges were granted to Genoese and Venetian merchants. Matthew Paris records a visit as a student by Master John of Basingstoke (died 1252). In 1258 Guy I accepted the title of duke from King Louis of France; the magnificence of the Athenian court of this period is noted by the Catalan chronicler Ramon Muntaner. On the death of Guy II in 1308, the duchy passed to his cousin Walter de Brienne. Walter's designs on Byzantine territories leagued the rulers of Constantinople, Neopatras, and Epirus against him, and he called to his aid the Catalan Company. Being unable later to rid himself of them, he precipitated the disastrous battle of Kopais, where in 1311 the Catalans totally destroyed the power and nobility of Frankish Greece.

The Grand Company now assumed sovereignty of Athens and Thebes, but placed Roger Deslau, one of the two noble survivors of Duke Walter's army, at their head. After pursuing a career of conquest in N Greece, they approached Frederick of Aragon, king of Sicily in 1326, with the result that his second son Manfred became duke and for sixty years the Duchy of Athens and Neopatras (as it was now styled) was misgoverned from Sicily by avaricious General Commissioners. In 1386 the Siculo-Catalans fell foul of Nerio Acciaioli, governor of Corinth, a member of that family which was 'plebian in Florence, potent in Naples, and sovereign in Greece' (Gibbon). Nerio seized Athens, Thebes and Levadia, and in 1394 received the title of duke from Ladislas, king of Naples. Captured by a band of Navarrese troops, he bought his ransom by rifling all the churches in his dominions.

Under his son Antony, Athens, protected by Venice, enjoyed forty years' peace, but Antony's weak cousin and successor, Nerio II (1435–53) held his duchy as a vassal of the Sultan. During his reign Athens was twice visited by Ciriaco de' Pizzicoli (better known as Cyriacus of Ancona), the antiquary. Demetrius Chalcondyles (1424–1511), the Renaissance scholar who published the *editio princeps* of Homer, was an Athenian. When Nerio's widow and Pietro Almerio, the Venetian governor of Nauplia and her new husband, seized the dukedom, the Athenians complained to the Sultan, who replaced Almerio by Franco Acciaioli, a nephew of Nerio. Franco banished his aunt, the ex-duchess, to Megara and had her murdered there, whereupon Pietro complained to the Porte. Mehmed II ordered Omar, son of Turahan, to seize the Acropolis, and annexed Attica to the Ottoman Empire in 1456. A guide book written by the so-called Vienna Anonymous, describes Athens in 1456–60. A Venetian raid in 1464 achieved nothing but the plunder of the city.

Nearly 400 years of Turkish rule followed, a peculiar result of which was the rehabilitation of the Orthodox Church, so long dispossessed by Rome. Athens was visited in 1672 by Père Babin, a French Capuchin, who drew the earliest extant plan, and in 1675 by Francis Vernon, who sent back to the Royal Society the first English account of the city. The same year Lord Winchilsea, then ambassador to the Porte, secured some architectural fragments. In 1676 came Spon and Wheler. In 1687 occurred the siege by Francesco Morosini, during which the Parthenon was shattered. Thenceforward until 1821, the conditions of Athens under the Turks is picturesquely described by Gibbon, who accuses the Athenians of his day of 'walking with supine indifference among the glorious ruins of

Acropolis. Venetian bombardment and explosion of the Parthenon in 1687. Engraving

antiquity'. The worst period of tyranny was experienced under Hadji Ali Haseki in 1775–95. After the appearance of Stuart and Revett's 'Antiquities of Athens' (1762), based on a visit of 1750, travellers to Athens became more numerous.

In 1821, soon after the outbreak in Patras of the War of Independence, the Greek general Odysseus seized Athens and the Acropolis. In 1826–27 the Acropolis, besieged by Reshid Pasha, was bravely defended by the klepht Gouras and after his death by the French general Fabvier. Vain attempts to raise the siege were made by Karaïskakis and after his death in 1827 by Admiral Cochrane and General Church. On 27 May 1827, the Acropolis was taken by the Turks and held until 12 April 1833. In 1834 Athens became the capital of liberated Greece.

During the First World War the city was occupied by British and French troops after some opposition by Royalist troops of the pro-German government. The population was greatly increased by the exchange of Greek and Turkish nationals in 1923. On 27 April 1941, German forces entered the capital unopposed after a campaign lasting three weeks, and Athens remained in their hands until October 1944. In December 1944 open Communist revolution broke out in the Theseion area after a demonstration had been fired on by police earlier the same morning in Sindagma Sq. After bitter street fighting British troops, with reinforcements, landed at Phaleron, eventually restored order and at a conference called by Churchill on Christmas Day an armistice was arranged whereby Archbishop Dhamaskinos became regent.

Topography. PREHISTORIC ATHENS. In Early Helladic times groups of settlers had lived within reach of the fortress, and Late Helladic chamber tombs have been found in the N and W slopes of the Areopagus hill and in the area which later became the agora. The Mycenaean royal city centred on the fortress of the Acropolis, where a 'Cyclopean' wall enclosed the palace complex, Homer's 'strong house of Erechtheus', but settlements and shrines extended S to the Ilissos. At an early date part of the N, S and W slopes of the Acropolis were enclosed by the Pelasgikon wall, but evidence of Sub-Mycenaean and Protogeometric graves shows a gradual spread of occupation towards the NW, where the Kerameikos became the chief necropolis.

THE ARCHAIC CITY. Peisistratid palatial occupation and the siting of a new temple perhaps in 566 BC for the Panathenaic festival must have lessened the living space on the Acropolis. The Pnyx and Mouseion hills were already occupied by houses in the 6C, and even before the Peisistratids the popular Kerameikos quarter was becoming the centre of Athenian life. It was the meeting-place of the assembly, the altar of the Twelve Gods was set up there, and the archons had their offices in the vicinity. By the end of the 6C the population seems to have resided wholly in the lower city. There was probably a city wall at this time but no archaeological evidence of it has ever been found.

CLASSICAL ATHENS. The Acropolis and much of the town outside was laid waste by the Persians in 480. After the battle of Plataea, Themistocles, who had begun to fortify Piraeus as early as 493, began a city wall on a course which endured until the time of Hadrian. Thucydides (1, 93) records its hasty erection with whatever material was at hand. No general plan of the sort adopted in Piraeus was ever made for Athens, and the narrow crooked streets remained.

Kimon finished the circuit; and the two Long Walls, connecting Athens with Piraeus, were completed under Pericles. Of the fifteen city gates located, the names of ten are known but not certainly identified. In the 440s Kallikrates completed the Phaleric Wall. Much of the monumental greatness of Athens dates from the third quarter of the 5C. The Academy, embellished by Kimon, became a favourite Athenian promenade. In 404 the walls were demolished at the Spartan command, and the Long Walls never rose again. Konon rebuilt the enceinte in 393, and Lycurgus (338–326) completed, rebuilt or embellished much of the city, modifying the Pnyx for the Assembly's use. The walls were shortened about this time by the erection of the Diateichisma, and the city flourished with gradual modifications until the Roman sack of 86 BC.

IMPERIAL ATHENS. Archaeologists have disagreed whether Hadrian extended the enceinte, but the discovery in 1959 near the Olympieion of a gate which confirms the E course of the Themistoclean wall suggests that Hadrianopolis was indeed an extension to the E and not merely the aggrandisement of an older quarter. Here were gymnasia, thermae, and the usual manifestations of Roman rule. Under Augustus a new market had been built E of the Agora; Hadrian added a huge library in the same area. He also built a reservoir on Lykabettos fed by a new acqueduct. A generation or so later Herodes Atticus founded his Odeion and reseated the decaying Stadium in marble. After the Herulians had destroyed most of Athens in 267, the Athenians lost confidence in the Roman army and withdrew behind the post-Herulian ('Valerian') wall enclosing the N slope of the Acropolis.

LATER TOPOGRAPHY. Christian Athens remained round the Acropolis where the Frankish dukes had their palace in the Propylaia. The Turks fortified the S slope of the Acropolis, Serpentzes turning the Odeion of Herodes Atticus into a redoubt. The later Turkish town was lightly walled by Haseki in 1778–80, using in the N the ruins of the ancient circuit. The modern city owes its basic inner plan to the Bavarian archtects of King Otho and its unplanned suburban development to its rapid growth in 1923.

GLOSSARY OF ART TERMS

AEGIS. Cuirass or shield with Gorgon's head and ring of snakes.

AGORA. Public square or market-place.

AMAZONOMACHIA. Combat of Greeks and Amazons.

AMBO (pl. *ambones*). Pulpit in a Christian basilica; two pulpits on opposite sides of a church from which the gospel and epistle were read.

ANTHEMION. Flower ornament.

APOTROPAION. A protective symbol to turn away evil.

BEMA. (*Anc.*) Rostrum; (*Byz.*) Chancel.

BRECCIA. A composite rock (pudding-stone).

CHITON. A tunic.

CHLAMYS. Light cloak worn by epheboi.

CHOROS. A hanging circle in metal or wood for the display of icons.

CHTHONIC. Dwelling in or under the ground.

CYMA (recta or reversa). A wave moulding with double curvature.

EPHEBOS. Greek youth under training (military, or university).

EPITAPHIOS. Ceremonial pall.

EROTES. Figures of Eros, god of love.

ESCHARA. Sacred hearth.

EXEDRA. Semicircular recess in a classical or Byzantine building.

GIGANTOMACHIA. Contest of Giants.

GYMNASION (in Mod Gk.). Grammar school.

HERM. Quadrangular pillar, usually adorned with a phallus, and surmounted by a bust.

HEROÖN. Shrine or chapel of a demigod or mortal.

HIMATION. An oblong cloak thrown over the left shoulder, and fastened over or under the right.

HOPLITE. Heavily armed foot-soldier.

HYPAETHRAL. Open to the sky.

ICONOSTASIS. Screen bearing icons.

KORE. Maiden; Archaic female figure.

KOUROS. Boy; Archaic male figure.

MEGARON. Hall of a Mycenaean palace or house.

NARTHEX. Vestibule of a Christian basilica.

NAUMACHIA. Mock naval combat for which the arena of an amphitheatre was flooded.

NYMPHAION. Sanctuary of the Nymphs.

ODEION. A concert hall, usually in the shape of a Greek theatre, but roofed.

OIKOS. A house.

OMPHALOS. A sacred stone, commemorating the 'centre of the earth' where Zeus' two eagles met.

OPUS ALEXANDRINUM. Mosaic design of black and red geometric figures on a white ground.

PANTOKRATOR. The Almighty.

PARECCLESIA. Chapel added to a Byzantine church.

PEPLOS. A mantle in one piece, worn draped by women.

PERIBOLOS. A precinct, but often archaeologically the circuit round it.

PETASOS. Broad-brimmed felt hat worn by epheboi.

PHIALE. Saucer or bowl.

PINAX. Flat plate, tablet, or panel.

PODIUM. Low wall or continuous pedestal carrying a colonnade or building.

POLYANDREION. Communal tomb.

POROS. A soft, coarse, conchiferous limestone (tufa).

PROPYLON, PROPYLAEA. Entrance gate to a temenos; in plural form when there is more than one door.

PROTHESIS. (*Anc.*) Laying out of a corpse; (*Byz.*) The setting forth of the oblation, or the chamber N of the sanctuary where this is done.

PUTEAL. Ornamental well-head.

QUADRIGA. Four-horsed chariot.

SIMANTRON. Block of wood or metal bar beaten as a call to divine service.

SPHENDONE. The rounded end of a stadium.

STOA. A porch or portico not attached to a larger building.

TEMENOS. A sacred enclosure.

THEME. (*Byz.*) A province.

THOLOS. A circular building.

THYMELE. Altar set up in a theatre.

TRANSENNA. Openwork grille at the entrance to a Byzantine chapel.

TRILITHON. Gateway made up of two jambs and a lintel.

TRIREME. Greek galley rowed by 3 banks of oars.

XOANON. Wooden image or idol.

I ATHENS

ATHENS (η Αθήνα), the capital of the Hellenic Republic (Ellinikí Dhimokratía), is situated in lat. 37° 58' N and long. 23° 43' E, 6.5km from the sea. The city, which now occupies the greater part of the Attic plain, is surrounded by an amphitheatre of mountains, nowhere far distant, and to the E, in Hymettos, barely 8km from the centre. At the 1981 census Greater Athens (Periféria Protevoússis), comprising 37 demes and 19 communes partly in the nome of Attikí and partly in that of Piraeus, numbered 3,027,331 inhabitants; of these the city proper, or deme of Athens, accounted for 885,737 and Piraeus for 196,389, while the remainder was distributed between their modern residential and industrial suburbs extending in every direction. Athens has thus engulfed the subordinate and almost isolated group of lesser hills, which more nearly defined the limits of the ancient city.

The northernmost of these hills, which are in reality fragments of the Anchesmos or Tourkovouni range, is Strephís. Immediately S rises the conical rock of Lykabettos, still called by its classical name. This remarkable hill is to Athens what Vesuvius is to Naples or Arthur's Seat to Edinburgh. From its summit the city is seen as on a map. To the SW of Lykabettos are five more hills, all of which were included in ancient Athens. Of these, the nearest is the Acropolis or citadel of Athens, rising abruptly to 156m, a little more than half the height of Lykabettos. To the W of the Acropolis are the Areopagus, the Pnyx, and the Hill of the Nymphs; and to the SW is the Mouseion.

Athens, although one of the most easterly cities of Europe and in spite of nearly 400 years of Turkish rule, is almost entirely western in appearance. A creation of the 19C and 20C, it was planned by the Bavarian architects of King Otho, who laid out a new street plan round the large village that then occupied the N slope of the Acropolis. Though its approaches are ugly and gimcrack, the centre with squares planted with exotic trees is by no means unattractive; in recent years a number of fine neoclassical buildings have been restored and both these and examples of inter-war public architecture are an interesting and attractive, though often neglected, feature of the city today; the best of the most recent buildings achieve a style appropriate to the strong light by successful use of deep balconies and white marble; while the splendour of its ancient monuments grouped about the dominating Acropolis, gives to Athens a distinction enduring time and change.

'Odhós' (Street) is often omitted in addresses; the practice has sometimes been followed here (with the abbreviations 'Od./Odd.'), except where the omission might cause confusion.

1 From Síndagma Square to the Acrópolis and the Agorá

BUS 230: by this route hurried tourists may quickly reach the Acropolis by road while seeing some of the more obvious sights of Athens on the way. For the traveller on foot whose immediate object is the Acropolis it is more rewarding to approach from the N side by plunging directly into the narrow streets of Plaka (Rte 6); the shortest way is by Od. Apóllonos and Od. Adhrianoú, where Od.

Mnesikléous leads to the path under the awe-inspiring cliff crowned by the Erechtheion.

Those on foot who wish to combine the S slope with the Acropolis itself may avoid the noisiest streets by taking Od. Níkis and Od. Kidhathenaíon to the Monument of Lysikrates. The buildings on the S slope will, however, be better appreciated from the Acropolis wall where their plan is more clearly apparent. This may prove sufficient for the casual visitor.—For the direct approach to the Agora, see Rte 4.

The centre of the visitors' quarter is Síndagma Square (3, 8; Πλατεία του Συντάγματος, or *Constitution Sq.*), a busy open space closed on the E by the palace from whose balcony in 1843 the constitution was proclaimed. The square itself, to the W and below the level of Amalia Avenue, bustles with the life of its hotels, cafés, air terminals and banks. The gardens are planted with orange trees, oleanders, and cypresses. The figures in bronze beside its walks are copies, presented by Lord Bute, of antique originals in the museum at Naples. The ancient *Stele* in the NW corner marked a boundary of the Garden of the Muses (see below). The *Hôtel Grande Bretagne*, built in 1842–43 as a private house for A. Demetriou by Theophilus von Hansen, was reconstructed in 1958 retaining some of the original features. It was the headquarters of the French School in 1856–74, and of the Greek, German, and British forces in turn during the Second World War. During Christmas eve, 1944, while Churchill was visiting strife-torn Athens, an attempt to blow up the hotel from the sewers was just foiled. Above Amalías Avenue, a paved hollow square, framed by trees, fronts the palace, in the retaining wall of which is placed a *Memorial to the Unknown Soldier*.

The bas-relief, depicting a dying Greek, was modelled on a figure from the Temple of Aphaía at Aegina now in the Munich collection; the adjacent texts are from Pericles' funeral oration. On the walls bronze shields celebrate Greek victories since 1821. The guard, drawn in turn from the armed services, is changed on Sunday mornings (11.00), and the square is used as a saluting base for national processions. From it a ceremonial marble staircase (1928) leads up to the ex-Royal palace (visitors ascend by the side roads).

Excavations during rebuilding round the square in 1957–61 brought to light 119 graves dating from Classical times when the area, which lay along the Themistoclean wall between the Acharnai and Diocharous gates, was a necropolis.

The *Lykeion*, or Lyceum, dedicated to Apollo, lay beyond the Diocharous gate at the foot of Lykabettos. Its grounds served as a parade-ground for the ephebes; before the time of Solon, the Polemarch had his offices here. Later Aristotle expounded his philosophy here; his disciples were dubbed 'Peripatetics' from their habit of walking as they discoursed. The trees of the Lyceum were cut down by Sulla to make siege-engines. The *Garden of the Muses*, or Mouseion, was given c 320 BC by Demetrios of Phaleron to Theophrastos, Aristotle's heir and successor at the Lyceum, who left it to the school.

The old **Royal Palace** (3, 8; *Pálaion Anáktoron*), since 1935 the seat of the GREEK PARLIAMENT (Βουλή; *Vouli*), is well situated on rising ground E of the square. Designed by Bavarian court architects, it was built in 1836–42, King Ludwig of Bavaria laying the first stone. It is in the early plain classicising style and the original interior decoration was in the Pompeian manner. The W front has a Doric portico of Pentelic marble. The interior was damaged by fire in 1910 and transformed in 1935.

After the senate was abolished in 1862, apart from an unsuccessful attempt in 1927–35 to revive the Upper House, Parliament consisted of one House only. During the military dictatorship of 1967–74 its functions were in abeyance.

LEOFÓROS VASILÍSSIS AMALÍAS (Queen Amalía Av.), a handsome boulevard where many suburban buses terminate, leads S alongside the *National Garden (*Ethnikós Kípos*; open daily to sunset). Designed by Queen Amalía for the palace and still referred to as the *Royal Gardens*, this is a favourite Athenian retreat from the summer sun. Its sub-tropical trees are irrigated by a channel that succeeds the aqueduct of Peisistratos; peacocks and waterfowl frequent its serpentine walks and ornamental ponds; and nightingales sing here in the spring. There is a *Botanical Museum* housed in a charming small pavilion (1857) with an imaginative display of all the trees, shrubs and plants in the garden.

In the garden are busts of the poets Solomós and Valaorítes, of Count John Capodistrias, and of Eynard, the Swiss philhellene. There are remains of an Early Christian basilica and mosaic. Farther N, behind the palace, are some remains of *Roman Baths* with large geometric mosaics, and traces survive of Hadrian's city wall.

Farther along (right), the **Russian Church** (*St. Nicodemus*, properly *Sotíra Likodhímou*; 7, 4) overlooks a small square. The church, the largest remaining medieval building in Athens, was founded shortly before 1031 by Stefan Likodemou (died 1045). Its monastic buildings, ruined by earthquake in 1701, were pulled down in 1780 to provide material for Hadji Ali Haseki's wall. Damaged by shell-fire in 1827, the church remained derelict until restored by the Russian government in 1852–56. The external walls have a terracotta frieze, and the wide dome rests on squinches. The detached belfry is a 19C addition; the great bell was a gift of Tsar Alexander II.

Under the church and square are remains of a Roman bath (2C AD); excavations in 1961 suggested its early adaptation as a place of Christian worship. An inscription of the 1C BC, still near the church where it was found, comes from the Gymnasium of the Lyceum (comp. above), with which this bath is probably to be associated.

Just beyond is the **English Church** (*St. Paul's*; 7, 5), designed by C.R. Cockerell in an undistinguished Gothic style in 1840–43. Within on the N side are a British funerary memorial of 1685, removed here from the Theseion, and a painted window to Sir Richard Church with an inscription by Gladstone. The E window commemorates the victims of the 'Dilessi murders' (1870). At 36 Amalias is the *Jewish Museum*, founded in 1977 to illustrate the heritage of the Jewish community in Greece whose origins go back to the 3C BC. On the opposite side of the avenue open the *Záppeion Gardens*, the S continuation of the National Garden. To the left of the entrance is a charming marble Pan by Yeoryios Demetriades and in the central avenue a figure of Varvakis, founder of the high school. The **Záppeion** (7, 6), founded by the cousins Zappas as a national exhibition hall, was built by Theophilus von Hansen in 1874–88 and renovated in 1959–60. The semicircular exterior has a handsome porticoed façade and encloses a circular colonnade surrounding an open court. In front are statues of the founders; beyond is a popular café with an open-air stage (evening cabaret).

The S side of the Záppeion Gardens is bounded by Leofóros Olgas (see Rte 7) which meets Amalía Avenue in a large open triangle, one of the busiest traffic centres in Athens. On the corner (left) stands a sentimental 19C group of Byron and Hellas, by Chapu and Falguière. On the far side is the **Arch of Hadrian** (7, 5), an isolated gateway in Pentelic marble erected by Hadrian c AD 132 to mark the limit of the

ancient city and the beginning of Novae Athenae or Hadrianopolis
(Rte 7). The façades, otherwise identical, bear differing inscriptions
on the frieze: that on the NW side towards the Acropolis reads 'This is
Athens, the ancient city of Theseus'; that on the SE side towards the
Olympieion records 'This is the city of Hadrian and not of Theseus'.
The gate is some way W of the line of the Themistoclean Wall; it was
incorporated in the 18C Turkish enceinte.

The gate is 18m high, 12·5m wide, and 2·3m thick, with an archway 6m across.
The piers of the arch were adorned with Corinthian columns, the bases and
consoles of which can be traced. Above the archway is an attic consisting of a
portico of four Corinthian columns with three bays, the middle one having a
pediment.—Behind is the *Olympieion* (Rte 7).

Odhós Lissikrátous leads W into Plaka (see Rte 6), passing the church
of *Ayía Aikateríni*. The ancient columns that front the palm-shaded
garden were probably reused as an earlier church façade in the 6C.
At the end of this street ran the STREET OF THE TRIPODS.

It was the custom of the victorious choregi to dedicate the tripods which they
had gained in dramatic contests to Dionysos. These tripods were erected either
in the precincts of the Theatre or (on special bases or in architectural settings) in
a street specially appropriated to them, which led in a semicircle round the E of
the hill from the Prytaneion to the Theatre. The tripods were placed over the
works of art, the kettle or cauldron forming a sort of roof. Pausanias singles out
for mention the Satyr of Praxiteles, no longer extant (torso of a copy in the
Louvre), but ignores the monument of Lysikrates. Such other foundations as
were located in 1921 and 1955 (to the number of seven) and 1980 have been left
in situ and covered again.

The well-preserved *Choregic Monument of Lysikrates is renowned
not only for its graceful detail, but as being the earliest building
known in which the Corinthian capital is used externally. A square
base of Piraeus stone 4m high, with a cornice of Eleusinian marble,
bears three circular steps of Hymettos marble. On this base six
monolithic Corinthian columns are arranged in a circle to support an
entablature crowned by a marble dome, wrought with great delicacy
from a single block; from the centre of the roof rises an elaborate
finial of acanthus-leaf carving, the support for the tripod itself. An
inscription on the architrave informs us that 'Lysikrates of Kikyna,
son of Lysitheides, was choregos; the tribe of Akamantis won the
victory with a chorus of boys; Theon played the flute; Lysiades of
Athens trained the chorus; Evainetos was archon' (334 BC). Round
the frieze is represented the story of Dionysos and the Tyrrhenian
pirates, whom he turned into dolphins. The whole of the superstructure is in Pentelic marble, except the curved panels (of Hymettian
marble), engaged between the columns that form the central drum.
Of these only the three showing a frieze of tripods are original.

The inside of the drum was never intended to be seen for the capitals are
unfinished within and there is no provision for light. However, the missing
panels were removed during the period (1669–1821) when the monument was
incorporated in the library of a French Capuchin convent. It was then known as
the 'Lantern of Demosthenes' from a belief that the orator prepared his
speeches in it. Byron, one of many English guests at the convent, is said to have
used it as a study; he wrote part of 'Childe Harold' here in 1810–11. On the
occupation of Athens by Omer Vrioni the convent was accidentally burned
down; the monument was freed and later properly restored in 1892 with French
funds. Recent excavations in the immediate vicinity of the monument have
uncovered a further section of the Street of the Tripods and the foundations of
other choregic monuments. Later finds include Roman burials and the remains
of an Early Christian basilica. To Monastiráki and the N side of the Acropolis,
see Rte 6.

The Street of the Tripods curved down to the main Propylaia of the Sanctuary of Dionysos (see below). Inside the curve, just E of the theatre, stood the **Odeion of Pericles**, built originally before 446 BC, burnt during the sack of Athens in 86 BC by Aristion, a general of Mithridates, who feared that Sulla might use the timbers of the roof for siege engines, and rebuilt in marble on the former plan by Ariobarzanes II, king of Cappadocia (65–52 BC). Its side has only recently been expropriated from beneath a jumble of poor houses, but investigations by the Greek Archaeological Society in 1914–31 proved it to be rectangular in plan, not circular as had been assumed from classical references to its being modelled on the tent of Xerxes. It was a large hall, terraced on the S side, with interior columns arranged in nine rows of ten, somewhat similar in plan to the Telesterion at Eleusis, and had a pyramidal roof with a lantern. The scene of the musical contests of the Panathenaic Festival, it had the reputation of being the best concert-hall in the Greek world; and rehearsals of the tragedies presented in the Theatre of Dionysos at the Great Dionysiac Festival were held in it.

You continue by the broad Od. Dhionissiou Areopayítou (named after St. Paul's convert, Dionysius the Areopagite). To the left (entrance in Od. Makriyiánni) is the *Centre for Acropolis Studies* and the site of the projected new Acropolis Museum (see p. 60); to the right an entrance to the **Excavations on the S slope of the Acropolis** (6, 6; there is also a gate above giving access to the Acropolis, which is sometimes open). Immediately within the gate we cross the line of the wall that once bounded the TEMENOS OF DIONYSOS ELE-UTHERIOS. Traces of the wall survive to the E, but the main entrance to the precinct from the Street of the Tripods (see above) has not been excavated.

The worship of Dionysos Eleutherios was introduced into Athens in the 6C BC from the then Boeotian city of Eleutherai. The festival of the Great Dionysia of the City, instituted by Peisistratos, which eclipsed the old festival of the Wine-press (Lenaia) held in the marshes, was characterised by the competing choruses of satyrs, clad in goatskins, who danced round the altar of the god and sang their 'goat songs'. These dithyrambic contests were the forerunners of Attic tragedy.

You pass the breccia foundations of a small 4C *Temple* consisting of pronaos and cella, built to re-house the chryselephantine statue of Dionysos by Alkamenes, seen by Pausanias; the great base on which it was placed remains. Nearer the theatre are scantier remnants of an *Older Temple* dating from the 6C. To the SE are foundations representing either the great altar or the base of a large votive dedication.

The **Theatre of Dionysos** was rebuilt in stone by Lycurgus in 342–326 BC to replace an earlier structure in which the masterpieces of Aeschylus, Sophocles, Euripides, and Aristophanes were first per-formed. Extensive modifications in Hellenistic and Roman times involved the re-use of old material so that the existing remains present a puzzling conglomeration of the work of 750 years. A programme of conservation and restoration now in progress was preceded by a careful survey of the site.

History. Archaeologists differ about the dating of much of the structure and historians of the Greek drama have reached no certain conclusions about the superstructure or internal layout of the skene before Roman times. The clearest exposition of the many problems can be found in A. W. Pickard-Cambridge: The Theatre of Dionysos in Athens (OUP, 1946) and may be supplemented by the reports of further investigations in 1951 and 1963.

It is probable that a circular *Orchestra*, or dancing ground, with a central altar, existed here in the 6C BC (though traces of a terrace-wall are all that survive from this period) and that by the beginning of the 5C spectators occupied wooden stands. Following an accident (c 500–470 BC) to a stand either here or in the agora, an earthen auditorium (*theatron*) was constructed. Here, against a background of wood and canvas, the great dramas of the Golden Age were performed. About the time of Pericles the auditorium assumed nearly its present shape, when supporting walls were built to the E and W; the seats were still probably of wood. The orchestra was moved a little to the N but remained circular, and a long foundation wall served both to retain the extended terrace and to support a wooden stage set. Immediately behind and slightly below this was built a stoa, connected to the orchestral area by a flight of steps and having an open colonnade on its S side.

A reconstruction in the 4C was probably finished c 330 BC by Lycurgus, when the theatron was rebuilt in stone in much the form it has today, and a permanent skene in stone, flanked by columned paraskenia, replaced the movable wooden sets. Plays continued to be acted at orchestral level but in Hellenistic times, when attention had passed irrevocably from ritual dancing to dramatic acting, a raised stage was added, supported by a stone proskenion. At the same time the paraskenia were taken back and the parodoi (side entrances) widened to give easier access to the auditorium.

The skene and stage were again rebuilt, possibly by T. Claudius Novius c AD 61. At some time the Roman stage was further extended over the parodoi to meet the auditorium, and a marble barrier erected round the orchestra to protect the audience from gladiatorial exhibitions. At a later period (?3C AD) the Bema of Phædrus was added in front of the Roman proskenion. Still later the reliefs on the bema were truncated and cemented over when the orchestra was turned into a watertight basin for the performance of naumachiæ.

Even in classical times the theatre was used for other purposes than drama. The presentation of crowns to distinguished citizens, the release of orphans from state control on their reaching man's estate, and other ceremonies served as curtain-raisers to the play. The golden crowns presented by independent foreign states and the tribute of subject states were displayed in the theatre. Annual cock-fights, instituted after the Persian wars, took place here. The Assembly, occasionally in the 4C (Thuc. VIII, 93) and regularly after the 3C, met here instead of in the Pnyx. Demetrios Poliorketes after making himself master of Athens (292 BC) here overawed the Assembly with a military display.

The AUDITORIUM retains roughly the form it assumed under Lycurgus when, on the W side, the outer wall of poros was added to the earlier buttressed wall of breccia. At the same time the supporting wall on the E, irregular in contour due to the proximity of the Odeion (see above), was extended to the rock above. Concentric tiers of seats, radiating fanwise from the orchestra, are separated into 13 wedges (kerkides; *Lat.* cunei) by narrow stairways. Some 25 tiers survive in part.

It is generally assumed that there were 64 tiers of stone seats divided by a postulated gangway (*diazoma*) into two sections of 32 rows each. Above this the *Peripatos* (cf. below) formed a second diazoma. An upper section of 14 more rows of seats, hewn from the rock, may have been a later addition; the higher remains are fragmentary. The seating capacity can hardly have exceeded 17,000, far short of Plato's estimate of 30,000 (Symposium).

The seats, made (except for the front row) of Piraeus limestone, are shaped so that one row of spectators did not incommode the next row: each person sat on the flat section in front (probably on a cushion), placing his feet in the trough hollowed behind the seat below. The front row consisted of 67 *Thrones* in Pentelic marble. Sixty remain in the theatre, of which 14 were found in place; the remainder have been restored with some certainty to their original positions. Each bears the name of the priest or dignitary for whom it was reserved; since some of the original inscriptions were replaced with later inscriptions, the thrones have been called replicas of the 1C BC. However, the style of the relief sculpture and both the design and workmanship of the thrones indicate that the entire front row dates from the time of Lycurgus. Distinguished by its more elaborate shape and fine sculpture is the *Throne of the Priest of Dionysos Eleutherios*, placed in the centre, exactly opposite the thymele, or altar of the god, which stood in the middle of the orchestra.

The throne is a beautifully carved armchair with lion's-claw feet. On the back, delicately worked in low relief, is a representation of two satyrs, supporting on their shoulders a yoke from which hangs a branch of grapes. In front is inscribed the name of the owner; above the inscription is a remarkable relief of two kneeling male figures in Persian costume, each of whom grasps a gryphon by the throat with one hand, lifting with the other a scimitar. On each arm is a beautiful figure in low relief of a winged boy conducting a cock-fight. The Throne of Hadrian occupied the large plinth just behind. The area in front of the seats drains into a channel surrounding the orchestra.—Statues of Roman emperors, tragic and comic poets, orators, statesmen, and philanthropists were numerous; the base of one of Menander, by Kephisodotos and Timarchos (sons of Praxiteles), stands at the NW corner of the skene.

The ORCHESTRA preserves today none of its classical appearance. The existing area, in the form of a slightly extended semicircle, represents the orchestra of the Roman rebuilding under Nero. The surface was then paved in marble slabs with a central rhombus made of smaller coloured pieces. Slabs also cover the Lycurgan drainage channel. Both these and the marble barrier protecting the auditorium are pierced with drainage holes, which were later stopped up (and the water channel blocked) when the theatre was used for mock sea-fights.

The so-called *Bema of Phædrus* stands in a mutilated condition for about half its length. This presumably represents the final front of the Roman stage. It takes its name from the dedicatory inscription on the slab that surmounts the uppermost of the four stone steps in the centre. The date of the inscription is doubtful; Phædrus is otherwise unknown; and the stone is not in its original place. The reliefs have been dated to the 2C AD, and almost certainly came from somewhere nearby. They portray scenes in the life of Dionysos, the last (westernmost) relief showing the God installed in his theatre on a gorgeous throne with the Acropolis and Parthenon in the background. The well-preserved crouching sileni were forced into place afterwards. When found in 1862 the figures were still plastered with cement from the waterproofing (see above).

Behind lie the foundations of earlier stage buildings. You can trace the Hellenistic proskenion, flanked by paraskenia, some truncated columns of which survive, and, farther back, the outline of the long stoa of Periclean date; but the remains between are too confused by late masonry, designed merely as support for the Roman skene, to aid any imaginative reconstruction in the mind of a layman, and admit of widely diverging interpretation by experts.

Above the theatre opens the **Panayía Chrysospilióttissa** or *Chapel of Our Lady of the Cavern*. On the walls are faded Byzantine paintings. Within, every evening, a solitary lamp is lit. Round the mouth of the cave the rock face is cut vertically to form a scarp known as the *Katatomé*. The entrance was masked, until Turkish gunfire destroyed it in 1827, by the *Choregic Monument of Thrasyllos*, erected in 320 BC by Thrasyllos, who dedicated the cavern to Dionysos. The monument took the form of a Doric portico raised on two steps. Three marble pilasters supported an architrave bearing the dedication, above which was a frieze adorned with eleven wreaths carved in relief; the tripod stood above the cornice. Fifty years later, when president of the Games (agonothetes), Thrasykles, son of Thrasyllos, added two further dedications commemorating similar victories of his own in choregic contests. The inscriptions may still be seen. A seated figure of Dionysos found above the monument, and now in the British Museum, was a Roman addition.—The two Corinthian *Columns* above the cavern also supported votive tripods; the cuttings for their feet in the triangular capitals may be seen from the top of the wall of Kimon. To the right is a *Sundial* in Pentelic marble, noted in the 15C Vienna Anonymous.

To the W of the theatre the ancient remains extend along the slope in two terraces. The upper terrace is supported by a massive retaining wall buttressed by a continuous row of arches (some 40 of which now provide from the road the most conspicuous feature of the area), over which ran the PERIPATOS, the main highway, nearly 5m wide, round the Acropolis. Steps descend to it from the upper part of the theatre. If you ascend from the orchestra, you see (left) the rectangular foundations of the *Choregic Monument of Nikias*, erected in 319 BC in the form of a prostyle hexastyle temple and demolished soon after AD 267 to provide material for fortifications. The stones were used in the Beulé Gate, where part of the inscription from the architrave can still be seen (cf. Rte 2); the full text read: 'Nikias, son of Nikodemos of Xypete, dedicated this monument after a victory as choregos with boys of the tribe of Kekropis; Pantaleon of Sikyon played the flute; the *'Elpenor'* of Timotheos was the song; Neaichmos was archon.

Above the peripatos and to the W of the theatre extends the pleasant **Asklepieíon**, or *Sanctuary of Asklepios in the City*, dedicated in 418 BC by Telemachos of Acharnai on a site already sacred to a water-god. The 5C sanctuary occupied the W portion of the terrace; in the 4C a new precinct was built to the E, extending to the theatre wall. Each contained a sacred spring, a temple and an altar, and an abaton or stoa. The most conspicuous remains within the temenos are, however, the walls of a large Byzantine *Church* of the 5C or 6C, where, probably under the patronage of SS. Cosmas and Damian, the cure continued under the Christian ægis.

The worship of Asklepios, which spread from Epidauros, was introduced into Athens on the occasion of the plague of 429 BC. The 'cure' followed a ritual, during which patients washed in the sacred spring, offered sacrifices at an altar, and then retired to the stoa where the mysterious process of incubation ('ἐγχοίμησις)was assisted by incense from the altars. This and religious excitement produced dreams, through the medium of which Asklepios was supposed to effect his cure. Many ex-voto tablets to Asklepios and Hygieia have been found showing the portion of the anatomy treated. These were affixed to a wall or inlaid in the columns; larger votive stelai, some showing the god visiting sick patients in their sleep, were fixed to the stoa steps (examples in the National Museum).

To the E, somewhat obscured by the Byzantine walls, can be traced the foundations of the later *Abaton*, consisting of a colonnade with 17 Doric columns and two interior galleries separated by another colonnade. The long plinth of Hymettian marble, the back wall to the E and the intermediate row of bases are all that remain *in situ*, but the stoa probably had two floors, the upper one being the *Enkoimeterion*, or dormitory of the sick. A narrow passage leads from the N gallery into a circular spring house hewn in the rock. The wonder-working nature of the sacred spring continues, and the ancient spring house is now a chapel which is kept locked.

At the W end of the stoa, probably under a baldachin roof, was the so-called *Bothros*, perhaps a sacrificial pit where blood was poured to chthonic divinities, but more likely the dwelling of the sacred snakes. In front of the stoa are the foundations of a small *Temple* in antis. In the W part of the temenos, which is bounded by the Pelasgikon wall, are the foundations of the smaller 5C *Stoa*. The *Old Spring* was contained in a fine 5C rectangular cistern of polygonal masonry, transformed by the Turks. Just to the S is another huge *Cistern*, probably of Byzantine date.

To the W of the Asklepieion the sanctuaries enumerated by Pausanias have disappeared beneath the Turkish fortifications. A path follows the general direction of the peripatos through confused remains round the top of the Odeion (see below) to the entrance of the Acropolis, though this gate is sometimes closed.

The arches of the peripatos road were formerly concealed by the so-called **Stoa of Eumenes**, which began c 9m from the Theatre of Dionysos and extended for 163m. At its W end it communicated with the Odeion by two doors. The impressive socle of its back wall is in Hymettian marble. The outer Doric colonnade had 64 columns.

This is assumed to be the colonnade built by Eumenes II, king of Pergamon (197–159 BC), who is recorded by Vitruvius (V, 9, 1) as having built a stoa near the theatre to serve as a shelter and promenade. Recent study (M. Korres) has shown close technical connections (similar marble, mason's marks) with buildings at Pergamon itself and parts of the structure may have been prefabricated there. In Roman times it was connected with the much later Odeion of Heródes Atticus and remained in use until the 3C when it was destroyed and the materials used in the Valerian wall. Column drums can be seen at No. 30 Veïkou. The Turks incorporated the remnants in their lower enceinte (Wall of Serpentzes) in 1687.

To the W of the stoa is the **Odeíon of Heródes Atticus**, built in honour of Regilla, wife of Herodes, who died in AD 160. It has the typical form of a Roman theatre with a seating capacity of 5000–6000, and was one of the last great public buildings erected in Athens.

The sudden rise to wealth of Julius Atticus, father of Herodes, is wittily related by Gibbon. Julius, who had accidentally found a vast treasure buried in an old house, anticipated the officiousness of informers by reporting his find to the emperor. On being told by Nerva to have no qualms about using—or abusing—fortune's gift, Julius devoted large sums to public works and to educating his son. Herodes, after a distinguished public career, including the consulship at Rome, retired to Athens and continued the munificence of his father, paying for projects in Troas, Delphi, and Corinth, as well as for the stadium and this Odeion in Athens. The Turks converted the Odeion into a redoubt, without, however, injuring its plan. The interior was excavated in 1857–58, when evidence showed that it had been destroyed by a fire. A large quantity of murex shells found at the same time suggests that the Byzantine Greeks had a factory there for Tyrian purple. The theatre is the scene of orchestral and operatic performances during the Athens Festival.

The massive *Façade* stands everywhere to the second storey and in places to the third, though the portico that stood in front has disappeared (mosaic excavated and re-covered). Entrance is made to either side through vestibules (traces of mosaics) leading to the parodoi. The stage wall is pierced by three doors and has eight niches for statues. Above are windows. Three steps of the E stair connecting the stage with the orchestra remain. The steeply-rising *Auditorium*, supported by a thick circular limestone wall, was roofed with cedar. It consists of a cavea, c 78m across, divided by a diazoma, below which are five wedges of seats and ten above. The seating was entirely restored in Pentelic marble in 1950–61, and the *Orchestra* repaved in blue and white slabs.

To the S of the Odeion, on either side of the modern entrance stairway, are remains (of various dates) including a *Sanctuary of the Nymphs*, excavated by the Greek Archaeological Service in 1955–59 and identified by its boundary stone. Loutrophoroi found date from the mid-7C; these were vessels used for the bridal bath and offered here afterwards as dedications.

Just beyond the Odeion is a busy junction. To the right a drive (no motor vehicles; car park opposite, in front of Dhionisos Restaurant) mounts to the entrance of the Acropolis. Ahead a panoramic avenue (access to Pnyx *son et lumière* seating and *Dora Stratou/Philopappos* theatre) circles Mouseion Hill to the Philopappos monument (see Rte 3). Between them Leofóros Apostólou Pávlou continues (c 1km) to the W entrance of the Agora (Rte 5).

2   The Acropolis

The Athenian **Acropolis** stands alone in its unique combination of grandeur, beauty, and historical associations. This rocky height, traditionally connected with the Pelasgi, was the original city (πόλις) and the abode of the early kings and their courts. It possessed also an irresistible attraction for the tyrants, Kylon making an abortive, and Peisistratos a successful, attempt to establish it as a fortified residence. After the fall of the Peisistratids, however, the Athenians lived entirely in the Lower City and resigned the Acropolis to their gods. It was sacked by the Persians in 480 BC. New walls built by Kimon and Pericles were followed by the great era of construction under Pericles, who was responsible for the array of buildings which, despite the vicissitudes of time, remain an inspiration to the world. It is particularly beautiful in the setting sun and by the light of the full moon.

The *Acropolis* is a rock of coarse semi-crystalline limestone and red schist, of very irregular form, measuring c 320m by 128m. Its summit (156m), to the NE of the Parthenon, is 91m above the general level of the city. From the summit two ridges run towards the W, the more important of them ending in the bastion of the Temple of Athena Nike, to the SW. The only accessible slope follows the depression between these two ridges. Elsewhere the hill is precipitous or even overhanging, with inaccessible clefts and caverns in the rock. The sheer descent on the S side, however, is largely artificial.

History. Natural springs have attracted man to the slopes of the Acropolis since Neolithic times (c 5000 BC) and the site was inhabited continuously throughout the Helladic periods. Towards the end of the Bronze Age (Late Helladic IIIB) the Mycenaean settlement was strengthened with a 'Cyclopean' rampart (sometimes loosely called the Pelasgic Wall), consisting of two facing walls of large undressed stones in more or less regular courses, with a core of rubble. It was filled in with clay and its thickness varied from 4·5m to 6·7m. The surviving fragments show that the wall followed a sinuous course adapted to the contour of the rocky height. A well-preserved section (4·3m) runs from the Propylaea to the S circuit wall. To the N the wall overhung the escarpment of the Long Rocks and is now mostly obscured by later walls; to the S and E it kept nearer to the ridge than the later wall of Kimon. The bastion on which the Temple of Athena Nike stands has a Mycenaean predecessor beneath which probably defended a principal W entrance akin to the Lion Gate at Mycenae. A postern gate to the NE, approached by narrow steps hewn in a natural cleft, which provided the entrance in Early and Middle Helladic times, was abandoned about this time. Farther W a secret reservoir, deep underground, was reached by eight flights of stairs, accessible only from the top of the Acropolis, thus securing an unassailable water supply for the Acropolis in time of siege. Explorations, made with great difficulty in 1937–38, showed that the reservoir dated from the latter half of the 13C BC and was in use for c 25 years only. Its existence was quite unknown in Classical times, when the lower flights were buried and the uppermost two flights of stairs were used to provide a secret exit from the Acropolis to the N slope. The principal Mycenaean building was the Royal Palace, Homer's 'strong house of Erechtheus', which stood somewhere on the N side probably in the region of the Old Temple of Athena. The Tomb of Kekrops, founder of the dynasty, was presumably just to the W. A few remains of Mycenaean dwellings exist on the N side, and tombs below.

At some later date a lower wall was constructed on the W slope to form a precinct similar to that at Tiryns. This wall was known as the Pelasgikon or Pelargikon, perhaps because it was built by the Attic Pelasgi (Hdt. VI, 137), perhaps from the storks which used to nest on the battlements. It was known later as the 'Enneapylon' (nine gates), but no trace of it remains and its course can only be inferred from literary references. Though this was dismantled after the fall of the Peisistratids in 510 BC the area enclosed by it remained unoccupied in obedience to the oracle of Delphi until refugees crowded in at the time of the Peloponnesian War.

Little is known of the Acropolis in the five centuries between the Mycenaean and Archaic periods, though continuity of the cults of Erechtheus, Kekrops, etc., suggests uninterrupted occupation. The original wall, the Kekropion, and the great altar of Athena seem to have survived until the Persian War. A Geometric temple to Athena is assumed to have stood on the same site as the Late Archaic Temple of Athena which replaced it 530–500 BC. Numerous fragments of architecture and of pedimental sculpture belonging to a sizeable poros lime-stone temple of the mid-6C BC have been found on the S side of the Acropolis between the Parthenon and the S wall. This temple has, rightly or wrongly, been identified with the *Hekatompedon* (or 'hundred-footer') to which ancient inscriptions refer. Because the inscriptions clearly name the Parthenon cella 'Hekatompedon' and use the same name for a pre-Parthenon building on the Acropolis, and because the architectural and sculptural remains were found in the immediate vicinity of the Parthenon, many archaeologists equate these remains with the Hekatompedon and consider it a predecessor of the Parthenon built on the Parthenon site; others consider that this material belongs to the building whose foundations were identified by Dörpfeld between the Parthenon and the Erechtheion (cf. below, *Old Temple of Athena*). Pedimental sculpture and other members of four small Archaic buildings have been found on the Acropolis; the better preserved fragments are displayed in the museum.

The victory of Marathon (490 BC) and the opening of new marble quarries on Mt Pentelikon stimulated a scheme, presumably stemming from Aristides, for an ambitious new temple (usually referred to as the Older or Pre-Parthenon). The surface area of the Acropolis was enlarged by building terraces with retaining walls filled in with debris from the demolished Hekatompedon. The new foundations in poros had been completed and work started on the columns when the Persian sack of 480/79 BC reduced the Acropolis to calcined ruins.

Essential cleaning up and patching up were undertaken directly after the battle of Plataea. The gateway was repaired and part of the cella of the Old Temple of Athena may have been restored as a Treasury. In accordance with an oath taken before Plataea, the sanctuaries were left in ruins as reminders of Persian impiety. The Persians had demolished enough of the fortification wall of the 13C BC to render it useless, and when the Acropolis north wall was rebuilt the Athenians created a perpetual reminder of Persian barbarism by incorporating remains of both the Old Temple of Athena and of the Older Parthenon near the top of the wall where they can be seen to this day. On the S side more terrace walls were undertaken and filled in with debris to extend the area of the Acropolis still further. The spoils of the Battle of the Eurymedon (460s BC) eventually enabled Kimon to undertake a more ambitious plan whereby a massive S wall was started. This was completed under Pericles and established the bastion, c 18m high, that still exists.

The decision to rebuild the Acropolis on a monumental scale was taken by Pericles about the time the peace treaty was signed with the Persians at Susa (448 BC). The Parthenon was finished in 438 BC and the Propylaia immediately begun. The Temple of Athena Nike and the Erechtheion followed. The latter was not finished until 395, and the final demolition of the restored Opisthodomos of the Old Athena Temple in 353 marks the end of the old order. From the time of Pericles until the death of Augustus (AD 14) the general appearance of the Acropolis underwent little change. Votive offerings in the form of shields were added to the Parthenon by Alexander the Great, and Antiochus Epiphanes added a gilded Gorgoneion to the S wall of the Acropolis. The siege of Sulla in 86 BC affected only the buildings of the S slope. The round Temple to Rome and Augustus, whose columns copy those of the Erechtheion, was built E of the Parthenon after 27 BC.

Claudius began the embellishment of the entrance c AD 52 with a monumental staircase (a typical manifestation of Roman grandeur), and Hadrian enriched many shrines. The building of the 'Beulé' Gate in the 3C marked the beginning of the second fortified period presaging damage and deterioration, and the Edict of Theodosius II in AD 429 dealt the final blow to pagan worship. Justinian converted the temples to Orthodox Christian churches, restored the military character of the citadel, and provided for the water supply of the garrison. The bronze Athena Promachos of Pheidias was removed to Constantinople before 900 to adorn the Hippodrome.

In 1204 the Acropolis was taken by the Marquess of Montferrat. At the end of the same year it was occupied and plundered by Otho de la Roche. In 1387 Nerio Acciaioli captured the citadel after a long siege. On Nerio's death, the succession was disputed; his son Antony occupied the Acropolis in 1403 after a 17-month siege. During his reign the Propylaia were converted into a Florentine palace. In 1458 Franco, last duke of Athens, surrendered the Acropolis after a two-year defence, to Omar, Attica having been annexed to Turkey in 1456.

To meet the threat of the extended use of cannon, the defences of the Acropolis were remodelled. In 1640 or 1656 a powder magazine in the Propylaia was struck by lightning, causing its first serious injury. After 1684 the Temple of Athena Nike was removed to make way for a new battery. On 21 September 1687, the Venetian army under Morosini landed at Piraeus, and on the 23rd two batteries opened fire on the works before the Propylaia. After an explosion in the Parthenon, a fire raged on the Acropolis for 48 hours. On 3 October the Turks capitulated, but in April 1688 they reoccupied the citadel and for the next century its ruins were obscured by a maze of little streets. In 1822 the Turkish garrison surrendered to the Greek insurgents; but in June 1827 the Acropolis was recovered after 11 months desultory siege by Reshid Pasha. The Turks now retained possession until after the end of the war when, in 1833, they were succeeded by a Bavarian garrison, which did not quit till 30 March 1835.

In 1801 Lord Elgin, then British Ambassador to the Porte, obtained permission in a firman to fix scaffolding, to excavate, to make casts and drawings, and to take away pieces of stone with inscriptions or figures. Whatever may be the opinion of his action, it should be appreciated that at the time fragments were being reduced to lime in the lime-kilns on the Acropolis; the sculptures which Elgin took away were at least spared the further ravages of time and of successive wars. A recent campaign by the Greek Government to have the sculptures returned to Greece is winning increasing support in Britain.

Excavations. Demolition of Turkish and Frankish structures began immediately in 1833, not without dissentient voices, one of the regents as early as 1835 opining that 'the archaeologists would destroy all the picturesque additions of the middle ages in their zeal to lay bare and restore the ancient monuments'; as indeed they have. Restoration and rearrangement of existing fragments continued to 1853, when Beulé uncovered the gate that bears his name. Burnouf discovered the Klepsydra spring in 1874 and Schliemann demolished the Frankish Tower in 1875. In 1876–85 the Greek Archaeological Society subsidised excavations by Kavvadias and Kawerau, when the surface of the Acropolis was investigated in many places to bedrock. Restorations and examinations of buildings in detail have gone on almost continuously ever since, with a mass of published reports.

By 1976 continuing damage to the Acropolis had reached unacceptable levels. There were three main causes: internal deterioration of the marble through the use of iron clamps and supports in 19C restoration works; external chemical changes wrought in the surfaces by sulphurous pollution from central heating and vehicle exhausts; and wear to surfaces by visitors' feet. Legislation has already reduced oil pollution. Motor vehicles are no longer permitted on the approaches. Severe restrictions are in force as to where visitors can walk: when new paths have been laid, a channelled round may have to be enforced. The former moonlight openings have ceased. Entry to all buildings is forbidden, except to parts of the Propylaia that are floored. A programme has been started to replace all iron by titanium, to remove much of the remaining original sculpture to controlled museum atmospheres, and replace it with copies (some supplied from British Museum casts of an earlier era). Work on the Erechtheion was completed in 1987, after 9 years. Restoration of the Parthenon started in 1983 and is expected to take c 12 years. Parts of the Propylaia and Temple of Athena Nike are also being treated.

In 1988 the *Centre for Acropolis Studies* was opened (see p. 53). The building itself, originally constructed in 1836 as a military hospital, and more recently (1920–75) used by the police, has been restored and will eventually become the core of a new museum complex (leading designs from competition displayed on first floor) housing all the finds from the Acropolis. At present it contains casts of the Parthenon sculptures, displays relating to conservation work on the Acropolis, and other temporary exhibitions. In the garden outside is a display of replicas of ancient lifting gear. Excavation trenches can be seen in the grounds and a section of the ancient remains is visible through a shaft in one of the ground floor passages. The finds have consisted mostly of Roman houses.

To explore the Acropolis thoroughly is thus almost impossible at present. A superficial tour can be made in 1½–2 hours by taking a route from the Beulé Gate through the Propylaia, circling the Parthenon, and visiting the Museum; then via the Belvedere and the Erechtheion back to the Beulé Gate. Though visitors will not be able to see everything described hereunder, it is hoped that the text in its present complete form will best serve the changing situation.

Approaches. A paved road, through gardens planned by Queen Amalia, leads up from Od. Dhionissíou Areopayítou (Rte 1). Paths lead from the Agora round the Areopagus, from the Odeíon of Ieródes Atticus and monuments on the S side (see Rte 1) and round the N slope from Plaka (see Rte 6).—**Admission.** Tickets are taken at the Beulé Gate or sometimes at a secondary gate to the S. Museum closed Monday till 11am. Refreshments are available below the entrance in summer; food may not be taken on to the Acropolis. There are lavatories in the grove below the ticket office, and by the NW corner of the Museum.

A. The Entrance

In Classical times the Panathenaic Way ended in a ramp going straight up from the level of the tourist post office to the gateway of the Propylaia with an inclination of one in four. On the modern approach you cross first the line of a medieval wall, then the Turkish wall of Serpentzes that ran N from the retaining wall of the theatre of Herodes Atticus. The ceremonial entrance by which you enter is known as the **Beulé Gate** after the French archaeologist who discovered it in 1852. A marble wall between two unequal pylons (the N one restored) is pierced by a trilithon gateway aligned with the central opening of the Propylaia. This had a defensive purpose and was paid for, c AD 280, by F. Septimus Marcellinus. The gate was built of stones from the destroyed Choregic Monument of Nikias. The name of Pantaleon of Sikyon, the flute-player, can be clearly read above the lintel; the remainder of the inscription is higher up. The inner face of the gate incorporates a grey slab carved with two victor's wreaths.

Within the gate parts of many levels exposed show that the way up was frequently modified. A few courses of polygonal walling lower down on the axis of the Propylaia are all that remains of the N retaining wall for the late-Archaic ramp of the Panathenaic way; in Pericles' day the ramp was widened to the full width of the central section of the Propylaia; by the time of Pausanias all save a central path for sacrificial animals had been concealed beneath a broad MARBLE STAIRCASE, some 73m long, erected within the Propylaia wings in AD 52 by Claudius and completed in its lower courses much later.

At the foot of the steps, just to the left of the Beulé Gate, are four fragments of an architrave, with doves, fillets, and an inscription, belonging to the *Shrine of Aphrodite Pandemos,* which stood below the SW corner of the hill (confirmed by excavations in 1960).

Half-way up the staircase is a natural landing from which a terrace opens to the N. Partly blocking this is the so-called *Monument of Agrippa,* identified by inscriptions on its face and on the landing below it. The colossal plinth, 8·8m high, has a shaft of Hymettos marble set off by a base moulding and cornice in poros (the foundation steps of conglomerate were not intended to be seen). It bore a quadriga. A partially effaced inscription on the W side under the Agrippa inscription records the original dedication, probably in 178 BC, to celebrate a Pergamene chariot victory in the Panathenaic Games. Cuttings in the top show that two chariot groups occupied the plinth at different dates. What happened to the original group depicting Eumenes II is not known. Later, according to Plutarch and Dio Cassius, the plinth bore statues to Antony and Cleopatra, which were blown down in 31 BC. The group to Marcus Agrippa was raised after his third consulship in 27 BC.

Behind the monument a terrace of the Periclean period extends below the N wing of the Propylaia. The mound on it consists of marble fragments, many inscribed, dating from the Turkish period. From the terrace there is an excellent *View of the Agora and Temple of Hephaistos; the course of the Panathenaic Way along the Wall of Valerian can be traced towards the Klepsydra spring which lies below the bastion. Here descends the late stairway (inaccessible) that begins from the terrace; emerging from the bastion beneath our feet by a Byzantine doorway, the steps follow a gully and enter a late-Roman well-house.

Klepsydra cannot be visited but can best be understood from this point. The spring, originally called *Empedo,* attracted Neolithic settlers and was early the centre of a cult of Nymphs. It issued from a small natural cave. Within this, c 460, a well-house with a deep *Draw-Basin* was built, and adjoining it a substantial structure, of which the paved floor and a wall survive. Part of the roof of the well-house fell in in the 1C BC, though the well was still usable in 37 BC when Mark Antony set out for Parthia taking (in obedience to an oracle) a bottle of water from Klepsydra. In the reign of Claudius a further fall ruined the building without rendering the water inaccessible. In Roman times a vaulted *Well-House* was built over the fallen roof of the original cave with a shaft driven to water level, and the whole sealed with concrete. The new structure was linked for the first time by a stair to the bastion above and was from that time accessible only from the Acropolis, though the overflow later fed a 6C cistern. At the time the new well-house was built, the court seems to have been abandoned, and later was covered by the Wall of Valerian. The Roman well-house received frescoes during its medieval transformation into a *Church of the Holy Apostles,* perhaps of the same period as the Byzantine door (see above). By 1822 all lay beneath a deposit of earth, though the spring itself bubbled up and served a Turkish fountain lower down the hill. After the Turks on the Acropolis had capitulated in 1822 for lack of water, the Greeks, searching for a water supply, found Klepsydra and repaired it, and in 1826 Gen. Odysseus Androutsos enclosed it in a bastion (demolished 1888). Its water served the Greek garrison throughout the siege of 1827. Excavations by Kavvadias in 1897 uncovered the paved court, but the American investigations of 1936–40 form the basis of modern study.—The remainder of the N slope is described in Rte 6.

From this point to the Propylaía you mount the modern zigzag ramp that resembles the Mycenaean and medieval approaches rather than the classical ramp.

The **Propylaía,** a monumental gateway, was designed by Mnesikles to replace an earlier entrance, its axis aligned to that of the Parthenon. It provides the only certain example before Hellenistic times of designing one building in direct relationship to another. The exact nature of the original plan is a matter of some dispute. Built in 437–432 BC, it was left incomplete at the beginning of the Peloponnesian War and the work was never resumed. Except for the foundations, and for certain decorative features in black Eleusinian stone, the construction is wholly of Pentelic marble. Discreet restorations have minimised the ravages of later history and a great part of the building still stands.

History. The Greeks gave the name of Propylon ('gate-building') to the entrance of a sanctuary, palace, or agora. The plural form Propylaia was reserved for more elaborate entrances. Earlier propylaia, probably to be ascribed to Peisistratos, but shown by the re-use of material from the Hekatompedon to date in their later form from 488–480 BC, were aligned differently from the existing structure. The Propylaia of Pericles (the existing edifice), begun upon the completion of the Parthenon, was hampered by political and religious agitation. It is possible that the original plan of Mnesikles was curtailed on the S in deference to the prejudices of the priests of the adjoining sanctuaries. The enormous cost was defrayed by grants from the Treasurers of Athena and Hephaistos, from the sale of old building material, from the rent of houses, and from private subscriptions, as well as by contributions from the Hellenotamiai, but Pericles was accused of squandering the funds of the Delian League on the embellishment of the Acropolis.

The Propylaia remained almost intact down to the 13C, being then used as the Byzantine episcopal palace. The dukes of Athens raised the N wing and used it as their chancery. Nerio Acciaioli made the propylaia his palace and erected the so-called Frankish Tower, 27·5m high, on the S side. The Turks covered the centre vestibule with a cupola and turned it into a magazine, the Aga making it his official residence. In the 17C it was struck by lightning and the magazine exploded with the result that the architraves of the E portico fell and were broken and two Ionic columns collapsed. The W façade and the celebrated ceiling were demolished in the Venetian bombardment of 1687. Later on a Turkish bastion was erected between the Bastion of Athena Nike and the S wing. Some columns were used to make lime. The building suffered again in the siege of 1827. In 1836 Pittakis removed the Frankish and Turkish additions, except the Tower, which was not taken down until 1875 (at the expense of Schliemann). Reconstruction of the central hall was undertaken in 1909–17 and the wings were restored after the Second World War.

The Propylaia comprise a central hall containing the portal and two wings flanking the approach. The CENTRAL HALL forms a rectangle 23·7m long and 18·2m wide, with side walls having antae at each end and Doric hexastyle porticoes facing E and W. It is divided two-thirds of the way through by the portal itself, to the W of which is a vestibule screened by an entrance portico. This *West Portico,* 19·8m wide, rests on four high steps, except in the middle, where the steps give place to a continuous ramp (transverse cuts for foothold visible at Roman level). Six sharp-fluted Doric columns are spaced to correspond with the five gateways of the portal. The two end columns stand to their full height (nearly 8·8m) and retain their capitals and portions of their architrave; other parts lie beneath the N colonnade.

Behind is the *Vestibule,* 13·7m deep, whose coffered ceiling of marble, 12m high and painted and gilt, earned the praise of Pausanias. The panels were supported on beams of 5·5m span, each weighing 11 tons, that rested on two rows of blunt-fluted Ionic columns flanking the central carriage way. The beams were reinforced with iron bars set in their upper face. The six Ionic columns were two-thirds the diameter of the Doric columns, and about 10 diameters (10·2m) high. One of the beautiful Ionic capitals has been restored to position, with a section of the coffered ceiling. Traces of the paint and star decoration can be seen on a well-preserved panel standing below. The *Portal* stands on a platform at the higher level of the E portico, and consists of five gateways, graded in size from the centre outwards. The paved ramp continues through the largest gateway in the centre, while the four side gateways are approached from the vestibule by flights of five steps, the topmost of black Eleusinian marble. The entrances had massive wooden gates. Three transverse steps are cut in the rock below the portal but these relics of an earlier entrance are now concealed by wooden planking.

The *East Portico* corresponds to that at the W, having six Doric columns of the same size and arrangement, but reduced in height by nearly a foot; it stands on a simple stylobate. The depth (5·8m) of the portico allowed the ceiling to be supported on beams laid parallel with the axis of the Propylaia, so that no inner colonnade was necessary. Each of the porticoes was surmounted by an entablature of triglyphs and unsculptured metopes supporting a pediment, but though pedimental sculpture was planned it was never started.

The N and S wings had Doric porticoes of three columns in antis, facing each other and at right angles to the W portico of the central hall; but whereas the N portico screens an important chamber, that to the S was left with nothing behind it. The wings had hip roofs. The NORTH WING is in a very perfect state. The architrave still has its plain frieze of triglyphs and metopes. The walls of the room at the back still stand; entered by a door and lighted by two windows in the partition wall, this room is called the *Pinakotheke* (picture gallery) from the pictures, many possibly by Polygnotos, that Pausanias saw there. The door and windows are not centred in the wall; most probably its original function room was as a room for ritual dining, where the standard arrangement of couches round the walls necessitated an off-centre doorway. The rough surface of the walls suggests that the pictures installed by the time of Pausanias were easel paintings. The joist-sockets of the storey added by the dukes of Athens are still visible.

The SOUTH WING appears from the outside to be the counterpart of the N Wing, but there is no chamber behind the portico, and the area of the portico itself is much smaller. The back wall stops opposite the third column, the W anta being a sham. At the SE corner the wall is slightly chamfered, so as not to interfere with the surviving section of the *Mycenaean Wall,* which bounded the Temenos of Artemis Brauronia. It has been suggested that the peculiar shape of this wing means that Mnesikles only temporarily abandoned his design, hoping to overcome the opposition of the priests to its completion. However, the corner is chamfered to ground level and later continuation would have been very difficult.—Above the S wing later stood the Tower of the Franks.

Mnesikles intended to add two E halls on the N and S sides of the central hall, which would have occupied the entire W end of the acropolis and given the Propylaia the same length exactly as the Parthenon. The existence of a cornice running round the two walls designed to form inner walls of the N hall on the S and W, and of other structural features (cf. below), proves that the NE hall was actually started; the SE hall, planned as the exact counterpart of its fellow, was abandoned at an early stage, though an anta exists at what would have been its NE corner. Both halls would have measured about 21m by 12m, much more spacious than the Pinakotheke.

The L-shaped foundations between the Mycenaean wall and the S wall of the S wing (which overlies them) represent a corner of the exedra that flanked the older Propylaia, forming a grandstand for the Panathenaic procession. Here may have stood the well-known 'Hekatompedon Inscription', cut in 485 BC on the reverse of an earlier metope, which enumerated prohibitions to visitors to the Acropolis.—The small trapezoidal enclosure to the S was a precinct of the Graces, associated probably with the worship of Hekate of the Tower, whose triple image by Alkamenes was located hereabouts by Pausanias.

The charming little *Temple of Athéna Níke (not accessible to visitors), called inaccurately *of Nike Apteros*' (wingless Victory), reached from the S wing of the Propylaia, stands on a precipitous platform, 8m high, projecting towards the W. The bastion originated as a Mycenaean outwork. In Peisistratid times it was consecrated to the worship of Athena Nike, being furnished with an altar and sanctuary, lost in the sack of 480 BC. In 449 a new *naiskos* (miniature temple) was decreed, with Kallikrates as architect, to celebrate the peace with Persia, and the following year the bastion was faced with poros. The present temple was built in 427–424. A theory that the Temple itself (rather than the naiskos) is referred to in the 449 decree, but not built until later, is now less persuasive.

The Temple of Athena Nike was thrown down by the Turks in 1686 in order to use the bastion as an artillery position, the pieces being used in the construction of another gun emplacement above the Beulé Gate. With the help of Stuart and Revett's drawings of a temple by the river Ilissos, designed by Kallikrates who may also have been responsible for the Nike temple, it was reconstructed piece by piece in 1836–42 by Ross, Schaubart, and Hansen, but again dismantled and rebuilt in 1936–40 in order to strengthen the bastion which had become unsafe. Present restoration work includes replacing the original sculptures with casts.

The temple, built entirely of Pentelic marble, stands with its W front along the W edge of the bastion on a stylobate of three steps measuring 5·5m by 3·5m. It consists of an almost square cella with an Ionic portico of four columns at either end. The fluted shafts are monolithic and the capitals closely resemble those of the Propylaia. A *Frieze*, 46cm broad, round the whole exterior of the building, is adorned with sculptures in high relief. It originally consisted of 14 slabs, four of which are in the British Museum (replaced by casts in cement). The genuine slabs, whose correct positions are uncertain, are badly weathered and being removed. Divinities (headless) occupy the E front. Athena may be distinguished by her shield; next to her appears to be Zeus. At the S corner are Peitho, Aphrodite, and Eros. Of the 22 figures which can be made out, 16 are female. The other sides bear scenes from the Battle of Plataea (479 BC); on the W front Athenians are fighting Boeotians and on the flanks Persians.

The cella housed a marble statue, reproduction of an archaic xoanon or wooden statue, probably destroyed by the Persians. The goddess held in her right hand a pomegranate, emblem of fertility, which indicated her pacific side, and in her left the helmet of the Athena of War. Her correct name was Athena Nike or Athena, bringer of victory. In Greek art the goddess Nike (Victory) was represented as a winged female; common tradition, confusing the two goddesses, supposed the statue of Athena Nike to be a wingless 'Victory' (Nike apteros). The story (retailed by Pausanias) grew up that the Athenians had deprived the Victory of wings to prevent her flying away.

The *Pyrgos,* or platform, on which the temple stands was paved with marble and surrounded by a marble parapet, sculptured in high relief and surmounted by a bronze screen. The grooves into which the slabs were bedded are still visible on the edge of the platform. Many fragments have been recovered and are now in the museum. The reliefs, which date from c 410 BC, represented a band of Winged Victories attendant upon Athena, and include the famous Victory adjusting her sandal.

At the top of the small flight of steps that gave access to this temple is a block of Hymettian marble with marks of an equestrian statue and a Greek inscription of c 457 BC, recording that it was dedicated by the cavalry and executed by Lykios of Eleutherai, son of Myron. The block appears to have been turned upside down and used for a statue of Germanicus when he visited Athens in AD 18. A second inscription (below the block) records this event.

If the air is clear, the platform commands a magnificent view (best at sunset) of Phaleron Bay, Piraeus, Salamis, Acro-Corinth and the mountains beyond it, Aegina, the E tongue of Argolis, with Idhra behind it, and the coast-line to the left towards Sounion. In the foreground the contour of the Pnyx is clearly seen.—This is the spot where, according to legend, Aegeus kept watch for the return of his son Theseus from his expedition against the Minotaur. Theseus, who had promised to hoist a white sail if he was successful instead of his usual black sail, forgot; Aegeus seeing the black sail, thought his son was dead and threw himself over the rock.

B.   Walk Inside the Walls

Note. The NW part of the Acropolis between the Propylaia and the Erechtheion is at present inaccessible. The full description has however been retained below.

Few visitors can resist walking straight from the Propylaia to the Parthenon; but you are strongly recommended to make a circuit of the Acropolis (when this is permitted) before approaching the Parthenon a second time. In Classical times the focus of attention was on the great statue of Athena while the direct approach to the Parthenon was channelled through a propylon; from the Propylaia all but the pediment of the Parthenon was hidden by intervening buildings.

Turning to the left beyond the Propylaia, you pass (left) the anta or pilaster of the projected N hall (cf. above). On the open ground to the left stood the chapel of the Frankish dukes, removed in 1860. From here you observe the beautifully regular but unfinished masonry of the Pinakotheke and the projection at the NW corner which is another indication of the unbuilt N hall. Walking E you cross an ancient drain, and farther on pass large *Cisterns*, probably built by Justinian c AD 530. You now bear towards the Acropolis wall, and at its next angle observe a flight of steps of Classical date descending from S to N. This may represent a *Secret Staircase* used annually by the Arrephoroi.

The Arrephoroi were two (or four) girls of noble birth between the ages of seven and eleven, chosen by the King-Archon to perform an obscure service in honour of Athena. Their duties (in addition to the weaving and the carrying of the Peplos) apparently consisted in carrying down by an underground passage to the Sanctuary of Aphrodite in the Gardens (not located) a burden whose contents were unknown. This they exchanged for another mysterious burden, which they brought back.

A platform above the steps gives a fine view towards Piraeus, with the Areopagus in the foreground and the 'Theseion' below. A few metres E a Turkish staircase, probably on an earlier course, descends from W to E, turns abruptly under the wall, and enters a cavern. Investigations were started here in 1937 in an attempt to find further evidence of the Arrephoroi; though unsuccessful in this, they unexpectedly uncovered traces (not now accessible) of a secret *Mycenaean Stairway*, hewn in the rock, partly in a natural cleft, partly underground, constructed in wood and stone in eight flights to a depth of 33·5m and leading to a natural spring.

The outer face of the acropolis wall at this point is composed of blocks from the entablature of the Old Temple of Athena: architraves, triglyphs, metopes, and cornices. A row of them is seen directly to the right as you stand at the wall behind the Turkish staircase.

You now pass between a Byzantine cistern which abuts on the Acropolis wall, and the Erechtheion. Built into the wall on the left are two of the unfinished drums intended for the columns of the Older Parthenon. Farther on are four others in a row. A flight of marble steps leads up to a platform, from which you can view a large section of the N wall, exposed when the korai, etc., were extracted from the fill. Here unfinished marble column drums and stylobate blocks from the Older Parthenon (490–480) are built into the wall. In the next deep excavation are the remains of the stairway in a rock gully which led down from the *Mycenaean Postern*. Beyond the far side of the chasm a few steps farther E there are poros drums and capitals (reddened by fire) from the Old Temple of Athena, and, to the left of the path farther on, other poros remains from the Old Temple of Athena including an inverted Doric capital with four rings above the fluting.

At the extreme end of the enclosure is the *Belvedere* (*View). By the steps are beautiful fragments of many periods. In the NE corner, behind the museum, a capacious Turkish storage jar stands on a well-preserved curving stretch of the Pelasgic wall.

Returning towards the Parthenon, you will notice (right) a large platform in the natural rock, which may have been the *Precinct of Zeus Poleios*. Immediately in front of the Parthenon, the architectural remains of the circular *Monopteros of Rome and Augustus* have been assembled on and around foundations which are still awaiting investigation. The conical roof was supported on nine Ionic columns. The inscribed architrave was recorded by Cyriacus of Ancona.

In front of the museum the parapet above the Wall of Kimon overlooks the Theatre of Dionysos (*View over the Olympieion and Stadium to Hymettos). Hereabouts Attalos I, king of Pergamon, erected four groups of sculpture (probably in bronze), representing the Gigantomachia, the Amazonomachia, the Battle of Marathon, and his own victory (in 230 BC) over the Gauls of Asia Minor. Plutarch relates that the statue of Dionysos from the Gigantomachia was blown by a high wind into the theatre below. Marble copies exist in various European museums.

Walking W along the massive *Wall of Kimon* (restored), you pass a triangular enclosure, where a cross wall of the Ergasterion is visible, and come near the SW corner of the Parthenon, to two deep pits revealing earlier walls.

The W front of the Parthenon is approached by a flight of nine steps cut in the rock, continued upwards by seven more in poros of which fragments survive. These served as a decorative retaining wall for the Parthenon W terrace and later were used for votive offerings, as is shown by some 38 rock cuttings where the various stelai were fixed. Before the steps at the W end stood the bull set up by the Council of the Areopagus. Below them was the Periclean *Entrance Court*, conjectured as part of Mnesikles' commission to tidy the Acropolis; rock cuttings suggest that it was entered on the N by a propylon. The court was closed on the S side by the *Chalkotheke*, or magazine of bronzes, dating from c 450 BC. The foundations show it to have been not quite oblong (c 41m by 14m), the E wall being slightly askew. It was later embellished with a N portico which encroached upon the steps leading to the Parthenon.

On the inner N wall are laid five fragments of a long base with inscriptions, from which it appears that they once bore statues by Sthennis and Leochares (350 BC). Roman inscriptions on the S face show that the bases were afterwards appropriated by Drusus, Tiberius, Augustus, Germanicus, and Trajan. Other pedestals, some detailed by Pausanias, lie hereabouts, and the area is further confused by modern ceiling blocks prepared to protect that part of the Parthenon frieze remaining *in situ* beneath the W peristyle.

To the W of the Chalkotheke and the Court lay the **Sanctuary of Artemis Brauronia,** the bear goddess, which took the form of a stoa with two projecting wings. Votive offerings, including a well-carved little Bear, have been found on the site (see Aristophanes, 'Lysistrata', 646), and inscriptions record the storage of others. Some of the inscriptions are copies of those found at the site of Brauron (*q.v.*), whence valuable votives were transferred at the beginning of the Peloponnesian war. Within the precinct, of which the foundations of the N and W walls (4C BC) can be easily traced, is the pedestal of a colossal bronze figure of the Trojan Horse by Strongylion. Its two marble blocks, c 1·8m long, bearing an inscription, were discovered in 1840; they lie nearly on a line with the E portico of the Propylaia.

The remnant of Mycenaean wall bounded the sanctuary on the W. Behind and below this, in the angle of the Propylaia, foundations remain of one corner of the pre-Periclean propylaia. By the corner column of Mnesikles' propylaia is the round *Pedestal* of a statue to Athena Hygieia, with clear traces of her feet and spear.

Plutarch ('Pericles', 13) tells that during the building of the Propylaia one of the workmen 'the quickest and handiest of them all' fell and was badly hurt, Pericles was told by Athena in a dream how to cure him, and in gratitude set up a bronze image of the goddess in her attribute of health-giver. Pliny adds the information that the remedy was the plant parthenion (feverfew), a pleasant punning conceit. Just E of the pedestal is an *Altar* to Hygieia, which Plutarch records as older than the statue.

In front of the Propylaia the surface of the rock is carefully roughened by transverse grooves, to give a foothold in the ascent to the Parthenon—a rise of c 12m. The numerous rectangular cuttings were occupied by pedestals of statues. On the right are rock-hewn steps ascending to the Sanctuary of Brauronian Artemis. The Sacred Way passed through the entrance court (see above), and along the N side of the Parthenon, to end at its E front.

Some 40 paces in front of the Propylaia are some foundations of poros on which stood the colossal bronze *Statue of Athena Promachos* by Pheidias. Blocks of the capping course of its pedestal, with huge egg-and-dart moulding, lie a little to the W. The statue, which Demosthenes calls 'the great bronze Athena' was finished c 458 BC as a trophy of Athenian valour in the Persian wars. Details of its form are safely known from the medieval description of Niketas Choniates as well as from contemporary medals. The goddess was represented standing with her right arm leaning on her spear, and holding in her left a shield, with figures in relief (battle of the Lapiths and Centaurs) designed by Parrhasios and wrought by Mys. In later times the epithet Promachos (Champion) was given the statue, to distinguish it from the statues of Virgin Athena in the Parthenon and of Athena Polias in the Erechtheion. It was c 9m high; the spear blade and helmet crest were visible to sailors coming from Sounion as they rounded Cape Zoster. The statue, removed to Constantinople at an uncertain date, was destroyed in a riot in 1203, because the superstitious people believed that her apparently beckoning hand (already lacking the spear) had summoned the invading Crusaders out of the W.

Farther E, opposite the seventh N column of the Parthenon and protected by a grating, is a rock-carved dedication to Fruit-bearing Earth (Ge Karpophoros). Here stood a personification, rising apparently from the ground, of Earth, praying for rain to Zeus.

C.   The Parthenon

The ****PARTHENON,** or *Temple of Athena Parthenos*, represents the
culmination of the Doric, indeed of the Classical, style of architecture; as a monument it has no equal. The temple was designed to
provide a new home for Athena, her fine new cult statue and the
continually increasing treasure. It was erected in 447–438 BC as the
cardinal feature of Pericles' plan. The loftiest building on the Acropolis, it is situated on its highest part, midway between E and W.
Under the order of Pheidias as 'surveyor-general' were the architects
Iktinos and Kallikrates, who built the Southern Long Wall. The most
celebrated sculptors in Athens, rivals or pupils of Pheidias, such as
Agorakritos and Alkamenes, worked on the pediments, the frieze,
and the metopes. Pheidias supervised, if he did not actually design,
the whole of the sculptures, reserving entirely to himself the creation
of the chryselephantine statue of Athena. The result is a peerless
blend of architecture and sculpture. (Amongst many works, see J.
Boardman, 'The Parthenon and its sculptures' (1985)). The Parthenon
was regarded, indeed, principally as an artistic masterpiece and as
the state treasury, and never replaced the Old Athena Temple or the
Erechtheion in the veneration of the Athenians as the holy place
sanctified by tradition.

The name Parthenon (Παρθενών), meaning the virgin's apartment,
originally applied to one room in the temple. Its first recorded
application to the whole building appears in the speeches of
Demosthenes. Before this the temple seems to have inherited the
sobriquet 'Hekatompedon' from its predecessors on the site. The
statue of Athena Polias became popularly though unofficially known
as Athena Parthenos.

Except for the roof (which was of wood) the Parthenon is built
entirely of Pentelic marble. The whole of the stylobate survives,
together with the columns of the peristyle and of the end porticoes,
though some are incomplete and some restored. The entablature at
the E and W ends, most of the W pediment, fragments of the E
pediment, and considerable portions of the walls of the W portico and
cella still stand.

History. At least four temples were built successively on the Parthenon site and
recent work (M. Korres) has suggested that the location of the building was
determined by the presence of an earlier shrine in the area of the N colonnade.
Rooftiles of the late 7C have been attributed to the first archaic temple here. The
second temple may have been the **Hekatompedon,** though fragments
attributed to it could belong with the Dörpfeld foundation (cf. below). Enough
architecture remains to show that the Hekatompedon was a peripteral temple of
the mid 6C BC which might be restored as 30m long. The interested visitor will
get an idea of Hekatompedon architecture by looking at a restoration of the
entablature set up behind the museum, outside, at the N corner. Pass round the
museum to the S wall of the Acropolis and stand by the low fence, looking into
the area between the S side of the museum and the S wall of the Acropolis.
There can be seen the mighty grey poros capitals of the Hekatompedon and,
behind them, fragments of the columns and other architecture stacked in an
oblong.

The scheme to replace the poros Hekatompedon, mooted perhaps after the
fall of the Tyrants, seems to have matured under Aristeides after the victory of
Marathon, just as new marble quarries were opened on Pentelikon. Remains of
the earlier building were used to build up a new terrace on the W and S (cf.
above). A massive limestone stereobate 76·8m by 31·4m, was bedded on the
rock, from which it rises in places by 22 courses of masonry. The marble
stylobate, the lower drums of still unfluted columns (6 × 16), and the first course
of the wall of the **Pre-Parthenon** were already *in situ* when in 480 the Persians

did their work of destruction. Marks of fire are still visible under the later stylobate (to the W near the N angle), as well as on the column-drums built into the acropolis N wall. Kimon enlarged the terrace on the S when he built his wall. 'The chief interest of this temple is that it initiated marble construction in Attica on a large scale, introduced the use of Ionic elements and the application of delicate refinements in upward curvature and column inclinations, and even contributed much of the material and many of the dimensions for the present Parthenon' (Dinsmoor).

Pericles proposed the erection of a new temple in Pentelic marble with a different columnar arrangement and somewhat wider and shorter than the existing base. It was brought more to the N and W so that the old foundations project 4·3m on the E and 1·7m on the S, while extra foundation courses were necessary on the N. Work on the **Parthenon** started in 447; in 438, at the Great Panathenaic Festival, the statue of Athena was dedicated in the cella; in 435 the opisthodomos was opened to receive the treasure, and in 434 the first inventories were made; the sculpture was complete by 432. Structurally the Parthenon remained virtually intact for 2000 years. New embellishments were added from time to time, such as the shields of gilded bronze presented by Alexander. In 305 BC, Demetrios Poliorketes desecrated the temple by turning the W portion into a residence for himself and his seraglio. In 298 he returned to besiege Lachares, who fled with the golden ornaments of the temple and the precious casing of the statue. The Parthenon was respected by the Romans, except that the statue had disappeared by the 5C AD. There are grounds for believing that the cult statue of Athena Parthenos was still in place until that time, when the Panathenaic festival was still being celebrated.

In the 6C AD the Parthenon was turned into a church. Under Justinian the edifice was dedicated at first to Saint Sophia (Holy Wisdom), then to the Virgin Mother of God (Theotokos), and became the metropolitan church of Athens. The entrance was made at the W end; the opisthodomos became the Byzantine pronaos and the Parthenon proper the narthex. The wall between the Parthenon proper and the cella was pierced with three doorways, two of which gave access to side staircases leading to the womens' galleries, which were erected over a colonnade, probably of Hellenistic date and from a building in the city of Athens but inserted into the Parthenon in the 4C AD. The walls were covered with frescoes and the ceiling replaced by a barrel-vaulted roof. The pronaos was converted into an apse to receive the altar. Vaults for the interment of the bishops were discovered under the floor in 1910. As the cathedral of the Frankish dukes, it followed the Latin rite in 1208–1458. It was later converted into a mosque, and a Byzantine bell-tower at the SW angle of the opisthodomos was converted into a minaret.

Jacques Carrey, a painter in the suite of the Marquis de Nointel, made (in 1674) over 400 drawings (now invaluable) of subsequently destroyed sculptures, and Spon and Wheler (in 1676) were the last travellers to see the Parthenon intact before the disaster of 1687. Carrey's drawings are preserved in the Bibliothèque Nationale in Paris. They include the pediment groups, a large portion of the frieze, and many of the metopes. On 26 September 1687, at 19.00 hrs, a mortar placed by Morosini on the Mouseion Hill was fired by a German lieutenant at the Parthenon, which the Turks were using as a powder magazine. The resulting explosion carried away practically the whole of the cella and its frieze, eight columns on the N side, and six on the S, together with their entablature; and the temple was cut into two ruinous halves. Morosini added to the damage, on gaining possession of the Acropolis, by attempting to remove from the W pediment the horses and chariot of Athena: the group fell during the process of removal and was smashed.

By 1766 a small mosque had been built within the ruins. With the revival of antiquarian interest, the Parthenon suffered further damage. The Comte de Choiseul-Gouffier removed to France in 1787 one detached piece of the frieze. His example was followed in 1801 by Lord Elgin, who secured an official permit 'to remove some blocks of stone with inscriptions and figures'. The artist Lusieri superintended the work of removing the greater part of the frieze, 15 of the metopes from the S side, the figures from the pediments, etc. In 1816 these 'Elgin Marbles' were placed in the British Museum.

As a result of its varied building history, the Parthenon now incorporates fragments of at least 40 other structures.

Restoration started in 1834–44. After the earthquake of 1894, Balanos replaced a few pieces of architrave and capitals on the W façade. In 1921–30, in the face of considerable opposition, he reconstructed the N peristyle. The new columns were made of Piraeic stone with a covering of concrete; this harmonises well with the ancient marble yet distinguishes the true from the false. Five missing capitals have, however, been replaced in Pentelic marble. The roofing of the W portico with copies in Pentelic marble of the original ceiling blocks was planned to protect the remaining section of the cella frieze, which today contrasts sadly with Elgin's casts. Many blocks were made and lie below the W façade; their erection awaits results of tests to determine whether the structure will now stand their weight. Further restoration work started in 1983 (see above) and some additional reconstruction—of the pronaos, as well as of a few stones of Justinian's church—is contemplated.

Exterior. The foundations are best studied on the S side, where the steps of the earlier temple may still be distinguished beneath the three marble steps that form the *Crepidoma* of the present temple. The Doric *Peristyle* consists of 46 columns (8 by 17), an octastyle arrangement matched only by the earlier Temple G at Selinus in Sicily. The columns, which have a base diameter of 1·9m, rise to a height of 10·4m. Each column is formed of 10–12 drums of varying height and has 20 shallow flutings.

A peculiarity of all Greek buildings of the best period, specially remarkable in the Parthenon, is the use of optical refinements executed with great mathematical precision. These include varying the breadth of the intercolumniation throughout the building, thickening the corner columns, and grading the spacing of the triglyphs. Lines that appear horizontal are in fact curved, and lines that appear vertical are slightly inclined. If you stand at one corner and look along the upper step, you will notice a perceptible rise in the centre giving to the whole pavement a convex character. The rise is less than 7·6cm in 30·8m on the fronts, and 2·6cm in 69·5m on the flanks, the latter giving a radius of curvature of c 5·5km. The rising curve is imparted to the entablature. The axes of the columns lean inwards to the extent of nearly 6·4cm in their height. The inclination can be detected by measuring the lowest drum of a corner-column, which will be found shorter on the inside than on the outside. The columns themselves have a convex entasis, or swelling, designed to correct the optical illusion by which straight tapered shafts appear concave.

The deep *Architrave* was adorned at a later date with gilded bronze shields, fourteen on the E front and eight on the W, between which were inscribed in bronze letters the names of the dedicators, the shields may have been presented by Alexander the Great in 334 BC after the battle of the Granicus. An inscription on the E front, relating to some honour conferred on the Emperor Nero by the Athenian people has been deciphered by means of the marks left by the nails. On the N and S sides were bronze nails or pegs for hanging festoons on days of festival. The *Frieze* above was decorated with triglyphs and metopes. The *Cornice* consisted of a slab overlapping the frieze, the projecting ledge of which supported the sculptures of the pediments. On its under side we notice mutules with guttæ. The upper part was surmounted by a beautiful hawksbeak moulding. The apex of the pediment, 18m above the stylobate, was crowned with an immense anthemion, or leaf ornament, as acroterion, of which a few fragments have been recovered. The wooden roof had tiles of Pentelic marble, from which the rainwater ran off without any gutter. At each of the four corners was a lion's head, purely ornamental since the mouth was not pierced, and the eaves were surmounted by palmette antefixes.

Details were brought into relief by polychrome decoration. Many mouldings retain traces of ornaments beautifully drawn; in some of the most protected parts the pigment itself remains. Strong colour seems to have been confined to the parts that were in shade. The intense whiteness of the columns, architraves, and broader surfaces was probably modified by some ochreous colour to such an extent only as to anticipate the rich golden hue produced by time on Pentelic marble. The channels of the triglyphs, or possibly the triglyphs themselves, were painted dark blue, as were also the six guttæ below them. The ceilings were adorned with deep blue panels and gilt stars.—In the British Museum is a coloured reconstruction of the NW corner of the Parthenon.

SCULPTURES. *Eastern Pediment.* We know from Pausanias (I, 24, 25) that the subject was the birth of Athena, but there is little left on the pediment, which was ruined when the Byzantine apse was built. Of the various fragments found, some are in the Acropolis Museum, more in the British Museum; a Roman puteal (well-head) in Madrid is believed to have been copied from the central group. (For recent discussion of the composition in detail, see A.J.A. 1967.)

The *Western Pediment* represented the contest of Athena and Poseidon for the possession of Attica. These sculptures, practically intact when Jacques Carrey made his drawings, were those destroyed by the clumsy avarice of Morosini.

The *Metopes* were originally 92 in number: 14 at either end and 32 on each side. Of these, 41 remain *in situ*, but with rare exceptions they are so battered as to be unintelligible. Their artistic value appears to have been very uneven. Fifteen are in the British Museum and one is in the Louvre. The remaining 35 are, with the exception of some fragments (in the Acropolis Museum, and in the Vatican Museum), entirely destroyed (the greater number in the explosion of 1687) and they are only imperfectly known from Carrey's drawings. The metopes in the British Museum and the Louvre are all from the S side, and illustrate the contest of the Lapiths and Centaurs at the marriage feast of Peirithoös. Those of the E front remain in position; they represent a Gigantomachia. The subject of the metopes of the W front appears to be an Amazonomachia. All the metopes seem to have been deliberately chiselled off in the (?) 6C–8C. A substantial section of one of the S metopes was discovered built into a late wall in the Theatre of Dionysos in 1989. Study of other fragments is in progress.

The **Interior** has been closed to visitors to protect the structure. Within the peripteral colonnade the ambulatory, 4·3m wide on the flanks and nearly 4·9m at the ends, is equipped with drainage channels. The ceiling was formed of coffered panels of marble, those at the ends supported by marble beams; four of these remain *in situ* at the W end, where restoration is in progress.

The SEKOS, or temple proper, stands on a socle raised two steps above the stylobate. Unlike the usual Doric temple of three chambers, it was divided by a blank partition wall into two halls, each with a portico of six Doric columns. The ends of the walls forming the sides terminate in antæ facing the portico columns. The Pronaos, or E portico, opened into the Cella and there were probably also windows between the two, while the Opisthodomos, facing W, fronted the Parthenon proper. Frieze, see below.

The CELLA or *Hekatompedos Naos* is presumed to have inherited its alternative name from an earlier building; its interior measurements are somewhat less than 100 Attic feet. An inner colonnade, formed (like those at Aegina and Paestum) of two storeys separated by an architrave and carried round three sides, supported beams for the roof and ceiling. Some of the circular marks left by the original column-bases are still visible, but the more obvious remains are from slenderer columns of Hellenistic date re-used here after a fire. Bronze barriers between the 23 lower columns formed an ambulatory from which privileged visitors (among them Pausanias) would view the great chryselephantine *Statue of Athena Polias,* by Pheidias. Its site is clearly located by an oblong space where the marble floor is economically replaced by plain Piraeic stone; it was placed in position in 432 BC.

Literary references, combined with extant reproductions, provide an accurate account of the work. Reproductions include the Varvakeion and Lenormant figures (National Archaeological Museum) and the Strangford shield (British Museum). The statue was of gold plate over an inner wooden frame and stood, with the pedestal, 11·9m high. The face, hands, and feet were of ivory (Plato, Hippias Major). The pupils of the eyes were of precious stones. The goddess stood upright, clad in a dress that reached to her feet; on her breast was the head of Medusa wrought in ivory; in her right hand she held a crowned Victory about four cubits high, and in the other a spear. Her helmet was surmounted by a sphinx, with griffins in relief on either side, representing the winged beasts that fought with the one-eyed Arimaspi for gold (cf. Hdt. III, 116). On her sandals was wrought the battle of the Centaurs and Lapiths. At her feet stood a shield, on the outside of which was represented in relief the battle of the Amazons with the Athenians: in this scene Pheidias introduced figures of himself and Pericles that got him into trouble with pious Athenians (Plutarch, 'Pericles'). On the inside was a representation of the Gigantomachia. Near the base of the spear was a serpent, perhaps Erichthonios. On the pedestal was wrought in relief the birth of Pandora. The dress and other ornaments, all of solid gold and weighing some 40 or 50 talents, were so contrived that the whole could be temporarily removed, in case of national emergency, without injuring the statue (Thuc. II, 13). The whole work was presumably designed to glow softly in subdued light from the doorway and limited windows. It became known as the *Athena Parthenos.*

The W wall was originally blank. Three doorways were made in it and all the interior columns were removed when the building was converted into a church. Beyond this wall lay the PARTHENON proper, a chamber of the same width as the cella but only 13·1m long, of which three walls still stand. Here four presumably Ionic columns (traces on four square slabs larger than the rest) supported the roof.

Many archaeologists have argued that Parthenon means the 'chamber of the maidens' (i.e. of the priestesses of Athena). This is borne out by information from Brauron. If it means the 'chamber of the maiden' (Athena herself), the fact that her statue was not placed there needs explanation.

The *Opisthodomos* corresponded to the pronaos in all its details, save that the columns were c 5cm thicker; they are probably fashioned from drums cut for the Pre-Parthenon. There are conspicuous traces here on the columns and antæ of the grating which separated the opisthodomos from the ambulatory. A relic of the days when the Parthenon was a mosque is the base of the minaret, below the level of the marble pavement at the SW corner, where a rough staircase mounts to the pediment. Some interesting relics are still visible from the time when the opisthodomos served as cathedral narthex: on the left pillar, Byzantine Greek inscriptions; to the right of the doorway, fragmentary wall-paintings. Between the second and third pillars from the N of the W peristyle a chequer-board is incised in the pavement.

It is believed that the opisthodomos served as treasury of the Delian League in succession to the 'Opisthodomos', part of the Old Temple of Athena.

Right round the outer walls of the sekos, just below the cornice and 11·9m above the stylobate, ran a continuous Ionic **Frieze.** Although much of its sculptural detail was destroyed by the explosion in 1687 and about 13·7m are altogether unrecorded, yet the existing 53·6m in Athens, together with 75·3m in the British Museum, out of a total length of 159·5m suffice with Carrey's drawings to give a tolerably adequate idea of the whole. Its uniform height is 99cm and its relief nowhere exceeds 5·7cm. It has generally been taken to represent the procession of celebrants at the Great Panathenaic Festival, though an attempt has recently been made, by equating the number of figures with the number of dead at Marathon, to proclaim the frieze a record of a specific heroising ceremony.

The *Greater Panathenaia,* traditionally founded by Erichthonios (see below) and renewed by Theseus, was refounded in the archonship of Hippokleides (566/565 BC) and turned into a ceremony of the first rank by Peisistratos. It occurred on every fourth anniversary of the goddess's birthday, in the month of Hekatombaion (August). Athletic, musical, and equestrian contests were held and the victors received Panathenaic prize amphorae filled with tax-free olive oil from the sacred olive trees. The main feature was the Procession, in which the new embroidered saffron peplos woven to drape an early wooden xoanon of Athena Polias was borne in state through the streets of Athens on a ship on wheels. The ship was manned by priests and priestesses wearing golden crowns and garlands of flowers (see Philostratus, Vit. Soph. II 1, 7). The chief citizens of Athens, the envoys from the allied states, and even resident aliens had a fixed part to play in the ceremony. The citizens were on this occasion allowed to bear arms without exciting suspicion—at any rate in the time of Hippias (Thuc. VI, 56). The peplos may have been woven by, and was certainly carried (at some part of the procession) by the Arrephoroi, the maids in waiting on Athena. The route of the procession was from the Pompeion in the Kerameikos to the Eleusinion then past the Pelargikon to the Pythion, where the ship was moored. It is probable that the procession halted outside the Parthenon or its predecessor and that the victors in the Panathenaic games there received their prize amphorae. The proceedings ended with a sacrifice on the Great Altar and in the depositing of the robe (at any rate latterly) in the Erechtheion.

The entire WEST FRIEZE, with the exception of three figures, remains *in situ,* and in surprisingly good state: the Athenian knights are seen putting on their sandals and cloaks, bridling their horses, mounting, and moving off under the marshals. Viewed from outside the W front of the building, it gives an excellent idea of the way in which the frieze was intended to be seen between the columns of the peristyle, the changing scenes, viewed successively between each pair of columns, giving a feeling of the movement and forward impetus of the procession.

Somewhat less than one-third of the N frieze and five slabs of the S frieze are in the Acropolis Museum (see below). The remainder is in London, together with all the extant remains of the E frieze (except for three slabs and sundry fragments in the Acropolis Museum, and eight slabs in the Louvre).

D.   The Erechtheíon

Looking towards the Erechtheíon from the N colonnade of the Parthenon you can see the foundations of a temple, published by Dörpfeld in 1886 and ever since its discovery 'the subject of endless controversy as to its identity, its date, its relation to its neighbours, and how long it continued in use' (Ida Thallon Hill). It is now generally called the **Old Temple of Athena** and is believed by Dinsmoor to be of Peisistratid date (529 BC is suggested by astronomical calculations from its orientation). Two column bases (once attributed to the Mycenaean megaron) are now ascribed to a Geometric predecessor but are not *in situ.* The temple is the only pre-Persian building in Athens of which complete foundations are extant; to it are ascribed Archaic sculptures (independently dated stylistically to c 525 BC), now in the museum. The building, amphidistyle (or perhaps prostyle) in antis with a peristyle of 12 columns by 6, was partially destroyed in the Persian sack and poros and marble remains of it were built into the N wall and used as fill for later terraces. The rear part of it seems to have survived to be rebuilt as a treasury; it may have been the 'Opisthodomos' referred to in the Kallias Decree (439 or 434) and the 'Megaron facing W' which Herodotus describes with smoke-blackened walls; it was dismantled (says Demosthenes) in 353 BC.

The **'Erechtheíon,** one of the most original specimens of Greek architecture, stands near the N edge of the rock, about midway between the E and W ends. Designed to succeed the Old Temple as the joint shrine of Athena and Poseidon-Erechtheus, it was finished after 395 BC and owes its curious plan to the sacrosanct nature of the associated sanctuaries that preceded it. Like the Parthenon, it became generally known by a name that originally applied only to one of its parts.

The **Legendary History** of the contest between Poseidon and Athena for possession of the Acropolis in the reign of Kekrops occurs in many ancient authors (cf. Hdt. VIII, 55; Apollodorus, Lib. III, xiv). Poseidon produced a 'sea' called Erechtheís and Athena an olive tree. Athena was judged the winner but was reconciled with Poseidon and henceforth they were worshipped together. Another myth tells of Erichthonios, born to Hephaistos and Earth, who was placed by his foster-mother Athena in a chest and committed to Pandrosos, daughter of Kekrops. Erichthonios, who had serpent attributes, grew up to expel Amphictyon and become king of Athens; to him is attributed the setting up of the xoanon to Athena and the institution of the Panathenaia. His grandson Erechtheus also became king of Athens. These myths and their dramatis personæ are indissolubly confused, but the sacred tokens (μαρτύρια) venerated in Classical times Athena's olive tree and the mark of Poseidon's trident—probably date at least from pre-Homeric times. At some time Poseidon and Erechtheus became identified with one another.

As historical fact we can say that the N side of the Acropolis became the centre of a group of cults, based on the worship of Athena and Poseidon-Erechtheus, all with elements in common and stemming probably from late Helladic times, since they grew up round the Mycenaean megaron. The tokens survived in Roman times and Dionysios of Halicarnassus locates the olive tree in the *Pandroseion*. Pausanias speaks of Poseidon's well of sea-water within the Erechtheíon. The *Kekropion*, or Tomb of Kekrops, was near by, and sacred snakes dwelt in the precinct. No archaeological evidence has been found to suggest a combined temple earlier than the Erechtheíon as we know it today.

History. The *Erechtheíon* formed part of the programme of Pericles. The construction was delayed by the Peloponnesian War, but the evidence of inscription proves that it was nearly ready in 409 BC and probably complete three years later. It was damaged by fire in 406 (Xenophon, Hellenica, I, 6, 1) and was not rebuilt until 395 or even later. Another fire caused damage in Augustan times, and the reconstruction incorporated some new features. The building was converted into a church about the 6C AD, and the greater part of the interior destroyed in the successive alterations. The Turks, in 1463, turned it into a harem for the wives of the Commandant of the Acropolis. It suffered from the acquisitiveness of Lord Elgin in 1801 and was damaged during the various sieges of the War of Independence. In 1838 Pittakis cleared some of the wall of rubbish; in 1842–44 Paccard restored the Portico of the Caryatids. A violent storm on 26 October 1852 blew down the upper part of the W façade with its engaged columns. In 1903–09 the exterior was virtually rebuilt by M. Balanos. Conservation and restoration work begun in 1979, was completed in 1987.

Curiosities. The temple must have been profoundly interesting to visitors. In addition to the tokens (see above) and the ancient xoanon and its lamp (see below), here also were a wooden Hermes, said to be an offering of Kekrops, a folding chair made by Daedalus, and some Persian spoils from Plataea, including the corselet of Masistius (of gold links) and the sword of Mardonius.

The Erechtheion is unique not only in plan but also in elevation since the foundations of its S and E walls stand nearly 2·7m above those on the N and W. No attempt was made to correct the various levels of the terrain on which it stands, and the exterior is manifestly that of a single building in spite of incorporating existing features at these differing levels. When seen from the E it has the appearance of an

Ionic prostyle temple with a hexastyle portico; behind the façade it is in fact a plain rectangle with a projecting porch on either flank.

The EASTERN PORTICO had six Ionic columns, on a stylobate of three marble steps, supporting a pediment without sculpture. Five columns with their architrave are standing; the sixth (at the N corner) was carried off by Lord Elgin. They are 6·7m high, including bases and capitals, and 0·8m in diameter at the base. The back wall of the portico, which had a central doorway and two windows, was pulled down to make way for the Byzantine apse. The S anta survives, while that to the N, reconstructed in 1909, lacks the capital (in the British Museum).

The INTERIOR is a tangle of late substructures, which have destroyed even the foundations of the Classical building. The modern traveller can only stand at the porches and use his imagination.

The description of Pausanias is unusually ambiguous, and even after considering beddings in the rock together with the original building specifications and progress reports, which survive on marble, archaeologists differ widely in their reconstruction of the classical interior. Previous views of the internal arrangement were challenged c 1970 by John Travlos, but his views have been questioned in their turn. Some of the argument centres on the route of the profane dog (Philochoros, Fr. 146).

The EASTERN CELLA was at a higher level and separated by a crosswall from the rest. It is not clear whether this or the WESTERN CELLA was the main cult chamber. In one of them were located three altars: of Poseidon-Erechtheus, of Hephaistos, and of the hero Boutes; also the thrones of their priests (the inscribed thrones of Boutes and Hephaistos are now outside). On the wall, says Pausanias, were portraits of the Boutad family from whom the priests of the cult were drawn. In the other cella was the highly venerated *Statue of Athena Polias,* in olive-wood. This was presumably removed to safety at Salamis in 480 BC and housed in a temporary building on the site after Plataea.

The goddess seems to have been represented as standing and armed (Aristophanes, 'Birds', 826–31). She held a round shield on which was the gorgon's head (Euripides, 'Electra', 1254–57). The sacred Peplos, renewed every four years at the Panathenaic Festival, was woven to adorn her shrine. The so-called Dresden statue of Athena is supposed to be a copy of this wooden image. In front of the statue burnt the golden lamp made by the ingenious Kallimachos with an asbestos wick that needed oil only once a year, and a brazen palm tree to serve as chimney. The lamp was tended by elderly widows; during the siege of Athens by Sulla in 86 BC it was allowed by Aristion to go out (Plutarch, 'Sulla', 13).

An enlarged cistern, cut deep into the rock in medieval or Turkish times, has destroyed most of the evidence which might have allowed a positive identification beneath the ante-chamber of the Erechtheís 'sea' (see above). The visible fragments of brick vault are medieval; the 'sea' or well was presumably covered with marble tiles and seen through a puteal. When the S wind blew the well gave forth the sound of waves.

To reach the North Porch you descend a modern staircase, replacing an ancient flight. The court enclosed between the stair and the building was paved and probably served a ritual purpose. The **`*`** **`*`**NORTH PORCH formed a lateral pronaos to the Erechtheion proper, hence its Greek description (πρόστασις ἡ πρὸς τοῦ θυρώματος). Formed of an elegant Ionic colonnade of four columns in front and one at each side, with its architrave, its frieze in dark blue Eleusinian marble, its panelled ceiling; and its richly decorated N door, this porch is one of the masterpieces of Attic art. The superstructure was restored from fragments that date from a Roman reconstruction. The porch protected the marks left perhaps by a thunderbolt, which are seen through a gap in the tiles as three holes in the rocky bottom of a crypt. A corresponding opening in the roof over this pit was purposely left on the analogy of leaving open to the sky places struck by lightning. By the gap stood the *Altar of the Thyechoös*, a priest important enough to have a place reserved in the theatre. He offered sacrifices of honey-cakes to Zeus Hypatos. An opening leads from the crypt into the basement of the temple. Here perhaps within the adyton surrounding the Tomb of Erechtheus dwelt the serpent guardian of the house (cf. Hdt. VIII, 41, and Plutarch, 'Themistocles', 10), for whom the honey-cakes served as food. The *North Doorway* is celebrated for the magnificent moulding of its Ionic decoration, though much of it consists of exact copies of Augustan date replacing the originals destroyed in a fire; the pierced centres of the rosettes are omitted. The inner linings are Byzantine additions.

From the N porch, which projects some way beyond the W façade of the building, a smaller opening leads down two steps into an outer court of the temple, no longer enclosed. This was the **Pandroseion,** or *Temenos of Pandrosos,* a precinct of uncertain boundaries containing a small temple. Here grew the *Sacred Olive of Athena.* Herodotus tells how it sprouted again after being burnt down by the Persians; the existing tree was planted on 22 February 1917, on Washington's birthday, by Bert Hodge Hill, near a fine ancient copper water-pipe which he excavated, and which he conjectured had been installed to supply water to something of especial importance. More to the S was a further precinct, the **Kekrópion.** The foundations of the Erechtheion were modified at the SW corner to avoid disturbing an earlier structure, the presumed *Tomb of Kekrops,* which was spanned by a single huge block, c 4·5m long and 1·5m deep.

Above rises the WEST FAÇADE of the temple, restored in 1904 (after being blown down in 1852) to the form it acquired in the 1C BC. It consists of a high basement, upon which were set engaged columns joined by a low solid wall with a parapet. The upper part of the intercolumniation was closed with wooden grilles, except above the Kekropion where it was left open, presumably for some important cult purpose. The original column-bases remain but everything above was renewed after the fire in Roman times to the existing design with three windows; even then, however, the S opening was left open. The S block of the entablature is a copy; the original removed in 1805, has been recovered defaced by Turkish inscriptions. It lies on the ground in front of the W façade.

The SOUTHERN PORTICO, or *Porch of the Caryatids,* consists of a solid marble wall, rising 1·8m above the peristyle of the Old Temple on which it is founded, surmounted by six statues of maidens (*korai*), rather over life-size, popularly known as Caryatids. The figures stand four in front and two behind, their long Ionic tunics draped like column flutings about their outer legs, on which their weight is thrown. They support an entablature which has capitals of a special decorative form and no frieze. At the close of the War of Independence only three of the caryatids remained in place, all much damaged; the second figure from the W, removed by Lord Elgin, was later replaced by a cast. All surviving originals have now been removed to the museum and the porch has been rebuilt with casts having a titanium core. The porch was entered through the E wall of the podium by narrow steps which seem unlikely to have served the needs of the public. The floor has disappeared, but the flat coffered

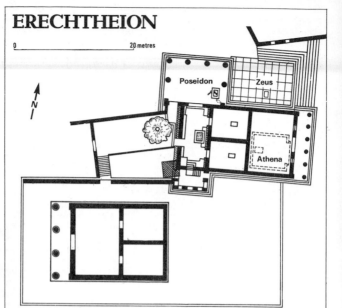

ERECHTHEION

0 _____ 20 metres

N

Poseidon

Zeus

Athena

after Dinsmoor and others

ceiling is nearly entire. A portal gave access by an awkward descending L-shaped stair to the W cella.

The idea of using statues in lieu of columns seems to have been borrowed from the Treasuries of the Knidians and Siphnians at Delphi. Vitruvius states that the sculptors took as models the girls of Karyai, in Laconia: hence the name Caryatids. Prof. Dinsmoor suggests that here the figures represent the Arrephoroi, bearing Athena's burdens on their heads.

The temple was given structural unity by its balancing pediments and by the emphatic nature of the *Frieze*, which, save where the roof of the N portico interrupted it, extended right round the building above the architrave. Unique in design, it consisted of coarse-grained Pentelic marble figures, cut in high relief and attached by bronze clamps to a ground of dark Eleusinian stone. Two large blocks of the background are still *in situ* above the columns of the E front; part of the frieze above the N porch also remains. The holes for fitting the sculptured figures are plainly visible. Of these only 112 small fragments have been recovered, mostly in bad condition; they are in the Acropolis Museum. The theme of the work is not known.

It must be remembered that here, as in the Parthenon, to the beauty of form was added the attraction of colour. The capitals of the columns were enriched with gilt bronze ornaments, and inlaid with coloured glass 'gems'. The panelled ceilings of the porticoes were painted blue and had gilt bronze stars.

E.   The Acropolis Museum

The *Acropolis Museum, founded in 1878 and reconstructed since the Second World War, was reopened in sections in 1956–61. It occupies the SE corner of the Acropolis and is sunk below the surface level of the rock in order not to interfere with the skyline. Started as the repository of finds collected haphazard on the citadel, it was greatly enriched by the systematic excavations of Kavvadias in 1885–90, when the whole of the rock was laid bare. With the exception of the bronzes and the vases (now in the National Museum), it contains all the portable objects discovered since 1834 on the Acropolis. As an education in the development of Attic sculpture, the collection is unique. The arrangement is roughly chronological.

Admission daily; closed Monday until 11am. Small charge for photography; cameras must otherwise be left in the vestibule. Concise Guide in English (1965); more detailed (also in English) by M. Brouskari, 'The Acropolis Museum: a descriptive catalogue', (1974). Students are referred to the 'Catalogue of the Acropolis Museum', 2 vols; (Cambridge), Vol. I (1912) by Guy Dickins, Vol. II (1912) by Stanley Casson, and to 'Archaic Marble Sculpture from the Acropolis' (1939) by Humfry Payne and G.M. Young. For the Parthenon sculptures, see above.

Outside the entrance (right) is 1347. Colossal marble owl.

VESTIBULE. 1338. Panel of a pedestal dedicated by Atarbos to commemorate a victory with his chorus in a Pyrrhic dance, which the youths are executing (late 4C); 1326. Quadrilateral base, with relief of an apobates (a soldier who leaps on and off a chariot at full speed); 2281. Male head; 1331. Youthful head (4C), possibly Alexander the Great; 1358. Statue of a woman and child (late 5C; much mutilated), perhaps the Prokne and Itys mentioned by Pausanias as being dedicated by Alkamenes.

You turn left. The first three rooms contain **Pedimental Sculpture**, in poros limestone or in imported island marble, from destroyed 6C buildings on the Acropolis. Much shows traces of the bright paint then favoured for accentuating the design and movement of the figures. ROOM I. 552, 554. Fragments of a leopard, in Hymettian marble, perhaps from the metopes of the Hekatompedon; 4572 is notable for its painting; 1. Pediment of a small building (c 570 BC; the oldest known relief from the Acropolis); it shows Herakles and the Hydra, with Iolaos driving his car; on the left is the crab sent by Hera to hamper the hero. 4. Lioness rending a small bull, one of the earliest groups; flanked by serpents (cf. below), it may have formed part of the centre of the W pediment of the Hekatompedon; 122. Lion's head in Hymettian marble; 701. Archaic head of a running Gorgon, perhaps the acroterion above the E pediment of the Hekatompedon.

ROOM II. In the doorway, 56. Owl; 41. Serpent's head. Within, 36, 35. Left and right portions of a pediment: left, Herakles and Triton (the head came to light in 1938); right, Typhon, a blue-bearded monster with three human heads and bodies ending in a serpent's tail (traces of vivid colouring); it has been suggested that the lions in the next room should be restored between these two to form the E pediment of the Hekatompedon; 2, 37, 40. Serpents from a pediment (cf. above); 9. Right half of an early pediment representing the Introduction of Herakles to Olympos; Iris presents him to Zeus who has Hera or Athena beside him; 624. *Moschophoros, a man bearing a calf on his shoulders, in Hymettian marble (c 570 BC), one of the earliest examples of native art in marble, still employing techniques suitable to working in limestone; an inscription on the base bears the name Rhombos. Triglyphs and cornice fragments. In a glass case, terracotta figurines found S of the Acropolis in 1955–59; 52. The 'Olive tree' Pediment, with its remarkable representation of a building: the masonry, roof-tiles, and other architectural details are lovingly rendered. On the left a single olive-tree stands within a walled precinct. Although the figures allow various interpretations, the temptation to recognise Athena's token, the Acropolis olive-tree, is hard to resist; 593. Kore, wearing chiton and Doric peplos (mid-6C); this is one of the earliest of these figures (see below); 575. Small quadriga (fragmentary) in Hymettian marble.

ROOM III. 3. Part of a colossal group of two lions attacking a bull, a remarkable 6C work which may have been the centre-piece of the E end of the Hekatompedon (cf. above).

Here also are two primitive korai (677, 619) executed in Naxian marble in the shape of the xoanon; one very stiff, once thought to be of Samian workmanship; the other headless; 618. Lower part of an enthroned female figure (note the modelling of the feet); 620, another, clumsily executed.

In ROOM IV are displayed the majority of the **Korai**, or maidens, perhaps the chief treasure (because unique as a group) of the museum. These female statues were dedicated as votive offerings to Athena in the course of the 6C BC in the precinct of one of her temples. Ruined in the sack of 480 and later scrupulously buried, they were discovered during excavations in 1882–86 mainly to the E of the Parthenon or NW of the Erechtheion. All the statues are clothed and painted, and each kore held an offering in one hand. Under the Peisistratids the Doric dress gradually gave way to the Ionic; you see in the statues the simple symmetry and contour of the woollen Doric peplos and chiton being replaced by the linen Ionic chiton worn with the himation. The new chiton, both thinner and more voluminous, posed new problems in modelling the body, the contour of which was more emphasised in some places by the thinner nature of the material and more covered in others by the increased drapery. The manner of wearing the himation gave a marked diagonal emphasis of line. Parallel to the sartorial changes we notice the developing naturalism of the features, including the losing of the archaic 'smile'. This development was once taken as the ascendancy of 'Attic' art over Ionic or island styles; but it seems likely to have been a development common to sculpture in general, more characteristic of a period than of a region. The korai are arranged with other works of their period, but the exact chronology of this period of Attic art and the importance of outside influences ('Ionic' or 'Samian') on it are still the subject of scholarly controversy.

The room divides into three sections. In the first: 1340. Head of a horse in Pentelic marble (? from a 5C votive relief); 581. Worshippers bringing a sacrificial sow to Athena. Grouped together are four works assigned to the same artist, probably called *Phaidimos*, including 679. The Peplos Kore (c 530 BC), so called from the girded Dorian peplos she wears over her chiton; it is famous alike for the facial expression and the preservation of the ancient colour and *590. Horseman (c 560 BC); the head is a good cast of the 'Rampin Head' in the Louvre first recognised by Humfry Payne in 1936 as belonging to this figure. This and a second statue (700 below) may be a memorial to Hippias and Hipparchos, the horse-racing sons of Peisistratos; *143. Hound; 69. Lion head, a spout from a cornice; 606. Horseman in Persian or Scythian dress, dedicated by someone with Northern interests (? Miltiades), c 520 BC.

702. Relief of Hermes, the three Graces, and a boy; 1343. Fragmentary relief of a bearded man, wearing the exomis (singlet); 669. Kore; the hair, the set of the eyes, and the modelling of the ears recall mid-6C styles, but the drapery shows important innovations; this is thought to be the earliest example of the chiton and himation pattern which became standard (? c 540).

In the second section: 700. Equestrian statue carved in one piece (pre-Persian); of the rider nothing survives above the hips; 665. Kouros (mid-6C), damaged by fire; the muscles are modelled with greater accuracy than usual at this period; 145. Small torso of a warrior, also marked by fire; 594. Kore (headless) of Ionian workmanship; an epiblema (shawl) is thrown over the himation and colours are freely used; 694. Nike, c 480 BC; 675. Kore, preserved with much original colour, having the high forehead and features characteristic of Chiot art; 673. Kore, probably by a Chiot artist; 190. Lamp in island marble decorated with four human and four animal heads.

The third part of the room is grouped about a fine selection of korai of the last quarter of the 6C BC: 682. The hair and dress afford a striking example of late-Peisistratid elaboration (c 525); the figure is still heavy and stiff; 1342. Chariot relief (cf. 1343, above). Korai: 684. The face is intellectual, the eyes straight, the mouth firm; 674. Shoulders finely modelled; although the head is too large, the face is most delicately rendered (near the end of the 6C); 670. Clad in simple chiton, with features showing a considerable advance in naturalism; 625. Seated Athena (headless), found at the N foot of the Acropolis, conjecturally identified with that by *Endoios*, seen by Pausanias. The goddess wears the Ionic chiton and appears, from the positon of the right foot, to have just sat down—an early example of such mobility. The aegis on her breast was coloured. Korai: 633, 685, and 595 all repay attention; *671. A severe beauty; 696. The 'Polos' kore; note the headdress and the simplicity of the hair.

ROOM V. Pedimental figures of the Gigantomachia from the Old Temple of Athena (c 525 BC). These are particularly striking from behind, though presumably never designed to be so seen: 631. Athena, attacking with lance, and snake aegis, newly restored; two terminal kneeling giants. Here also are *681. 'Kore of Antenor', the largest of the Korai, with unusual vertical emphasis of the drapery, and (left) a base which may or may not belong to it; the base bears the dedication of Nearchos, the donor, and of the sculptor *Antenor* (both Attic work in island marble c 525 BC); 1360. Kore, damaged by fire, but beautiful and elegant.

At the entrance to the alcove, 683 (left), a curious Kore, disproportionate and heavy; 597 (right). Youth riding a hippalektryon; 6476 A and B, two terracotta Korai. In the alcove, seven cases of choice pottery and terracottas, mostly from excavations of 1955–59 in the Sanctuary of the Nymphs, and archaic *Marble fragments from the Acropolis. Particularly interesting, in addition, are the original cedarwood blocks from the centre holes of column drums.

ROOM VI is devoted to the 'severe' style, a stage in the emergence of the Classical style from the Archaic. Most characteristic is *698. The Kritian Boy (c 480 BC); the weight is at last correctly posed and the body liberated from archaic stiffness; the confident modelling and bodily proportions of the early classical style are already felt; it is now proven beyond doubt that head and body belong together; 695. Relief, 'Mourning Athena'; *689. Head of a Kouros, delicately modelled; 697. Forequarters of a horse, in a more developed style than No. 700 (above); 692. Torso of a young boy; 699. Male head (Pheidian school?); 599. Male torso; 688. Kore; 302. Torso; 67. Pinax with painting of a warrior running; 690. Nike.

In ROOM VII are arranged the mutilated fragments from the **Parthenon Pediments**: their probable relative positions can be seen from the plaster models constructed in 1896–1904 from the then available evidence: Pausanias' description, the Madrid 'puteal', Carrey's drawings, portions in the British Museum, etc. Reconstructions using full size casts of the surviving pieces can be seen in the Centre for Acropolis Studies. The composition of the W pediment is tolerably certain; that of the E end considerably less so, since the central 12·2m was destroyed in the Christian alterations; most of the figures still extant in Carrey's day are in London (cf. 'Blue Guide London').—WEST PEDIMENT. The subject is the contest of Athena and Poseidon. 882. Head of a horse from Athena's team (*contra* the exhibit label); 884. Head from Poseidon's team, with hoofs, etc.; 1363. Seated goddess (= Figure U); 880. Hermes (H); 881. Selene (N); (in case, unnumbered = Figures B, C)) Kekrops and daughter (?); 885. Part of torso of Poseidon fitted to a cast of another piece in London (M); 887. Torso and leg from the statue of Ilissos (A); (unnumbered) Reclining draped figure, Procris (?) (W). etc.—EAST PEDIMENT. The birth of Athena.

Also in this room are 705. Metope, Centaur carrying off a Lapith woman; 727, 720. Centaurs' heads, from the S metopes of the Parthenon; 1309. Head of a young girl.

In ROOM VIII, admirably lit and mounted at eye level, is all the detached part of the ****Parthenon Frieze** that remains in Athens. Many of the slabs were blown clear in the explosion and buried, thus escaping Lord Elgin. The slabs have been arranged in correct order; their original positions are indicated on a wall diagram. The subject is the Panathenaic procession (cf. above).

Since the frieze is displayed on an inside instead of an outside wall for which it was designed the relative positions are reversed: the sculptures from the N side of the Parthenon are on the S wall and vice versa. They lead up to the three remaining slabs of the East Frieze on the E wall. West frieze (*in situ*), see above.

You start at the W door of the room and proceed along the long S wall. Here are 13 slabs out of the 42 which composed the *North Frieze*. The beginning of the procession on this side (corner slab and the following 12 pieces) is all in London. *862, 861, 863 (adjoining slabs) portray horses and riders, very spirited; one is turning and apparently being exhorted by a marshal to close up. The next three (872, 859, gap, 871) form a group from the chariot procession (just over half-way along the cella); one chariot has an apobates; an official directs; 874. Youth leading horses. Two adjoining slabs (875, 876) depict thallophoroi (bearers of olive branches), and another (875), from farther along, lyre-players. The remaining three slabs are from the head of the procession (alternate slabs are missing): *864. Four epheboi carrying hydriai; the expressions and drapery are exquisite; 860. Four men with rams; 857. Youths leading sacrificial heifers.—The *South Frieze* fragments, five in number, begin opposite by the anta on the N wall: 866–69. Four slabs from near the W end, depicting horses and riders; 873. Magistrates and two women. On the adjacent wall to the left of the door follow three slabs (797, 877, *856) from the right side of the *East Frieze* of the Parthenon: nearly all the remaining slabs, which show the ceremony of the peplos, are in London. The third, well-preserved, shows three of the twelve gods attending the Theoxenia, probably Poseidon, Apollo, and Artemis.

In the SW corner of the room are displayed the surviving thirteen slabs of the parapet that extended round three sides of the Temple of Athena Nike. This parapet was executed in high relief by a number of artists between 421 and 407 BC; the scenes represent winged *VICTORIES at their various tasks, among them the well-known Victory adjusting her sandal (973); 972(r.) has been thought by Paionios, sculptor of the Nike from Olympia .—On the upper part of the central anta are placed fragments of the ERECHTHEION FRIEZE. The marble statues, attached to a background of blue Eleusinian marble, were commissioned at 60 drachmas apiece from a number of sculptors, whose names are known from the building records of 408 BC; 1075. Presentation of Erichthonios.

In ROOM IX have been placed four of the six Caryatids from the Erechtheion porch (one is in the British Museum, one being conserved), seen through a transparent screen behind which they have a sterile atmosphere. Also here (but possibly to be moved) are later sculptures, mostly fragmentary: 1339. 'Lenormant' relief of a trireme (c 400 BC), with two finials and a colossal head; 1333. Relief of Athena receiving Hera, symbolising Samos, with the text of a treaty between Athens and Samos (405 BC), defaced under the Thirty Tyrants, and re-engraved two years later when Samos also had meanwhile suffered a change of government.

3 The Areópagus, Mouseíon, Pnyx, and Hill of the Nymphs

The WEST SLOPE OF THE ACROPOLIS, now covered by ornamental groves, has never been systematically explored, though Dörpfeld unearthed a street and part of the quarter flanking it (see below) in the valley to the W where Leofóros Apostólou Pávlou now runs. This he took to be the Panathenaic Way; but the agora excavations (Rte 5) have conclusively proved that the processional approach from the Agora to the Acropolis passed to the E of the Areopagus. The saddle that links the Areopagus spur to the Acropolis, may have been the site of the earliest agora of the Archaïc period.

A flight of rock-hewn steps mounts to the **Areópagus** (6, 5; 115m), the low hill that gave name to a council of nobles which became at once the senate and the supreme judicial court; with the rise of democracy, it gradually lost its powers.

History. The name, commonly derived (cf. Euripides, 'Elektra', 1258) from the tradition that Ares was tried here by the other Gods for the murder of Halirrhothios, more likely signifies the Hill of Curses (arai). Here Aeschylus placed the camp of the Amazons ('Eumenides', 681–706). The Persians encamped on the hill when they besieged the Acropolis in 480 BC (Hdt. VIII, 52). The 7C council of elders, composed entirely of the Eupatridai became known as the *Council of the Areopagus* (ἡ Βουλὴ ἡ εξ 'Αρείου Πάγου) to distinguish it from later councils. Its original and most important function was the conduct of criminal justice, particularly in cases of murder and manslaughter; but in the aristocratic days it became the governing body of the state. The archons were ex-officio members, or, according to Plutarch (Pericles), became members on quitting office. The Assembly of the people was at this time merely the recording machine for the decisions of the Areopagus. Solon transferred its powers of administration and legislation to the Assembly; but he made the Areopagus the protector of the constitution and the guardian of the laws, with control over the magistrates and the censorship of morals. Under Ephialtes (c 461 BC) censorship and control over the magistrates were transferred to the people, and the jurisdiction of the Areopagus limited once again to cases of homicide. Aeschylus, in the Eumenides, 458 BC, described the trial of Orestes on the Areopagus for the murder of his mother Klytemnestra, and the institution of the Court of the Areopagus—the implication being that this was its proper function and that the restriction of its powers thereto was strictly correct.

In the 4C BC the Areopagus dealt also with crimes of treason and corruption, notable cases being the trials of the deserters after Chaeronea in 338, of Demosthenes in 324, and of the courtesan Phryne. It was in existence during the Empire. In AD 51 St. Paul (Acts xvii, 22–34) delivered 'in the midst of Mars' Hill' the sermon on the Unknown God, which converted the senator Dionysius (St. Dionysius the Areopagite, patron saint of Athens).

On the artificially levelled summit of the hill are remains of beddings in the rock for the walls of a small edifice, probably connected with the formalities of the tribunal. Bishop Wordsworth started the tradition that these were rock-hewn seats. 'The unwrought stones', says Pausanias (I, 28, 5) 'on which the accused and accusers stand are named respectively the Stone of Injury (ὕβρις) and the Stone of Ruthlessness'(ἀναιδεία; cf. Euripides, 'Iphigeneia in Tauris', 961).

Looking down from the summit you can trace the ruins of the 16C church of *St. Dionysios the Areopagite* (see above), which stood (as did its predecessors) on a level platform beneath the N side of the hill. This is believed by Prof. E. Vanderpool to be the site of the court's sessions. Lower down the N slope four ruined *Mycenaean Chamber-tombs* (explored in 1939 and 1947; see Agora Museum) yielded gold rosettes, ivory toilet boxes, swords, etc, etc, suggesting royal burials of the second quarter of the 14C BC. Tradition places the **Cave of the Furies** beneath the NE brow of the hill. A spring here was locally credited with medicinal virtues in recent times. Like the Theseion, the precinct of the cave was a recognised sanctuary for murderers and fugitive slaves. Kylon's fellow-conspirators were killed within it in abuse of the right of sanctuary. People acquitted by the court of the Areopagus were wont to sacrifice at the cave. Within the enclosure stood the Tomb of Oedipus, the possession of which was long regarded as essential to the safety of Athens. The closing scene of the 'Eumenides' of Aeschylus is set in the cave.

The Areopagus also affords the most illuminating general view of the Agora. A path descends the E side of the Areopagus past the Cave of the Furies (see above) to join the road bordering the S gate of the Agora excavations.

From the Areopagus you descend the Acropolis approach road to Leofóros Dhionissíou Areopayítou. To the SW, by the Dionysos Restaurant, paths mount the tree-clad slopes of the **Mouseíon** (148m), a hill which throughout history has played a strategic role in the fortunes of Athens. A Greco-Roman tradition derives its name from Musæus, the poet-disciple of Orpheus; it was more likely the *Hill of the Muses* who, in their character of Oreades, may have had a shrine here.

The Themistoclean Wall climbed its gentle E slope, followed the top of its sheer S face (visible traces), and joined the Southern Long Wall near its W extremity. The later Diateichisma (see below) ran NW from the summit. In 294 BC, Demetrios Poliorketes built a fort to command the Piraeus road; it changed hands four times in the ensuing struggles. From the hill Morosini bombarded the Acropolis in 1687. At the end of November 1916, Greek royalist forces occupied the ground here, and on 1 December fired on Allied troops. It was again a scene of activity during the coup of 21 April 1967.

On the summit stands the **Monument of Philópappus**, built in AD 114–116 by the Athenians in honour of C. Julius Antiochus Philopappus, a prince of Commagene (Northern Syria), who had a distinguished career both as an Athenian citizen and as a Roman consul and prætor. The monument, of Pentelic marble, consisted of a rectangular tomb with a slightly concave façade 12·2m high. Intact in 1436 when Cyriacus of Ancona saw it, it later became ruinous. The *Façade*, which faces the Acropolis, is decorated with a frieze showing Philopappus as consul (AD 109) driving in his chariot. Above are four Corinthian pilasters which frame three niches. The central niche contains the statue of Philopappus as an Athenian citizen of the Deme of Besa; the left one his grandfather Antiochus IV Epiphanes, last king of Commagene (dethroned by Vespasian); the right one, according to Cyriacus of Ancona, held the statue of Seleukos I Nikator, the Macedonian founder of the dynasty. On the left central pilaster is inscribed in Latin the deceased's cursus honorum at Rome; on the right, in Greek, were his princely titles.—The tomb, traces of which are visible, lay behind the façade.

The *View from the monument, especially at sunset (often windy), is particularly fine, embracing the Parthenon, Hymettus, the Attic Plain with its encircling mountains, and the Saronic Gulf.

A paved path descending directly towards the Observatory (a little W of N) along the ridge of the hill follows the **Diateíchisma**, the lower courses of which are visible for most of the way. Built to shorten the city's fortifications after the slighting of the Long Walls had made Themistocles' original line untenable, this cross wall was formerly attributed to Kleon on the evidence of Aristophanes ('Knights', 817–8), but is now securely dated on evidence from excavation to the end of the 4C BC. To it was joined the *Fort of Poliorketes* (cf. above), of which the remains of a tower 10m square, can be seen c 70m N of the Philopappus monument; the foundations of another may be traced at a lower level to the NE.

The region enclosed by the two diateichismata formed the ancient quarters of *Koile* and *Melite*. It is occupied by a very large number of **Ancient Dwellings**, once thought to represent the region of the Pelasgic *Kranaa*; but archaeological evidence does not support any great antiquity. They belong for the most part to the 5C BC. This quarter, then entirely within the city walls, became overpopulated at the time of the Peloponnesian War, when the Athenians flocked from the country into the city (Thuc. II, 14); but it was deserted before the end of the 3C BC. In the Roman era these old dwellings and cisterns were used as tombs. They lie thick on the ground on both flanks of the hills. The ruins include rooms, niches, terraces, flights of steps, and cisterns. Often two or three walls of the buildings were formed by excavation in the rock. Nearly 60 cisterns, large pear-shaped excavations, may be observed; they vary in depth from 4m to 6m. Seven rock-hewn seats, in an elevated spot c 137m W of the wall, may possibly represent an ancient court of justice. In the bottom of the valley are extensive traces (cart-ruts) of an ancient road that led SW from the Ayios Dhimitrios gate (see below).

The path follows the wall down to the modern drive that serves the *Philopappus Theatre* on the SW flank of Mouseion hill. Here on the foundations of the N tower of the *'Dipylon above the Gates'* (S tower excavated in 1936 and filled in again) stands the little chapel of *Ayios Dhimítrios Loumbardhiáris*. The name (from loumbardha or canon) is derived from a miracle attributed to the saint in which a Turkish canon, located on the Acropolis, was struck by lightning at the moment it was about to open fire on his congregation. The chapel has some surviving Byzantine frescoes. The restoration of the building and attractive refurbishment of the surrounding area (including pleasant outdoor cafeteria) is the work (1951–57) of the leading architect Dhimitrios Pikionis, his students and local artists. The gate (cf. above), wrongly identified from a late 4C BC inscription, is not a dipylon. The so-called *Tomb of Kimon*, which served in later times as the tomb of a certain Zosimianos, is really a rock-dwelling of the 5C BC. In the cliff-face, a little to the S, is the equally misnamed PRISON OF SOCRATES, another such dwelling having no proven connection whatever with the philosopher. It consists of three rooms, one with a sloping ceiling, and a bottle-shaped cistern once independent of the rest.

Above Ayios Dhimítrios rises the *Hill of the Pnyx* (109m), in Classical times popularly called 'The Rocks' (αἱ Πέτραι). On its NE slope, 27·5m from the top, is the site of the **Pnyx**, approached by a path (right, also serving the *Son et lumière* seating on the Pnyx), past Ay. Dhimítrios, the meeting-place of the Assembly, or Ecclesia (Ἐκκλησία), firmly identified by the discovery in the 19C of its boundary stone (inscribed ΟΡΟΣ ΠΥΚΝΟΣ) and scientifically investigated by Kourouniotes and Homer Thompson between 1930 and 1936. With the establishment of democracy under Kleisthenes the Assembly changed its venue from the Agora to the Pnyx, where its deliberations could not be overlooked; they were thus held, significantly perhaps, above instead of below the Areopagus. Here the great statesmen of the 5C and early 4C, among them Aristides, Themistocles, Pericles and Demosthenes, held their audience.

The word *Pnyx* (ἡ Πνύξ, gen. Πυχνός) means the place where people were tightly packed (πυχνός, compact, dense, crowded). The 'tight-packing' must have had special reference to the single entrance, as there was room inside for four or five times the number of legislators. The Assembly was presided over by the Prytaneis (see the Agora). The citizens, 5000 of whom were needed to form a quorum, were hustled towards the Pnyx by Scythian archers who held across the Agora and neighbouring streets cords daubed with wet red paint in order to hurry up the laggards, and to prevent any citizen from 'cutting' a meeting. There was only one entrance. Here the arrivals were scrutinised so that no unauthorised person should slip in. No person not a citizen was allowed to attend without special authority. Citizens marked with the red paint forfeited their allowance.

Three periods of construction have been confirmed. In the first, c 500 BC, the seating faced N and the bema S towards the sea, a natural adaptation of the

Pnyx. Hypothetical reconstruction with Panathenaic stadium, c 329 BC

configuration of the ground. Under the Thirty Tyrants (403 BC) the arrangements were reversed so that the bema faced to landward because, according to Plutarch ('Themistocles', 19, 4), they thought oligarchy less distasteful to farmers than to mariners. The retaining wall of this period, uncovered in 1930–31, was of poor masonry and carelessly constructed. Most of the extant remains date from the last period; this was first thought to be of Hadrianic date but is now attributed to a comprehensive plan of Lycurgus for the embellishment of the site (cf. below). The buildings planned to accompany the new auditorium were left unfinished and the Assembly seems to have migrated to the Theatre of Dionysos.

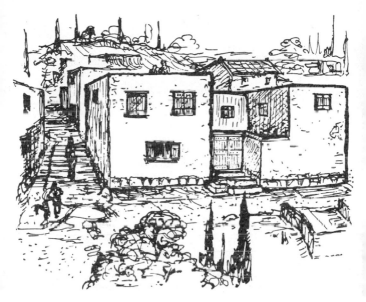

Pnyx. Reconstruction of Classical houses

The Pnyx is a huge artificial terrace in the form of a semicircle, the ends of which joined a perpendicular wall of rock, a man-made scarp forming the base-line. The semicircle, 198·5m round, is formed by a colossal *Retaining Wall*, 1·8m thick, built of trapezoidal blocks quarried in the fashioning of the scarp. The blocks, one of which is 4m long and 1·8m high, are remarkably well jointed without the use of mortar. About one-third of the wall, now diminished to a height of 4·5m, remains, at the central part of the arc. Its object was to keep in place the gigantic embankment of earth which was built to convert the natural downward slope of the ground into an upward slope, so that the area had the form of a crude theatre. The ravages of time and the mutilation of the retaining wall have restored the natural slope of the earth, which still, however, lies in places 1·8m above the top of what is left of the wall. The single entrance to the Pnyx of the third period was by a flight of steps on the N side of the wall. The remains of a second and concentric wall exist ten yards within the outer wall below present ground level; this belongs to the second period.

The *Auditorium* presumably had a shallow slope like a scallop-shell, but there is no material evidence for seating of any kind or even for a floor other than of earth.

The perpendicular wall of rock that forms a base-line of 118·8m is hewn in two sections which make an obtuse angle (158°) at the centre, where it is highest (4·6m). At the angle is a three-stepped platform, 0·9m high, 9·4m wide, and projecting 6·4m from the wall, which formed the *Bema* or tribune, from which the orators spoke. The sockets of the balustrade that surrounded it are still visible. It is crowned by a cube of rock 1·8m high and 3m sq. with a flight of five steps at either side. Round its base was a ledge for votive or legislative tablets.

In the wall of rock, 12m to the left of the Bema, is a large niche, surrounded by over 50 smaller ones. Twelve marble tablets, found by Lord Aberdeen in 1803 in the ground below them, are now in the British Museum, and others have been recovered since. Most of them are ex-votos dedicated by women to Zeus Hypsistos and date from Roman times.

Above the Bema is a broad terrace levelled from the rock. In the centre, in line with the tribune, is a bedding probably for a monumental *Altar*, flanked by rock-cut benches, perhaps the seats of the prytaneis. Farther back another bedding in the rock may mark the site of the *Heliotropion*, or sundial, erected by the astronomer Meton in 433 BC. At a higher level are beddings for foundations of two large 'stoas'. The *West Stoa* measures 148m by 18m, and would have had 54 columns. The *East Stoa*, 21·5m by 6m, was begun on a different alignment and in its second form accords with the placing of a smaller central building, perhaps a *Propylon*. These three structures are dated to the third quarter of the 4C BC and have been conjectured to represent a scheme of Lycurgus, c 330–326 BC, for the comfort of the Assembly. A recent reappraisal (A.J.A. 1985) of the site has however suggested that the 'stoas' actually form part of the Lycurgan Panathenaic stadium, of which no archaeological indication has ever been found on the site of the later stadium (cf. below). In this case, the two rectangular foundations were not for stoas but for earth embankments on which the spectators would have stood to watch contests taking place on the levelled terrace immediately in front.

Soon after these buildings were begun, a decision was taken to carry the Diateichisma (see above) through the site. The wall did not survive long at this point, being replaced by a parallel wall of white poros with towers, traces of which can be seen to the S and W. This probably strengthened a weak point in the circuit at the time the Long Walls and the outer diateichisma were finally abandoned as a defensive line (c 200 BC).

To the N of the Pnyx, rises the so-called **Hill of the Nymphs** (104m), a modern name borrowed from the dedication to the Nymphs carved on a rock inside the Observatory garden. The slopes of the hill are covered with ancient foundations, in the midst of which stands the little rock-cut church of *Ayía Marína* attached to the SE corner of its multi-domed modern successor. Recent work has revealed frescoes in several layers going back to the 13C. On the rock below the church, is a 6C inscription written from right to left, which marks the limit of the Precinct of Zeus ("Ορος Διός). On the summit of the hill stands the conspicuous *Observatory* (Asteroskopíon), founded by Baron Sinas in 1842, which is open to visitors on the last Friday of the month. A second building, with a large telescope, was added in 1905, and a seismological station in 1957.

Behind the observatory a path leads towards a radio station. To the right (c 70m) is the *'Little Pnyx'*, a small rock-cut assembly place. Traces of the *Northern Long Wall* may be seen close by. A long depression to the W, partly filled up, is generally identified with the *Barathron,* the ancient Athenian place of execution.

Returning past the observatory and descending to Leofóros Apostólou Pávlou (cf. below), you face two gates: to the left an entrance to the *Agora* excavations (Rte 5); to the right access to a tract of ground excavated by Dörpfeld in 1892–97. His contentions that he had discovered here the Temple of Dionysos in the Marshes and the true Enneakrounos were based on topographical suppositions about the location of the Agora which have since been conclusively disproved. DÖRPFELD'S EXCAVATIONS are now largely overgrown and their identification, though interesting to the scholar, need not delay the ordinary visitor.

An ANCIENT ROAD, c 4m wide, equipped with a gutter and bordered by walls of polygonal masonry, is laid bare for some 228·5m. It was possibly the principal street of the demo of Molito. To the right stood a *Lesche* (club) identified from inscriptions. Farther on is a private house with a record of two mortgages (for 1000 and 210 drachmæ respectively) inscribed on its outer wall in letters of the 4C BC. On the other side of the ancient road is an early triangular precinct, not the Dionysion in Limnai, but very possibly the *Heroon of Herakles Alexikakos.* The site, which is 1·0m below the level of the road, is covered with later buildings which have no connection with it. In the S corner is a small *Temple.* In the middle of the adjoining courtyard are the foundations, in poros, of a square base which may have supported the statue of Herakles by Ageladas (Scholiast to Aristophanes, Frogs 501). In the NW corner is a building formerly identified by Dörpfeld with the *Lenaion,* i.e. the building which enclosed the Sacred Wine Press (Λήναιον). The remains of a wine press were found here. Overlying the Greek remains and extending a little to the E are the foundations of a Roman basilica, identified from the long inscription (2C AD) on a column, which relates to the religious guild of the Iobacchoi, as their clubhouse or *Baccheion.* Farther on, on the same side of the road, are the ruins of the *Amyneion,* a small shrine to the hero Amynos, the assistant of Asklepios, of which Sophocles held the priesthood. Inside are a temple and a well which was fed by a conduit from the main fountain.

Opposite are remains of the great WATER SYSTEM OF PEISISTRATOS, which Dörpfeld asserted were those of the Enneakrounos. These are partly beneath the modern avenue and partly on its far side. At the foot of the Pnyx is a small square chamber hewn out of the rock, with a niche from which water still occasionally flows. It feeds a smaller round basin, also rock-hewn, a few feet lower down. This primitive supply, later covered by a Roman well-house, was identified by Dörpfeld with the Fountain of Kallirrhoë (cf. Rte 7). In the time of Solon, the yield was supplemented by cutting connecting channels from neighbouring water-courses on the Acropolis and Mouseion hills. A much more important undertaking, attributed to Peisistratos, was the construction of an *Aqueduct* nearly 5km long, which led from the valley of the Ilissos under the present National Garden to the foot of the W slopes of the Acropolis. It ended in a large square *Cistern,* hewn like the others from the rock, from which pipes lead to a spacious *Square,* where stones belonging to a fountain base have been found.

The ancient road goes on some way farther S and SE along the line of the aqueduct, and then bends NE towards the Acropolis. A footpath from the Amyneion leads through the pine-trees to the foot of the Areopagus where you started.

Leofóros Apostólou Pávlou continues NW past public gardens. A side-road, on the bend, approaches *Ayios Athanásios,* beyond which a footbridge leads to the entrance gate of the Kerameikos (Rte 4).

4   From Síndagma Square to the Agorá and the Kerameikós

Bus No. 026 from Leofóros Amalías, via Mitropóleos, returning via Ermoú.

From Sindagma Square the long OD. ERMOÚ (Hermes St.), lined at first with fashion and textile shops, runs straight W for nearly 1·5m, dividing the old city in two; as it descends it changes character, being devoted to the furnishing and building trades. In a large square to the S (off Mitropóleos) stands the **Cathedral** (7, 3), built in 1840–55 out of the material of 72 demolished churches and from the design of four architects. The resultant incongruity is not, therefore, surprising. Since 1864 the Metropolitan Archbishop of Athens has been the chief dignitary of the independent Greek Orthodox Church. To the left of the W entrance is the tomb of the Patriarch Gregory transferred from Odessa in 1871, fifty years after his execution at Constantinople. To the S stands the **Small Metropolis,** or old cathedral, known also as *Panayia Gorgoepikoös* and *Ayios Eleftherios.* In its present form it dates from the 12C, though legend attributes its foundation to the Empress Irene c 787. Its external dimensions are only 12·2m by 7·6m; the cupola is under 12m high. The walls of the church are artfully constructed entirely of ancient architectural blocks and reliefs, some inscribed, and of reliefs from an earlier church or churches of the 6–7C. On the W side above the arch over the door is a calendar of the Attic state festivals (? 2C AD). Each festival is represented by symbolic figures or objects in relief; signs of the zodiac indicated the time sequence. One of the Maltese crosses added by the Christians has blotted out the sole known representation of the Panathenaic ship; its wheels are visible to the right of the second cross from the left.

Outside the S wall lies a block of grey marble 2·1m long and ·6m wide, known as the Stone of Cana, with a late Greek inscription recording its use at the Marriage Feast of Cana of Galilee. It was discovered at Elatea, in Phocis.— Behind the Apse: inscriptions and tablets, archaic relief with dancing figures.— N side: ancient votive tablets.

The modernised church of *St Andrew* at the top of Od. Filothéis to the S is now the chapel of the archbishop's palace.

About 450m W of Sindagma Square Od. Ermoú divides to form a little square round the tiny church called *Kapnikaréa* (7, 3). The origin of its name is doubtful, as is the inevitable attribution of its foundation to the Empress Irene. The existing cruciform structure, of stone with the usual courses of brick, cannot be older than the 11C; the porch, the exo-narthex and the parecclesion (or N chapel) were added in the 13C. Saved from demolition in 1834 by Ludwig of Bavaria, the building was carefully restored by the university and is its official church. The dome is supported by four columns with Roman capitals.

You cross Od. Aiólou (Rte 8), overshadowed at its S end by the towering rock of the Acropolis, then skirt the N side of Monastiráki Square (Rte 6). To the right lies the district of PSIRÍ, less appealing than Plaka though still maintaining its irregular street plan. In Od. Ayías Théklas No. 11 was the scene of Byron's ten-week stay on his first arrival in Athens in 1809; he later immortalised the 13-year-old daughter of the house, Teresa Makris, as the Maid of Athens. Farther N, on the corner of Evripídhou and Menándrou streets, is the chapel of *Ayios Ioannis stin Kolona,* built round an unfluted Roman column with a Corinthian capital which projects through the roof. The column, probably from a gymnasium dedicated to Apollo, has reputedly the power of curing fevers.

Off the S side of Od. Ermoú lies the little Plateía Avisinías with the *'Flea Market'* (Sunday mornings). The antiquities (especially coins) are not always what they seem. Metal-workers practice their traditional craft in Od. Iféstou, to the E. Od. Astingos, its W continuation, is named after Frank Abney Hastings, the English philhellene who was mortally wounded at Aitoliko. Nearby, *Ayios Filippos* stands above the railway cutting near the N entrance to the *Agora* (see Rte 5). This may be conveniently visited on the return.

The church of the *Asomáton* (6, 3), freed in 1960 of its 19C additions, closes the N side of the square fronting Thissíon Station. Beyond this, Od. Ermoú continues alongside the excavations of the Kerameikós. In the street flanking their E end is a *Synagogue* with a marble 'classical' façade.—On the far side of the railway some traces of the city walls can be seen to the W of the church of *Ayios Athanásios* (6, 3); the church and adjacent cottages utilise ancient rock-cut foundations.

The **Kerameikós** (6, 1; excellent guidebook by U. Knigge (1990), available at the site in German or Greek and to appear in English) includes the ruins of the Dipylon and Sacred Gates and excavations made outside the walls in the ancient *Cemetery of the Kerameikos.* Here roads from Piraeus, Eleusis, and Boeotia converged upon that from the Academy, so that most ancient travellers entered the city by this way. The brook Eridanos flows from E to W across the area, which is frequently waterlogged; frogs abound and tortoises may be seen. The place Kerameikos is said by Pausanias (I, 3, 1) to take its name from the hero Keramos, a supposed son of Dionysos and Ariadne.

Cemeteries existed in the Kerameikos district at least from the 12C BC. By the 7C a line seems to have been drawn between the *Inner Kerameikos*, a quarter of potters and smiths, and the *Outer Kerameikos*, but it was the building of the city wall that conclusively separated the two. Few burials later than this are found in the inner area, as thenceforward it became usual (just as later in Rome) to bury the dead outside the enceinte along roads leading from the city gates. The importance of the W entrance to the city was enhanced by the Dionysiac and Eleusinian processions which passed through it and by that of the Panathenaia which set out from it. In consequence the Academy Road outside the Gate of Thria (later the Dipylon) had perhaps already by the 6C become the **Demosion Sema,** the official burial area of the Athenian war dead, reserved for state tombs and cenotaphs of individuals or polyandreia for groups of battle heroes. Here were the graves of Pericles, Thrasyboulos, Konon, Zeno, Harmodios and Aristogeiton, and other worthies. Thucydides tells how 'when the remains have been laid in the earth, some man of known ability and high reputation, chosen by the city, delivers a suitable oration over them'. From a platform here Pericles delivered the famous oration (Thuc. II, 35–46) on those who died in the first year of the Peloponnesian War. The remainder of the ground was available to all classes, including slaves.

Many tomb monuments removed in the 19C are in the National Archaeological Museum. The Greek Archaeological Society began excavations in 1863, continuing at intervals until 1913. In 1913–41 the German Archaeological Institute conducted excavations directed by A. Brückner and K. Kübler. In 1956 the Greek government requested the Institute to resume responsibility for the Kerameikos site and further intensive work began under the direction of D. Öhly. New excavations have been initiated; the old areas have been reinvestigated, conserved and landscaped; the museum, built with funds donated by Gustav Oberlaender (1867–1936), a German-American silk-stocking manufacturer, has been renovated and expanded. The Academy Road, whose course lies largely beneath modern houses, has not been properly explored, though many casual finds are in the National Archaeological Museum. The sector that has been cleared lies S of the main Kerameikos and consists of an extension to

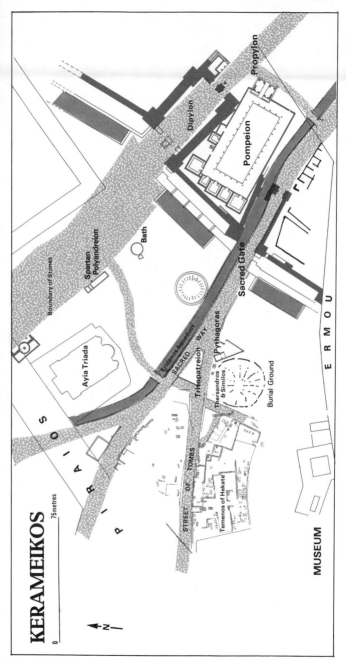

the SW made at the beginning of the 4C BC. Most of its tombs were destroyed for material to repair the city walls after the battle of Chaeronea (338 BC), but those remaining were covered by successive layers of earth and later tombs to a depth of 6–9m, and so were untouched by the extensive siege work of Sulla in 86 BC.

Half-right inside the entrance on top of a mound is a plan of orientation with a view over the whole site. From it can be clearly identified the Wall of Themistocles with its later outwork and sectional moats. Of the wall only the bottom course of masonry is Themistoclean. On top of this in blue 'acropolis' stone are two courses of Konon's wall, then, in creamy limestone, two courses of a Demosthenian renewal, further courses attributable to Lycurgus, and, to the right, in long and short work, masonry of the period of Justinian.

A path descends to give a closer view of the double **City Walls,** which here occupy a frontage of c 183m, interrupted by the Dipylon and the Sacred Gate. The inner line of wall was built by Themistocles in 479 and rebuilt by Konon in 394. It is only 2–2·4m thick and consists of one course of poros blocks (truly Themistoclean) and two rows of well jointed polygonal blocks of blue limestone (Kononian), interspersed with hastily reused marbles, with a core of rubble. The upper part was of unbaked brick. The outer breastwork, with moat, was of later date, and may have been contemporary with the Dipylon. It is 4·3m thick and has facings of regularly cut blocks of conglomerate, with an earthen core. To the SW of the Sacred Gate both are fairly well preserved, the 'Themistoclean' wall with its later superstructures being 4m high in places and the outer wall still higher. Plutarch's contention that Sulla, before he stormed Athens in 86 BC, razed the whole section of the wall between the Sacred and the Piraeic Gates indicates that earlier socles were by this time below ground level.

The **Sacred Gate** ('Ἱερὰ Πύλη) spanned both the Sacred Way to Eleusis and the Eridanos brook. In the Themistoclean period an inner gate was constructed 10m inside the circuit wall. The road was protected on the S by a high wall which joined the enceinte in a massive tower, and a matching tower was added to the E exit of the gate in the 4C BC. The water, which presumably bore the sewage from the Agora area, was conveyed in a vaulted channel.

A well-preserved section of the WALL OF KONON, in rusticated polygonal masonry on the Themistoclean line, runs NE between the Dipylon and the Sacred Gate. About 2·5m short of the gate is a *Boundary Stone,* inscribed perpendicularly ΟΡΟΣ ΚΕΡΑΜΕΙΚΟΥ; this is one of several found at different points of the Kerameikos boundary. The space between the two gates was occupied by the **Pompeíon,** a place of preparation for processions (πομπαί), which served as a storehouse for the heavy vehicles and other paraphernalia used in the Panathenaic festival. It was adorned with painted portraits of the comic poets and a bronze statue of Socrates by Lysippus, and in emergency served as a centre for distributing corn. The Greek edifice of the 4C BC consisted of a court surrounded by a colonnade of six columns by thirteen, known to have been a haunt of Diogenes. The orthostats in Hymettian marble of the E wall and of part of the S wall still stand. Off the N and W sides project six small dining-rooms. A simple *Propylon* in the E corner, which gave access from the city, preserves its plan complete. Prominent are the metal clamps joining the marble blocks, wheelruts, and the holes for door fittings.

The classical Pompeion was destroyed in Sulla's siege, evidence of which survives in the shape of stone balls from his catapults. A new building occupying the same area was erected on massive concrete foundations in the time of Antoninus Pius. This was basilican in form, divided by two rows of 11 pilasters, and its most prominent remaining features are the buttresses of its S wall. It was destroyed in turn during the Herulian raid of 267. The plans of both can be best appreciated from an artificial terrace in the SE corner of the excavated area.

The **Dípylon** (Δίπυλον, double gateway), was the main gate of the city. Not only was it larger than any of the others, but it received the greatest volume of traffic. A broad thoroughfare known as the Dromos (now built over), bordered with gymnasia and porticoes, ascended direct to the Agora (cf. Rte 5). Outwards, an important avenue led to the Academy, with a branch road to the *Hamaxitos*, the busy old road to Piraeus. This last intersected the *Sacred Way*, which led from the Sacred Gate (see below) to Eleusis, where high roads ran W to Megara and N to Boeotia.

History. The Dipylon was built at the end of the 4C BC, on the exact plan of its predecessor, the Themistoclean gate of 479 BC, known as the Thriasian Gate (cf. Plutarch, 'Pericles', 30) which was so-called because it led to Thria, a deme near Eleusis. Known also as the Keramic Gate, it provided the favourite, though not the most direct, way to or from the Piraeus, as it avoided the hills and led straight into the heart of the city. In 200 BC Philip V of Macedon, furiously attacking Athens for siding with Pergamon and Rome against him, penetrated the court and extricated himself with some difficulty (Livy XXXI, 24).

The Dipylon gateway was strategically placed at the end of a deep court c 13·5m long and 7m broad, open on the W and protected by flanking towers. A considerable portion of the SW tower is preserved. This is nearly 7·5m sq. and is built of large blocks of conglomerate cased with limestone, very well worked. The *Court* was flanked by thick ramparts. The two gates are separated by a central pier, behind which is a square base supporting a round marble altar dedicated to Zeus Herkeios, Hermes, and Akamas (eponymous hero of the tribe of Akamantis). To the E of the entrance was a classical fountain-house behind which are preserved the first few of the steps leading up to the NE tower. The *Outer Gate*, added to the defences in the 1C BC, was set back c 8m from the city wall and was divided vertically by a stone pier c 11m wide; the openings on either side were 3·5m wide. The marble base of a monument stands outside the pier.

The Apotheke or dig-house lies beyond (no adm.).

The **Kerameikos Cemetery** lay outside the Dipylon and extended alongside the two principal adjoining roads. Part of the area is being slowly cleared. At present the ACADEMY ROAD offers little on the spot to justify its fame. Opposite the late *Sarcophagus of Philotera*, to the left of the road are scanty remains of a *Bath-house* of the 5C BC, the earliest of its kind yet discovered. Also to the left of the road is a *Polyandreion* which was found to contain the skeletons of 13 Spartan officers who fell fighting in the civil war in 403. Two of the bodies in the central chamber were named on an inscribed marble slab as Chairon and Thibrachos (mentioned by Xenophon); the third was probably the Olympic victor Lakrates. Here and to the NW of the church are two original *Boundary Stones*. Where the road disappears below the modern Od. Piraiós, is an elaborate grave monument formerly known as the Tomb of Chabrias, of c 350 BC, half excavated.

Literary evidence, casual finds, and excavations at intervals to the N augment our knowledge of the road. Identified post holes are believed to come from the wooden stands erected for spectators of the annual torch races in honour of the dead. Inscriptions have been found from the polyandreia of the battles of Potidaea, the Hellespont, and Corinth. About 185m NW of the Dipylon lay the *Peribolos of Artemis Kalliste*, identified with walls discovered at No. 11 Od. Plataíon, where votive reliefs came to light in 1922. For the *Academy of Plato* (c 1km NW of the Dipylon), see below.

Retracing your steps, keeping the church on your right, you cross the excavations where c 8000 ostraka (discarded from the Agora in ancient times) came to light in 1966, cross over the Eridanos and reach the *Tritopatreion* in the angle of the SACRED WAY (ΙΕΡΑ ΟΔΟΣ) and the so-called Street of the Tombs. Beyond the excavated area the present-day Ierá Odós follows the line of the ancient Sacred Way all the way to Eleusis. The Tritopatreis were perhaps deities connected with ancestor worship and three boundary stones warn of their sacred precinct.

Kerameikos. Funeral plot with grave stelai, etc.

Opposite, on the S side, stand the stelai of Pythagoras, consul (proxenos) of Athens at Selymbria in Thrace (early 5C BC) placed on a stepped pyramid of interesting geometrical proportions, and of the Corcyraean envoys, Thersandros and Simylos, who came to Athens at the outbreak of the Peloponnesian War (Thucydides, I, xxii); their tomb furniture in the museum indicates a 5C grave, though the monument was refurbished in the early 4C and the lettering of the stele is of that date.

Behind these ambassadorial stelai rises an enormous *Grave Mound* which was erected for two foreign dignitaries (ambassadors?) in the third quarter of the 6C BC. Opposite them, on the N side of the sacred way and beyond the Eridanos, there is a further large grave mound which was partly surrounded by a wall in the 4C. Its origin dates to the 7C BC and it may have belonged to the old Attic clan of the Kerykoi. It was the burial place of the herald Anthemokritos, of the same clan, who was murdered in Megara shortly before the beginning of the Peloponnesian War and whose grave is often mentioned by ancient writers (e.g. Pausanias, I, 36, 3). Adjoining it to the W are several grave tumuli, including one with the 'stele of the myrtles' and a large mound of the second half of the 5C BC.

The **Street of the Tombs** is a planned funerary avenue (cf. Rhamnous), begun c 394 BC. The street, 8m wide, has been excavated for 91·5m. On either side of the street the cemetery was divided into plots reserved for wealthy citizens (both Athenian citizens and metics). About 20 of these plots have been discovered, divided into distinct terraces (especially on the S side).

All types of funerary monument common in the 4C are represented: the plain *stele* with palmette anthemion; more elaborate *stelai* with reliefs enclosed in a frame, culminating in the *naïskos*, or *ædicula*, where the sculptural frame achieves architectural proportions; the *column* surmounted by a device or animal; and the great marble *lekythoi* (with one handle) and *loutrophoroi* (with two handles; used for unmarried persons), which enjoyed special favour in the 4C. In 317 BC Demetrios of Phaleron limited memorials to a plain *trapeza* (slab) or a *kioniskos* (or cippus; a small undecorated column). A few wells here and there provided the necessary water for the funeral rites.

To the left stands the **Memorial of Dexíleos**, the 20-year-old son of Lysanias of Thorikos, who was one of the 'five knights' killed in action at Corinth in 394 BC. On a massive conglomerate base stands a crescent of poros on which the inscribed monument was set off by two sirens. The marble relief (cast *in situ*) represents the young man in the act of despatching a prostrate adversary. The lance, horse, trappings, and bridle were of bronze. The tall stele crowned with a palmette commemorates Lysanias and a smaller one (behind) Melitta, brother and sister of Dexileos; a trapeza tombstone bears the names of Lysanias, another brother, and his family.

The adjacent plot of the brothers Agathon and Sosikrates of Herakleia contains the *Ædicula of Korallion*, wife of Agathon, as well as the tall *Stele of Agathon and Sosikrates.*—The *Monument of Dionysios of Kollytos* is an ædicula without relief backed by a pillar stele, which supports a conspicuously fine bull, in Pentelic marble.— In the plot of *Lysimachos of Acharnai*, with retaining walls of excellent polygonal masonry, are a Molossian Dog in Hymettian marble and a pudgy Roman sepulchral relief representing a funeral feast on the banks of the Styx, with Charon in attendance. The temenos of Nikostrates and Kephisodoros occupies the angle of a lateral road mounting to the *Temenos of Artemis Soteira*, a precinct long attributed to the worship of Hekate.

Returning along the NORTH SIDE of the Street of Tombs you see first the concession of Eubios of Potamos, with the *Stele of Euphrosyne* (c 386), sister of Eubios, and the *Monument of Bion* (his nephew) in the form of a Doric column surmounted by a loutrophoros. The plot of *Koroibos of Melite* contains his own stele, the *Loutrophoros of Kleidemos*, his grandson, and a facsimile of the ædicula of Hegeso, his wife. Beyond are the stelai of *Samakion* and *Menes* (on horseback). Farther over the *Ædicula of Eukoline*, a little girl with her dog; and the *Ædicula of Aristion*, a boy with a pet bird and a slave holding a strigil; below is a mourning siren, supported by kneeling figures. On the side of the mound on which stood the church of Ayia Triada can be seen the small *trapezai* of *Hipparete*,

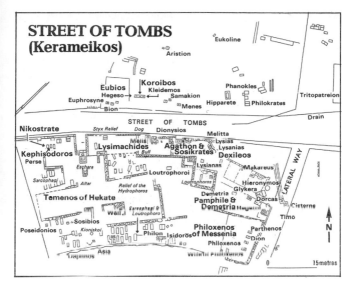

granddaughter of Alcibiades, and of *Phanokles of Leukenoe* and *Philokrates of Kydathenaion*.

In the LATERAL WAY, to the S, are the graves of two actors, *Makareus* and *Hieronymos*. The plot of Demetria and Pamphile includes the fine Ædicula of *Pamphile* represented as a seated figure beside her sister Demetria, who is standing. Beyond is the reservation of the family of *Philoxenos of Messenia* with a statue of his wife and three trapezai, one for himself and two for his sons; also tombstones of slaves.

The **Oberlaender Museum**. ROOM I. SCULPTURE recovered from the Themistoclean Wall: *Dexileos Monument (cf. above); P 1130, *Stele of Ampharete holding her infant grandchild, with beautifully executed drapery (5C BC); I 190, Base of a grave monument (c 515 BC) for the Carian *Tymnes*, son of Skylax, with three lines in Greek and one in Carian; Skylax may be the famous Carian captain, the earliest explorer of the Indus region and of the coasts of the Indian Ocean and Red Sea; P 105, Sphinx (c 550 BC), acroterion of a grave stele; P 1001, Base (c 560 BC) with four horsemen in relief on the front, found in S tower of Dipylon, perhaps the base for the famous Discophoros relief in the National Museum; P 1051, Horse and rider (c 520 BC); P 1052, Seated man, grave monument of c 530 BC, both in the Themistoclean Wall; P 1054, Boxer Stele (c 550 BC): head of boxer with cauliflower ear and thongs of glove tied round his wrist; P 1169, Stele of Eupheros (5C BC), grave relief of youth with strigil; P 1132, Grave stele of warrior with staff and sword (c 570–560 BC).

ROOM II contains terracotta figures and choice *Vases of all kinds of the Sub-Mycenaean, Protogeometric, Geometric and Protoattic periods (11–7C), part of a most important collection, from which the definitive dating of the period has been largely deduced. Among these are the earliest pictorial representation (a horse: the 'Ur-Pferd') on a pot since Mycenaean times, and a bronze bowl of Phoenician

workmanship (late-9C BC), 'the earliest confidently dated Near
Eastern art object found in Greece' (Akurgal).

ROOMS III AND IV. Grave groups of the Archaic, Classical, and
Hellenistic periods, containing black-figured and red-figured pottery
of well-known painters (Amasis, Kleophrades), terracotta figurines
including 'four exquisite figures attached to a base' (Higgins);
ostraka, from a find of about 18,000, naming Themistocles and other
famous citizens.

Beyond the entrance to the Kerameikos excavation, the buildings of the former
gas works are being restored for conversion into a Museum of Industrial
Archaeology.

The Academy, made famous by Plato's school of philosophy, was a
sacred wood c 2 stadia in diameter, situated at the end of an avenue
(cf. above) 6 stadia from the Dipylon. Pious walkers wishing to follow
as nearly as possible the avenue's course should take Od. Plataíon or
the parallel Od. Salamínos (2, 5) and their extensions from the NW
side of the Kerameikos (2·5km). The church of Ayios Yeóryios on the
corner of Palamidhíou, two-thirds of the way along, stands on the
ancient road, which has been located at many points. *Ayios Trífon*,
standing in Kolokínthou off the N side of the main Corinth road,

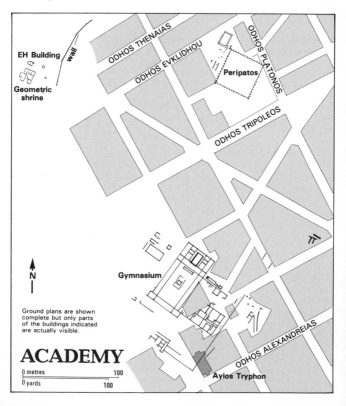

marks the S corner of the **Academy of Plato**, whose positon was confirmed in 1966 by the discovery *in situ* of a boundary-stone dated to c 500 BC. The area is more easily reached by bus No. 051 from Od. Veranzérou via Kolonós.

The hill of *Kolonos Hippios* (56m), the refuge of Oedipus, the flowers of which are celebrated by Sophocles' chorus (Oed. Col., 688–719), lies to the E of Od. Lenormán, enveloped by the city. On its bare top, above the trees, tombstones commemorate Charles Lenormant (1802–59) and Karl Ottfried Müller (1797–1840), two archaeologists who died in Athens.

In 1985, the excavation of an underpass for Od. Lenormán to cross Od. Konstantinoupóleos led to important archaeological discoveries close to the ancient road from the Erian gate to Hippios Kolonos—a large cemetery, mainly Archaic and Classical in date, and the debris of pottery factories which made vases and votives, some of them for the cemeteries. Study of the finds is expected to throw light on the organisation of pottery production. One of the workshops in the vicinity was evidently that of the Haimon Painter, whose work is already known from other sources.

The ACADEMY, more correctly the *Hekademeia*, was traditionally founded by Hekademos, who told the Dioscuri where their sister Helen was hidden; hence, in gratitude to Hekademos, the Lacedaemonians always spared it when they invaded Attica (Plutarch, 'Theseus', 32). Twelve sacred olive-trees, supposed to be offshoots of Athena's tree on the Acropolis, grew here. In the 6C BC Hipparchos built a wall round the Academy (perhaps that which has been located), and excavations have shown that the Kephissos was diverted at about this time. Kimon converted the place 'from a bare, dry, and dusty spot into a well-watered grove, with shady walks and racecourses' (Plutarch, 'Kimon', 13). It was a gymnasium in the time of Aristophanes ('Clouds' 1002). Plato taught here from c 388 BC, while dwelling between the Academy and the hill of Kolonos; he was buried on his estate. Sulla cut down the Academy trees to make siege engines in 86 BC, but the damage was immediately made good since Cicero, who visited Athens in 79 BC, here sets the scene of one of his philosophical dialogues ('De Finibus'). Funeral games in honour of the dead buried in the Kerameikos were held in the Academy, where also was an Altar of Prometheus, the goal of torch-races from Athens. Excavations, begun in 1929–40 by the Greek architect P. Aristophron, were continued by members of the Greek Archaeological Society. There are now three main areas of excavation forming a triangle some 230m apart.

The entrance to one is in Od. Thenaías near the bus terminus. Here the W wall of the *Peribolos* (? the Ἱππάρχου Τειχίον) has been laid bare for about 137m. During the clearance of debris inside the wall many schoolboys' slates came to light, bearing inscriptions (with the names of Demosthenes and Sophocles) of the late-5C or early-4C BC. The most surprising discoveries, however, have been of pre-Classical date and outside the wall. An early Helladic dwelling may indeed be the *House of Hekademos*, since a short distance to the S is a large *Heroön* of the Geometric period (8–7C), extraordinarily preserved since it is built entirely of mud brick, with seven rooms and an eschara nearly 1·5m in diameter, which served presumably for his cult. Unearthed in 1956, this is now protected by a metal roof. Many fine vases have been found in the area, which is honeycombed with graves from pre-Mycenaean times and later cremation burials. A large circular *Well*, of excellent masonry, inscribed round the mouth, has been reconstructed here.

In a second enclosure, to the SE near Ay. Trífon, are the excavated remains of a *Gymnasium* of the late Hellenistic or Early Roman period.

In the third area between Odd. Evkleídhou and Tripóleos are parts of the re-excavated (1979–80) *Square Peristyle*, sometimes thought to be the *Peripatos* frequented by Plato and Aristotle. The building itself belongs to the later 4C but there is evidence of earlier activity on the site, in the Late Geometric and Archaic periods. Some Roman buildings have been excavated nearby.

5　The 'Theseíon' and the Agorá

Approaches. There are three entrances to the Agora: at the SW corner from Leof. Apostólou Pávlou (Thissíon terminus of bus No. 230, cf. Rte 1); from the N side by bridge over the railway from Od. Adhrianoú (cf. Rte 4); from the S side near the Church of the Holy Apostles (cf. Rte 3).—An excellent 'Guide to the Excavations and Museum', published in English by the American School, is available (4th edn 1990), as well as a series of booklets explaining various aspects of the agora.

The upper gallery of the Stoa of Attalos has six plans showing the topography of ancient Athens and five stages in the development of the Agora; these are augmented by a model reproducing the agora at its greatest extent (2C AD). Having got your bearings, you can begin with either the Theseion temple or the agora square itself, reserving the museum till later. Lavatories and iced water are available in the Stoa of Attalos (railway end).

ARCHAEOLOGICAL NOTE. The approximate location of the Agora had been demonstrated as early as 1859–62, from the identification of the Stoa of Attalos by the Greek Archaeological Society and the interpretation of ancient texts. Haphazard digs were made by Greeks and Germans between 1859 and 1897 where remains showed above the surface, and when the Athens–Piraeus railway was extended through a cutting in 1890–91. In 1931–40 the American School of Classical Studies, with the financial backing of John D. Rockefeller, Jr, undertook systematic excavations under Prof. T. Leslie Shear. They were continued in 1946–67 under Prof. Homer Thompson and since 1968 under T. Leslie Shear Jr. Professor John McK. Camp is Resident Director. The area between the railway and the Acropolis and the Areopagus was declared an archaeological zone by law; some 350 dilapidated 19C houses were expropriated and demolished and 300,000 tons of accumulated deposit sifted and removed until the whole area had been excavated to classical, and part of it to prehistoric, levels. Of the area investigated about two-thirds is now open to the public, the enclosure including the Agora, the buildings bounding its W, S, and E sides, and the hill of Kolonos Agoraios to the W. Excavations started in 1970 in a further expropriated zone beyond the railway revealed the *Stoa Basileios*, and in 1980 the *Stoa Poikile*.

The so-called **'Theseíon'** (Agora Pl. 5) that crowns the low knoll of *Kolonos Agoraios* is now identified with the *Temple of Hephaistos and Athena* noted by Pausanias, although the misnomer, applied as early as the Vienna Anonymous MS, is not likely to be easily displaced from popular usage. The * *Hephaisteíon*, as it should rightly be called, is the most complete example remaining of a Doric hexastyle temple. Together with some other temples which exhibit closely similar characteristics, it may be the work of the so-called 'Theseum Architect'. Archaeological and stylistic grounds alike support the foundation date of 449 BC suggested by Prof. Dinsmoor. It thus opens the great period of reconstruction following the Persian peace.

The temple was mistaken in the Middle Ages, on the evidence of its metopes, for the heroön erected by Kimon c 475 BC to receive the bones of Theseus recovered from Skyros. Excavation has shown that the Hephaisteion stands appropriately amid foundries and metal-workers' shops; sherds have fixed its dates within narrow limits; and its position is unequivocally located by Pausanias. The true Theseion, which ancient sources located on the Acropolis N slope, has not yet been found.

The temple, adapted to Christian use probably in the 7C with the addition of an apse, was further modified c 1300, when it became the *Church of Ay. Yeoryios*, by the construction of a concrete interior vault. A later apse survived till 1835, though in Turkish times the liturgy was celebrated here only once a year, hence its late nickname ἀκαμάτης (the idler). The last services held in it were a Te Deum to celebrate King Otho's arrival in the newly founded capital on 13 Dec 1834, and a centenary Te Deum in 1934. The surroundings of the building were explored in 1936–37 and the cella and peristyle excavated in 1939.

The temple consists of a cella, with pronaos and opisthodomos, both distyle in antis, surrounded by a peristyle of 34 columns (6 by 13). Except for the lowest step of poros it is built entirely of marble, the structure in Pentelic, the sculptured members in Parian. The EXTERIOR lacks only the roof and, save for the sculpture, is excellently preserved. The columns are slighter than those of the Parthenon, though the entablature is heavier; the same optical refinements are incorporated. The pronaos (to the E) is arranged unusually with the antae in line with the third columns of the peristyle; the E pteroma is given special emphasis by the sculptural arrangement. The ten *Metopes* of the E front depict nine of the twelve Labours of Herakles: those omitted are the Augean Stables, the Stymphalian Birds, and the Cretan Bull. The metopes above the E pteroma, four on each flank, show eight exploits of Theseus; the remainder are blank.

The subject of the W pediment may have been a Centauromachia. That of the E pediment is not known; in the lower colonnade of the Stoa of Attalos are displayed fragments attributed to this pediment and conjecturally restored as the Apotheosis of Herakles.

INTERIOR. The EAST PTEROMA is still covered by its coffered ceiling. Its importance is emphasised within as without by its sculpture, here an Ionic *Frieze* of heroic combat which extends beyond the antae to bridge the ambulatory and return above the columns of the peristyle. Since the E wall was removed and the columns of the *Pronaos* re-erected in 1936–37, the CELLA, with its barrel vault, strikes an uneasy balance between its pagan origin and its dedication to St George. Its proportions were altered during construction, probably under the influence of Iktinos, and a surface treated to take plaster begun inside, presumably in preparation for frescoes, was never completed. The composition of the interior colonnade is still a matter of scholarly controversy. The walls bear sepulchral slabs dating from 896 to 1103, parts of a 'Stone Chronicle' listing events in 1555–1800, graffiti of British visitors (1675), and memorials to others who died in Greece in the 17–19C, when the building seems to have been used as a Protestant cemetery. That of George Watson (died 1810) bears a defaced Latin epitaph by Byron. The marble floor was ruined in the Middle Ages when graves were dug through it. Two blocks of Eleusinian limestone, which bore the cult statues by Alkamenes erected c 420, were recovered from the E wall in 1936 and restored to position; the clay moulds, perhaps used to cast the statues themselves, came to light 9m from the temple.

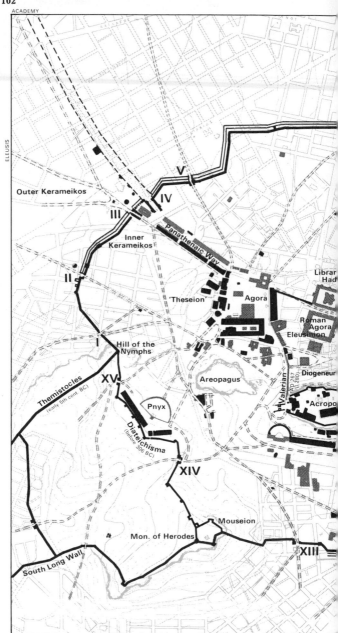

ACADEMY

ELEUSIS

Outer Kerameikos

V

IV

III

Inner
Kerameikos

Panathenaic Way

II

'Theseion'

Agora

Librar
Had

Roman
Agora
Eleusinion

Hill of the
Nymphs

I

Areopagus

Diogeneu

XV

Valerian
AD 267
(1 280)

Themistocles
(early 5th cent BC)

Pnyx

Acropo

Diateichisma
(before 306 BC)

XIV

Mouseion

Mon. of Herodes

XIII

South Long Wall

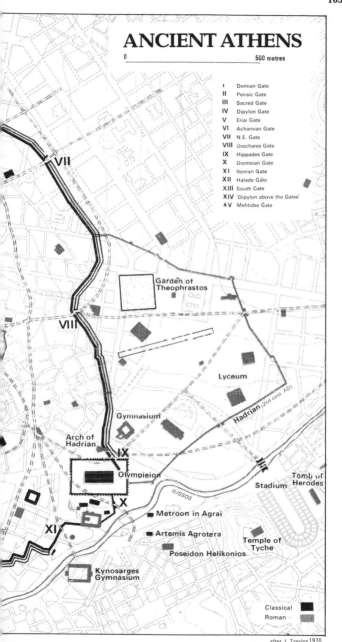

ANCIENT ATHENS

0   500 metres

I	Demian Gate
II	Peiraic Gate
III	Sacred Gate
IV	Dipylon Gate
V	Eriai Gate
VI	Acharnian Gate
VII	N.E. Gate
VIII	Diochares Gate
IX	Hippades Gate
X	Diomeian Gate
XI	Itonian Gate
XII	Halade Gate
XIII	South Gate
XIV	'Dipylon above the Gates'
XV	Melitides Gate

VII

Garden of
Theophrastos

VIII

Lyceum

Gymnasium

Hadrian (2nd cent. AD)

Arch of
Hadrian

IX

Olympieion

ILISSOS

X

Stadium

Tomb of
Herodes

XI

Metroon in Agrai

Artemis Agrotera

Temple of
Tyche

Poseidon Helikonios

Kynosarges
Gymnasium

Classical
Roman

after J. Travlos 1970

In the 3C BC–1C AD a formal garden, planted in sunken flower-pots, bordered the S, W, and N sides of the temple. It has been replanted as far as knowledge permits with plants known to have been there in antiquity (e.g. pomegranate and myrtle).—To the N are scanty remains of a large Hellenistic building conjectured to be the *State Arsenal*.

The **ˑAGORÁ** (ʼΑγορὰ = assembly), or *Kerameikos Agora*, was the assembly-place *par excellence* where the citizens of Athens met daily in the open air for all purposes of community life. In early days the scene of athletic displays and dramatic competitions, it became the recognised venue for the transaction of business or the discussion of philosophy. In its small compass traders rubbed shoulders with administrators in the shadow of buildings and an ever-increasing number of monuments bearing witness to their past achievements. St. Paul disputed in the Agora daily with those who met with him (Acts xvii, 17).

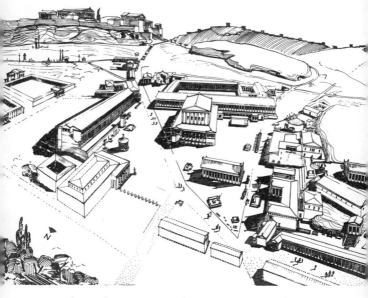

Agora. Reconstruction of area in 2C AD

History. The site, which has been occupied since the Protogeometric period, developed slowly in the 6C BC as the main square of the city, probably in succession to a site nearer the entrance to the Acropolis. The earliest Council house is known to date from the time of Solon, and the Peisistratid tyrants laid on a water supply. A great drain was built in the time of Kleisthenes, whose constitutional reforms necessitated much reconstruction, most of it swept away in the Persian sack of 480 BC. The new agora seems to have been well in hand before Pericles' time, since Kimon is known to have embellished it with plane trees. A large addition made in c 300 BC to the E side of the square was removed in the time of Attalos, king of Pergamon (159–138 BC), when the agora was replanned in the more formal style in vogue in Asia Minor. Stoas bounded it on the E and S. The agora seems to have survived Sulla's sack in 86 BC and, with the addition to the centre in the reign of Augustus of an Odeion and a temple, retained its identity with minor changes until the Herulian raid of AD 267 laid it waste. For the next century and a half the site lay outside the new fortification, the mis-named Valerian wall, which was largely built of stones from the shattered agora. When the old outer walls were re-established in the 5C part of the site was occupied by a large gymnasium which went out of use in the 6C (possibly to be identified with the University closed down in 529). Abandoned until the 10C, the area was covered by successive dwellings throughout Byzantine, Frankish, and Turkish times, its only public monument of this period being the little church that survives.

Ancient Institutions. The people of Attica belonged to four phylae (tribes), or clans, whose identity survived the union under Athens, while their territory comprised three districts known as the Plain (Pediake), the Coast (Paralia), and the Hill (Diakria). The population was early divided also into three classes, *Eupatridai*, or nobles; *Georgoi* and *Agroikoi*, or farmers (of hill and plain); and *Demiourgoi*, or artisans, all of whom were *ipso facto* equal members of the *Ekklesia*, or Assembly. The arable land held by free men was immemorially inalienable from their family or clan. A fourth class of freemen without civic rights, known as *Hektemoroi*, included agricultural labourers. At an early date, possibly about the time of the Dorian invasion, the kings of Athens had been overthrown by the Medontid family, who held the hereditary office of *Archon* (regent) for life. Power gradually passed to the *Areopagus*, or Council of Nobles, who supervised the three executive archons elected by the Assembly: the *Basileus*, the *Polemarch*, and the *Eponymos*, whose functions were, broadly speaking, respectively religious, military, and civil. The Archon Eponymos was chief magistrate and nominal head of the polis, or city-state, and after these offices were restricted in 683 BC to yearly tenure, also gave his name to the year. On relinquishing office Archons automatically became life members of the Areopagus. Later their number was increased to nine by the addition of six recording judges (*Thesmothetai*). The aristocracy monopolised political office though after Kylon's unsuccessful attempt to usurp power and the consequent war with Megara, popular discontent extorted Draco's legal code in 621 BC. The harsh law of property that allowed a debtor's person to be taken in pledge still reduced many peasants to slavery, but a Court of Appeal of 51 judges (*Ephetai*) was instituted to deal with cases of bloodshed.

Towards the end of the century new classes (the *Timocracy*) were emerging, founded on wealth gained in commerce or agriculture, and a new division of the people, based on landed property qualification, was made. The highest class was now the *Pentakosiomedimnoi* (those whose income was equivalent to 500 medimni of corn); next came the *Hippeis* or Knights (300–500 medimni) from whose ranks came wartime cavalry; and below them the *Zeugitai* or Yeomen (those with a pair of oxen) who in war became Hoplites, or infantrymen. The fourth estate of peasants and artisans (*Thetes*) were excluded from the Assembly but paid no taxes. In war they became oarsmen and marines.

Solon, who became Archon Eponymos in 594 BC, promulgated the Seisachtheia, cancelling all debts involving the person of the debtor. He retained the classes of the Timocracy, limited election to archonship to the highest class, but enfranchised the Thetes. He increased the judicial dignity of the Areopagus while transferring its deliberative functions to the Assembly, and created a new Council of Four Hundred (*Boule*), upon which devolved in effect the transaction of the business of the Assembly. The Thetes were excluded from the Boule. Popular tribunals (*Heliaia* or Heliasts) were enrolled by lot so that justice would be impartial to rich and poor alike. Magistrates were made answerable at the end of their term of office to the Heliaia. Despite Solon's reforms party strife between the clans (including the returned Alkmaeonids) caused thirty years of anarchy, which ended in the constitutional tyranny of the polemarch Peisistratos. Under his benevolent dictatorship the reforms of democracy were preserved, and Herodotus (1, 59) acknowledges that he 'administered the state according to the established usage and his arrangements were wise and salutary'.

After the overthrow of his more despotic son, Hippias, the Alkmaeonid Kleisthenes (c 508 BC) reorganised the tribes. Finding Attica composed of c 140 *Demes* or parishes, he altered their traditional division into three *Districts*: the City ("Αστυ), the Coast (Παραλία), and the Inland (Μεσογεία), and to stamp out their old regional rivalries, he regrouped the inhabitants. In each of the Districts the Demes were divided into ten *Trittyes*; three trittyes, one from each district, went to form a new tribe, named after a hero, thus forming ten new *Tribes* independent of old clannish loyalties. The old Council of 400 became a *Council of 500* composed of 50 deputies from each tribe, elected annually by lot. The deputies of each tribe held office in rotation for about five weeks in the year as *Prytaneis*, or Presidents. They chose one of their number by lot as *Epistates* (Chief President), who with nine *Proedroi* as assistants, and a *Grammateus*

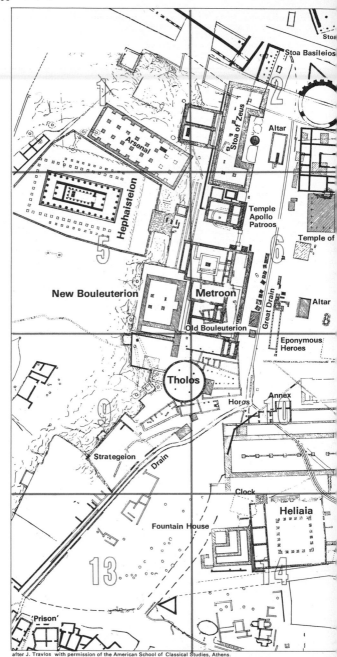

after J. Travlos with permission of the American School of Classical Studies, Athens.

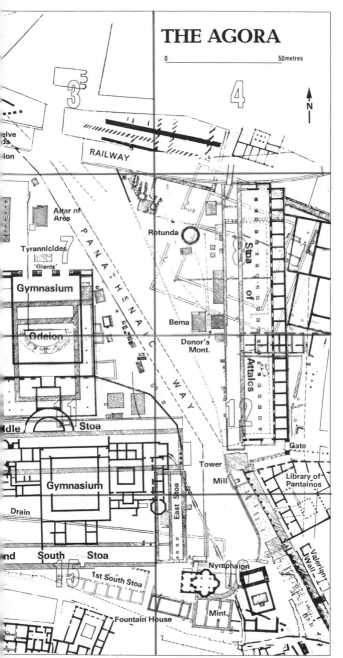

THE AGORA

0 _____ 50 metres

N

RAILWAY

Altar of Ares

Tyrannicides

'Giants'

Gymnasium

Odeion

Rotunda

Stoa

of

Bema

Donor's Mont.

Attalos

Middle Stoa

Gymnasium

Stoa

East Stoa

Tower

Mill

Gato

Library of Pantainos

Drain

South Stoa

1st South Stoa

Nymphaion

Mint

Valerian Wall

Fountain House

PANATHENAIC WAY

(secretary), not of their body, formed the *Prytaneia*, or Presidential Committee. The Prytaneis presided also over the meetings of the Ekklesia, which was the ultimate authority without whose sanction no bill could be passed into law. By the institution of *Ostracism*, a ten years' banishment without loss of rights (used between 487 and 417), the duty of guarding the state against the plots of potential tyrants was transferred from the Areopagus to the sovereign people. Philochoros tells how in such cases 'the Agora was fenced with boards, ten entrances being left, through which the citizens entered by tribes to cast their votes; the nine archons and the Boule presided'. The classes of the Timocracy were retained; below the rank of citizen were the Metics (Μέτοικοι), or resident aliens, and slaves.

In 487 BC the power of the nine archons was reduced by the institution of their election by lot. Before this date the Polemarch had acted as Commander-in-Chief, assisted by the ten tribal generals; henceforward the *Ten Generals* (Strategoi), elected every year one for each tribe, became not only the supreme commanders of the army and navy (one or more being named by the Assembly to lead each expedition), but were also the dominant magistrates in the political field. Pericles was elected general every year from 443 till his death in 429 and to this fact he owed his unique position. To Pericles and his older contemporary Ephialtes is due the completion of Athenian democracy. Nearly all the powers of the Areopagus were transferred to the Assembly. The archonship, no longer confined to the two higher classes, became a paid office, having little political power, and pay was also introduced for the Council and the Jurymen. By the time of the Peloponnesian War all property ceased to be entailed.

You descend a path towards the SW corner of the excavated area. Near the junction of the two branches of the great drain (see below) stands the **Hóros** (Pl. 10), or *Boundary Stone*, inscribed in Attic characters of the 5C BC with the legend 'I am the boundary stone of the Agora'. This was necessary because the square was a sacred precinct from which certain classes of convicted persons were barred; citizens entering it performed a purificatory rite. At a higher level immediately to the S is the stump of a marble pedestal of the 1C AD, which probably supported a *Perirrhanterion* or holy-water stoup.

The boundary stone is set against a contemporary wall belonging to a row of dwellings or shops. The discovery here of hobnails and of a black glazed cup dating to the third quarter of the 5C BC and bearing the name of its owner, Simon, makes it likely that here really was the *Shop of the Cobbler Simon*, where, according to Diogenes Laertius, Socrates spent much of his time.

The WEST SIDE of the agora was flanked by a group of public buildings. The circular foundations of the **Thólos** (Pl. 5), discovered in 1934 much farther N than had been expected, provided the first certain fixed point for the topography of the Agora. Built c 465 BC, this is the 'Prytanikon', also known from its roof as the *Skias*, or parasol, where, as Aristotle records, the fifty Prytaneis dined daily at the public expense and offered sacrifice before their deliberations. Here their chairman (epistates) and the third of his colleagues who were on duty also slept (Aristotle, 'Constitution of Athens', 44) and the building became the effective headquarters of Athenian government. A set of standard weights and measures were kept here; they are now in the museum.

A porch was added to the original rotunda at the time of Augustus. The six columns that supported the roof (three stumps *in situ*) were cut down during the reign of Hadrian when a single-span roof was substituted. At the same time the floor of mosaic chips (1C AD), part of which remains uncovered, was overlaid by marble slabs. The original clay floor is 45cm below the surface, and, save for a few blocks of poros, the visible outer wall is a restoration. Fragments remain to the N of a small room that served as a kitchen.

The foundations of the **New Bouleutérion** (Pl. 5), or Council House, lie to the NW on a platform cut back into the hill of Kolonos. Here the Boule met under the Prytaneis to prepare legislation for the Assembly. The building apparently replaced its predecessor at the end of the 5C BC. A formal S Portico was added by Lycurgus, together with an Ionic *Propylon* facing the agora, the two being connected by a passage along the S front of the old Bouleuterion. The *Old Bouleuterion*, a square building erected for the Council of 500 soon after its inception by Kleisthenes, replaced a still earlier edifice of the time of Solon. When the council moved to its new chamber, the old building was used to store official documents. Parallel with its N side was a small archaic *Temple* which was destroyed by the Persians. This is presumed to have been dedicated to the Mother of the Gods, since her worship seems to have survived on this spot until, in the late 2C BC, a **Metróön** (Pl. 6), consisting of four rooms with a colonnade fronting the square, was built on the site. This had the dual function of *Sanctuary of the Mother of the Gods* (2nd room from the S) and *Repository of State Archives*, which seems, like the library at Pergamon, to have had quarters (N end) for a superintendent. The mosaic pavement in the third room from the S dates from a transformation in the 5C AD.

In front of the Metroön is a row of foundations for monuments. At its NE corner are monument bases carelessly made up in Christian times of reused material. Here has been re-erected a headless *Statue of Hadrian* (AD 117–138) found in the great drain. It is identified by the decoration of the corselet, which bears a crowned Athena standing upon the wolf suckling Romulus and Remus, a symbol of the captive taking the captor captive. The statue is probably contemporary with the emperor.

The *Great Drain of Kleisthenes*, aligned with the Old Bouleuterion, and beautifully constructed of polygonal blocks of limestone, channelled the waters from the hills on the SW towards the Eridanos brook to the N. The two branches that flow into it near the boundary stone were dug in the 4C BC or later. Beyond the drain, remains of a fenced enclosure round a long base locate the *Monument (or Peribolos) of the Eponymous Heroes*. The 4C base, on which stood statues of the ten legendary heroes chosen for Kleisthenes by the Delphic oracle as 'founders' of his ten tribes, was extended several times after 307 BC as additional 'tribes' were created. It bore also two tripods. The sides of the plinth were used as a notice-board for official announcements and for proposed new legislation (cf. Demosthenes, XXIV, 23).

A little to the E again is an *Altar (? Zeus Agoraios)*, of 4C workmanship, known by the identifying letters of its parts to have been moved in the mid-1C, presumably from the Pnyx, where a cutting of exactly similar size has been located.

The gap below the Hephaisteion was never completely closed by buildings. Before the Metroön was built, four rows of stone slabs, of which blocks remain, extended N from the Bouleuterion, serving perhaps as a *synedrion* (meeting-place). In early Imperial times a grandiose stairway was erected as an approach to the Hephaisteion.

Beyond the gap stood the *Temple of Apollo Patroös* (Pl. 6), a small structure, tetrastyle in antis, of c 330 BC, with conglomerate foundations and walls in the late polygonal style. The two Omphaloi may have stood beneath its porch. The statue of Apollo by Euphranor, that stood within, is probably that found in 1907 and now in the Stoa of Attalos.

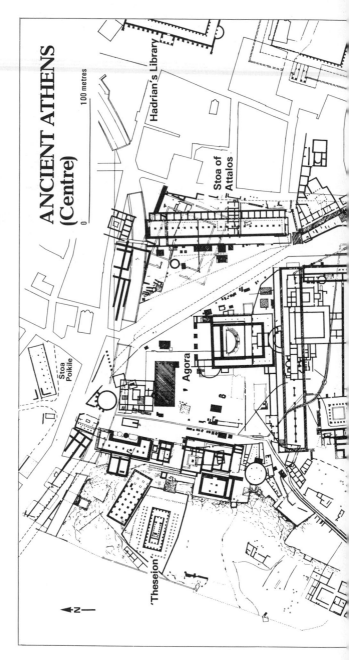

ANCIENT ATHENS
(Centre)

0   100 metres

N

'Theseion'

Stoa
Poikile

Agora

Stoa of
Attalos

Hadrian's Library

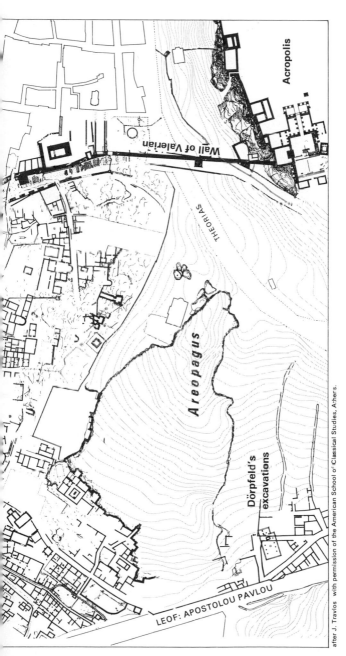

Acropolis

Wall of Valerian

THEORIAS

Areopagus

Dörpfeld's excavations

LEOF: APOSTOLOU PAVLOU

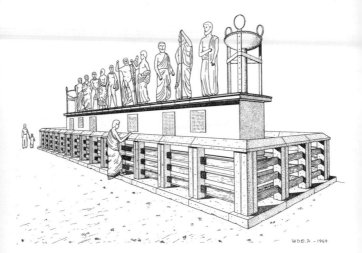

Agora. Monument of the Eponymous Heroes.
Reconstruction

Apollo 'Patroös', that is the father of Ion, was specially worshipped by the
Athenians who counted themselves of Ionian descent. He was patron deity of
state administration; before him magistrates were sworn and citizens registered. A 6C temple on the site was destroyed by the Persians and apparently left
derelict in accordance with the Plataean oath for more than a century. The
casting pit for the bronze 6C cult statue (a kouros) was discovered in front of the
temple and fragments of the terracotta mould are in the museum.

Adjoining are the remains of a slightly earlier cella, identified from
the inscription on the altar with the *Temple of Zeus Phratrios and
Athena Phratria*, the deities of the ancestral religious brotherhoods,
or phratries. The foundations at the E end supported a porch added
to the 4C cella in the mid-2C BC.

To the N the poros foundations of the **Stoa of Zeus Eleuthérios**
extend to the railway, the cutting of which destroyed the N wing. The
portico, which had two projecting wings, was built by unknown
architects c 430 BC to honour Zeus as saviour of the Athenians from
the Persians. Externally of the Doric order, with marble acroteria on
the gables of the wings (flying Nike in the museum), the building had
Ionic columns within. It was decorated, according to Pausanias, with
paintings by Euphranor. Under its colonnade citizens transacted
their private business. Socrates is known to have discussed philosophy here with his friends. An annexe was added behind in the
1C AD.

The piled marble fragments in front mark the site of superposed altars of the 6C
and (?) 3C BC.

The whole of the NORTH SIDE of the agora, lying beyond the railway, is to be laid bare, but will only gradually become accessible to the public. At its NW angle the *Dromos* (cf. Rte 4), or Panathenaic Way, entered from the Dipylon. The street between the gate and the Agora was lined with porticoes fronted by bronze statues of the famous. Here you can imagine the popular and crowded markets of the day, the money-changers, barbers' shops, and bustle of the most commercial part of the city (cf. Lysias, XXIV, 20: Theophrastos, 'Characters'). Here also lay the *House of Pulytion*, where Alcibiades played the hierophant in the parody of the Eleusinian mysteries (Plut., 'Alcibiades' XIX) before the mutilation of the herms (see below). Between the Pompeion and the Stoa of Zeus lay the *Sanctuary of Demeter, Kore, and Iakchos* with statues of them by Praxiteles (Pausanias, I, 2, 4); a damaged monumental base, signed by Praxiteles, found built into a wall N of the railway, is in the museum.

The 1970 excavations immediately uncovered the **Stoa Basileíos**, or Royal Portico, where the Archon Basileus held his court. A clear cut identification is provided by the text of Pausanias (I, 3, 1), and the discovery in the expected spot of the 'Lithos'—'the Stone' par excellence—on which the archons took their oath of office. A surprisingly small building, with a colonnaded façade of eight Doric columns, it can be dated c 500 BC, perhaps rebuilt on the original lines after the Persian sack of 480 BC. It survived with alterations until AD 400. Two porches were added in the late-5C probably expressly to house the revised statutes of Solon and of Draco. Here occasionally the Council of the Areopagus met—perhaps even when it heard St. Paul. A number of sockets for herms can be seen at the N end, and many herm fragments have been recovered. A base *in situ* records prize-winners in the Epilenaia, a drama festival possibly held in front of the Royal Stoa. To the E stood a small crossroads shrine of the 5C. Also in the area was the *Leokoreion* near which, while marshalling the Panathenaic procession, Hipparchos was assassinated in 514 BC by Harmodius and Aristogeiton.

Of the two large groups commemorating the Tyrannicides, only a fragment from an inscribed base has been recovered. The earlier group by Antenor (c 505 BC) was carried off by the Persians. A replacement was fashioned by Kritias and Nesiotes in 476 BC, and after the original had been returned from Persepolis by Alexander the Great, both groups stood together in the *Orchestra of the Agora*. This early open circle designed for ritual dancing was thus closely related both to the Royal Stoa and the assassination spot, but its exact location is uncertain.

Between the Stoa Basileios and the Stoa Poikile (see below) stood a row of *Herms*, celebrating with epigrams Kimon's great victories over the Persians. On the eve of the Sicilian expedition (415 BC) the Athenians were profoundly shocked by the wholesale mutilation of these figures (Thuc. VI, 27–61), and they believed that the outrage was a prelude to an attempt on the constitution. Alcibiades was charged with being the ringleader, recalled from Sicily, and (in his absence) sentenced to death. About 40 fragments listing his personal possessions, confiscated by the state and sold at public auction, have been recovered from the Eleusinion. An inscription naming a 'Stoa of the Herms' was unearthed in 1962.

Excavations (visible from street) in 1980–82, beneath a demolished building on the N side of Od. Adhrianoú, uncovered the W end of the **Stóa Poíkile**, or painted portico, founded c 460 BC by Peisianax (Kimon's brother-in-law), after whom it was sometimes called. Here Zeno taught his disciples, who thus acquired the name Stoics. The building was decorated with battle scenes (Marathon, Troy, etc.), painted by the leading artists of the 5C BC, including Polygnotos,

Mikon, and Panainos, brother of Pheidias. Their work was probably executed on wooden plaques; some blocks fitted with iron spikes (now in the museum) are believed to be from the wall against which they were fixed. The paintings, seen by Pausanias, had disappeared before AD 402. In this stoa were also displayed bronze shields captured from the Spartans at Sphakteria in 425 BC, a fine example of which is displayed in the museum.

The stoa (12·4m deep) is in the Doric order, with Ionic columns in the interior. To the W, partially over the steps of the building, are massive square piers, probably the supports of the gate on which Pausanias saw a trophy set up by the Athenian cavalry to celebrate a victory over the Macedonian Pleistarchos in 303/2 BC.

Further W lie the remains of a handsome altar of island marble, built c 500 BC and repaired in the second half of the 5C. From Pausanias' account, it should be part of the sanctuary of *Aphrodite Ourania*.

Immediately E of the Altar of Zeus is a late-Roman building, a rectangular structure of unknown purpose on massive concrete foundations. Its NE angle lies over the **Períbolos of the Twelve Gods** (Pl. 3), much of which is obscured by the railway, but which has been investigated and firmly identified by an inscription found *in situ*. The *Altar*, was set up by Peisistratos the Younger in 521 BC within a fenced enclosure. Situated in the open section of the Agora bordering the Panathenaic Way, it was the 'London Stone' of Athens where road distances were measured. A recognised place of sanctuary, it may possibly be the '*Altar of Pity*' seen by Pausanias.

The Twelve were not synonymous with the twelve Olympian gods but represent a local Athenian grouping.—Remains of a 6C Eschara, or ground altar, to the S may mark the *Altar of Aiakos*, mentioned by Herodotus (V, 89).

E of the Peribolos, a line of stone sockets set across the Panathenaic Way held wooden posts which formed part of the starting mechanism for races that were originally held here during the festival (cf. Corinth).

The site of the TEMPLE OF ARES (Pl. 6) has been marked in gravel. Some architectural fragments have been arranged at its W extremity and foundation blocks are visible at the E end. These bear Roman masons' marks showing that the temple, which markedly resembled the Hephaisteion and is ascribed to the same architect, was removed to this site in the Augustan period possibly from Acharnai. Foundations of a large altar can be seen to the E.

To the S the construction known to 19C archaeologists as the '*Stoa of the Giants*' marks the N limit of two huge interrelated structures, the **Agrippeíon** (Pl. 7), or *Odeion of Agrippa*, and a much later *Gymnasium*.

The site may perhaps be equated with the *Perischoinisma*, where some public functions (ostracism, etc.) continued until c 15 BC, when an *Odeion*, or concert-hall was endowed by M. Vipsanius Agrippa, son-in-law of the Emperor Augustus, on the site. Shortly after Pausanias saw it in this form, its roof collapsed, but in the reign of Antoninus Pius (c AD 150) it was rebuilt on a smaller scale, probably as a lecture-hall. This was consumed by fire in the Herulian sack of 267 and much of the masonry used in the 'Valerian' wall. About AD 400 a vast *Gymnasium* rose on the site extending well to the S; this was perhaps the principal seat of the university until its closure in 529.

The ODEION, which was roofed by a single span c 24·5m wide, was surrounded on three sides by a two-storeyed portico and entered from the stoa to the S. Traces can be seen of the lower storey. Of the

Auditorium, which seated c 1000 people, only a few marble seats are preserved, together with some of the polychrome paving of the *Orchestra* floor. The remains of the *Skene* have been buttressed with modern walling. The position of the façade of the Antonine rebuilding is marked by two seated figures (? philosophers) which formed part of its sculptural ornament. The '*Giants*', two of which are in fact Tritons, were reused in the façade of the 5C GYMNASIUM. Copied from figures on the Parthenon pediments, they also belonged originally to the second Odeion, where (being then six in number) they supported the architrave of the remodelled N façade. The great *Rectangular Court*, behind the gymnasium's façade, can be traced by its rough wall.

To the S, reached by a rectangular lobby and a semicircular corridor, is a *Square Court*, with a *Bath-House* on the W, and on the E a third *Small Court*, surrounded by well-preserved rooms, which may have served as the administrative offices of the university. The whole of this S complex lies athwart earlier stoas (see below) now believed to have fulfilled the same function.

You cross the PANATHENAIC WAY, here marked by its stone water channel and lined with bases of unidentified monuments. The processional road crossed diagonally in front of the Stoa of Attalos, where it had a gravel surface, passed in front of the Library of Pantainos (see below), where in later times it was paved, and climbed the slope of the Acropolis on a ramp.

The E side of the agora is closed by the ***Stoa of Attalos** (Pl. 12), dedicated as the AGORA MUSEUM by King Paul in 1956. Erected by Attalos II, king of Pergamon (158–138 BC), as the inscription (recovered in 1861) on the architrave records, it was used for promenades, for watching the Panathenaic Procession and events in the Agora, and for retail trade, and is mentioned by Athenaeus alone of classical writers. Pausanias ignores it. The stoa was sacked in AD 267, but the ruins were incorporated in the Valerian wall so that the N end survived throughout the ages to roof height, and sufficient of its plan and members were recovered to make an accurate restoration possible. The building was reconstructed on its old foundations in 1953–56 with materials from the same sources as those originally used, the expense being defrayed by private donors in the United States. The façade is of Pentelic marble, the remainder of creamy limestone from an ancient quarry in Piraeus.

Excavations beneath the foundations uncovered graves of the Mycenaean and Protogeometric periods and later wells. The earliest building on the site (late 5C BC), consisting of an irregular court surrounded by small rooms, was found to contain bronze voting discs for jurors. It is conjectured to have been the *Parabyston*, or Court of the Eleven, a petty sessions court for offenders taken in flagrante delicto. This was superseded as part of the Lycurgan improvements by an edifice c 59·5m sq., which probably served the same function. The Stoa of Attalos survived in part from late-Roman to Turkish times incorporated in a rampart, its rooms being filled with rubble. An oblong tower was built at the N end, another in the middle of the building. At the SW corner stood a gate, the N tower of which was converted into the chapel of *Panayia Pyrgiotissa* (Our Lady of the Tower), now demolished.

The stoa, a two-storeyed building 116·4m long and 20m wide, has a colonnade of 45 columns, Doric below, double Ionic above, closed by a low balustrade. Within, the portico is divided lengthwise into two aisles by a row of 22 columns, Ionic on the ground floor, Pergamene above. Twenty-one rectangular chambers designed as shops opened from the back of the portico on each floor; each had a door opening on to the inner aisle and a loophole in the back wall. The arrangement has been modified in the reconstruction. The exterior staircase at the N end has been restored as originally planned; below it an exedra with a marble bench is entered through an arched opening (the earliest known use of a visible arch in an Athenian building). The S end follows the alterations that were made at the end of the 1C AD (cf. below). In front of the centre of the stoa are a *Bema* and the base of the *Donor's Monument*, more than 100 blocks of which have been recovered from the dismantled Valerian wall. It resembled the monument of Agrippa on the Acropolis and bore, about the level of the second storey of the stoa, a bronze quadriga. It was later re-dedicated to the Emperor Tiberius. Other statues stood against the terrace wall to the N.

The ancient design has been somewhat modified internally to house c 180,000 finds from the Agora excavations; the vast majority of these form study collections (available to specialists on application) on the upper floor and in the basement, where there is a unique library of 7500 documents on stone.

The **Agora Museum.** The GROUND FLOOR contains a selection of the most notable pieces of the collection. Beneath the portico is displayed **Marble *Sculpture**. AT THE S END: S 2154, Apollo Citharoedos (350–325 BC), conjecturally the cult statue of Apollo Patroös by Euphranor; I 4165, Base for statues of Demeter and Kore; note signature of Praxiteles; the monument was dedicated by Kleiokrateia, daughter of Polyeuktos the Teithrasian (the 41st oration of Demosthenes concerns a lawsuit about Polyeuktos's estate).— ALONG THE WALL: S 2038–39 & I 6628, The Iliad and Odyssey personified and inscribed base for the first, group of the 2C AD, signed by Jason the Athenian on one of the long lower lappets of the Iliad's cuirass; Odeion stage front restored (model); S 1882, Aphrodite (c 420 BC); S 182, 'Nereid' acroterion (c 400 BC); I 7154, Cave of Pan relief, inscribed (c 320 BC); S 429, Acroterion group of Hephaisteion (c 415 BC), flanked by fragments attrib. to the E pediment of the temple; S 1232, Torso of Athena (5C BC); I 7167, Rider relief (early 4C BC), commemorating victory won by the tribe Leontis in the anthippasia, the cavalry contest of the Panathenaic Games; S 676, 679, 870, 1072, Reliefs from the Ares temple frieze (c 420 BC); S 654, Torso of Athena (second half 5C BC).—AT THE N END: S 657, Portrait statue of a magistrate (end 5C AD); this elaborate but lifeless piece may be compared with S 312, the Nike acroterion from the SE corner of the Stoa of Zeus Eleutherios (c 400 BC), a vivid flamboyant figure with drapery billowing in the wind.—ALONG THE INNER COLONNADE: IG 112, 3781, Base of a statue of Karneades, founder of the new Athenian Academy, under whom the dedicators of the statue, the future Attalos II and Ariarathes V, king of Cappadocia, studied as princes; S 270, Roman copy of portrait of Herodotus; S 1654, Nymph with water jar, copy of a famous 5C statue of Aphrodite; S 2354, Head of goddess, faithful replica of a classical original, extraordinarily close to the Nike of Paionios; S 2094, Head of goddess (c 430 BC), by an Attic sculptor of the first rank; *I 6524, Stele inscribed with a law of 336 BC against tyranny (the relief represents Democracy crowning the Demos of Athens).

The *EXHIBITION GALLERY, occupying the length of ten shops, is arranged chronologically and demonstrates the almost unbroken occupation of the site from Neolithic to Turkish times. Representative pottery of all periods is attractively displayed. Case 1. Neolithic vases found in wells on the N slope of the Acropolis, the earliest evidence of habitation (note the red polished jar of the 4th millennium BC).

Objects from royal chamber-tombs of the 14C BC on the N slope of the Areopagus: Case 4 (right) Mycenaean bronze sword; Case 5 (left), BI 511, Ivory *Toilet-box carved with griffins bringing down stags. Burials of various periods, urn, grave and pithos. Cases 13–18. Pottery of the Geometric period from burials and sacrificial pyres (model chariot, child's boots, etc.). Contents of the grave of a rich Athenian lady of c 850 BC. Case 23 (right), Clay mould for casting a bronze statue of Apollo (6C BC). Heads of Herms. On the right are three inscriptions: I 2729. Rules of the library of Pantainos; I 4809. Dues owed to Athens in 421 BC by the tributary cities of the Hellespont; I 4120. List of 6C BC Eponymous Archons, including the names of Hippias, Kleisthenes, and Miltiades for successive years (525–523 BC). I 3872. Fragment of a base belonging to the second group of Tyrannicides. *P 1231. Kneeling boy, terracotta oil flask in the form of an athlete binding his hair with the victor's fillet (540–530 BC). To the left (Cases 26–28), standard weights and measures; objects from a court of justice: bronze voting discs (cf. above); klepsydra, or water clock, in terracotta (5C BC), designed to measure the time allowed for pleadings (cf. Aristotle, 'Constitution of Athens'); I 3967. Part of a kleroterion for selection by lot using numbered balls.

There follow cases (30–32) of choice black-and-red figured *Vases, attributed to particular vase-painters and potters: P 12628. Alabastron, by the *Amasis Painter* (mid-6C BC); P 24114, P24110. Two cups assigned to *Epiktetos*. Cups: P 1272. Youth jumping using halteres; P 1273. Youth reclining; P 1274. Youth playing the game of cottabus; P 23165, P 24102, P24116, P 24115. Four cups attributed to *Chairas* (c 500 BC); P 24113. Kylix signed by *Gorgos* (c 510 BC), possibly providing the real name of the Berlin Painter, depicting Achilles and Memnon the Ethiopian in combat; P 24131. Kylix by *Epiktetos*; Calyx-krater (by *Exekias*, c 530 BC), the earliest known example of this form, found in a well on the N slope of the Acropolis; the paintings show the introduction of Herakles to Olympos and Greeks and Trojans fighting for the body of Patroclus.

*B 30. Bronze Nike head of 430 BC. The head was originally plated with sheets of gold over silver, which must have been hammered on to the modelled surface of the bronze. Edges of the sheets were bent down in the channels and securely keyed by a packing of solid gold. This may still be seen behind each ear and at the back of the neck.

To the left, B 262. Huge bronze shield, captured by the Athenians from the Spartans at Sphakteria (Pylos), 425 BC, crudely inscribed ΑΘΗΝΑΙΟΙ ΑΠΟ ΛΑΚΕΔΑΙΜΟΝΙΩΝ ΕΚ ΠΥΛΟ. Child's commode (or 'potty') in terracotta (early 6C BC). Case 38 contains Ostraka (sherds used in secret ballots by citizens recommending banishment) of 487–417 BC with the names of Aristides the Just, Themistocles, Kimon, and Pericles as candidates for ostracism. Case 39. Household grills and ovens in terracotta. Case 42. A few of the 75,000 coins (mainly 6C BC to 6C AD) found in the Agora, including four in gold (Persian Daric, 465–425 BC; Alexander the Great, 336–323 BC; Silvestro Valiero, 1694–1700; and Napoleon III, 1854). BI 236. Statuette in ivory, reconstituted from fragments; this is a replica (2C AD) of the Apollo Lykeios of Praxiteles. Among the sculptural fragments to the left is (S 922) a miniature copy of the cult image of the Mother of the Gods by Agorakritos.

The far end of the museum is devoted to Hellenistic pottery, Roman terracottas, including a toy animal on wheels, lamps from the 7C BC illustrating a return after 14 centuries of evolution to the crude design of the original, Roman portrait busts; Byzantine and Venetian ceramics (portrait of a Doge). *S 221. Young

Satyr in marble, a copy of the 2C AD of a Hellenistic prototype. Mosaic pavement from a house of the 5C AD.

The *Rotunda*, or Monopteros, in front of the N part of the Stoa may have been an ornamental fountain. The green marble columns probably supported a brick dome.

To the S of the Stoa of Attalos, the misnamed **'Valerian' Wall** (Pls, pp. 106–7, 110–11) is a Roman fortification built with stone from buildings partially destroyed in the Herulian sack of AD 267 (when the Emperor Valerian was already dead). An inscription attributes it to Claudius Illyrius. The large tower at the N end of the standing curtain was one of two forming a gate. The wall, which has now been largely dismantled in order to recover the precious earlier inscriptions incorporated in it, followed the line of the façade of the destroyed **Library of Pantainos**, erected before AD 102 at the expense of Titus Flavius Pantainos, who dedicated it to Athena Polias and the Emperor Trajan (inscription from the lintel of the main door exposed). A portico of nine Ionic columns faced the road (graffiti suggest youthful readers) and gave on to rooms grouped round a peristyle; the principal rooms lay to the E.

Between the library and the stoa a street led E towards the Roman market through an *Arch* provided with a small fountain. The construction of this right-of-way necessitated modifications to the S end of the Stoa of Attalos.—Remains of a *Water-Mill* of the 5–6C AD and of its well-built conduit can be traced on the outer side of the Valerian wall.

At the SE corner of the Agora a temple was erected in Augustan times from materials brought from a Doric building at Thorikos. Its hexastyle porch was cleared in 1959.

Beyond the fenced enclosure the *Panathenaic Way* continues upward, showing well-preserved paving of the 2C AD. The site of the *Eleusinion*, about halfway up on the E side, has been identified by the discovery of reliefs, inscriptions, and cult pottery (kernoi) relating to the worship of Demeter and Kore.

Near the SE gate is the pretty **Church of the Holy Apostles** (Pl. 16), stripped in 1954–57 of 19C additions and restored by the American School to its form of c 1020. Within the narthex are 17C wall-paintings from the demolished church of St Spiridon. Of the four Roman columns that supported the dome, one of the originals remains; the other three are copies.

Beneath and to the E of the church are the remains of a *Nymphaion*, a fountain-house with a semicircular outer wall, similar to that at Olympia built by Herodes Atticus. Its construction necessitated the demolition of the N half of a building dated to c 400 BC, identified with the *Argyrokopeion*, the mint of Athens, where the famous 'Owls' that became the accepted coinage of the Eastern Mediterranean for 200 years may have come from, though only bronze coins have so far been found. To the N, bordering the modern road (which retains a course from the Bronze Age), are remains of a *Fountain-House* (the Enneakrounos of Pausanias), probably erected by Peisistratos. This road ran along the back of the *First South Stoa*, which, from the 5C to the 2C BC, dominated the S side of the Agora, probably as administrative offices. At its W end the ground plan has been recovered of a large structure which survived, with alterations, from the mid-6C BC to the sack of Sulla. This is tentatively identified as the *Heliaia*. In the 4C BC the building had a *Water Clock* attached to its N side, which probably told the time by means of a float on a column of water. Another *Fountain-House* stands to the SW.

In the 2C BC the S side of the Agora was entirely remodelled. This was achieved by constructing the MIDDLE STOA (Pl. 11) a portico open on both sides and divided lengthwise by a screen wall. Over 137m long, it was the largest edifice of the Agora, extending from the Panathenaic Way to the Tholos, in front of which it was raised on a high podium. The red conglomerate foundations are best seen at the W end (where the floor level is indicated) and members of the poros colonnade, which had unfluted Doric columns, will be noted at the NE corner. The N terrace of the stoa provided access to the Odeion (cf. above). In Hadrian's time a small annex of the Metroön was built against the podium opposite the Tholos. The *East Stoa* and *Second South Stoa* completed the Hellenistic project, much of which has been obscured by the Roman gymnasium.

To the W of the Middle Stoa near the Tholos are scanty remains of a large building of the 5C BC, perhaps the *Strategeion*, headquarters of the Ten Generals.

SW of the Strategeion you can continue for c 100m on the line of an ancient road into an area between the agora proper and that of Dörpfeld's excavations, where a building has been identified (not without controversy) as the *State Prison* (desmoterion) (see plan of ancient Athens) where Socrates met his death by drinking hemlock, as described by Plato ('Phaedo'). The compound consists of eight small 'cells' to left and right of a central passage which leads to an inner yard. To the left of the entrance a block of rooms (possibly two-storeyed) at an oblique angle to the passage could have belonged to the prison administration. Two of the 'cells' are linked, fitting the two-roomed setting of Socrates' final hours. Small flasks found in the excavations would have been suitable for storage of hemlock.

6   Pláka

The name **Pláka** seems to be of recent origin and is unsatisfactorily derived either from the Albanian *pliaka* (old), or from a *plaque* said to have marked the crossing of its principal streets (see below). The area it describes has no official boundaries but may be said to comprise that part of the old town extending between Od. Ermoú and the N and NE slopes of the Acropolis, corresponding to the ancient deme of KYDATHENAION and including four small districts once known as *Rizokastro, Brizaki, Alikokou,* and *Anaphiotika*. In Turkish times much of this area was called *Gorgopikos* after the little cathedral. Its narrow undulating lanes have no pattern but follow the configuration of the terrain, rising in steps in the higher sector. The principal streets are Adhrianoú and Kidhathenaion, which still follow Turkish (perhaps ancient) courses. The houses, several of which have been excellently restored, date for the most part from the mid 10C and despite popular occupation often proclaim their patrician origin. Many of them are occupied by tavernas. The best time for sightseeing is in the morning.

Plateía Monastirakíou, or **Monastiráki Square** (6, 4), opens from the S side of Od. Ermoú (Rte 4); from the Agora it may be quickly reached by following Od. Adhrianoú (right; see below) from the N exit. Here is Monastirion station (usually called like the square Monastiráki), where the Piraeus railway is still underground. In the square stands the church of the *Pantanassa*, or Great Monastery, commonly called MONASTIRAKI (the diminutive) because of its smallness. An aisled basilica of the 10C with an elliptical cupola, it was badly restored in 1911.

At the SE corner, dominating the square, is the former **Mosque of Tzistarakis**, built in 1759 by the Voivode Tzistarakis, when a column of the Olympieion was sacrificed in its construction. An open loggia, approached by steps, precedes a plain square building surmounted by a heavy octagon; its minaret was razed after 1821. Used for years as a prison, it became a museum in 1918. It was reopened in 1958 under the directorship of Mme P. Zora as the *Museum of Greek Popular Art* (at present closed for restoration).

The narrow Od. Pandróssou, which runs E towards the cathedral, masking the N wall of Hadrian's Library, is the principal relic of the Turkish *Bazaar*, now occupied by antique dealers, shoemakers and tourist shops; the Albanian tsarouchia (scarlet boots with turned-up toes) can be bought here. Iféstou, the other way, runs to the original Flea Market (see Rte 4).

Beyond stands the chief surviving portion of the so-called *Stoa of Hadrian*, a vast façade of the Library of Hadrian (see below). The marble W wall had at the centre a simple propylon, standing forward of antæ and approached by six steps, the only entrance so far discovered. The left portion survives as far as the jamb of the doorway; the mosaic to the left adorned the little chapel of *Ayios Asomatos sta Skalia* that adjoined the porch until the late 19C. The porch was flanked on either side by seven unfluted columns of Karystos marble standing slightly forward of the wall and supporting on Corinthian capitals an architrave which returns over each column. The finely preserved section N of the porch remains.—Od. Areos, lined with booths of workers in old rubber and basketry, continues towards the Acropolis.

A few paces to the left is the *Taxiarkhon* (6, 4), or Church of the Archangels, rebuilt after a fire in 1832, which houses a much venerated ikon, the Panayia Grigorousa. Excavations in Od. Poikílis (right) show the Roman way from the new market (see below) to the Agora; a house in this street, described by Chateaubriand as 'a splendid museum', after his reception here by Fauvel, the French consul, in 1806, is now ruinous.

To the left stands the *Gate of Athena Archegetis*, the main entrance to the Roman market (see below), set a little S of centre in the W wall. It consists of an outer Doric portico with four columns supporting an entablature and pediment, most of which is still in position. This stood just foward of the main wall, its antæ forming the ends of two side walls which were carried back to the inner colonnade of the market to form a vestibule. Within this a double porch of two columns between antæ formed the gate proper.

A worn inscription on the architrave records the dedication of the building to Athena Archegetis, and states that its erection was due to the generosity of Julius Caesar and of Augustus during the archonship of Nikias. On the central acroterion, as is known from the inscription (lost) that it bore, stood a statue of Lucius Caesar, son of Agrippa and Augustus's daughter Julia, who was adopted by Augustus in 17 BC and died in AD 2. The gateway was doubtless erected between these dates. On the N jamb of the doorway is engraved the celebrated edict of Hadrian regulating the sale of oil and the excise duty thereon.

The site of the Roman agora, which is entered from the NE corner, was partially excavated in the 19C. Just within the gate (right) are the foundations of a large *Public Latrine* of the 1C AD. The *Tower of the Winds* (6, 4), properly the *Horologion of Andronikos Kyrrhestes*, stands beyond, just outside the market enclosure. Built in the 2 or 1C BC by the astronomer Andronikos of Kyrrhos (authorities disagree whether this is the Syrian or the Macedonian town), it served the triple purpose of sundial, water-clock, and weather-vane. The tower, which stands on a base of three steps, takes the form of a marble octagon with a pyramidal roof of marble slabs held together by a round keystone. Each face accurately marks a cardinal point and is adorned with a relief representing the wind blowing from that direction. On the NE and NW faces were porches of two fluted

Corinthian columns with peculiarly simple and graceful capitals. Fragments of the NW entablature have been reassembled close by. The tower, according to Vitruvius (I, 6, 4), was originally surmounted by a revolving bronze Triton holding a wand, which pointed out the face corresponding to the prevailing wind.

The eight figures are represented as winged and floating almost horizontally through the air. Beginning at the N side and proceeding clockwise: N, Boreas, in a thick sleeved mantle, with folds blustering in the air, and high-laced buskins, blows a twisted shell; NE, Kaikias empties a shield full of hailstones; E, Apeliotes exhibits flowers and fruit; SE, Euros, with his right arm muffled in his mantle, threatens a hurricane; S, Notos, emptying an urn, is producing a shower; SW, Lips, driving before him the stern ornament of a ship, promises a rapid voyage; W, Zephyros showers into the air a lapful of flowers; NW, Skiron bears a bronze vessel of charcoal in his hands, with which he dries up rivers.—Beneath the figures of the winds are traced the lines of eight sundials.

Attached to the S face is a reservoir in the form of a semicircular turret, from which water could be released in a slow steady stream to run the clock works. Through the doors in the porches can be seen the ancient pavement of white marble, scored with circular channels for a parapet and other channels so far unexplained. At present miscellaneous finds from all over Athens are stored here, obscuring some of the detail of the interior. Some restoration has recently (1988) been undertaken.

In Turkish times the tower was occupied as a Tekke by dervishes. The arches of Hymettian marble on a massive base to the S form the façade of a building dedicated to Athena Archegetis and the Divi Augusti in the 1C AD. The function of the building, formerly wrongly identified as the Agoranomion (office of the Magistrates of the Market), is not known.

At a lower level to the W extends the **Roman Market**, the S half of which is revealed. This was a large rectangle c 111m by 96m, bounded by a poros wall (early 1C BC), within which, on the S side at least, a (probably Doric) colonnade flanked central blocks of rooms. Later (? under Hadrian) an Ionic *Peristyle* was added within, having unfluted columns of Hymettian marble with bases, capitals, and epistyle of Pentelic. The central area was bordered by a deep drainage gully and later paved in marble (in places still *in situ*). To reach this you descend the five steps to the *South-East Propylon*, which, though smaller and later, has a similar plan to the W gate (see above). It is neither on the central axis of the market, nor at right angles to the wall. Its lower portion is well preserved, though the columns are all broken off 2·4–3m from the pavement. It is flanked by a row of shops, of which five have been explored, when inscriptions were found on the floor or on columns giving the names of the shopkeepers. The area is occasionally used as a venue for concerts in the summer.

The mosque, now used as an archaeological workshop, that occupies the corner of the site, dates from the late-15C and is probably the *Fetihie Cami*, or Victory Mosque, built to celebrate the Turkish conquest. From time to time visiting Sheikhs perform their devotions here.

On the corner of Od. Aiólou all that remains of the *Medresse*, or seminary, is a ruined gate bearing a Turkish inscription that records its foundation by Mehmet Fakri in 1721. Here, a century later, the

cadi Haci Khalil dissuaded the Turks from a general massacre of
male Greeks in Attica. In Dhiogénous is the new (1991) *Museum of
Greek Folk Music*. Also in Aiólou is the **Library of Hadrian** (6, 4),
closed to the public. The E wall is buttressed by six Corinthian
pilasters and originally presented an unbroken face to the street; the
ancient entrance was in the marble W façade (cf. above). The
building consisted of a huge rectangular wall of poros, c 122m by
82m, portions of which survive on three sides, which enclosed a
cloistered court adorned with a 'hundred splendid columns'
(Pausanias) of Phrygian marble (long since vanished). In the N and S
walks three recesses opened in the outer walls, the central one
rectangular, the side ones semicircular. On the E side the main block
of five rooms was ranged along the cloister. The central chamber,
which was entered through a porch of four columns, housed the
Library proper. In the E wall is a large central niche with four smaller
ones on each side, which held the bookshelves—an arrangement
similar to that of the library of Pergamon. The rooms on each side
were probably (like those in the contemporary library at Alexandria)
workrooms and repositories for archives. The W end of the building
has been cleared and conserved (from 1982).

The interior of the quadrangle was doubtless laid out as a garden, with a long
central reservoir or pool. About AD 410 a square building, either a lecture hall
or a church, quatrefoil in plan, was erected by the governor Herculius over the E
end of the pool. Its NE angle stands to c 2·7m and some mosaic fragments of the
exedræ survive. This building was replaced in the 6C, by a basilica which,
under the Byzantines, became the *Megáli Panayía*, or church of Great St. Mary,
and survived in a later modification until 1885.—Much of the market site was
occupied by a bazar through which passed Od. Adhrianoú, divided since the
excavations into two parts.

You cross the pleasant square opposite, and from Od. Adhrianoú
climb the picturesque Od. Mnesikléous to the little 14C church of the
Transfiguration (Μεταμόρφωσις του Σωτήρος), known as *Sotiráki*.
This stands just beneath the Acropolis but below the level of the
ancient *Peripatos*, which here divided the official precincts of the
lower slope from the primitive sanctuaries above.

Close by is the **Kanellópoulos Museum** (closed Monday) opened in
1976. An English guidebook is available: M. Brouskari, 'The Paul
and Alexandra Kanellopoulos Museum', 1985. The 19C mansion has
been tastefully restored and the interior arranged functionally to
display the eclectic family *Collection of antiquities of all periods. It
is especially rich in bronzes, jewellery and everyday objects. The
ground floor and basement have a variety of Byzantine and Late
Antique material. On the ground floor: vases, bronzes, crosses and
jewellery. In the basement: ikons, bread stamps, jewellery, liturgical
accoutrements, silver bowls, crosses, furniture, etc., as well as huge
blocks of an Archaic wall. On ground floor landing: embroideries,
etc. On first floor: prehistoric (including Mycenaean) and Geometric
vases and bronzes; Near-eastern and Cypriot objects. On top floor:
Archaic and Classical vases and major and minor sculpture.

Od. Theorías, a modern road, runs (right) to the entrance of the
Acropolis.

The daunting **North Slope of the Acropolis** (no adm.), occupied in Neolithic
times and known in antiquity as the LONG ROCKS, repays inspection from this
level. Here the primitive deities of vegetation and fertility cults which survived
from the remotest times into the Classical period were worshipped. A decree of
415 BC, forbidding the erection of altars within the Pelargikon area, may
represent an attempt to restrict these rites. Later writers pointedly ignore or
mock these survivals of popular belief. The area was investigated by the Greek

Archaeological Society and the American School in 1931–39, when a mass of black-figured pottery was discovered, together with many objects apparently thrown down from the Acropolis; these included the Erechtheion accounts, the Opisthodomos inventory, the accounts for the Athena Promachos statue, about 200 ostraka inscribed with Themistocles' name, and a calyx-krater of Exekias.

At the W end, above Klepsydra (cf. Rte 2) are four *Caves*. The first is little more than a niche with rock-cut seats. In the second (B), somewhat larger, have been found a number of tablets (of Roman date) dedicated to Apollo Hypo-akraios by archons taking the oath of office. The third (Γ), which is separated from the second only by a spur, has been suggested as the place where the Pythiasts watched for the flash of lightning from Mt Parnes before starting the procession to Delphi. The narrow tunnel-like cave (Z), above which later stood a chapel of St Athanasios, is identified with the *Cave of Pan*. Herodotus (VI, 105) tells how the worship of Pan was revived after his appearance to Pheidippides in 490 BC. This cave is referred to by Euripides ('Ion' 938) and Aristophanes ('Lysistrata' 911). Farther E cult reliefs with phallic and fertility emblems were discovered as well as fragments of a frieze of Erotes which may have decorated the temenos wall. On a large boulder is inscribed a boundary mark of the Peripatos. The huge *Cave* in the E face of the Acropolis rock has not been fully explored though much pottery came to light here in 1936.

Just to the N of the Sotiraki, No. 5 in Od. Thólou, is the *Old University*, a building dating from the Venetian occupation, used as public offices by the Turks, and rebuilt with a third storey by Cleanthes in 1830; here the university functioned in 1837–41. It has recently been excellently restored and will become a *Museum of the University*, with accommodation also for seminars and educational programmes. *Ayioi Anárgyroi* (6, 6), a little farther E, is by tradition associated with the Athenian orphan who became the Empress Irene (762–803), reigning alone in Byzantium after the death in 797 of Leo IV, her husband. The Sarandapichos family, to which she belonged, is said to have come from this district. The church, remodelled in the 17C, serves the pleasant monastery Metokhi tou Panayiou Tafou, a dependency of the Holy Sepulchre at Jerusalem. The Byzantine chapel of *Ayios Nikólaos Rangavás* (7, 5) stands at the corner of Od. Pritaníou. The site of the Prytaneion itself (the official centre of the city where the sacred flame was kept burning) has not yet been found. Some slight remains to the N of Od. Kirístou are tentatively identified with the Diogeneum. Overlooking this street, at the corner of Od. Fléssa, are the rooms in which Caroline, Princess of Wales, was entertained in 1816.

You descend to ODHÓS ADHRIANOÚ. No. 96, built under the Turks by the Benizelos archons, is perhaps the oldest surviving house in Athens. The family name survives in Od. Venizélou, which descends from here to the Cathedral (Rte 4). Follow Adhrianoú, where, in a house built c 1780, lived George Finlay (1799–1875), the historian. The *Demotic School* at the corner of Od. Fléssa occupies the site of the 'Mosque of the Column', which became for Morosini's Lutheran gunners (for a short time in 1687) the first Protestant Church in Greece. The *Hill Memorial School*, at the corner of Thoukidhídhou and Nikodhímou streets, to the NE, was founded in 1831 by John Henry Hill (died 1882), an American missionary. You continue to the Monument of Lysikrates (Rte 1) or turn left into Od. Kidathenaíon, where, at No. 27 (garden) Ludwig of Bavaria stayed in 1835. Many of the neighbouring houses date from this period.

At No. 17 has been installed the **Museum of Greek Folk Art** (closed Monday; free). The collection of embroidery, ranging from Coptic cloths of the 2C AD to local fabrics of the Greek islands, is outstanding. Two magnificent *epitaphioi* (processional palls) date from the 17C. Displayed are gold and silver ware from Asia Minor, ikons, and jewellery of barbaric splendour which emphasises the affinity of Greek medieval art with the Balkans and Near East.

From the little shaded *Plateia* (cafés; 7, 5) you can descend NE towards Sindagma Square.

7   From the Arch of Hadrian to the Benáki Museum

Immediately behind the Arch of Hadrian (Rte 1) extends the archaeological park (entrance in Leofóros Vasilíssis Olgas) surrounding the Temple of Olympian Zeus. To the left are the remains of a *House* of the 4C BC; a cast marks the site where a fine relief (now in the National Museum) was discovered. A second *House* of the same period, with traces of a pebble mosaic floor, is partly overlaid by **Roman Thermae** of AD 124–31, of excellent construction, having four public halls with mosaic floors and the usual three bath chambers off the S side. It apparently survived into the 7C AD.

Farther on, excavations at a lower level have revealed part of the *Themistoclean Wall* (c 479 BC), incorporating drums from the Peisistratid Olympieion, with the *Hippades Gate*, a defensive ditch added in the late 4C BC, and a stretch of ancient road. The ground plan of the *Basilica at the Olympieion* or St. Nicholas of the Columns, a church built of classical fragments in the late 5C, was recovered in 1949 between the baths and the peribolos.

The SANCTUARY OF OLYMPIAN ZEUS occupies an artificial terrace supported by a *Peribolos* of square Piraeic stones buttressed at regular intervals. Except near the propylon and at the SE corner, where the buttresses and arched drains date largely from the time of Hadrian, this retaining wall is mostly a work of restoration. It measures 205m by 129m, making a perimeter (as indicated by Pausanias) of 4 stadia. The ground plan of its principal entrance, a Doric *Propylon*, has been clarified by restoration.

In the centre stand the majestic remains of the **Olympieíon**, or *Temple of Olympian Zeus*, the largest temple in Greece. It took 700 years to complete, 'a great victory of time', as Philostratus happily describes it. Livy says 'it is the only temple on earth of a size adequate to the greatness of the god', though it was in fact exceeded in extent by temples to other gods at Agrigento and Selinus in Sicily, and at Ephesus and Miletus in Asia Minor.

History. Scanty remains of a small shrine have been discovered with vaults beneath an exit through a subterranean passage to the Ilissos. This may account for the tradition that a temple was founded here by Deukalion over the chasm through which the waters receded after the flood. Pausanias relates that in commemoration of this event an annual sacrifice of flour mixed with honey was thrown into the cleft. Peisistratos seems to have been the first to undertake the construction of a temple on a grand scale, possibly, as Aristotle suggests ('Politics'), to keep the people too busy to indulge in plots. Work ceased before the stylobate was complete when Hippias went into exile and much of the masonry was used in the Themistoclean wall (cf. above). In 174 BC Antiochus Ephiphanes, king of Syria, resumed building to a new design by Cossutius, a Roman architect, who substituted the Corinthian for the Doric order. Work was again interrupted at the entablature stage and put back further in 86 BC, when Sulla carried off some of the shafts and capitals to Rome for the Capitoline Temple. The honour of its completion was reserved for Hadrian who dedicated the temple on his second visit to Athens c AD 130 and set up a chryselephantine statue of the god within the cella (a copy of that by Pheidias at Olympia), as well as a colossal statue of himself. Cyriacus of Ancona (c 1450) noted 21 standing columns with their architraves. In 1760 the Turkish governor converted one to lime for the construction of a new mosque; the great storm of 26 October 1852 overthrew another.

The **Temple** stands on a stylobate (107·8m by 41m) of three steps, the lower two of poros from the original foundation, the upper one of marble (partially restored in 1960–61). The foundations, which were laid by Peisistratos, exhibit the same curvilinear features as those of the Parthenon. Dipteral octastyle in arrangement with an extra row of columns at each end, the temple had 20 columns at each side, making 104 in all. Of these 13 survive in a group with part of the architrave at the SE, and two farther W. They are of Pentelic marble with 16 fluted flutings. The fallen column, which was blown down in 1852, shows clearly the construction of base, 16 column drums, and capital in two sections. Its base diameter is 1·7m, and height 17m. The capitals are beautifully carved. The original height of the front is estimated at 27·4m. The stones comprising the architrave weigh up to 23 tons; in the Middle Ages a stylite lived on the architrave that still covers the two W columns of the SE group. The remains are not sufficient to determine the plan of the cella, though Vitruvius records it as hypæthral. The ruin is popularly known as Kolónnes (columns); the columns are floodlit in summer.

You leave Leofóros Singroú (Rte 12) to the right and take Od. Athanassíou Dhiákou to (5 minutes) the *Kallirrhói Bridge* over the seasonal Ilissos. An older bridge, surviving beneath, is well seen from Kallirrhoi (see below).

The **Ilissos** (Ιλισός) flows from two sources on the slopes of Hymettos, one at Kaisarīani, the other at St. John Theologos. The united branches, diminished since Classical times and now either underground or canalised, flow on the S side of the city and, passing to the S of the Mouseion, descend to the Bay of Phaleron.

The district extending outside the S wall of the city along the river bank was anciently known as KEPOI, the Gardens. To the SW of the Olympieion lay the *Pythion 'on the Wall'*. Two large fragments (now in the National Museum), found on the right bank of the Ilissos, have been certainly identified with the Altar of Apollo Pythios by their inscription, a dedication to Peisistratos the Younger, which is quoted in full by Thucydides (VI, 54). Further finds in 1965–68 below Od. Iosíf ton Rógon may locate the site.

Beyond the river lay the district known as DIOMEIA. Downstream, c 275m below the bridge, is the presumed site (excavated by the British School in 1896–97 and recent rescue excavations) of the *Gymnasium of Kynosarges*. An inscription naming Kynosarges has been found near the church of Ay Pandeleimon.

Just above the bridge somewhat artificially contrived is the *Kallirrhoi*, a shallow fall where the Ilissos flows over a ridge of rock. The traditional name, which dates back at least to Byzantine times, recalls that of the ancient **Kallirhóë Spring** (8, 5), but the locality has drastically altered since Classical times. In 1896 floods swept away remains of ancient masonry and even altered the contour of the rock. The course of the river has now been irretrievably interfered with and its waters have largely vanished underground. On the S bank, beyond the modern chapel of Ayía Fotiní, a much eroded figure of Pan adorns a right-angled chamber hewn out of the rock.

Extending towards the Olympieion is the 'ILISSOS AREA' excavated by Threpsiades in 1956–67 during the covering of the Ilissos and the construction of the Ardhitós highway. The area is traversed by a section of the Valerian Wall, for the building of which most of the ancient structures were quarried. The gate here may be that of

Aigeus (cf. Plutarch, 'Theseus', xii). Foundations remain of a temple of late date (mostly under the road) and, between this and the Olympieion Temenos wall, of three buildings of some importance amid a confusion of ruins. These are from E to W: the *Precinct of Kronos and Rhea*, with prominent foundations of a Doric temple ascribed to the 2C AD; a much larger Doric temple of the 5C BC, which had a peristyle of 13 columns by 6, perhaps to be identified with the *Temple of Apollo Delphinios*; and a civic structure in archaic polygonal masonry believed to be the *Law court of the Delphinion*.

From the S end of the bridge Od. Anapáfseos mounts to the main gate of the *Próto Nekrotafíon Athinón*, the principal Cemetery of Athens. Here, in sumptuous tombs, generally in Classical styles and decorated by the best sculptors of the day, are buried many celebrated Greeks of the 19C and 20C. Among heroes of the War of Independence are the generalissimo, Sir Richard Church (1784–1873), and Kolokotronis (1770–1843), as well as Makriyannis and Androutsos. Writers include Rangavis (1810–92), Panayiotis Soutsos (1800–68) and the statesman-historian Trikoupis (died 1896). Averoff (see below), Singros (died 1899), and Antoine Benaki, benefactors of the city, lie here. *The Mausoleum of Heinrich Schliemann* (1822–90), the archaeologist, is decorated with Trojan scenes in bas-relief, while the *Tomb of Adolf Furtwängler* (1853–1907) bears a marble copy of a sphinx he unearthed at Aegina.

On the S side of the Ardhitós highway, near Od. D. Koutoula, are the remains of the terrace wall of a temple, known to antiquaries as the *Temple by the Ilissos*, which was discovered and drawn by Stuart and Revett in 1751–55 but destroyed in 1778 by the Turks. It appears to have been constructed before the Temple of Athena Nike from the same specificiations of Kallikrates, and may be the Temple of Artemis Agrotera. It became an orthodox church but was abandoned after a Roman mass had been said there in 1674.

To avoid the noisier Ardhitós highway you can return by footpath to LEOFÓROS VASILÍSSIS OLGAS (7, 6), an attractive avenue that skirts the S side of the Zappeion Gardens (Rte 1). To the right, between the avenues, are the *Tennis Club*, the *Olympic Swimming Pool* (ΟΛΥΜΠΙΑΚΟΝ ΚΟΛΥΜΒΗΤΗΡΙΟΝ), and the *Ethnikos Athletic Club*. The athletic track occupies the site (once an island in the river) where stood the '*Basilica by the Ilissos*' (mosaics in Byz. Mus). The countryside hereabouts was lyrically described by Plato at the beginning of the 'Phædrus'. The two highways join below the hill of *Ardhitós*.

On the hill, the former **Ardettos**, or *Helikon*, where the Heliasts came to take their oath, are some scanty foundations (no adm.) assigned to the *Temple of Fortune*, erected by Herodes Atticus. On the opposite height beyond the Stadium some ruins (no adm.) are presumed (from an inscription *in situ* in archaistic letters to the 'Marathonian Hero') to be the *Tomb of Herodes*, who died at Marathon but was given a public funeral at Athens.

The **Stadium** (Στάδιον; 8, 5) occupies a natural valley between these two low hills, which is closed at the S end by an artificial embankment to form the semicircular sphendone. Faithfully restored in 1896–1906 by Anastasios Metaxas, it has the normal plan of a Greek stadium and corresponds to the description of Pausanias, who saw the gleaming Pentelic marble of the first restoration as we see the pristine whiteness of the second. The Plateía tou Stadhíou bears a statue of Averoff (1867–1930), the benefactor who financed the work.

History. Lycurgus may have constructed the stadium in its original form in 330 BC (but see pp. 86–8) to provide for the contests of the Panthenaic Festival. On the occasion of Hadrian's presidency a thousand wild beasts were baited in the arena. The stadium was reseated in marble by Herodes Atticus for the Games of AD 144. In the course of centuries' use as a quarry, the marble all but disappeared. Ernst Ziller cleared the site in 1869–70 at first at his own expense, later with the support of George I of the Hellenes. In 1895, for the forthcoming revival of the Olympic Games, Yeoryios Averoff, a wealthy Greek of Alexandria, emulating Herodes, undertook to restore the marble. The sphendone was provided with seats in time for the first modern Games of 1896, and the work was completed for the extra 'Olympic' Games, held out of series as a 10th anniversary celebration in 1906 and visited by Edward VII.

The *Arena*, in the form of an elongated horseshoe, measures 204m by 33m. As restored it comprises a modern running track (at high level) with provision in the centre for athletic and gymnastic contests. On the E side a tunnel, c 3m high, admits competitors and officials from the changing rooms.

In ancient times the course was a straight track measuring one stade of 600 Greek feet whence the name stadion. The Greek foot varied slightly from place to place, but the Athenian track seems to have measured c 185m. It was divided down the centre by a row of pillars, of which four, in the form of double hermae, have been recovered. The finishing point was in front of the sphendone, which was surmounted by a Doric stoa to provide shelter for the top corridor. A Corinthian propylon (restored, but since removed) formed a ceremonial entrance at the open end.

The course is enclosed by a low marble parapet, behind which a paved promenade 2·7m wide, follows the circuit. Rainwater is channelled through gratings in the pavement into an arched drain of brick. A wall, 1·6m high, forms the substructure of the tier of the *Auditorium*, thus affording the spectators a clear view over the parapet. The side tiers are slightly curved to give better visibility. Twenty-nine narrow flights of steps (12 on each side and 5 in the sphendone) lead from the promenade to the seats. These are arranged in 47 tiers, divided into two blocks by a *diazoma*, or gangway, behind the 24th row. The seats are of the same simple pattern as those in the Theatre of Dionysos. The seating capacity is 60,000. A block on the S side and the front row of the sphendone provide more comfortable accommodation for honoured patrons and royal occasions.

Across the square, at the SE entrance to the Zappeion Gardens, stand a bronze statue of a discus thrower (1927) and a huge equestrian figure, also in bronze, of Karaïskakis, by Michael Tombros (1966).

Leofóros Konstandínou continues NE to meet Leofóros Vasilíssis Sofías (see Rte 10). An important Dark Age cemetery was found here during the construction of new barracks in 1975. The area has since been converted into a pleasant park.

Opposite the stadium Od. Iródhou Attikoú runs between the E side of the National Gardens and the modest former **Palace** (8, 3), residence of the king after the restoration of 1935 and more recently of the president. The picturesque Evzones have their barracks at the top of the street, which emerges into Leofóros Vasilíssis Sofías (Rte 10).

Just opposite in the avenue is the ***Benáki Museum** (8, 3; open mornings only; closed Tuesday), containing the fruits of 35 years eclectic collecting by Antoine Benaki. In 1931, having arranged his collection in the family town house, Benaki endowed the museum and presented it to the state. Later gifts have been accepted. Particularly interesting are the classical antiquities from Egypt (Benaki's birthplace), the items of Islamic art, the collection of icons and the folk costumes.

The museum is at present subject to partial closures and rearrangements, pending refurbishment of an adjoining building as a extension. The first floor is not accessible at the time of writing. A good guide by the director A. Delivorrias, 'Guide to the Benaki Museum' (1988) is useful and well illustrated but does not reflect exactly the present arrangement of the collections. There is a well-stocked museum shop, and refreshment facilities are available, though the pleasant terrace cafeteria on the second floor is closed at present.

Entry is through the garden and by the door facing Vasilíssis Sofías. The ENTRANCE HALL contains prints, paintings, jewellery and furniture, classical marble grave lekythoi, displays of recent acquisitions and of replicas for sale in the shop. The GROUND FLOOR presents a roughly chronological display of the ancient and medieval arts. You turn left to Room 1: prehistoric antiquities including two gold cups of the Bronze Age (c 3000 BC) from N Euboea and a Mycenaean gold cup with hounds in relief. Room 2: Archaic, Classical and Hellenistic pottery, terracottas, gold etc. Room 3: Roman jewellery, ivories, mummy portraits (in encaustic technique); items of Coptic Art, including textiles; some Early Christian and Byzantine objects, including a 14C Macedonian icon. Room 4: Early Christian and Byzantine pottery, icons, silverware, textiles.

Room 5: The furthest section is arranged as a Moslem reception hall with original 17C mosaic, etc. from Cairo, and ceramic decorations, including so-called 'Rhodian' ware (16C) which in fact comes from Nicaea in Asia Minor. Ranged against the wall are funerary monuments of the 10–11C bearing Cufic inscriptions. The other sections of the room contain a rich collection of fine Islamic pottery, metalwork, glass; Turkish armour; Brusa velvets. Room 6: Byzantine paintings, icons and manuscripts including two works of the Cretan painter Domenicos Theotokopoulos, better known as El Greco. On the right is his earliest known work, The Adoration of the Magi (c 1560); on the left, The Evangelist Luke. Rooms 7–9: ecclesiastical furniture (17–19C), vestments, church jewellery, some of it brought back from Asia Minor and Thrace by refugees in 1922; and icons, mostly post-Byzantine.

The BASEMENT rooms are devoted to a unique display of Greek regional *Costume and popular art including the bonnet of Theresa Makri, Byron's Maid of Athens.

8   From Monastiráki to the National Museum

From Monastiráki (Rte 6) the broad ODHÓS ATHINÁS strikes N straight to Omonia Square. Crowds throng the vegetable and meat markets that line its southern half and extend into the narrow turnings on either side. Ironmongery and cheap shoes and clothing are sold. You take the narrower ODHÓS AIÓLOU, a popular shopping street, parallel to the E where excavations in 1961–62 disclosed tombs of c 500 BC. On the right is *Ayia Irini* (with fine music) with a colourful market of nurserymen on the N side.

About 450m farther on, beyond Od. Sofokléous, opens the PLATEÍA DHIMARKHEÍOU (formerly KOTZIA), which, since the demolition in 1937 of the Municipal Theatre, extends to Od. Athinás. To the left stands a mansion by Ziller which for many years housed the main post office. The severe *Dhimarkhíon*, or Town Hall, in Athinás to the W, faces the *National Bank of Greece* (Ethnikí Trápeza tis Elládhos). In an adjacent plot extensive remains of the ancient city wall were discovered. The square has recently been completely cleared in advance of redevelopment allowing full archaeological investigation of an area which lies just outside the Acharnian Gate of the ancient city. Finds have ranged in date from the Geometric to Roman periods and include burials, roads and, most impressive, a series of potters' establishments, better preserved than any known to date. At present the foundations of Ziller's theatre are exposed in the W (larger) part of the plot. The NE corner, which is securely fenced and will be preserved, includes roads, tombs and the reddened remains of kilns. Od. Aiólou continues N, crosses Stadium St. (Od. Stadhíou) (Rte 10), and passing E of Omónia Sq. becomes Od. Patissíon (see below).

The Mela mansion (later the post office). Drawing by E. Ziller, 1884

Od. Athinás leads directly to **Omónia Square** (3, 3; Πλατεία της Ομονοίας), the busy centre of commercial Athens, where eight important roads converge. Its name (Concord Sq.) commemorates the reconciliation of two warring 19C political factions. Its fountain is ringed by undistinguished buildings. Escalators lead down to the main station of the Piraeus–Athens–Kifissia Railway (E.H.Σ), where shops, cafés, banks, a post office and an information office of the National Tourist Organisation surround the concourse.

Immediately to the left the broad ODHÓS PIRAIÓS (also called Pan. Tsáldari) begins its straight course to the port of Athens. Many treasures, now in the National Museum, have been found during building operations along its route; but nothing of interest survives above the surface, and the depressing street has been largely superseded as a highway by the boulevards to the S.

Plateía Koumoundhoúrou (Eleftherías), with its bus terminal, lies off Piraiós, about 800m from Omónia.

To the W, Od. Ayíou Konstandínou, lined with electrical and record shops, descends to the large modern church of *Ayios Konstandinos*, in front of which is the booking-office for bus services to the Peloponnese. Opposite stands the *National Theatre*.

Larissa Station of the Greek State Railways and the *Peloponnisos Station* lie c 1km NW.

Od. Patissíon (cf. above), alternatively named Od. Ikosiokhtó Oktovríou (28th. October), an uninteresting modern thoroughfare, passes to the W of PLATEÍA KÁNNINGOS (3, 3), with a busy local bus terminus, where stands a *Statue of Canning* by Chantrey (1834), erected here in 1931 to honour the British minister's services to Greek independence. The plinth, marked by shrapnel, also celebrates a descendant who fell in Greece in 1941. The street continues N to the **Polytekhneíon** (Εθνικόν Μετσοβίον Πολυτεχνείον), designed by Kaftandzoglou and built of Pentelic marble in 1862–80. Two side pavilions in Doric style form propylæa to the main block, where an Ionic upper storey is superimposed on the lower Doric. Here the *School of Fine Arts* and the *Polytechnic School* jointly constitute an institution having university status and teaching the practical and artistic subjects not recognised by the Panepistimion. In 1973 student occupation of the Polytechnic buildings, brutally ended by the police, was the focus of opposition to the military regime, which fell the following year.

You pass the **National Archaeological Museum** (see below), with its shady garden (café), beyond which (c 1km from Omonia) you reach the Plateia Areos at the SW corner of the **Pedhíon Areos** (3, 2; 'Champ de Mars'). Before the main entrance to this pleasant park stands an equestrian *Statue of Constantine I*. An avenue to the N of this (running E–W) is flanked by busts of heroes and martyrs of the Revolution of 1821.

On the S side of the park, facing Leofóros Alexándras, is a *War Memorial* (1952) in Pentelic marble erected 'to the memory of soldiers of Britain, Australia, and New Zealand, who fought for the liberty of Greece'. Three cenotaphs (each with a bowl for a sacred flame) bear the arms of the three Commonwealth countries; behind, a Greek lion sits on a plinth of steps before a column bearing a statue of Athena. Her left arm holds a shield, the right arm is lacking since the spear it held was struck by lightning. In the park, near the chapel of Ayios Kharalambos is a *Monument to the 'Sacred Battalion'* (Ieros Lokhos), an irregular brigade of students commanded by A. Ypsilanti, which was unnecessarily sacrificed in 1821 in a skirmish at Dragashan in Romania.—At the NE end of the park stands the EVELPÍDHON, formerly the military academy and now housing the main law courts. The fine building, now restored, was designed by Ziller and erected at the expense of Averoff in 1889–94. In front stands a bronze *Statue of a Youth* (1940), by Athanasios Apartis, cast in Paris and since damaged by bullets.

9   The National Archaeological Museum

Approaches. Trolley-bus/bus No. 2, 12 or 3 from Sindagma Sq. to the museum which is in Od. Patissíon (Rte 8), 450m N of Omonia Sq., and a short walk from Plateía Kánningos. Electric railway (1 stop) from Monastiráki to Omónia. No direct service from the Acropolis.

Admission. Closed Monday. A printed catalogue to the Sculpture (1968) and good illustrated souvenir volumes are available in English; guide to the Prehistoric collections, at present only in French and German. These and slides and postcards are sold in the entrance hall.
Cafés. In gardens outside museum and in museum basement off the central ATRIUM (see plan and Room 20), below; access also from entrance hall).
Shop. In basement, with access from entrance hall. Casts and replicas of objects in the museum collections are sold, also a selection of books on sites, museums etc.

The **NATIONAL ARCHAEOLOGICAL MUSEUM** (3, 2; Εθνικόν Αρχαιολογικόν Μουσείον) contains an outstanding collection of masterpieces from excavations throughout Greece. All periods of pagan antiquity are included but new finds are now brought here only where no regional museum has a prior claim: Cretan antiquities, for example, are retained in Herakleion and other local museums and barely represented in Athens. The museum, erected in 1866–89, and extended to the E with a large new wing in 1925–39, forms a vast rectangle round an inner cross. The façade comprises an Ionic portico flanked by open galleries with plain square pilasters; the wings at either end are marked by plain pediments.

Arrangement. The first collection of antiquities formed in Athens was exhibited at the Theseion, which received sculptures transferred from Aegina in 1834. Both the Tower of the Winds and the Library of Hadrian served as repositories for occasional finds. The systematic excavations undertaken by the Greek Archaeological Society and the explorations by the British, French, German and American Schools at Athens led to the construction of the present building. For safety during the Second World War the collections were scattered. After the war the museum was entirely redecorated, alterations were made to the structure, and a whole new wing was available. For the first time the collections are being arranged as a whole; some rooms will inevitably be found closed, but the final arrangement, which is basically chronological, is predicated by the room numbering. From the entrance hall you proceed by the N wing to the central gallery, then usually visit whatever is accessible in the new wing. After making the round of the upper floor (pottery galleries open mornings only), you will eventually regain the entrance by the S wing. Here and there private bequests and donations, or finds from a particular excavation preserved complete, break the sequence. The splendid display, started by the late Dr Christos Karouzos (Director 1942–64) and Mrs Semni Karousos, and continued by subsequent directors, is still inadequately labelled even in Greek.

You cross the vestibule and enter the **Hall of Mycenaean Antiquities** (ROOM 4). In this great room are grouped the results of excavations at Mycenae and at other Mycenaean sites from 1876 to the present day. Chief among the splendid treasures are the contents of the six shaft graves from Grave Circle A at Mycenae, five excavated by Schliemann and the sixth by Stamatakis; these are now rivalled in fame by objects from Vaphio and in archaeological importance by more recent finds from elsewhere.

The cases are numbered in sequence round the room without regard to content; we follow the logical progression of the room, giving case numbers only for easy identification. Every case merits detailed study; only the outstanding or unique objects are indicated below. The numbers of the objects themselves correspond with the catalogue raisonné of G. Karo, 'Die Schacht-Gräber von Mykenai' (Munich, 1930).

Within the doors (right and left), two cases of miscellaneous finds from chamber tombs excavated in 1886–87 and 1892–99 outside the Acropolis of Mycenae. CASE 26 (right) contains an ivory head (T 27) wearing a helmet of boar's tusks (cf. below).—CASE 1 (left): Seal-rings; jewellery; 2947. Small bull in gold; sword-blades and hilts. In the next case (CASE 2) similar finds from Wace's excavations of 1921–23: outstanding are the bone objects, especially T 518; seal-stones; helmet of boar's tusk pieces.—In CASE 25, on the right, begins the material from GRAVE CIRCLE A. Contents of *1st Shaft Grave* (three women; 1550–1500 BC) and of *2nd Shaft Grave* (one man; 1580–1550 BC): Gold diadem and cup, arms, fine vases. To left and right of the room are displayed four of the stelai from the grave circle, carved with hunting scenes (of the 17 stelai found, 11 were so decorated).

There follows a group of five cases containing the most valuable objects from the 3rd, 4th and 5th Shaft Graves. In the centre: CASE 27 (*4th Grave*, the richest: three men and two women; 1580–1550 BC): Three bronze **Dagger blades inlaid in gold, silver, and niello with hunting scenes: 394, 395. Lions hunting and being hunted; 765. River scene (? the Nile) with cheetahs retrieving duck; 253, 254, 259. Three portrait masks in gold leaf; 252. Breastplate (plain); *Gold cups of varied designs (note No. 427 behind); **481. Silver rhyton with gold foil rim and handles and repoussé decoration depicting the siege of a maritime town; *412. Gold libation cup with two handles reaching to the foot of the stem and ornamented with falcons (not doves); it recalled to Schliemann Nestor's cup in Homer (Il. XI, 632–5); **Bull's head in silver with gold horns and a gold rosette; Seal rings; 555–70. Symbolic knots moulded in pottery; leg bones with gold ornaments attached.—CASE 24 (right; same grave): Gold diadems and cups; 388. Base silver rhyton in the form of a stag or reindeer (possibly of Hittite workmanship); 273. Lion-head rhyton in gold; headbands and (263) bracelet in gold; three gold pins, one (245) with a spirited reproduction of a goat; golden ornaments in the form of an octopus; three models of temple fronts, in gold, each with an altar surmounted by horns of consecration; on the two corners are doves with outstretched wings. Clasps and buttons; sword-blades and daggers.— Beyond, CASE 23 contains objects from the *3rd Grave* (three women and two children; see also Cases 10 & 11): Gold **Diadems and discs; these may have been affixed to wooden coffins, long since vanished, but more likely were used for personal adornment. Recumbent lions in gold repoussé; pair of scales in gold leaf; three gold seals engraved with a lion fight and a single combat; 116–8. Engraved gems; Gold pin, portraying a goddess of Minoan type, with thick silver shaft.—To the left of the room CASES 3 & 4 are devoted to the *5th Grave* (three men; 1580–1500 BC): *Gold mask of a man, bearded and moustached. Schliemann claimed, having removed this mask, to 'have gazed upon the face of Agamemnon'; breastplate adorned in spirals; swords (one with chased gold hilt); *656. Cup with repoussé lions; *629. Large gold cup; hexagonal wooden box overlaid with gold panels (in a remarkable state of preservation); 829, 854. Vases (in alabaster) of great elegance; sword pommel of alabaster; *Daggers and swords with blades inlaid with gold and silver or patterned with volutes of gold; 829. Ostrich egg adorned with dolphins in alabaster; 312. Sycamore box.

Two low CASES (28 and 29) placed back to back in the centre contain gold objects from the 3rd grave, notably the sheets that covered the bodies of two royal infants; small jugs, boxes, and ornaments; below, huge bronze bowl.—Lesser objects from the 4th and 6th shaft graves are displayed in CASE 22 (right): 389. Elaborate vase with three handles of Cretan alabaster; 552. Decorated ostrich egg; metal shield of Minoan type (in miniature; c 30cm high); ceramic vases of fine shape with interesting decoration. Beyond, in CASE 21, are miscellaneous finds from the Acropolis of Mycenae, including elaborately shaped pottery figurines and (2665, 2666) painted plaques; 4573. Blue monkey with cartouche.—On the opposite side of the room (CASES 5 and 6) is a selection of the finds from GRAVE CIRCLE B (1650–1550 BC) discovered in 1952–55. The graves here were generally poorer. Note however the rock-crystal duck vase, the cruder mask, and the sword-hilt.

Against a blue wall (right) are displayed a female head in limestone, perhaps from a sphinx (13C BC); a painted decorated plaque; and a stele originally incised, later covered with plaster and painted. There follow two cases of miscellaneous finds of Late Helladic date (1500–1200 BC) from Mycenae: CASE 30 (centre): Four gold vases with dogs' heads on the handles and a gold cup; two large rings or seals, one very elaborate; 991. Small recumbent lion of gold; *Group of two women and a child in ivory; inlaid handles; vases, and alabaster pommels most accurately shaped.—CASE 7 (left): Bronze mirror with an ivory handle; small carved plaques in ivory; bronze pins.—The low central CASE 31 contains ivory *Panels from furniture boxes, etc., and inscribed clay tablets from the House of Shields at

Mycenae; below is a vase of unusual shape. On the opposite wall CASE 20 has pottery, figurines, bronze weapons and jewellery from the important 12C cemetery at Perati in East Attica. Next to it stands the 'Warrior Vase' found by Schliemann. This is a large vase (c 1200 BC) painted dark red on light yellow. On one side is a line of six armed soldiers marching in single file away from a woman who bids them farewell. On the handles are modelled animal heads. Beyond the vase are two restored pillars from the 'Treasury of Atreus'. Other pieces of the pillars are similarly restored in the British Museum.

The remainder of the room is devoted to other Mycenaean sites. On the left side of the Hall, CASE 8. Finds excavated at Pylos before the site museum was founded: two daggers, one (**8340) in a wonderful state of preservation with repoussé gold hilt and inlaid blade; bronze mirror with ivory handle; ivory comb, seals, and ornaments. The low CASE 9, adjacent, contains some of the many calcined clay tablets with inscriptions in Cretan Linear B script.— Mounted on a partition wall are fragments of wall-paintings from the old (1350 BC) and later (1300 1200 BC) palace at Tiryns. Beyond (left), two CASES (10 and 11) of objects from Prosymna are placed either side of a table of large jars (that with the octopuses on the left has many Minoan parallels at Heraklion). The smaller pottery in the cases (from chamber-tombs and Middle Helladic graves) is particularly varied and graceful.

In the centre of the room, in CASE 32, are the famous **Gold cups (15C BC; subject of countless reproductions) from the beehive tomb at Vaphio dug up in 1889: 1758. Capture of wild bulls with nets; 1759. Trapping bulls with a decoy cow. Other finds from the same site: engraved gems; shallow silver cup with gilded rim and bowl. To the right (CASE 19) are miscellaneous objects from Mycenaean sites in Attica including Athens, Brauron, Markopoulo, Salamis, and an interesting vase in the form of a boot from Voula.

CASE 12 (Left: *Spata*), Ivory comb, tablets, and boar's tusk (restored). CASE 18 (right). Objects found in the tholos tomb at *Menidhi*: musical instruments in ivory, including a lyre (restored), cylindrical box with sheep carved in relief on its sides and lid; glass ornaments; engraved gems; stirrup vases.—The last centre CASE (33) is devoted to gold and silver cups, swords, etc. from *Midea* (Argolis), while the remaining five cases contain objects from *Nauplia* (13), *Mycenae* (14; three wall *Paintings), *Tiryns* (15), *Skopelos* (16), and (17) a selection of vase fragments from Mycenae chosen for their unusual representations of animal and human figures. CASE 15 includes the 'Tiryns Treasure', the loot of a tomb robber who had buried it, found in 1915 in a house of the lower town; the objects date from 1500 1100 BC: 6208, a huge seal-ring, is especially notable. Against the end wall (left) are recently discovered frescoes of the 13C BC from the cult centre at Mycenae: Goddess (?); figure-of-eight shields; (right) fragment of carved stone decoration from the Treasury of Atreus at Mycenae.

To the left and right of the Mycenaean Hall are long narrow rooms devoted to earlier antiquities. In that to the left (R. 5), objects of **Neolithic and Helladic** cultures from Thessaly (Dimini and Sesklo), Orchomenos, Attica (Ayios Kosmas, Rafina, Nea Makri) and Poliokhni on Lemnos, the latter having ceramic affinities with Troy. A case of objects from Troy itself was presented by Sophie Schliemann. To the right (R. 6), Cycladic objects from the islands: particularly important are finds from Phylakopi (Melos) with characteristic painted pottery showing Cretan influence, and the well-known Flying-fish fresco; vases from Syros; *Statuettes of male figures playing musical instruments, in Parian marble (2400–2200 BC), from Keros; and the contents of tombs found intact on Naxos.

You return to the vestibule and enter the NORTH WING, where seven rooms contain **Archaic Sculpture**. Free-standing sculpture of the 7–6C BC has two principal types: the *Kouros* or youth, represented nude with one leg forward of the other, and the *Kore* or maiden, portrayed draped. The form may derive from the xoanon, or ancient wooden statue; the stiff position of the arms, held tightly to the body, being dictated in wood-carving by the available shape of the timber. But many of the conventions show marked affinities with Egyptian and Phoenician models.

ROOM 7. In the centre, 804. Huge sepulchral amphora in ripe Geometric style (c 760 BC) found in the Kerameikos area (the like became known from the provenance as 'Dipylon vases'): on it are represented the prothesis (laying-out) and lamentation over the dead. In glass cases behind, 770–79. Geometric pottery and four ivory statuettes from the same grave, one from a Syrian model. 57. Statue of a goddess (?; c 630 BC) found at Ayioryitika near Tripolis; 1. Statue of Artemis found at Delos, the work of a Naxian sculptor (c 630 BC); the inscription on the left side records its dedication by Nikandre of Naxos; 2869. Part of a limestone relief in the 'Dædalic' style, possibly a metope of a temple (Mycenae; c 650–630 BC), one of the oldest monumental stone reliefs of continental Greece; 56. Grave monument of Kitylos and Dermis, set up by Amphalkes; work of a Boeotian sculptor (mid-6C BC), found at Tanagra. In the doorway, 16513. Archaic bronze flautist from Samos (cast solid).—ROOM 8. Kouros figures and fragments. Dominating the room, 2720. Colossal Kouros from the earlier Temple of Poseidon at Sounion (c 600 BC), newly restored. 3645. Torso of another; 71. Torso of an Athenian youth (590–580 BC) from Kerameikos; 3372. The 'Dipylon Head' from a Kouros funeral monument in the Kerameikos, remarkable Attic work of c 610 BC. The hand (3965) in the wall case is from the same work. 353. The 'Piraeus Amphora', funerary vase of 630–620 BC (chariot scenes); 15. Head of a kouros from the Sanctuary of Ptoan Apollo, of crude Boeotian technique (c 580 BC).

Off ROOM 8 open three small rooms containing sculpture of the 6C, with exceptional recent finds. ROOM 9. *1558. Kouros from Melos; 22. Kore; 21. Winged Nike, both from Delos; 10. Kouros from Sanctuary of Apollo at Ptoön; 73. Torso of Kore (Aegina, 570 BC); *4889. Myrrhinous Kore (c 590 BC), found in 1972 with a kouros (see below). The lead ring found with it fitted a known base inscribed Phrasikleia and signed by Aristion of Paros.—ROOM 10, beyond: 28. Sphinx (Spata, c 570); 76. Sphinx (Piraeus, c 540 BC); *38. Fragment of grave stele of a discophoros, of great vitality, executed in Parian marble by an Attic sculptor c 560 BC (Kerameikos); *4890. Myrrhinous Kouros (cf. above); 2687, 2891. Tall stele and crowning sphinx from the Kerameikos; the stele, typical of the 6C style, was hastily chipped back for use in the Themistoclean Wall (the two parts may not belong together).—In ROOM 10A are *1906. Kouros from Volomandra (Kalivia), a charming Attic work of c 550 BC; 14. Unfinished kouros from Naxos showing tool marks; 18232. Bronze vessel with sculptured handles; 4871. Head of Kouros.

Return to ROOM 11. In the centre, 3686. Kouros from Keos, local work of 530 BC. Round this are grouped marble sculptures and steles: 8. Kouros from Thera; 3728. Well-preserved Herm from Siphnos (c 520 BC); 1673. Part of pediment, perhaps from the precinct of Pythian Apollo; the other half is in the Metropolitan Museum (N.Y.); 27. Head of a woman with red hair and earrings, from Eleusis; 30. Grave stele of Lyseas erected by his father Semon (c 500 BC) found at Velanideza in 1838: the faded painting is reproduced in the adjacent copy; 26, 25. Ex-voto Korai figures from Eleusis, remarkable for their drapery; 31. Lower part of a stele of a horseman with well-preserved painted decoration, found in Aeolus St. (c 500 BC); *29. Funeral stele in Pentelic marble representing the warrior Aristion and signed by Aristokles (Velanideza); this is a typical stele of the period, narrow and crowned with a palmette, bearing a formalised relief of the dead person in a characteristic attitude; the full-length figure retains traces of colour. 3072. Mask of Dionysos; *3071. Grave stele of a hoplite found in Stamata (c 525 BC); 13. Kouros found at Megara (c 540 BC); 93. Marble discus dedicated to Aeneas 'the wise and excellent physician' (c 550 BC); 81. Base of a grave monument (c 550 BC) found in Vourva; only the feet of the statue of Phaidimos' daughter survive above the inscription; 41. Crowning member of a grave stele showing the squire of the deceased youth on horseback, carved in a very low relief.

You enter ROOM 13, a long hall in which the most striking work stands at the far end before a screen: *3851, the *Anávyssos Kouros*, found in 1936; the middle step of the base, found near by in 1938, has the inscription 'Stop and lament at the tomb of the dead Kroisos whom furious Ares slew when he was fighting in the forefront'. Though in archaic posture, its mobility and modelling suggest a date of c 520 BC. Other Kouroi in the room: 12, 20. Both from the Sanctuary of Apollo at Ptoön in Boeotia (end of 6C BC); 9. A coarse work from Orchomenos; *3938. Sepulchral statue unearthed near Keratea during the German occupation and smuggled to Athens; it represents the young Aristodikos (Attic work of c 500 BC); *16365. Bronze statuette of Apollo from Sparta (end of 6C BC). Other fragments include: 32. Sepulchral stele of two youths, Agathon and Aristokrates, from Thespiai (500 BC); 1926. Pair of stone halteres (jumping weights) of archaic type from Corinth; 89, 2823, 2826. Slabs decorated with reliefs, probably from a tomb, cut back for use in the Themistoclean Wall in 478 BC. At the far end (right and behind the screen) are two celebrated bases with reliefs on three sides, found in 1922 in a section of the wall of Themistocles. *3477. In front, six nude epheboi playing a ball game with curved sticks, strongly resembling modern hockey; left and right sides, chariot scenes (c 490 BC); *3476. In front, nude epheboi practising wrestling, jumping, and throwing the javelin; left side, six epheboi playing a ball game; right side, four clothed epheboi starting a fight between a dog and a cat (c 510 BC). To the left of the far door, 796. Acroterion of stele (Cycladic, c 440 BC). To the right of door: 36. Fragment of a relief, notable for the finely executed detail of its drapery (Attic, c 500 BC).

ROOM 12 leads off towards the front of the building. SCULPTURE FROM THE TEMPLE OF APHAIA AT AEGINA. 1933–38. Warriors' heads from the first version (c 500 BC) of the E pediment; for some reason unknown the figures were later replaced by new ones (now in Munich) and the heads buried; 1959. Relief of a running hoplite (end of 6C BC) found near the 'Theseion'; 1605. 'The Daphni Torso'; 3711. Seated marble figure, draped; 782. Palmette from a stele of c 500 BC; 3687. 'Kouros of the Ilissos' (early 5C).

5C Sculpture. ROOM 14 is devoted to funerary stelai or GRAVE MONUMENTS of provincial origin. The period here represented, during which the sculptured stele developed from a single figure to a group composition, is almost entirely lacking in Attica, probably due to a decree of Kleisthenes (c 509) prohibiting unnecessary expenditure on grave monuments. In the centre: *3990. Fragment of votive medallion of Parian marble, unique in form, found at Melos in 1937;

the expressive relief may represent Aphrodite, and is dated stylistically to 460 BC; 11761. Bronze Warrior, damaged but fine.

Round the walls (left to right): 734. Stele of Ekkedamos, found at Larissa (local work of c 440); 39. Stele, signed by Alxenor of Naxos, found at Orchomenos (Boeotia); 739. Stele of Amphotto, found at Pyri, near Thebes, work of a Boeotian artist c 440 BC; 735. Stele found at Vonitsa (c 460); 3344. Votive relief of a boy victor crowning himself (Cape Sounion, c 470); 741. Stele of a youth wearing the petasos and holding a hare, 733. Stele of Polyxena (both local Thessalian work); 4478–9. Ionic capitals from Sounion.

The principal masterpiece of ROOM 15 stands in the centre: * *15161. *Poseidon*, a powerful bronze of heroic proportions salvaged from the sea off Cape Artemision in 1928. This is an original work of c 450 BC possibly by the sculptor Kalamis; the god held, and is poised to hurl, a trident. It is surrounded by 5C marbles. Within the door (left) is the famous *Relief from Eleusis* (126) representing Triptolemos receiving the ears of corn from Demeter, while Kore crowns him with a garland. This grand work in very low relief and somewhat hieratic style belongs to the period (c 440 BC) immediately preceding the highest development of Greek sculpture.

To the left, 742. Grave relief of a youth from Thespiai (Boeotia), work of a local artist influenced by Ionic prototypes (c 440 BC); the inscription shows re-use in Roman times when the hair was probably restyled; 54. Base with sculptured reliefs; 1732. Hebe (mutilated) found near the Temple of Ares in the Agora, probably the central acroterion of the temple. On the other side of the room are various heads: 1825. Stele of a boy; 1385. Relief (fragmentary) of an idealised youth standing behind his horse; 828. Thespian stele (c 440); the hero, with chlamys flying, rides a galloping horse.

Beyond the great bronze, 332. Head of Hermes, from Piraeus, perhaps by Euphron (440 BC). To the left, 1664. Roman copies of statues of Theseus and the Minotaur. At the far end of the gallery, 248. Roman copy in marble of another bronze youth of the school of Kalamis (found in the Olympieion in 1888); 45. The 'Omphalos' Apollo, misnamed from the base (46, in the corner) found with it in the theatre of Dionysos; it is a copy (2C AD) of an original bronze by Kalamis.

You enter (ROOM 16) the HALL OF CLASSICAL GRAVE MONUMENTS where are displayed examples of Attic work of the late 5C when Kleisthenes' decree had lapsed.

Attic grave reliefs, starting again c 440 BC, continue all the provincial developments. Four main types may be distinguished: narrow stelai, sometimes in the form of a pilaster crowned by palmettes or the like, with a rectangular 'picture' in low relief, often with the addition of rosettes; monuments in the form of a vase ornamented in low relief; broad stelai with sculptured family groups, terminating in a cornice or pediment; lastly the great naïskos monuments (or *ædiculae*) of the 4C (cf. below) with increased emphasis on the temple-like character of the architectural frame.

Opposite the doorway stands (4485) the wonderful *Myrrhine Lekythos*, found in Sindagma Sq. and acquired in 1960 from the Vouros mansion; Hermes Psychopompos leads Myrrhine to the river of Acheron while her living relatives look on (c 420 BC). Also in the centre are: 14498. Red-figured Pelike by the painter Polion (420–410 BC), found on the Sacred Way near the Botanic Garden; it contained a cremation burial; 3709. Stele from the Kerameikos, unusual in having reliefs (lion and lioness) on both sides; 4502. Marble *Base on which stood a lekythos or loutrophoros; the reliefs show Hermes Psychopompos, the dead maiden receiving apples picked by a youth

(? Elysian Fields), and a bearded priest with a knife (found in Athens). *715. Tombstone of Pentelic marble (c 430 BC, perhaps by Agorakritos), in high relief and surmounted by a superb frieze of palmettes and lilies; the youth bids farewell while his small grieving slave leans sadly on a pillar bearing a (?) cat below a birdcage.

Round the walls: 711. Stele of a woman seated in high-backed chair, in a severe style probably not Attic (found at Piraeus); 766. Stele of Aristylla, erected by her parents (Piraeus c 440 BC); 716. Later stele from Piraeus, notable for the expressions of grief of the mourners; painted stelai, with names incised but no relief; 714. Early naïskos from Piraeus (c 390 BC); 1858. Upper part of a stele in low relief showing the profile of a young girl; 910. Similar: 3845. Stele of Mnesagora and her little brother Nicochares, erected by their parents (found at Anagyrous, Vari); 713. Stele of Lysander; Chairestrate (? the boy's mother), standing, offers him a bird; 37. Fragment of striking life-size figure from Kythnos, by an island sculptor; 880. Two old men shake hands, while a little girl offers her hand too (Piraeus c 435 BC); 712. Attic stele of the family of Iphistiadai, with facing lions on the fronton.

ROOM 17 displays CLASSICAL VOTIVE SCULPTURE, selected examples of the work of practised sculptors of the 5C. In the centre, *1783. Double relief found near New Phaleron station; on one side the local hero Echelos carrying off his bride Basile in a chariot, with Hermes in the role of nymphagogos (best man); on the other, Artemis with gods and nymphs, 1500. Offering to Dionysos by actors holding masks (from Piraeus); 254. Attic marble statue of a young athlete from Eleusis (4C BC; probably after an original by Polykleitos); 176. Young girl, from Piraeus. Round the walls: 199. Statuette of a young man found at Rhamnous, dedicated by Lysikleides, son of Epandrides; 203–214. Fragments of sculptures from the base of the statue of Nemesis at Rhamnous, by Agorakritos of Paros, pupil of Pheidias (430–420 BC). Architectural sculpture from the Heraion at Argos is displayed on two sides of the room: fragmentary metopes, cornice with lion's head spouts, and reliefs of cuckoos, Hera's bird; 1571. Head of Hera, by Argive sculptor of Polykleitan school; 226. Stele of a priestess of Apollo found at Mantinea, possibly the famous Diotima of the Symposium of Plato (c 410 BC); 2756. *Relief dedicated by Xenokrateia, showing her leading the little Xeniades to the river-god Kephissos who greets him; to the left and right are Apollo and Acheloös (c 400 BC, from the same sanctuary as 1783), 1391. Relief of an apobates, from the Amphiaraion.

ROOM 20 leads off from ROOM 17 (turn right; to the left is ROOM 19). Votive reliefs; 1394. Ephebos with horses, showing influence of the Parthenon frieze (430–420 BC); 1329, dedicated to Pan and the Nymphs, from the S side of the Acropolis; 3572. Persephone seated with Demeter standing (c 430 BC); 309. Funeral banquet; 223. Small torso of Apollo (copy of 2C BC). The remainder of the room is devoted to copies deriving from works of *Pheidias* (and his school), notably the Athena Parthenos: 1612. Torso of Apollo, Roman copy of a lost original by Pheidias; 200–202. Statuettes from Eleusis, copies of figures from the W pediment of the Parthenon. At the far end, 129. The *Varvakeion Athena*, so called because discovered near the School of that name in 1880. This statuette is a reduced copy dating from the 2C or 3C AD (at one-twelfth of the original) of the great chryselephantine statue of Pheidias though in itself it is disappointing and the workmanship, careful enough in its way, lacks inspiration. Nearly all the features of the original seem to be reproduced: Athena's right hand (in which she holds the winged victory) is here, however, resting on a pillar of no known order, possibly following a late addition made (after damage ?) to Pheidias' work. 4491. Part of a colossal head of Athena, from the workshop of Agorakritos; 177. Head of a goddess, copy of another chryselephantine statue of the 5C (found in the Herodes theatre); 128. The *Lenormant Athena*, an unfinished copy in miniature from the Roman period of Pheidias' statue; 3718. Athena of the Pnyx; copy (2C AD) of the head of a colossal statue in the style of the master.

R. 19. 3854. Relief of youths (in the Pyrrhic dance); 1811. Aphrodite, copy (1C AD) of a bronze original, perhaps by Kallimachos; 3949. Copy of the cult statue of Nemesis at Rhamnous by Agorakritos (Roman; found in Athens, 1934); 3569. Head of Aphrodite, a contemporary replica in miniature of an Attic bronze (c 420 BC); 3043. Acroterion (c 410 BC); 4531. Choregic relief with masks (5C BC) from Dhionisos.

Steps lead down from R. 20 to the charming ATRIUM, with a mosaic of Medusa in the centre. The surrounding colonnade shelters moving 4C grave stelai of children and Roman sarcophagi, as well as much-eroded marble statuary recovered from the sea off Antikythera (cf. below).

At the far end is an entrance to the pleasant café.

In ROOM 18 are displayed LATE-5C AND EARLY-4C SEPULCHRAL MONUMENTS. *3624. *Stele of Hegeso*, c 400 BC, from the Kerameikos cemetery, a masterpiece perhaps by Kallimachos himself; Hegeso seated examines a necklace (originally painted in) from a trinket-box held by her maid. 3472. Funeral stele of Theano, wife of Ktesileos of Erythrai (Athens; late 5C BC). Two marble lekythoi (835. Rider and hoplites; the background, perhaps an addition, is delicately sketched in but unfinished; 2584). Round the walls: 765. Stele of Mika and Dion from the Kerameikos; 2744, 754. Parts of the War Memorial erected by the city of Athens in honour of hoplites and cavalry who fell near Corinth and at Koroneia in 394 BC, found NE of the Dipylon; the list includes the name of Dexileos; 902. Stele of Tynnias, from Piraeus; 831. Stele of Phrasikleia; 3790. Stele of a young mother, from Psikhiko; Case of Attic white-ground lekythoi of the same period; 723. Stele of Polyxene; *717. Stele from Kerameikos; a young girl bids farewell to her parents; 752. Stele of Demokleides, son of Demetrios, a hoplite lost in a naval battle; 718. Grave relief of Ameinokleia from Piraeus (360–350 BC); 724. Stele of Phainarete; 13789. Bronze funeral kalpis (ash jar; 5C); 1822. Funeral stele of a woman, by a Peloponnesian sculptor (420–410 BC), found near Omonia Square.

ROOM 21 (Central Hall). In the centre, *15177. *Horse and Jockey of Artemision*, a lively masterpiece in bronze of the 2C BC, found with the statue of Poseidon, and pieced together from many fragments. The jockey is winning a race at full gallop; note, on the horse's right hind leg below the rump, brand markings of ownership. *1826. *Diadoumenos:* a good copy of c 100 BC of a lost bronze original by Polykleitos, found at Delos. The support with the false attributes of Apollo is an addition of the copyist. 3622. The 'Matron of Herculaneum', copy of a Greek work attributed to Lysippos; the best known copy of this work was found at Herculaneum. 218. Hermes of Andros, found at Palaiopolis (Andros); copy in Parian marble of an Attic original of the school of Praxiteles. 720. Sepulchral relief of Melite from Piraeus (mid-4C BC); 2308. Epikranion; 3964. Stele of Pausimache (Attic, c 370 BC); *3708. Base of a grave stele (early 4C BC) with reliefs of a rider fighting a hoplite, found near the Academy of Plato.

Since rearrangement is still proceeding in the New Wing, it is better to see next the rooms that are open there (and at least the Thera frescoes on the upper floor, see below) before continuing to ROOM 22, even though this breaks the intended sequence.

Beyond the colonnade, ROOM 34, HALL OF THE ALTAR, connecting the old museum with the new wing, is arranged to suggest an open-air sanctuary. In the centre, 1495. Altar dedicated by the Boule near the Agora to Aphrodite Hegemone and the Graces. Grouped round it are reliefs of differing provenance and quality. To the left: 303. Triple Hekate, Goddess of the crossroads (late Roman) found at Epidauros; 252. Pan holding the syrinx, from Sparta; another example of the same subject (3534) stands farther on; 4465, 4466. Attic reliefs (4C BC) dedicated to the nymphs, found in the Cave of the Nymphs, Mt Pentelikon; 1778. Attic relief dedicated to Zeus Meilichios (3C BC), found near the Ilissos. At the end of the room, to either side, 2756, 1783. Two limestone bases (end of 5C BC) bearing the inscriptions of the dedicators surmounted by casts of the votive reliefs now in the Classical gallery (see below). Returning along the other side, 227. Torso, copy of the 1C BC from the same original as the Aphrodite of

NATIONAL ARCHAEOLOGICAL MUSEUM

Arles now in the Louvre. 1451–52. Reliefs (4C BC): Erotes carrying incense-burners, from the sanctuary of Aphrodite and Eros on the N slope of the Acropolis.

You enter (left) the NEW WING, where the arrangement is still unfinished. ROOM 36. The **Karapános Collection**, the fruits of excavations by K. Karapános in 1875–77 at Dodona and elsewhere, with later finds from the same sites. The original collection, presented to the State in 1902, is particularly rich in small bronze objects, of which the most outstanding are noted. On a pedestal in front of the door: 27, 16547. Bronze horseman; the horse was recovered in 1956. *First Case* (right): Bronze strips with inscriptions of decrees, treaties, manumissions, etc., and leaden strips with questions asked of the Oracle at Dodona and answers similarly inscribed; the strips were varnished with some preservative. Cheek-shields. The *Second Case* contains votive figures dedicated to the god of the oracle: 22. Satyr; 31. Zeus hurling a thunderbolt; 54. Ram; on the shelf below, 70. Hand holding a dove; 166. Cheek-piece of an ancient bronze helmet, of exquisite hammered work probably Corinthian (early 4C BC); bottom shelf, Helmet. On a pedestal, 25. Woman playing the double flute. In the *Third Case* (right) are delightful animal figures, and (557) Bronze frying-pan. In a *Wall Case*, beyond: Archaic terracotta figures of Artemis from Corfu.—The *First Case* (left) contains 24. Statuette of a runner, c 530 BC; 36. Horseman. In the *Third Case* is a finely wrought statue of a warrior (550 BC). Beside, on a pedestal, a fine 5C statuette of Zeus hurling his thunderbolt. Farther on, mounted on a reconstruction in wood, bronze wheelhubs and decoration of a Roman state chariot. At the end of the room, 965. Attic gravestone, slave handing open jewel-box to her lady (330 BC).

ROOM 37 is the first of the BRONZE ROOMS to be opened. To left, case with finds and reconstructions demonstrating ancient casting etc. techniques. The other cases have a fine range of votive offerings (human and animal figures, jewellery, vessels, weapons) from various parts of Greece: Boeotia (including the Ptoön sanctuary), Macedonia, Thessaly and the North, Crete (the Idaean cave). In the centre, the *Marathon Boy*, a fine late 4C bronze statue recovered from the sea in Marathon Bay.

Rooms 38–39 and 46–47 are no longer in use; 40 is being prepared for a further display of bronzes; 41–45 are used for temporary exhibitions, often of great interest. The bronze statues from Piraeus, formerly on display here are now in the Piraeus Museum (cf. below).

First Floor, see below.

You now return to the central hall and continue in the SOUTH WING. ROOM 22. SCULPTURES FROM EPIDAUROS. All the fragments formerly at Epidauros were brought together here by N. Yalouris. The room is at present (1991) undergoing refurbishment and the sculptures are not accessible. Figures from the W pediment of the Temple of Asklepios at Epidauros (c 380 BC); the positions of the three acroteria are shown; one depicts Penthesilea, queen of the Amazons. The fragments from the E pediment, which represented the capture of Troy, include the Nike (or Eros) of the central acroterion, probably by Timotheos. 173. Relief panel showing Asklepios.—RR. 23–24. 4C FUNERARY MONUMENTS notably (in R. 23) *869. 'Stele of the Ilissos', commemorating a young hunter; his father stands at the right, a little slave sits at his master's feet (c 340 BC; possibly by Skopas); *870. Grave relief of two women, Attic work of the mid-4C BC; (in R. 24) 823, 824. Scythian archers, probably from the monument of an officer (Kerameikos; ? from the tomb of Lysimachides of Acharnai); 1488. Stele with bilingual inscription in Greek and Phoenician and an unusual theme; 3716. Seated women (note the drapery; 380 BC); 2574. Monument of Alexos of Sounion (c 320 BC).—RR 26–28. VOTIVE AND RECORD RELIEFS from various parts of Greece, also some free-standing sculpture. In Room 25, dedications to the nymphs, cave-shaped; 1479. Record of handing over of sacred funds of

Athena by the Tameiai in 398/7 BC; free-standing votive figures of children from the Temple of Eileithuia at Agrai by the Ilissos, 3C; several reliefs dedicated to Asklepios, usually showing the God and members of his family, with worshippers; 1378. Craftsman's relief, with helmets and tools; 258. Head and torso of the *Asklepios of Mounychia*; 1377. Unusual relief, with side piece, to Asklepios. In Room 26, several reliefs from the Amphiaraion, including 3526. Worshipper with huge votive leg, presumably a thank-offering for a cure; 304. Odd distorted figures of children (freestanding). In Room 27, 1487. figure with polos, two sphinxes, with Near-Eastern connections; 3405, 3873, 1503. Feasting reliefs. At the end of the room, 701. A large headless free-standing figure; 1613. Seated figure; 1555 etc. Reliefs dedicated to Cybele, shown seated in a deep frame, with lions and (sometimes) a patera (dish); 1540 is a double version.

You return to the main galleries.

ROOM 28 is devoted to late Classical sculpture. LAST FUNERARY MONUMENTS OF ATTICA comprise the first group: 738. Monument of Aristonautes (c 310 BC), a realistic armed figure depicted in full relief in a deep naïskos; 803, 804. Pair of marble lions from the Kerameikos; *4484. Large relief of a small negro trying to control a spirited horse (c 300 BC) found near Larissa station (Athens) in 1948; 1005. The latest known Attic tomb-relief before the prohibition of 307 BC, found in the Kerameikos (the drapery is astonishing). In the centre of the room: 13396. **Ephebos of Antikythera** (bronze; c 340 BC), found in 1900 at the bottom of the sea; this is possibly the Paris of the sculptor *Euphranor*. The eyes are inlaid and the lashes fashioned from bronze plate. The famous bronze is surrounded by originals and later marble copies of works of the same period: 178–80. Boar's and warriors' heads from the Temple of Athena Alea at Tegea (? W Pediment), by *Skopas* (c 340 BC), almost the only surviving certain work of one of the greatest Greek sculptors. The expression of emotion contrasts with the 5C calm and foreshadows the agonies of the Hellenistic school of Pergamon; 182 (? also by Skopas). Head of Ariadne; 323. Head of Asklepios. *3602. Hygieia from Tegea (? by Skopas).

ROOM 29, FIRST HELLENISTIC SCULPTURE ROOM. Centre (right), 247. Fighting Gaul, from Delos (c 200 BC); (left), 231. Statue of Themis, goddess of Justice, from Rhamnous (by Chairestratos; early 3C BC). To the left, 239. Young Satyr (Lamia; 3C BC); 215–217. Three reliefs found at Mantineia, representing the musical contest of Apollo and Marsyas, perhaps the bases of a group of Leto and her Children, executed by Praxiteles and noted by Pausanias; 245. Dionysos embracing a Satyr (unfinished; late 4C); 327. Head of Demosthenes, found in 1849 in the Royal Garden, a late copy of a bronze by Polyeuktos; Heads of a colossal group by Damophon from Lykosoura.

ROOM 30. *13400. Portrait head of a philosopher (bronze), found in the sea off Antikythera (3C BC) and other fragments from the statue; 2772. Statuette of Ianiskos playing with a goose (3C BC), found at Lilaia; *6439. Portrait of a boxer from Olympia, uncompromisingly naturalistic; possibly the head of a bronze statue of the athlete Satyros by the Athenian sculptor Silanion (c 340 BC); the lips are inlaid; *3266. Portrait head from a statue, from the Stoa of Attalos (c 150 BC); 3556. Ariarathes V (c 120 BC); 235. Poseidon of Melos (of Parian marble; c 140 BC); *14612. Head from Delos (bronze), a lifelike portrait of a man torn by doubts, of c 100 BC; *351. Portrait of a (?) Thracian priest, a fine Attic work of the end of the Hellenistic period (1C BC); 3485. 'The little refugee', a child holding a dog (brought from Asia Minor in 1922); 232. Aristonoe, a priestess of

Nemesis, dedicated by her son Hierokles at Rhamnous; 3335. Aphrodite defending her honour from Pan (the so-called 'Slipper Slapper'—well-preserved but inartistic), from the House of the Poseidoniastai at Delos, c 100 BC; 1829. Artemis, also from Delos; 457. Head of a youth (late 1C BC); 259, 260. Two relief slabs from the Theatre of Dionysos, depicting (?) Horai, with wind-blown drapery.

Rooms 31–3 (which included Roman material) are at present closed for rearrangement.

In R. 32 was previously displayed the **Hélène Stathátos Collection**, presented in 1957, consisting of objects of all periods from the Bronze Age to Byzantine times from Thessaly, Chalcidice, and Macedonia, and a most precious array of ancient *Jewellery and gold ornament. Unique are a breast ornament in gold of the 3C BC from Thessaly, consisting of a medallion of Aphrodite in relief surrounded by a network of fine chain; and a naïskos (c 300 BC) in gold, set with precious stones, depicting Dionysos and a Satyr. No finds similar to these have ever been recorded in any scientific excavation. Unique also is St. 332. Red-figured ceramic in the shape of an egg. Among small bronzes are (St. 328) an Archaic kriophoros and (St. 316) a graceful doe. Also a fine bronze helmet of Illyrian type, with a gold funeral mask, which perhaps belong together. In ROOM 33 a display of sculpture of the Roman period is in preparation.

The FIRST FLOOR, approached from the central hall (cf. above), is devoted to **Pottery**, mainly of post-Mycenaean date with a few typical earlier pieces; in general, earlier pottery is displayed on the ground floor with other contemporary objects. Classical vase-painting is represented by a daunting array of examples, of all shapes and great mythological interest, and generally of high quality. If few rank with the greatest masterpieces now in the major museums of Europe and America, they have the special advantage of being entirely free of foreign admixture. The collection, which is beautifully displayed in chronological sequence, is unique for the **Early Vases**.

VESTIBULE. Typical pithos, with plain bands in relief, of the Minoan period in Crete, found at Knossos (1878) before systematic excavations were undertaken there; other large storage jars; cast of a votive relief (from the Acropolis), depicting a potter offering two cups to Athena Ergane, goddess of industry; case of prehistoric pottery from various places and periods.

Off the centre of the vestibule has been mounted a temporary exhibition of recent finds from **Akrotiri on Thira** (Blue Guide Greece, Rte 73); these are eventually to be accommodated on the island. The first room contains an extensive display of Cycladic and imported Minoan pottery of the early Late Bronze Age (16C BC). Especially attractive are some of the pictorial scenes (vegetation, dolphins, birds). Also stone vessels and bronze objects (sickles, scale balances etc.). The second room has the spectacular **Frescoes**: swallows and lilies in a rocky landscape; monkeys; antelopes and boxing children (perhaps juxtaposed to compare rites of passages in the human and animal kingdoms); fisherman with catch; priestess; *ikrion* (stern cabin from ship)—the motif visible on the 'ship fresco'; part of a frieze c 6m long showing a maritime procession from one coastal town to another (perhaps in celebration of the Annual Resumption of Navigation after the close winter season); from the same room (in the 'West House') and the same fresco series are a sub-tropical landscape and a battle by a town, with warriors on the shore. The state of preservation of these paintings is unique in the Aegean Bronze Age. They are clearly based on Cretan models for both technique and subject but there are also local Cycladic (and possibly Mycenaean) features. Their full significance for our understanding of the representational art of this period is only beginning to be properly appreciated.

You leave the Akrotiri exhibition and turn left into the vase rooms.

ROOM I. Characteristic pottery of the **Bronze Age** (3rd–2nd millennium BC), showing the first attempts at painting in the Aegean, together with Mycenaean idols; note the lily and papyrus motives derived from Cretan models and ultimately from Egypt. **Protogeometric and Geometric Pottery** (10–7C).

In the upheaval following the Mycenaean downfall, as pottery deteriorated into 'sub-Mycenaean', designs grew more stylised and perfunctory and were reduced to geometric patterns. About 1025 BC, a new pottery style developed. This *Protogeometric* style, though it involved no change of actual technique and though it made use of the previous shapes and decorative motives, was important because it was the first sign of a new spirit, creative instead of decadent (cf. the works of V.R. Desborough). The style is common to the whole of Greece (disseminated, perhaps by Attic seamen?), but Attic invention soon becomes dominant and Athens emerges for the first time as the artistic centre of the Greek world. At the beginning of the period vase-painters use simple decorative motives, circles, and semicircles drawn in dark glaze on the light surface of the clay. Later, in the full *Geometric* style, which brings in new vase types with broad bases, potters begin to cover the greater part of the surface with black glaze; the decoration, at first restricted to zones filled with circles and linear patterns arranged in panels, later covers the whole vase in horizontal bands. In the 8C the human figure begins to take a prominent place in vase decoration, chiefly on large sepulchral amphorae and kraters. Scenes generally show the prothesis (laying out of the dead), the ekphora (funeral procession), and funeral games, especially chariot racing. This period coincides with the historical unification of Attica under Athens. The leading artist of the age is the so-called 'Dipylon Painter' of the Kerameikos.

To the left of the room, typical examples, standing alone, add emphasis to the general exposition. Against the wall (right): progression of 10–9C (Proto- and Early Geometric) vases, at first with simple geometric motifs; the first appearance of the meander (218) and of the swastika are seen; designs cover larger areas and show increased mastery of technique; more elaborately decorated pottery. In the centre, 216. Amphora. To the left, Geometric vases of the 9–8C. To the right, free-standing, are two Amphorae from the Kerameikos, with overall geometric decoration, one with serpents in relief on the handles; in the large case at right angles to them: 169, 186, 201–202. Fine examples of the Geometric style (8C), including a bronze tripod that supported a kalpis (cremation urn); beyond, a case with many figured fragments. In the case on the left wall: vases from excavations (1935) on Mt Hymettos; 192. Oinochoë with a graffito in primitive Greek characters of the 8C, reading 'He who dances better than the other dancers will receive this'. 17935 (beyond). Painted Geometric amphora with chariot race and helmeted warriors. Case: contemporary bronze and terracotta figurines, and pyxides. Further case of mature Geometric pottery (8C). Between the pillars, *803. Large late Geometric amphora of the 'Dipylon' type from the Kerameikos, with typical scenes of prothesis and ekphora (c 750 BC).

In the long vestibule to the next room, various large works in the Ripe Geometric style: 810. Vase in the form of a bowl (frieze of men and four-horse chariot) on an ornamental stand with four bands of painting; 894. Tall amphora with two friezes: chariots, with warriors, and procession of warriors.

ROOMS II AND III are mainly devoted to **7C Ceramics** of the style known generally as *Orientalising* and in its regional application as *Protoattic.*

By the end of the 8C Geometric art becomes perfunctory. The old precision of drawing is neglected but often for the sake of giving the whole composition movement and pictorial coherence. In the 7C Greek colonists penetrated the Black Sea and ranged to Sicily and beyond, making close contacts with both Egyptian and Phoenician culture. Greek painters come under the rejuvenating influence of oriental motifs. Linear patterns are replaced by lotus and palmette ornaments, trees, birds, animals (often in hieratic stance), chimaeras, gorgons, sphinxes, etc. (cf. the grave monuments of Archaic sculpture). Mythological subjects are increasingly depicted: at first centaurs and monsters, later heroic myths distortedly reflecting a memory of the great Mycenaean days, transmitted in Homeric poetry.

Along the right wall: Empedocleous Bequest (Geometric). Early 7C vases showing the beginning of oriental influences: 313. *Analatos Hydria*, having mixed decoration, Geometric on the neck, Orientalising on the shoulder, with a choral scene on the body; Amphora painted with scene of a warrior's departure, perhaps Hector and Andromache. In the centre: a case of late Geometric pottery then, on its own, a fine krater by the Hirschfeld Painter. Case of regional Geometric pottery. To right, case of Corinthian aryballoi showing (right to left) the evolution of the shape. In the centre, 220. Huge amphora from Thebes; metopes depict a bird of prey and Artemis as mistress of the brute creation. Returning along the left wall: contents of a tomb from Pyri, near Thebes; Boeotian figurines; 13257. Priest-king seated on a throne; 228. Boeotian stamnos with horse and lion metopes; 15424. Protoattic krater of the earliest Orientalising style from Phaleron (early 7C). Case of Boeotian and Euboean pottery: note *14481. Clay cart in the form of a horse on wheels carrying six amphoræ (Euboea; ? 9C). To the left as you pass into the next room, 238. Attic louterion from Thebes; the centaurs have human forelegs, an early conception; 14497. The *Kynosarges Amphora.*

ROOM III. Four cases in the left-hand corner contain 7C ware from Crete (12509 shows Egyptian influence); from Naxos, Santorin, and Rhodes (12717. Oinochoë decorated with lotus flowers and realistic gazelles); from other Aegean islands; and from Cyprus (17376. Chariot with three figures in pottery). In front are four fine amphorae from Melos: *911. Two Muses (?) in chariot, accompanied by Apollo and Artemis; on neck, combat of Ajax and Odysseus over the arms of Achilles; *354. On neck, meeting of Hermes and Iole; on body, Herakles mounting chariot in which Iole is accompanied by Eurytos and Antiope, her father and mother; the colouring is rich and the ornamentation elaborate.—You pass into the main body of the room. To the left, Tanagra vases. To the right, Ripe Protoattic pottery: on the middle stand, three kraters from a tomb at Anagyrous, near Vari, probably all by the same painter (c 620 BC) and clearly occupying a position midway between the Orientalising and Black-figure styles; 16384. Prometheus bound and Herakles shooting the eagle. Opposite stands 221. *The Siren Amphora* (c 630 BC) with black figures on a yellow-grey ground. In the last case to the left, 16391. Amphora, a good example of several showing Chimaera and Bellerophon. At the end of the room, *1002. *The Nessos Amphora*, still archaic but with many of the techniques later brought to perfection in black- and red-figure work; on the neck, the struggle of Herakles with the Centaur, Nessos; below, the three Gorgons (Medusa has already been beheaded by Perseus) (from the Kerameikos; c 600 BC).

ROOM IV. Three cases inside the door (right) contain miscellaneous finds from the *Heraion of Argos*, both pottery and bronzes, covering many centuries. The large amphora in front comes from a cemetery near the Academy of Plato (c 570 BC). A group of cases opposite the door contains examples of the **Early Black-Figured Style**, several signed by the painter *Sophilos* (590–580 BC): 15499. Fragmentary *Lebes, representing the funeral games of Patroklos, found near Pharsala; another, similarly signed, Marriage of Thetis and Peleus; others from the Acropolis by the 'Gorgon painter'. 12587. Krater, by *Sophilos*, Herakles and Nereus; in both style and subject it recalls the poros pediment from the Acropolis; 991. Loutrophoros from Vourva, by the same; on stand, 1036. Amphora, a late work by *Sophilos* found in the Tumulus at Marathon.

The *Black-Figure* technique, which is first clearly distinguished in Protocorinthian pottery, neglects outline drawing in favour of silhouette. The design is laid on the reddish clay with some addition of incised lines. Later the black is improved to the brilliant Attic glaze, and white (for women's flesh) and dark red paint are added. Decorated patterns are reduced until only the body of the vase has importance, usually adorned with paired subjects on opposing sides.

Continuing clockwise round the room: Vases and terracotta figurines from graves in Boeotia (early 6C); pottery of Corinthian workmanship, 7C and 6C from the Heraion at Perachora (cf. below).

In the last case (left), ivories from the Temple of Artemis Orthia at Sparta (late 8C or early 7C BC) of material imported from Syria or Phoenicia; lead figurines of the same provenance. On the end wall, terracotta metopes from the archaic Temple of Apollo at Thermon in Aetolia, with painted decoration by Corinthian artists (c 630 BC); above, antefixes from the same temple. On the right wall, two cases of Protocorinthian pottery: notable are 295. Bombyle (for pouring a drop at a time) and vases showing Bacchic or Dionysiac scenes; 664 has the earliest known representation of Dionysos (last quarter of the 7C). Model temples in terracotta (8C Geometric) from the Heraion at Perachora. Bronzes and model Archaic house (7C) from the Heraion of Argos. In the centre group of cases: Bronzes from the Sanctuary of Athena of the Brazen House (Chalkioikos), and ivories from the Temple of Artemis Orthia, both at Sparta. Portions of tempera painting on wood from Corinth (520–500 BC).

In ROOM V you are able to compare and contrast works of the mid-6C BC from Attica, the Islands, and Asia Minor.

In the course of this century **Attic Black-Figured Vases** win all the markets from Corinth. New shapes (e.g. the kylix) are invented; old shapes are refined as pottery is increasingly demanded for practical household use by the aristocratic society of the Peisistratid period and for export all over the expanding Greek world. A characteristic technique is the use of incision; mythological scenes are treated with increasing naturalness and humanity; scenes from everyday life become more usual. Known artists of the period include Kleitias (570–560), Phrynos, Nearchos, Lydos, Exekias (540–530), and the 'Amasis Painter'.

Of shapes there was a variety for different uses. To name the most important: at a 6C or 5C banquet wine was mixed in the *krater*, ladled out with the *kyathos*, distributed in the *oinochoë* or *olpe*, and drunk out of a *kylix, kantharos, kotyle, skyphos,* or *rhyton*. A *psykter* served for refrigeration. The *stamnos* and *amphora* were used for storing wine or oil, libations were poured with a *phiale*, scents or oils were carried in a *lekythos, alabastron,* or *aryballos*, water in a *hydria*. A *loutrophoros* was used for lustral waters at weddings and funerals.

Inside the door (left), vases, many with scenes from the myth of Herakles; *404. Lekythos (Rape of Helen), found at Tanagra, by the 'Amasis Painter', c 530 BC; 567. Another with satyr watching a maiden. Beyond is displayed a terracotta model (7C) of a funeral chariot from the Anagyrous necropolis: mourning women surround the bier; the small figure on the pall may represent the spirit of the dead; a rider escorts the procession. On a stand, Attic black-figured lebes: Greeks and Trojans fighting (560 BC). In a case including early-6C Corinthian ware, 559. Amphora foreshadowing the Panathenaic type with flute-player and jockey; 521. Olpe, Akamos in chariot; the horses' names are inscribed.

The centre case and the remaining three cases on the left contain Athenian vases of thematic interest: In the centre, 445 (kylix). Epheboi with instructors; 493 (lekythos). Sacrifice scene; 1054 (kylix). Monkey on a horse's neck; 1055. Aryballos with inscription 'Kealtes painted me, Mnesikleides gave me to Phokis' (c 550 BC). In the second, fragments found on the Acropolis including pieces by major painters—Kleitias, Lydos, Nearchos (a fine piece with Achilles and horses), the Amasis Painter. In the fourth, 2410–7. Plaques (pinax) by *Exekias*, part of a frieze from an erection over a tomb; two Ionian sarcophagi and pottery from Klazomenai (near Smyrna; late and early 6C); Etruscan vases in terracotta or bronze. Finds from the islands, notably 3886. Funeral stele with low relief of a man holding a lance, with inscriptions written in Greek characters but in an unknown language, from Lemnos.

ROOM VI. On the left, Lekythoi with mythological scenes: 488. Death of Aktaion; others depict Theseus and the Minotaur, Thetis and Peleus, etc. In the next case, excellent Attic examples of the *Black-figured style (some, unusually, on a white ground): 1134. Dionysos, Apollo and Hermes; 1124. Theseus slaying the Marathonian bull (?); 550. Peleus bringing the young Achilles to Cheiron. 1045. Oinochoë made by *Xenokles* and painted by *Kleisophos*, Bacchanalian scene (found in the Theatre of Dionysos).

The black-figured ware continues on the right side of the room. In the first case, amid other lekythoi on a yellow ground: 1129. Satyrs torturing Lamia, legendary queen of Libya, realistically violent; 1125. The chariot of Amphiaraos is swallowed up by the earth (490 BC). On a stand, 19312. *Panathenaic Amphora* (prize given at the Games, which remained by tradition in black-figure to the end), with boxing scenes, etc. Further case with material from Acropolis, including that of name painters.

Black-figured decoration reaches its peak c 540 BC and gives way to **Red-Figured Pottery**, in which the decoration is left in the ground colour and the background filled with black (a technique already started by 530). Detail is rendered in thin glazed lines. As complete mastery of draughtmanship is attained, figures lose the archaic stiffness and the art reaches perfection in the time of Pericles. Accessory colours, sparingly used in the 5C, are increasingly added in the 4C. Contemporaneously from c 460 develops white-ground ware (cf. below), with designs at first in black glaze, later in matt polychromy.

The free-standing *Calyx-Krater (Theseus and the Minotaur; by *Syriskos*, c 480 BC), in the centre of the room, begins the display of RED-FIGURED VASES. The case beyond (left) shows early examples: 15002. Alabastron signed by *Pasiades*; 1409. Kylix signed by *Pamphaios*; 1628. Kylix (helmeted hoplite), signed by *Phintias*. On the opposite side of the room, in wall-case: Vases found on the Acropolis, mostly dedicated to Athena by the artists themselves (e.g. pyxis by *Makron*). At end (left), case of Attic red-figured lekythoi.

ROOM VII contains red-figured pottery of mature style and some white-ground vases. On pedestal, 9683. Pelike, Herakles killing the attendants of the Egyptian king Busiris, by the 'Pan Painter' (470 BC); Vase, by *Polygnotos*, representing the poetess Sappho and her pupils. Here, continued in ROOM VIII, begins the unrivalled collection of ***White-Ground Lekythoi**, sepulchral vases from Athens and Eretria, with polychrome designs on a white ground.

The commonest subjects are: Offerings at the Tomb; Prothesis, or Lying-in-State; Burial in the Tomb; and Descent into Hades. In the last the deceased is conducted by Hermes to the Styx, where Charon awaits him with his boat. The purest style coincides with the rebuilding of the Acropolis (450–430), after which follows a period of freer design with the addition of red and purple lines, related to developments in wall-painting. The gems are by the *'Achilles Painter'*, a contemporary of Pheidias, and by contemporaries of *Parrhasios* (420–400). The custom of placing white lekythoi on the funeral stele or in the grave stops at the beginning of the 4C. The references in the 'Ecclesiazusae' of Aristophanes (392 BC) are contemporary with the 'Triglyph Painter' whose work ends the series.

In ROOM VIII, against the end wall is a long new case with examples of two specialised shapes, the *chous* and the *nuptial lebes*, the former used at festivals of Dionysos, the latter in marriage ceremonies.

In ROOM IX are displayed a selection of red-figured vases of various provenance (5C–3C), some of them chosen more for the fascinating themes depicted (Dionysiac, Kabeiroi, etc.) than for fineness of execution. At the far end are a group of mixed red-and white-figured calyx kraters; black-figured Panathenaic amphorae (cf. above; Athena on one side; a scene of the contest for which the vase was a prize, on the other); by the door, the 'Niinnion Pinax' from Eleusis, with cult scenes

The unrivalled ***Numismatic Collection** in the S wing begins with Mycenaean bronze talents in a form recalling the double-axe (cf. Il. xxiii, 852); hoard of iron spits (used as currency) and weighing standard found in the Heraion of Argos in 1894, perhaps those dedicated by Pheidon of Argos (according to Herakleides of Pontus) when he introduced his coinage there after the Lydian model. Among c. 400,000 coins (only a few poorly displayed) all the principal types are represented: incuse in electrum with a heraldic design (7C BC); in gold and silver, bearing a religious motif (gods, etc.) from the mid 6C; the famous Classical 'Owls of Athens'; tetradrachms of Philip of Macedon and Alexander the Great with inscriptions, and a fine range of later portrait types.

The **Epigraphic Collection** (entered through a courtyard from Od. Tósitsa), a classical library in stone, comprises some of the most important historical records found in excavations, including decrees, laws, building records, inventories, treaties, etc. Among them are the *Troezen Stele*, with a text of Themistocles' decree of 480, ordering the evacuation of Athens and the naval preparations which led to the battle of Salamis.

10 From Omónia Square to Ambelókipoi

The whole of this route, which comprises the most important thoroughfares of Athens, is followed by trolley-bus No. 3.

From Omónia Square (Rte 8) as far as Síndagma Square a choice of two routes is offered by Stadium St and University St, which run parallel in a SE direction. Both are one-way streets, the former in the direction described.

ODHÓS STADHÍOU (in 1945–55 renamed Churchill St), one side of the triangle of streets laid out by Kleanthes and Schaubert in 1834, takes its name from its alignment with the stadium (nowadays hidden by the trees of the National Garden). It is a busy street, commercial at the N end, with fashionable hotels and cafés farther S. To the left, between Odd. Santarósa and Arsáki, the offical Printing Press (1836, with many subsequent alterations, restoration in progress) bears a plaque commemorating the centenary (1925) of the death at Pylos of the Italian philhellene Santorre Santarosa. Beyond, the impressive extension to the Arsakeion (see below, Panepistemíou (Venizélou)) incorporates the *Stoa Orféas*. Half-way along Stadhíou, opposite the wide Od. Koraí (left), which affords a sight of the University (see below), the large PLATEÍA KLAFTHMÓNOS opens to the right. During rebuilding operations in this square in 1960–61 a large section of the classical *City Wall* was discovered, part of which is visible in an office building on the NW side. At the W corner is the cruciform **Ayioi Theódori** (3, 7), the most attractive Byzantine church in Athens. Founded in 1049 or 1065 (inscription in W wall), it was entirely rebuilt in stone with brick courses and Cufic decoration in the 12C, as an inscription above the W door records. The belfry is a later addition. The humble two-storeyed building with the balcony on the SE side of the square was *King Otho's Palace* and is now an attractive *Museum of the City of Athens in the 19C* (open Monday, Wednesday, Friday mornings). The building retains its original character, decoration (restored) and furnishings. There is a good collection of prints. Off the S corner of the square is the fashionable modern church of *Ayios Yeoryios*, with the hall of the Parnassos Literary Society opposite.

Farther on, on the corner of Plateía Kolokotrónis is the fine OTE building (A. Metaxas, c 1931). In the triangular Plateia stands an equestrian *Statue of Kolokotronis*, a copy of that in Nauplia by L. Sokhos; the reliefs on the plinth repay examination. Behind is the PALAIA VOULI, a building designed by Boulanger in 1858 to house the National Assembly and finished (with modifications due to the suppression of the Upper House) in 1874. On its steps Theodoros Deliyannis, three times Prime Minister, was assassinated in 1905. In ten rooms on the ground floor is arranged the **National Historical Museum** (closed Monday). The display, which is chronological, includes the ceremonial sword of the Emperor Leo V (813–20); helmets (14–16C) found in the castle at Khalkis; and a painting on wood of the Battle of Lepanto, probably by a Kephalonian eyewitness. Among the extensive collection of portraits, arms, and relics of the War of 1821–28 are objects recovered from Navarino Bay and Byron's helmet and sword; *David d'Angers'*, Girl weeping for the death of Botzaris; and a splendid series of small watercolours of the first five years of Otto's reign by Ludwig Kölnberger. The study of King George I is preserved and royal portraits, photographs, etc. of campaigning monarchs. Temporary exhibitions occupy the upper galleries round the *Chamber*.

Shortly beyond, the street bends to enter the lower side of *Síndagma Square* (Rte 1). Continuation, see below.

If you take the alternative LEOFÓROS ELEFTHERÍOU VENIZÉLOU, formerly and still normally called *Panepistimíou* (University St.), you pass (left) the Art Deco *Rex Theatre* (A. Cassandra and L. Boni, 1937) and (right) the site of the *Arsakeion*, built for a girls' school and training college, founded in 1836 by Apostolos Arsaki (see Rte 15), and until recently used as law courts. The classical building by Kaftandzoglou (1848) which succeeded it is now being restored and will eventually house the Supreme Court. Before the Arsakeion and extending into Stadhíou is its extension (white) built by Ziller (1900). On the other side of the road from the Arsakeion complex, at No. 40 the Mortgage Bank of Greece occupies an attractive Neoclassical building which has been imaginatively extended (A. Kalligas, 1980) upwards and inwards (shopping centre). Farther on an important group of buildings is fronted by formal gardens.

In the centre stands the **University** (Πανεπιστήμιον; 3, 6), built in 1839–42 by the Danish architect Christian Hansen. It is the least disturbing of the neo-Greek buildings, the polychrome decoration having been used with discretion. The handsome Ionic portico is of Pentelic marble; its upper part is frescoed with groups of ancient Greek authors. In front stands a statue of Gladstone, to the left and right of the steps are Capodistrias and the philologist Koraï, and before the façade are the poet Rhigas and the patriarch Gregory.

The University is modelled on the German system and is governed by a Council (Σύγκλητος) and by a Rector (Πρύτανις), elected annually from among the professors. It comprises five faculties (Σχολαί) of theology, law, medicine, philosophy, and science, each under its Curator (Κοσμήτωρ). The teaching staff of 1289 consists of Professors (Καθηγηταί), ordinary and extraordinary (Τακτικοί and Εκτακοι), and of Lecturers (Υφηγηταί). The Students (Φοιτηταί; 44, 438) mostly read law or medicine. Other faculties are provided by the Polytechnic Institute—Connected with the university are scientific museums (at 33 Akadhimías); laboratories and scientific institutes at Goúdhi; a Library (see below); a Botanic Garden, a herbarium at Haïdhári, near Dhafní, several hospitals and clinics, and the Observatory.

To the left is the **National Library** (3, 6), planned by Theophilus von Hansen and built of Pentelic marble in 1887–91 at the expense of P. Vallianos of Kephalonia, whose statue stands in front. The classical style is used with sufficient freedom for the building to look more than a pastiche. Adm. free daily, except holidays, 09.00–13.00 and 17.00–20.00.

In 1903 the contents of the National Library and the University Library were brought together in this building. It contains c 500,000 printed books and 3500 MSS. The 700 MSS from Thessalian convents include two 10C or 11C Gospels, richly illuminated.

On the far side of the University is the **Hellenic Academy** (3, 6), built in 1859, at the expense of Baron Sinas, to the designs of von Hansen. A pastiche in the style of the Erechtheion, it is entirely faced with Pentelic marble, and is adorned with Ionic columns and sculptured pediments. The façade is painted and gilt after the manner of the buildings of classical antiquity, but the effect is 'academic' in every sense of the word.

The colossal figures of Athena and Apollo, which occupy two lofty and unhappy Ionic columns in front, are by the Greek sculptor Drosos, who was responsible also for the figures in the pediment as well as for the seated statues of Plato and Socrates on each side of the entrance and for the statue of Baron Sinas in the hall.

Just beyond the Academy are the *Eye Hospital* (Οφθαλμοιατρείον), designed in a Byzantine style (1847–51) by von Hansen, and the *Roman Catholic Church*, a large Italianate basilica (1870) to a design by Klentze, dedicated to 'St Denis', the composite Western version of the Areopagite. Both buildings were completed by Kaftandzoglou; they face the dignified *Bank of Greece*. Beyond the *Archaeological Society* (founded 1837), *Schliemann's House* (left) may be identified by the inscription on the loggia (ΙΛΙΟΥ ΜΕΛΑΘΡΟΝ: Palace of Troy); its pleasing Renaissance style (by Ziller; 1878) was castigated by the neo-Greek Kaftandzoglou as 'an incurable leprosy'. From 1928 until recently it has housed the Areopagos, or Supreme Court of Appeal, an institution reconstituted in 1834. It has now been restored and will shortly become the *Numismatic Museum*.

The corner with Vourkourestíou (right) is occupied by the enormous MTS building (A. Cassandra and L. Boni, 1928–30) which incorporates Zonar's zakharoplasteion and the Pallas cinema, both of which show the influence of Art Deco in their interiors.

At the NE corner of Síndagma Square you turn left alongside Parliament House into the aristocratic LEOFÓROS VASSILÍSSIS SOFÍAS, lined on the N with embassies and ministries. Hymettos rises ahead.

From the left enters Leofóros Akadhimías (once briefly renamed after Roosevelt), a busy avenue that starts at Canning Sq. (Rte 8) and runs parallel to Panepistemíou (Venizélou). Immediately behind the University, a former hospital (1837, though the wings are later additions) is now well restored as the *Cultural Centre* of the city of Athens. It provides a venue for classes and other cultural events. Beyond, in the Pink Building, the Kostis Palamas building of the University of Athens (entrance from Od. Sína; open Monday–Friday 9–3.30) there is a *Theatre Museum*, with collections illustrating the ancient and modern Greek stage. Here are sets for various plays, the reconstructed dressing-room of Katina Paxinou, and a library. In Od. Kanári, just above its junction with Akadhimías, is the *Film Archive of Greece* (Tainiothíki tis Elládhos), with material relating to the history of the Greek cinema; films are also shown.

You pass the **Benaki Museum** (Rte 7) and (right) the imposing *Officers Club* of the Greek armed services. To the left the fashionable district of Kolonaki (see p. 157) rises on the S slope of Lykabettos. To the right, in the long triangle formed by Vassilíssis Sofías and Leofóros Konstandínou is a large and pleasant park.

The *Byzantine Museum* (4, *8*;) occupies the *Villa Ilissia*, built in a Florentine style in 1848 by Stamatis Kleanthes for the eccentric Sophie de Marbois, duchesse de Plaisance (1785–1854). Here the circle she received included David d'Angers, Edmond About, and Théophile Gautier. The museum was installed in 1930.

You cross a large COURT, in the centre of which is a Phiale, a reproduction of a fountain represented in one of the Daphni mosaics. The mosaic before it is of the 4C, and the font came from the church of the Apostoloi in the Agora. The sculptural fragments to the right are from basilicas of the 5–7C, while those to the left came from 9–15C churches. A secondary court (also right) has a display of architectural members (many decorated) in chronological order. Below the arcades of the wings are (right) mosaics (Heron killing a snake) from the Basilica by the Ilissos (5C), and (left) window panels from houses in Tinos and other Cycladic islands.

The Right Wing is closed at present but will contain the *Loverdos Collection* of ikons.

VESTIBULE. Characteristic examples of early Christian sculpture of the 4–6C: columns, capitals, etc. The doorway in the centre is from the Church of Ay. Dhimitrios in Salonika. Below, Bust of a Priestess (?; 4C) bearing the inscription ΙΣΒΑΡΔΙΑ. To either side, inscribed fragments of a cornice from the Acropolis. Sculptured remains of tombs.—You turn right. ROOM II reproduces a 5–6C **Basilica** in the form of a rectangle divided into nave and aisles by two rows of columns. The nave ends in an apse separated from the *Naos* by transennae and a central free-standing arch. Round the apse is the *Synthronon* (sedilia) with the *Cathedra* (priest's throne) in the centre. Below the marble Altar (*Hiera trapeza*, a square table, with a central circular depression, borne on four columns) is a reliquary in the form of a model sarcophagus sunk into a cruciform depression. To the right of the nave are a plaster copy of an *Ambo* from Salonika and a prothesis table in marble (4C) with sculptured reliefs of animals in a Hellenistic tradition. Round the walls are placed fragments of SCULPTURE from this and other churches. Right Aisle: 92. Christ the Good Shepherd in the guise of a boy (4C; from Old Corinth); 95. Relief of the Nativity, with charming animals; 113. Carved wooden cross. Beneath the arcade: 27. Prothesis table in marble, with reliefs of hunting scenes and Hellenistic heads (4C). Left Aisle: 93. Orpheus surrounded by wild animals; 35. Griffins; epigraphs.

From this aisle opens ROOM III, devoted entirely to **Sculpture** of the main Byzantine period (9–15C). Against the left (W) wall are three marble ikons of the Virgin: in the centre, 148. Virgin as fountain of life, a stiff and formal creation of the 10C or 11C; to either side, 147. Virgin 'Hodegetria' (13–14C), and 149. Virgin 'Orans' (11–12C), each surmounted by a marble arch (152, 154) with representations of the Descent into Hell (from 13C Franco-Byzantine tombs). Round the lower part of the walls are relief slabs of the 9–12C (from iconostaseis), showing typical Byzantine motifs influenced strongly by the Orient: 159. Lion devouring a gazelle. Above those on the N wall are reliefs with mythological subjects, probably used in secular decoration: 176. Hercules and the Erymanthian boar; 177. Gerene, queen of the Pygmies; 178. Centaur playing a lyre. In the centre of the E wall, 150. Marble plaque with a painting on wax of three apostles, from Moni Vlatadon (Salonika). This is framed in (155) a great arch, surmounted by (251) a slab bearing scenes of the Nativity, both of which formed part of the entrance of a Franco-Byzantine church. Flanking them are two capitals, one (217) bearing monograms referring to Irene, the Athenian empress of Constantinople (AD 797–802). The S wall is devoted to reliefs of the Frankish period: 250. St. John the Baptist, from Zante; heads of Venetian doges from Corfu.

ROOM IV reproduces a cruciform **Church**, with a cupola, of 11C Byzantine type. The plan is square with the dome supported on two columns and two pilasters. Between the latter a marble screen (*templon*) separates the nave from the sanctuary. This templon consists of a sculptured architrave (copy of that from the Erechtheion) resting on pillars with capitals, and the lower part is filled in with sculptured panels. In the centre under the dome is a slab with a sculptured eagle (*to omphalion*). The sanctuary floor is decorated in *opus Alexandrinum*. The carvings (of finer workmanship than those in R. III) came from Athenian churches.

From here you enter ROOM V, a reproduction of a **Post-Byzantine church** in a plain square building (of mosque type) with a flat ceiling. The decoration, mostly 18C, is rococo with marked Turkish influence. The *Iconostasis* is of wood, sculptured and gilded, and panelled with painted ikons; it was reconstructed from pieces from Kephalonia and Ithaca. The bishop's *Throne* was brought by refugees from Asia Minor in 1923. The *Epitaphios*, from Kimolos, was used in the procession of the Dormition of the Virgin. From the ceiling hangs the *Choros*, a huge circle of sculptured wooden plaques. Round the walls frescoes from destroyed churches in Atalanta, Delphi, and Athens (Ay. Filothei).

FIRST FLOOR (reached from the portico). The *Vestibule* and the next two rooms contain **Ikons**, the sacred images of the Orthodox religion. Scenes and figures are treated without any concern for natural realism in a formal and hieratic manner. The artist is as far as possible subordinated to an established tradition of representation in an attempt to materialise a spiritual vision of the basic truths of the Christian faith. Thus the ikon is believed to embody an inspired truth which can exalt the worshipper. ROOM II (right) contains the oldest and finest panel paintings, including a number of works of the 14–15C dating from the Palaeologian 'renaissance'.

198. St. George (15C) from Asia Minor; 191. Virgin and Child (14C); 157. Double sided: Crucifixion (12C, with 13C additions), backed by Virgin and Child (15C); 100. Mystical Virgin, holding Christ in both hands; 134. Illustration of the hymn, 'For Thee rejoices' surrounded by Passion scenes (Cappadocian; 16C); 89. St. George (13C), a painted bas-relief in wood from Kastoria; 176. St. Anthony, expressive; 177. Theotokos Hodegetria; *169. Double sided, Crucifixion, fine work of the Palaeologian period; 246. Crucifixion, showing Florentine influence; 145 (mosaic). Theotokos Glykophilousa (14C) from Trilia (Tirilye) on the Sea of Marmara; 2162. Archangel Michael, of the Classical school of Constantinople (14C); 85. St. Marina, combining simple composition and spiritual feeling; 32. Chrysobulon of the Emp. Andronikos II conferring privileges on the diocese of Monemvasia (1301); 188. Christ Pantokrator; 185. Wisdom of God, from Salonika. Case by door: Evangile and Cross of Alexis Comnenus of Trebizond. In the centre cases: Liturgical rotuli, bibles, and documents.

ROOM III. Frescoes from churches no longer extant at Merenda, Tanagra, Lakonia, Naxos etc.; minor arts (pottery flasks and lamps, bread stamps, glass, crucifixes, metal vessels, jewellery).—In ROOM IV (MINOR ARTS) are exhibited objects in metal, wood and ivory, also pottery from the excavation of the basilica of Ay. Dhimitrios at Salonika.—ROOM V. Vestments arranged to show their chronological development, including Coptic work of 5–7C; croziers; *685. Epitaphios of Salonika, magnificent embroidery of the 14C, made, perhaps, in Constantinople.

Adjacent is the imposing **War Museum** (adm. free; closed Monday), erected during the military dictatorship to demonstrate the prowess of Greek arms through the ages. The early galleries are cleverly embellished with reproductions from many Greek museums of sculptured battle scenes, armour, and armaments, as well as helmets and other excavated artefacts and graphic battle plans.—HALL A. Mycenaean to Classical periods.—HALL B. Campaigns of Alexander the Great, with explanatory maps.—HALL Γ. Byzantine wars.—HALL Δ. 'Tourkokratia' (Turkish Occupation) with good prints.—HALL E. The 'Epanastasis' or uprising of 1821–28.—HALL Z. The period 1828–1908 is well documented by contemporary maps.—HALL H. Balkan wars.—HALL Θ. *First World War. 1912–13.—HALL I. 1919–22; Italian War of 1940; and German occupation of 1941.

Greek arms (Middle East, Italy, etc) in the Second World War occupy Galleries of the MEZZANINE FLOOR. Uniforms are displayed in the BASEMENT. On the GROUND FLOOR, Turkish weapons; early firearms, and 19C dress armour.—Outside are a tank and seven aircraft, including a restored Farman biplane of 1912 and a 'Spitfire'; heavy artillery and missiles.

Beyond the next cross-roads (left) a small public garden (café) fronts the *Evanghelismós Hospital*, founded in 1881. A new wing with 483 beds was built in 1983, a gift of John Diamantis Pateras. The benefaction by John Pateras has been marked by the renaming of this section of Od. Alopekís. Behind are grouped the *Marásleion*, which combines the function of secondary school and teachers' training college (original building D. Kallias 1906, girls' college (Αριστοτελής) addition by N. Mitsakis and others c 1930), and the British and American Schools (5, 5).

The **British School of Archaeology** (opened in 1886), though founded primarily to promote the study of Greek archaeology, includes within its province 'research into the language, literature, history, religion, or art of Greece in ancient, mediaeval or modern times'. The results of its studies are published in the 'Annual of the British School at Athens'. The school is celebrated for excavations at Knossos, Perachora, Mycenae and elsewhere. The *Penrose*

Library (c 60,000 vols) is reserved for members of the school, but applications for reader's tickets (fee per session) from students with a suitable letter of introduction will be considered by the Assistant Director. The *Marc and Ismene Fitch Laboratory* was added in 1974. The **American School of Classical Studies** (1882), adjoining, has similar aims and publishes its findings both in its journal 'Hesperia' and in the 'American Journal of Archaeology'. Its most spectacular recent work has been in the Athenian agora, at Corinth, and at Isthmia. The excellent GENNADEION LIBRARY, donated to the school by a former Greek minister in London, is housed, a little higher up the S slope of Lykabettos, in a tasteful building with a central portico of eight columns in antis and two wings. It was erected by the Carnegie Foundation and opened in 1926.—Close by, to the SE, is the formerly monastic *Moní Petráki*, founded by a 17C doctor and now, much restored, given over to a theological seminary. The church (14C) has frescoes of 1719 by George Markos of Argos.

The conspicuous *Hilton Hotel* (5, 7), with a huge incised carving by John Móralis, stands at the important junction of Leofóros Vasilíssis Sofías with Leofóros Konstandínou.

On the corner of the latter street, opposite the side of the Hilton Hotel, is the **Ethniké Pinakothéke** (National Picture Gallery) and **Aléxandros Soútzos Museum** (closed Monday). This museum is devoted to 19 and 20C Greek painting and sculpture. It is not a museum of contemporary Greek art

There are two important collections of contemporary Greek art in the Athens area: the *Vorrés Museum* in Paianía (tel. 664–2639) and the *Pieridhes Museum* in Glifádha (tel. 856–3090). Because of restricted opening hours, it is advisable to check by phone before visiting.

It was established in 1954 by the consolidation of the former National Gallery, founded in 1900, and the Alexandros Soutzos legacy, bequeathed to the Greek nation in 1886 for the founding of a museum of painting. It was the donor's wish that the museum be named after his father, Alexandros Soutzos. Also bequeathed were the Soutzos numismatic and art collections. This endowment lay unexploited until 1954. Construction finally started in 1964 and the museum was inaugurated in 1976.

The permanent collection consists primarily of 19C and 20C Greek art, although there are European acquisitions, for instance a considerable collection of prints and engravings by Dürer, Goya and Manet (not on public view). Certain rooms, such as the entrance hall, the main mezzanine (off to the left of the entrance) and the lower floor, are devoted to temporary exhibitions. The Pinakotheke programme includes concerts, musical recitals, dance performances, etc.

From the high-ceilinged hall, visitors pass across an enclosed ramp, where a series of paintings donated by 20C French masters, including Picasso, Albert Marquet, Utrillo and Picabia, are hung. These were gifts to the Greek people, commemorating their liberation from the German occupation. A sculpture by *Réné Magritte*, The Therapist (1967), is also exhibited here. The ramp leads to the main wing.

The first floor is devoted to 20C painting. The section opposite the stairs is the *N. Khatzikyriakos-Ghikas Room*. This artist was born in Athens in 1906, and is considered to be the main exponent of the Cubist style in Greece. The exhibit represents a good retrospective of his work, which dates from 1927 (Open Door) to the present. Oddly, Khatzikyriakos-Ghikas passed through a surrealistic stage (Barracks; 1927) prior to his Cubism. His most fecund and significant years were the 1950s, as seen in Athenian Balcony (1955) and Sunflower and Trellis (1956).

Across from the Ghikas room is the section comprising Greek painting from 1900 to c 1950, a period characterised by a pluralism of expression. In contrast to the 19C, when most Greek artists culled their inspiration from the Munich School, the 20C art scene in Greece had essentially three sources: the Byzantine and Classical heritage, the folk and popular tradition, and the contemporary European mainstream.

Some of the more significant artists of this period are: *Alekos Kontoglou* (? 1898–1965), who came to Greece from Asia Minor in 1922. He was one of the first artists in Greece to draw directly on his Byzantine heritage. Much of his early painting of secular themes was executed in the Byzantine manner (see the wall paintings at his home in Kypriadi; 1927). In his later work he concentrated primarily on ecclesiastical decoration and hagiography. *Constantinos Maleas* (1879–1928) and *Spiros Papaloukas* (1892–1957) demonstrated the initial influences of Parisian art in Greece. This can be seen particularly in their treatment of light and of the flat surfaces of colour as, for instance, in Maleas' Monemvasia. *George Bouzianis* (1885–1959), the leading exponent of Expressionism in Greece, studied in Paris and subsequently in Munich. Curiously, his palette differs from that of the German Expressionists—his is dark and sombre. *Yannis Tsarouchis* (1910–89) was influenced both by the popular tradition and by modern trends which he combined to create original paintings with a vital local character (see, for instance, his Cafeneion 'To Neon'; 1935). In his early work *Yannis Moralis* (1916–) drew on Classical prototypes for the human figure (see Mourning). His later, more abstract work again shows Classical derivation in the innate balance and equilibrium of composition. *Nikos Engonopoulos* (1910–86), also a poet, was the most important representative of Surrealism in Greece (see Theatre). His bold bright colours produce a more joyous version of Surrealism. *Alexos Kontouplos* (1905–75) is important as the painter who introduced abstract art to Greece after 1950. However, his later paintings were never entirely abstract—some recognisable form or image was usually included. *Yannis Spyropoulos* (1912–), Greece's foremost abstract artist, won international acclaim after being awarded the Unesco prize at the 1960 Venice Biennale. His predominantly dark and heavily textured paintings are flat, without spatial depth, and have well-structured and tectonic compositions.

Visitors wishing to see the collection in chronological order should start at the far end of Floor 2 and make their way back towards the entrance.

The mezzanine between the first and second floors has a small collection of works by the self-taught primitive painter *Theophilos* (1878–1934), now widely and highly acclaimed. Of interest is the manner in which this artist interprets religious, popular and mythological themes. His naive and detailed style is replete with narrative.

The rooms to the right on the second floor are devoted to Greek 19C painting. The last room in this section has a heterogeneous collection of post-Byzantine icons of the Cretan-Italian and Ionian schools, and *El Greco's* Concert of Angels (detail), St. Francis of Assisi, and a Crucifixion. Also exhibited is *Eugène Delacroix's* small but exquisite painting, A Greek Warrior (1856).

The 19C section can be divided roughly into two groups: the Greek mainstream and genre, comprised mainly of historical, seascape and portrait painting. THE GREEK MAINSTREAM: the most important painters are N. Lytras (1832–1904), N. Gyzis (1842–1901) and G. Iakovides (1853–1932). The first two, educated in Germany, reflect a style of painting influenced directly by the Munich school. Gyzis, in particular, emulates the German Romantic movement in choice of subject, sobre palette and, often, a turbulent brushstroke (Destruction at Psara; 1878). Lytras excelled when painting scenes and characters from the café, the street, and family life. His work is altogether lighter and less anguished than that of Gyzis. Iakovides paints in the tradition of Lytras but with more impressionistic results in both colour and execution (Children's Concert; 1900).

GENRE. *Historical*: T. Vryzakis (1814–78) is the main interpreter of this epic style, depicting scenes from the Greek War of Independence. Of particular interest to English visitors is the painting of Lord Byron at Messolongi (1861). *Seascapes*: the chief exponents in the latter part of the 19C were C. Volanakis (1837–1907), I. Altamouras (1852–78) and V. Khatzis (1870–1915), who are represented by an ample collection of interesting and often lovely seascapes and admirably executed naval battles. *Portraits*: late 18C portraits in the collection are by N. Koutouzes (1741–1813) and N. Kantounis (1767–1834), both from the Ionian island of Zante. Other portraitists represented are E. Economou (1823–1887) and N. Kounellakis (1828–69). These indifferent and somewhat dour depictions show the influence of Italian painting, via the Ionian school, in both manner and mood.

On the same floor, to the left of the ramp, is the *G. Parthenis Room*, which holds a comprehensive retrospective exhibit of this Alexandria-born artist (1878–1967) who, in effect, bridged Greek 19C and 20C painting. His influence on Greek painting has been considerable: he established the Impressionist style and introduced Art Nouveau elements. He painted many themes—religious, mythological, and landscape. His later painting, influenced by Byzantine art, has a spiritual and idealist character (Musicians; 1930–35).

19C and 20C Sculpture. To visit the sculpture section, return to the main entrance and take the stairs down through the main mezzanine to the lower floor. These lead to the Sculpture Garden and Sculpture Hall. The Garden, devoted to 20C sculpture, is the most attractive section of the exhibit. Amongst an otherwise all-Greek collection is *Rodin's* beautiful bronze, The Prodigal Son (1909). Noteworthy are Zalonga, by G. Zongolopoulos (1903–), Acrocorinth (1965) by K. Loukopoulos (1908–), and the abstract constructivist sculptures by Philolaos (1923–) and K. Koulentianos (1918–). (The last two live and work in Paris.) The recently opened Sculpture Hall is a long, narrow, elegant building, very much like a classical Greek stoa, with a glass façade allowing the visitor to see the exhibits from the garden, and *vice versa*. On entering the building, the left-hand section houses the 19C collection—including work by Y. Halepas (1851–1937)—while the right-hand section holds the 20C material. Probably the most important 19C sculptors are P. Prosalentis (1784–1837), who worked chiefly in marble (particularly lovely is his Plato; 1815), D. Philippotis (1834–1920), and T. Vroutos (1843–1909), who also worked in marble. While Prosalentis preferred realistic themes taken from daily life, Philippotis and Vroutos drew on subjects from mythology (e.g. Echo; 1887). Vroutos' work is executed in the tradition of classical sculpture except perhaps when he indulged in sculptural acrobatics and produced precariously balanced works like The Spirit of Copernicus (1877).

Y. Halepas is considered to be one of Greece's most important and creative sculptors. Among his commissions were several tombstones, of which the best known is The Sleeping Maiden in the Athens First Cemetery. At the Pinakotheke the collection of small clay works such as Secret (1925) and Aphrodite (1931), in which the subject consists of a head or bust combined with a small figurine, reveal a strange co-existence of clumsiness and vitality—in effect, a schizophrenic co-existence. (The sculptor was mentally disturbed and spent several periods in hospital.) The small clay works by Halepas have an implicit inner tension which imbues them with a forceful presence.

Most noteworthy amongst the 20C sculptors in the sculpture gallery are: M. Tombros (1889–1974), who worked in marble and bronze; M. Lelakis (1907–), whose interesting wooden abstract forms are labyrinthine and free (Rhythm; 1959–74); C. Kapralos (1909–) (Horse's Head); A. Apartis (1889–1972); A. Apergis (1909–86), and K. Andreou (1917–) who, like the Greek-Parisians mentioned above, makes abstract constructivist sculpture from welded metal sheets.

Nearly 1km farther out, on the left, is the imposing *Hall of the Friends of Music*, begun in 1976 and nearing completion (1991). Just before this, a lane leads off (left) into the *Párko Eleftherías*, with an Arts Centre (Κέντρο Τεχνών: exhibitions; pleasant café). It also contains a *Museum of Eleftherios Venizelos*, with personal effects, photographs, documents and books related to the statesman, whose statue stands in the park. Next is the *United States Embassy*, an imposing building in marble and glass attractively landscaped, by Walter Gropius and H. Morse Payne Jr (1960–61). The road continues to *Ambelókipoi*, where it meets Leofóros Alexándras, a dual highway from Pedhíon Areos (Rte 8). A little farther on below the 'Athens Tower' (Pírgos Athenón) the road to Marathon and the Mesogeion divides from Kifissia Avenue (Rte 17B).

11 Lykabettos

The ascent of Lykabettos, which takes c 45 minutes from Sindagma Squre, is best made in the early morning or late afternoon when the superb view is clearest.

A theatre, on the N side of the hill is a venue for plays and concerts in the summer. The theatre can be reached by road from Od. Sarandapíkhou, the *peripherique* of Likavittós.

Approaches. From N, by any turnings (steep) leading S from Od. Asklipíou (buses from centre, Panepistemíou, to Ippokrátous terminal (ΙΠΠΟΚΡΑΤΟΥΣ) (025, 026 etc.). From S, on foot by stepped path from top of Od. Loukianoú; by funicular railway (easiest) from the top of Od. Ploutárchou (terminus of bus 023 from centre, Akadhimías via Kolonáki Square); by taxi to theatre and shorter climb (stepped path). Other less formal paths may be found through the woods.

There is a café/restaurant on the summit (not cheap); another (pleasant) lower down on the SW approach (cf. below).

Lykabettos (Λυκαβηττός; in modern Greek parlance *Likavittós*; 4, 4) is the highest (277m) of the hills of Athens, and the S termination of the Anchesmos range. Although perhaps the most conspicuous feature of the Athenian landscape, it gets its only classical reference in the 'Clouds' of Aristophanes. Formerly the NE surburban limit of the city, it is now an island in a sea of houses. The slopes are wooded, thanks to the Philodhasiko Society of Greece, and many pleasant approaches by shady but sometimes steep paths may be made, especially from the S side.

According to legend, Lykabettos was a rock which Athena was carrying to Athens to form a bulwark for her citadel; in her surprise at hearing that, in defiance of her injunction, Aglauros and Herse had looked into the chest containing Erechtheus, she dropped it.

Ascending from the N (by Asklipíou etc.) you can see, in Od. Dhidhótou (named after Ambroise Firmin Didot, the French publisher and philhellene) the

École Française d'Athènes, the oldest archaeological school in Greece, founded in 1846 and removed to this site in 1874. Edmond About was a student in 1851–53. The French School has explored sites in Asia Minor as well as in Greece where it is perhaps most celebrated for its work at Delphi and Delos. Its journal 'Bulletin de Correspondance Hellénique' is of the first archaeological importance. Just behind rises *Skhistí Pétra*, a curiously shaped rock (called by the Germans *Frog's Mouth*) easily climbed in a few minutes from its S side. Behind it ascends a road built to serve a *Wireless Station* of the Royal Hellenic Air Force which occupied the W slopes of Lykabettos until 1961. In 1941 this was the Operations Centre of the Greek Air Force and formed King George's last H.Q. on the mainland before he retired to Crete in the face of the German advance. Here also are sited the ceremonial cannon used for royal salutes.

On the S the funicular railway, in a tunnel c 200m long and opened in 1965, provides direct access to the summit.

You are better advised to make on foot the steep approach from the SW. From the Benáki Museum (Rte 7) the short Od. Koubári leads to the PLATEÍA KOLONAKÍOU, centre of the most fashionable district of Athens. On the right is the *British Council*, with an excellent library with lending facilities for residents only.

From the SE corner of the square, at 4 Od. Neofítou Doúka, reached via Od. Kapsáli, is the headquarters of the N.P. Goulandris Foundation and the **Museum of Cycladic and Ancient Greek Art** (closed Sunday and Tuesday), opened in 1986 by Mrs Dolly Goulandris, in memory of her husband. The museum has fine objects of ancient art from prehistoric to Roman times and is particularly rich in marble figurines and other material of the Cycladic Early Bronze Age. GROUND FLOOR. Explanatory panels; a few Early Cycladic items including important pieces purchased in 1990 at the disposal of the Erlenmeyer collection in London—one may be a cult statue; shop; garden and cafeteria; FIRST FLOOR. Cycladic (mostly Early Bronze Age) pottery, marble vases and figures (mostly of modest size but one 1.40m high), metal weapons and vessels, some obsidian; SECOND FLOOR. Material of prehistoric (non-Cycladic) to Hellenistic periods—pottery, terracottas, jewellery and other metalwork, glass; THIRD FLOOR. Temporary exhibitions (1991: 'Naxos in the 3rd millennium BC'); FOURTH FLOOR. The C. Politis collection of prehistoric and classical art.

From the NE corner of the plateia a short ascent leads to the *Dhexamení*, or reservoir of the old Town Aqueduct, a Roman work begun by Hadrian and completed by Antoninus Pius. It was recommissioned in 1840, restored in 1869, and again in 1929, when the ancient aqueduct leading from Tatoï was brought up to date. It is now ancillary to the reservoir on Tourkovouni, served by the Marathon pipeline. Here at Epiphany takes place the ceremony of the Blessing of the Waters. From the top of Od. Loukianoú a zigzag path, passing near the chapel of *St. Isidore* (16C), mounts to the little 19C chapel of *Ayios Yeoryios* on the summit, which commands a magnificent *Panorama of Athens and Attica. The Acropolis is however more effectively seen from the steps (café) on the way up, where its matchless marble ruins stand out against the sea.

12 New Pháleron and Piraeus

Approaches from Athens. BY RAIL, by the Piraeus Electric Railway (EHΣ) from *Omonia*, 11km in 20 minutes. Trains every 7 minutes; intermediate stations: *Monastirion* (2, 8), *Thission* (2, 8), *Petrálona*, *El. Venizélou/Tavrós*, *Kallithéa*, *Moskháton*, *Néon Fáliron*.—The State Railway lines do not carry local passengers.

BY ROAD. The shortest route to Piraeus (9km) is by the old Od. Piraiós, followed by bus No. 049 (from Omonia Sq.), which traverses the dreary industrial suburbs of Petrálona and Réndis. The EHΣ (green) bus (No. 040 from Sindagma Sq.) takes Leofóros Singroú, then diverges via *Kallithéa* to reach Phaleron Bay at Tzitzifiés. Leofóros Ilissoú follows the course of the Ilissos to link the Stadium with Kallithéa.—The pleasantest route (11km) is by Leofóros Singroú and Phaleron Bay, described below.

From the Olympieion (Rte 7), two of whose columns dominate the head of the road, LEOFÓROS ANDRÉAS SINGROÚ (7, 7), an imposing dual highway named after the philanthropist Singros (1830–99) runs straight to the coast. You soon pass the *Fix Brewery* (now derelict), scene of sharp fighting in 1944, then cross the Ilissos and its boulevard (Rte 7) by a viaduct with good retrospective views of Philopappos Hill and the Acropolis.—2·5km *Ayios Sostis* (left), a church built by Queen Olga as a thank-offering after an abortive attempt on the life of George I in 1897. Running between Kallithea and the large refugee suburb of *Nea Smirni* (New Smyrna), and passing (left) the *Intercontinental*, *Ledra Marriot* and *Athens Chandris Hotels* and the *Planetarium*, the avenue reaches Phaleron Bay at (6km) the *Racecourse*. You turn right along the shore, now recovering from former squalour and pollution by the main sewer outfall from Athens and with much land recently reclaimed from the sea.—7km *Tzitzifiés* (Hotels, C) is noted for tavernas with bouzouki music.

PHALERON BAY, a shallow and exposed roadstead, stretches from the peninsula of Munychia on the W to the headland of Old Phaleron (Rte 13) on the E. Here until the beginning of the 5C BC the Athenians beached their triremes, and the gently sloping sands were traditionally held to be the departure place of Theseus for Crete and of the Athenian contingent to Troy. In 1929–39 flying-boats of Imperial Airways en route to India and Australia called at a station opposite the racecourse; an earlier seaplane service of Società Aero-Espresso Italiana from Brindisi to Istanbul had called since 1926. Warships of the Greek Navy or of visiting fleets may often be seen anchored offshore.

8km **Néon Fáliron**, or *New Phaleron* (*Hotels* C, and others), founded in 1875 as a seaside resort. It lies along the low sandy shore, anciently marshy and called *Halipedon*, on either bank of the Kifissos, the position of which is now marked only by a street name. The *Anglo-French Cemetery*, behind the Karaïskakis Stadium, N of the railway station, contains monuments to sailors who died in Piraeus in 1855–59. The area is now dominated by the vast (126m × 28m) and impressive boat-shaped *Stadium of Peace and Friendship*, completed in 1985. Set in 3·25 hectares of land, with tennis courts, marina, etc., the building comprises an indoor stadium with a seating capacity of 16,000, concert and recreation halls and facilities for all indoor sport.—From New Phaleron you can follow the railway and Od. Skilítsi to meet the old Athens–Piraeus road (Pl. 8) or, by Od. Tzavéla and Plateía Ippodhamías, reach the central harbour of (11km) *Piraeus*.

PIRAEUS (Πειραιεύς), in modern parlance *Piraiévs* (commonly accusative Peiraiá), is now, as in classical times, the port of Athens. The town (196,389 inhab.), which owes its rebirth to the choice of

Athens as capital in 1834, is with its suburbs the third largest in Greece (476,304). It is the seat of a bishop and an important naval and commercial shipping base. Piraeus proper occupies a rocky spur-shaped promontory or double peninsula, joined to the mainland at the NE by a stretch of low ground. The SW part of the peninsula, called *Akti*, is joined to the E part by an isthmus which separates the Great Harbour (*Kantharos*) from the circular Pashalimáni (the ancient name *Zea* is also commonly used). Farther E, below the hill of Kastella (*Munychia*) is the still smaller harbour of Tourkolímano. The spine of the peninsula divides the modern town into the more fashionable quarter to the S and E, well supplied with restaurants and places of amusement, and a commercial sector surrounding the main harbour. Beyond this the mainland extensions, including *Dhrapetsóna* and *Níkaia* form the most important manufacturing centre in Greece, with more than a hundred factories, cotton mills, distilleries, soap works, and metal foundries.

The modern town follows the rectangular plan of its ancient predecessor, of which visible remains are scanty and, save to the professional archaeologist, unrewarding. The visitor is better employed in a tour of the harbours, where the interest is equally divided between the seafaring bustle of a busy Mediterranean port, the considerable remains of ancient installations, and the varied views of the Saronic Gulf from the indented coastline. On summer evenings Piraeus is agreeably cooler than Athens.

A recent study of the ancient city is R. Garland, 'The Piraeus', 1987; new discoveries can be traced through 'Archaeological Reports' (see Bibliography, above).

Boat Quays. Akti Poseidhónos (Pl. 3) to Aegina, Poros, Idhra, and Spetsai; **Plateía Karaískákis** (Pl. 3) for hydroplanes to Aegina.—**Pashalimáni** (Pl. 11) for hydroplanes to Poros, Idhra, Spetsai and the Peloponnese.

Railway Station. ΕΗΣ (Pl. 3), for Athens and Kifissia.

Restaurants. Along waterfront at Tourkolímano (seafood, some expensive), also on Akti Themistokléous.

Post Office (Pl. 7). Od. Fílonos.

Tourist Police. At corner of Akti Miaoúlis and Filellínon.

Buses. From Electric Railway Station; 20 (circular) to *Kastélla* and *Tourkolímano*; also to *New Phaleron, Custom House*. From Plateía Koraí (Pl. 7); **040** (green) to *Athens* (Filellínon); 904/905 (circular) to *Akte*. From Leofóros Ethnikís Antistáseos (Pl 7) to *Athens* (Omonia; **049**), *Glifadha* (**149**) and suburbs. From Plateía Karaískákl (Pl. 3) to Piraeus suburbs.

Shipping Offices. *Adriatica, Greek Line, Turkish Maritime Lines*, all TANPY Building, 19 Aktí Miaoúlis; *Kavounides*, 33 Aktí Miaoúlis; *Karageorgis*, 10 Aktí Kondíli; *Epirotiki*, 87 Aktí Miaoúlis; *Hellenic Mediterranean Lines*, Electric Station Building; *American Export Lines*, 33 Aktí Miaoúlis; *Mediterranean Sun Lines*, 5 Sakhtoúri; *Libra Maritime*, 65 Aktí Miaoúlis.

Steamer and Hydroplane Services (less frequently in winter; quays see above). Argossaronikos to *Aegina* (2–3 times per hour), continuing (many times daily) to *Methana* and *Poros*, and (3–4 times daily) to *Idhra, Ermioni*, and *Spetsai*; twice weekly to *Leonidhion*.

Car Hire. *Hertz*, 9–11 Ay. Nikólaos, facing Custom House (Pl. 6).

Festival. *Blessing of the Waters* at Epiphany (6 January).

History. *Piraeus*, originally an island, was still isolated in archaic times by the marshes of Halipedon. While Corinth and Aegina remained the principal maritime powers the Athenians kept their triremes on the beach at Phaleron Bay, which was in full view of the city while Piraeus was not. Hippias began to fortify Munychia c 510 BC. When Themistocles created an Athenian fleet of 200 ships, he chose Piraeus as its base, beginning in 493 BC the ambitious scheme of fortification which was to include the whole of the double peninsula and the approaches from Athens. By the outbreak of the Peloponnesian War (431 BC), the three Long Walls (see below) were complete. At its close the Phaleric Wall had fallen into decay, and the conditions of peace offered by Lysander after the defeat of Athens at Aegospotami (405) included the destruction of the remaining Long Walls as well as the walls of both cities. The population of Piraeus at the zenith of Athenian power consisted largely of Metics (μέτοικοι), or resident aliens, who controlled much of its manufacture and trade, and introduced strange cults, giving the city its cosmopolitan and radical character. Thrasyboulos sought the support of the citizens of Piraeus in 403, launching his *coup d'état* against the Thirty from Munychia. Munychia became the chief seat of the Macedonian garrison which controlled Athens in 322–229 save for brief intervals (liberation by Demetrios Poliorketes, 307–294). By 200 BC, when Philip V of Macedon again attacked Athens, the Long Walls had been abandoned, though Piraeus itself (its walls repaired by Eurykleides and Mikion, c 306–298) was flourishing as a commercial centre, and the Roman garrison used it as a base. In 86 BC Sulla ravaged the city, destroying the arsenal and the docks; but though Strabo dismisses it as an unimportant village, it seems to have revived early in the Imperial era, and could still serve as a base for Constantine's fleet in AD 322. After Alaric's raid in 396 it lost all importance. In 1040 Harold Hardrada, the Viking, in the service of the Byzantine emperor, disembarked at Piraeus to suppress an Athenian insurrection. In medieval times the town was known as *Porto Leone* (cf. below) and by the Turks as Aslanliman. When, in 1834, Athens became the capital of Greece hardly a house stood in Piraeus. Resettled by islanders with the trading instincts of the ancient Metics, it grew rapidly through the 19C, playing a large part in the revival of Athens. The population which did not exceed 4000 in 1840, rose from 11,000 in 1870 to 75,000 in 1907. The refugee settlement of 1922 increased it threefold. In 1854–59 Piraeus was occupied by an Anglo-French fleet to prevent Greek nationalists embarrassing Turkey, an allied power in the Crimean War. In the Second World War the port was put out of action and 11 ships sunk on the first night of the German air attack (6 April 1941) when the moored 'Clan Fraser' carrying 200 tons of TNT, and two other ammunition ships, blew up. Fully restored, it provides a port of call for most steamship lines operating in the E Mediterranean and is the focus of Greek services to the islands.—The opening scene of Plato's *Republic* is set in Piraeus, at the house of the aged Kephalos.

Defences of Ancient Piraeus. The LONG WALLS, sometimes called the 'Legs' (τὰ σκέλη), formed part of the original fortification scheme of Themistocles. The *First* or *Northern Long Wall* (7km long) ran from Athens to Piraeus, the *Second* or *Phaleric Long Wall* (6·5km long) from Athens to the E end of Phaleron Bay. The walls were completed c 456 BC. (Thucydides I, 108). A *Third* or *Southern Long Wall*, parallel with the first and of the same length, was built by Kallikrates under the direction of Pericles to guard against the possibility of a surprise landing in Phaleron Bay. The Northern and Southern Long Walls, starting from two points in the outer wall of the Piraeus, converged to within 183m of each other and then ran parallel to the region of Pnyx hill (cf. Rte 3). Between them ran a road. A second road, probably the 'carriage-road' (ἁμαξιτός) mentioned by Xenophon (Hellenica II, 4, 10), ran outside the Northern Long Wall. The direct modern road (Od. Piraiós, above) follows the Northern Long Wall for much of its course, the Electric Railway the Southern Long Wall. Sections of both can be seen between the Karaïskákis Stadium and Od. Piraiós (left) and in front of the Klostoufantourgoú School.

The Themistoclean *City Wall* guarded all three harbours; fortified entrances by each, forming part of the circuit, were probably closed by chains. The W half of Akte was excluded from the defences which crossed the peninsula from NW to SE. On the landward quarter they followed the solid land behind the Halai marsh, and on the side nearest Athens the contour of the ground, making a circuit of 60 stadia (Thucydides II, 13). The rebuilding of the walls is commonly credited to Konon (Xenophon, Hell. IV, 8), though an inscription has shown that this was started before his victory at Knidos and the work was probably finished only after 346 (Demosthenes XIX, 125). The defences were shortened on the N side by carrying the wall across the Choma (see below) to Eëtioneia, but the circuit was extended round the whole of Akte.

Under Pericles the *City* itself was laid out by Hippodamos of Miletus on a chessboard plan with a spacious agora at the centre. Special attention was paid to the needs of the fleet, no less than 1000 talents being spent on the construction of *Ship-sheds* and dry docks. Demosthenes considered the ship-sheds of Piraeus worthy of mention in company with the Parthenon and the Propylaea. In 330–322 BC they numbered 372, of which 196 were in Zea, 82 in

Asklepios treats a patient. Relief sculpture from Piraeus

Munychia, and 94 in Kantharos. This corresponds roughly with the strength of the Athenian navy under Lycurgus (c 400 ships), who completed the work by the construction in the Harbour of Zea of a NAVAL ARSENAL or SKEUOTHEKE (Σκευοθήκη), designed by the architect *Philo* in 346–329 BC (see below).

Od. Skilítsi and Od. Ippodhamías (cf. above) converge at the PLATEÍA IPPODHÁMOU, with a busy hardware market, then roads lead W to the Electric Railway Station and SW to the main harbour.

Just off Skilítsi, c 90m E of Plateía Ippodhámou, are the remains of the *Asty Gate*, where the Hamaxitos, or 'carriage-road' (see above), entered the city. Its Themistoclean round towers were later rebuilt on a square plan. Many neighbouring buildings incorporate classical masonry from the Long Walls. A little to the E are foundations of a second gate and of a sanctuary. Near the Merchant Navy School in Od. Evanghelistrías, and in Od. Kódhrou, further sections of the defences can be traced.

At the heart of maritime Piraeus at the E angle of the **Great Harbour** stands the *Dhimarkhíon* (Pl. 7), or Town Hall, in front of which is a clock, a local landmark ('to rolóï'). Immediately in front along Akti Poseidhónos moor the small steamers that ply to ports in the Saronic Gulf. To the SW along AKTI MIAOÚLI extend the liner berths (adm. restricted) with the *Passenger Terminal* and *Custom House* (Pl. 6). Here and in PLATEÍA KARAÏSKÁKIS (Pl. 3), to the N beyond the lively Bazar, are situated the offices of shipping companies. From the open quay alongside the square and the mole to the W depart ships plying to the Peloponnese and the Greek islands, as well as those making calls at Greek ports before continuing to Italy.

The modern harbour corresponds very nearly to the ancient KANTHAROS ('goblet'), which was divided, then as now, between naval and commercial shipping. To the navy was reserved the shore of Eëtioneia (see below) and the N shore of Akti beyond the custom house (then a temple site); these locations are still favoured by warships. The *Emporion*, or commercial quay, coincided with the modern berths along Akti Miaoúlis and Plateía Karaïskákis (cf. above). A jetty, called the *Diazeugma*, divided it into two, roughly where the Passenger Terminal now stands. Five stoas lined the quay, traces of one of which have been found c 140m from the quay SE of the custom house; other vestiges of the Emporion are visible in the foundations of the church of *Ayia Triadha* (Pl. 7). The short S mole projecting from Plateía Karaïskákis corresponds to the ancient *Choma*, the point of assembly where, on the eve of naval expeditions, the trierarchs had to report to the Council of 500 (when the first three to arrive were rewarded). The Trierarchy, instituted by Themistocles, was a form of taxation whereby the state provided the bare hulls of new warships, while the duty of fitting the galley, launching it and training the oarsmen, fell by rotation on the richest citizens. The Trierarch sailed with his ship and was responsible for its repair during his term of office.—The ancient harbour was guarded after 337 BC by two moles, extending respectively from the S end of Eëtioneia (still surviving in part) and from the N shore of Akte, leaving an entrance, 50m wide, guarded by towers or lighthouses. Nowadays an *Outer Harbour*, beyond this, formed by the construction of two breakwaters in 1902, shelters naval stores and yards, coal wharves, and a dry dock (cf. below).

NORTH-WESTERN QUARTER. Such vestiges of classical buildings as remain on the peninsula of Eëtioneia are scattered among factories, railway sidings, and somewhat rough popular quarters. Enthusiastic antiquaries may take Akti Kalimasíou from Plateía Karaïskákis (taxi advisable, but driver will need guidance; tram or bus to Larissa Station) and, leaving on the right the *Stations* of the Piraeus Electric Railway and S P A P, follow the dreary Akti Kondhíli behind the wharves that line the inner harbour, or *Limin Alon*. Anciently a miry lagoon called the *Halai* or *Kophos Limen* (κωφὸς λιμήν; 'silent harbour'), this is a relic of the marshes that once surrounded Piraeus. The ancient fortifications may at first have run to shoreward of it; later they crossed its entrance. Beyond *Larissa Station* of the State Railway extends the peninsula of **Eëtioneia** ('Ηετιώνεια), called by Thucydides 'the mole of Piraeus'. This peninsula was included in the Themistoclean circuit, which enclosed also the inlet of Krommydaron. Theramenes in 411 BC gave Eëtioneia separate fortifications but tore them down later owing to a change of policy (cf. Thuc. VIII, 92). The 4C walls enclosed only the peninsula. Railway sidings cross the road (traces, 3–3·6m thick, of the *Wall of Konon*) to enter the modern quays which have obliterated the ancient shipbuilding yards (νεώρια) and slipways (νεώξοικοι). Beyond the rails (right), at the entrance to Od. Monímon Dhexamenón, is a little hill (16m) on which are the remains of the 4C *Aphrodision*, a sanctuary dedicated to Aphrodite Euploia, goddess of navigation. This was closely ringed by Konon's wall, of which the *Aphrodision Gate* (excavated by the French School in 1887) can be traced just to the NW; its towers are more than 9m in diameter. The *Inlet of Krommydaron*, now the Monimai Dhexamenai (dry docks), yielded five marble altars in 1866, one with a Phoenician inscription. To the W are some vestiges of the *Themistoclean Wall*, slighter than that of Konon. Beyond, in the suburb of *Dhrapetsóna*, an obelisk in the Anastáseos cemetery commemorates French naval dead of the First World War.

From the Town Hall Leofófros Yeoryíou tou Prótou leads shortly to the *Tinan Gardens*, laid out in 1854 by a French admiral. Opposite stands the CATHEDRAL (Pl. 7; *Ayia Triadha*), gutted in 1944 and rebuilt in 1958–62 in its former style. On the corner of Od. Fílonos in July 1959 workmen digging a drain suddenly uncovered a bronze hand; careful excavation brought to light the unique collection of statuary now in the Piraeus museum. It is believed that this formed part of Sulla's loot, stored away in 86 BC in a commercial stoa for shipment to Rome and overlooked. Farther on in Plateía Koraï is the *Municipal Theatre*. The broad Leofóros Iróön Polytekhníou leads SW along the spine of the peninsula, passing between pleasant gardens; streets at right angles lead (right) to Akti Miaoúlis and (left) to Pashalimáni (see below). On the right, between Od. Skouzé and Od. Fillellínon is an archaeological park.

Descending Od. Khariláou Trikoúpi (left) towards Pashalimáni, you come to (Pl. 6) the newly refurbished (1981) **Archaeological Museum**, with interesting material, excellently displayed. You enter up steps from the street. (The rooms are unnumbered.) In the VESTIBULE, a statue of Hermes of the 2C AD. Through the vestibule, you enter a HALL with fine *Neoclassical reliefs of Amazonomachies from Kifissia, c AD 200. Lion stele from Moschato, 400 BC. A gallery to the right, off the hall, contains funerary urns and stelai, also Roman sculpture, including Heads of the Emperors Claudius (1163) and

Trajan (276). Beyond the main hall, the last room downstairs contains a massive funerary monument from Kallithea with relief (Amazonomachy, Zoömachy) and free-standing commemorative sculptures, c 400 BC.

The Piraeus Kouros, c 500 BC

Returning to the main hall, you ascend the stairs to the UPPER FLOOR. To the left, off the vestibule, a large gallery has funerary stelai of the 5 and 4C BC, also an East Greek archaic kore of cylindrical shape (c 580 BC). Beyond the vestibule, you will find, in the small HALL, Roman herms. Through the hall, you approach the superb ***Piraeus Kouros**, the oldest known hollow-cast bronze statue of large scale, found with the clay filling and iron supports preserved inside. It was almost certainly a cult statue of Apollo, who held a bow in one hand. It may be from a NE Peloponnesian workshop of c 530–520 BC (? Kanachos of Sikyon). The room to the left contains other fine bronzes from the same cache as the Piraeus Kouros (see above): *Athena, her helmet decorated with griffins and owls, 350–300 BC; *Artemis, with quiver on her shoulder; smaller statue of some deity; bronze mask. In the room to the right the display centres on a seated cult statue of Cybele with remains (feet) of a lion beside her, set within the restored outline of the temple in which they were found (original excavated in Moskhaton c 1975); small votive reliefs are also incorporated in the reconstruction. Also shown is an altar and various free-standing and relief sculptures including the famous scene of Asklepios treating a patient.

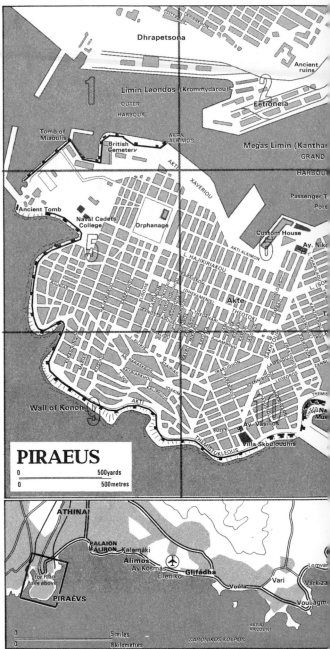

PIRAEUS

0 — 500 yards
0 — 500 metres

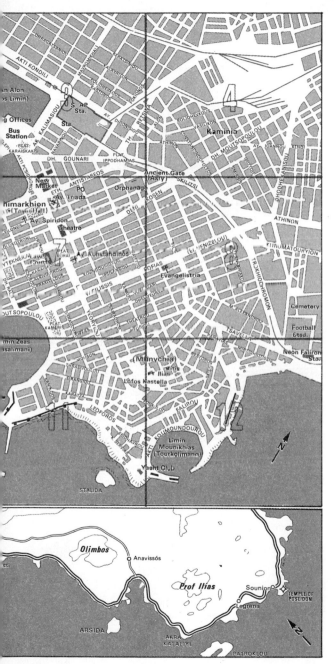

Next to the museum are the scanty remains of the **Theatre of Zea**, a Hellenistic edifice of the 2C BC which (unusually) was not altered in the Roman period. The rock-hewn cavea was divided by 14 flights of steps. The orchestra, better preserved, is surrounded by a covered channel.

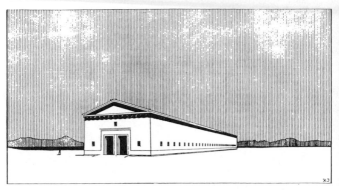

Perspectival view of the Arsenal restored (K. Jeppesen)

In a building plot at Ipsilántou 170, near the junction with Bouboulínas is a section of the SKEUOTHEKE or *Arsenal of Philo* (see above) found in 1988. The architect's complete specification for the building was discovered in 1882 (model in the Naval Museum).

You reach **Pashalimáni** (Pl. 11), the ancient harbour of ZEA, a land-locked basin connected with the sea by a channel c 200m by 100m, lined on either side by the ancient walls, which terminate at the inner end of the channel in two short moles. The port was occupied by 196 *Ship-sheds*, spread fanwise round the bay; many traces of these may be seen, particularly in the basement of a block of flats on the E side. On the W side the construction of an outer yacht basin, incorporating

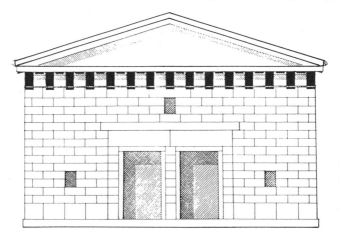

The front of the Arsenal restored (K. Jeppesen)

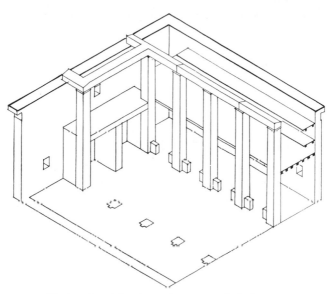

The interior of the Arsenal as restored (K. Jeppesen)

the bay to the W, has modified the shore line and narrowed the entrance to Zea.

Excavations in 1885 revealed the plan of the Ship-sheds. The flat beach round the basin was enclosed by a wall, c. 1.5m from the water's edge, which formed the back of the sheds. These, with an average breadth of 6·4m extended at right angles to it, each was separated from its neighbour by plain columns of Piraeic limestone, which supported the roofs (probably of wood). Between the columns the rock was hollowed out to form slipways which descended some way into the water (model in the Naval Museum).

The YACHT BASIN is generally crowded with large sea-going craft. Behind the reclaimed shoreline below Aktí Themistokléous a new **Naval Museum of Greece** (ΝΑΥΤΙΚΟΝ ΜΟΥΣΕΙΟΝ ΤΗΣ ΕΛΛΑΔΟΣ) faces a formal garden in which are displayed guns, conning towers, torpedo tubes, etc. The main door is to the right, but entrance more normally to the left. Opposite the main entrance the building incoporates part of the Themistoclean wall; to the right, carvings and models of ancient ships, including a fine trireme; representations of the Battle of Salamis in the Peloponnesian War. Returning, the order is chronological with Byzantine battles and Lepanto explained by drawings and plans. Among interesting documents is a letter from Nelson dated from New York in 1782. In the War of Independence emphasis is placed on the careers of admirals Miaoulis, Kanaris, etc. and the Battle of Navarino. Later Greek naval exploits (e.g. the 'Averof' and 'Elli') are celebrated, and the course of Greek naval warfare to the present day shown by relics salvaged from the sea, pictures, uniforms, flags, and ship models.

The *Averof*, launched in 1910 at Leghorn and flagship of the Greek fleet until 1951 has a permanent berth nearby and can be visited (evenings 18.30–20.30).

In the other direction the landing-stage for liberty-boats of visiting fleets continues the harbour's tradition as the *Stratiotiki Limen* (Military Port). Here the shaded PLATEÍA KANÁRIS (Pl. 7) is a favourite promenade.

The promontory to the SE ends in a salient of the fortification where there was a series of wells (φρέατοι). Here was possibly *Phreattys*, where sat the criminal court that tried those charged with homicide committed abroad. The judges sat on the shore while the accused pleaded from a boat in order not to pollute the land.

On the neck of the peninsula is the site of the *Asklepieion*, or Sanctuary of Asklepios Munychios, from which bas-reliefs were recovered in 1886 (see Piraeus Museum).

The cliff to the E of the salient is the alleged site of the SERANGEION (σήραγξ, a hollow rock). Here have been found the remains of *Baths* hollowed out of the rock and paved with mosaic: the main bath, with three apses, is connected with the sea by a passage through the rock 11·8m long; to the E is the cloak room with 18 compartments for the bathers' clothes. The place is now a restaurant.

The road to New Phaleron here quits the shore and passes below *Kastélla*, the terraced quarter occupying the slopes of the hill that rises to the left. Ancient quarries have been discovered in the area. The HILL OF MUNYCHIA (85m; 10 minutes walk), the Acropolis of Piraeus, commands all three harbours and *Views of Phaleron Bay and the Saronic Gulf. In 403 BC Thrasyboulus made it the base of his operations against the Thirty Tyrants, then in possession of Athens. Here in 1827 Karaïskákis was killed during an abortive campaign led by Sir Richard Church, designed to relieve the Greek garrison of the Athenian acropolis. Gen. Thomas Gordon held Munychia from February until May, but the defeat of an attempted attack on Athens made from Phaleron Bay put an end to the expedition and the siege. The modern chapel of *Ayios Elias*, near the summit, marks the site not of the Temple of Artemis Munychia but of *Bendis*, a celebrated sanctuary. About 90m W is the upper entrance to a flight of 165 steps, known as the *Cavern of Arethusa*, which leads to the stuccoed subterranean galleries that held the water supply of the citadel (65·5m deep). On the W slope of the hill (discovered in 1880, but now covered up) was the ancient *Theatre of Dionysos* referred to by Thucydides (VIII, 93).—From Munychia, Leofóros Yeoryíou tou Prótou (cf. above) descends to the main harbour. Halfway down stands a charming marble group of Mother and Child (1959).

Keep to the cliffs above the popular beach which faces the rocky islet of *Stalídha*, then descend past the *Yacht Club of Greece* (Ναυτικός Ομιλος Ελλαδός). During its construction in 1935 large unworked blocks belonging to the fortress of Hippias were unearthed and inscribed sherds from (?) the *Temple of Artemis Munychia*. The picturesque yacht basin of *Tourkolímano (Pl. 12), gay with coloured sails and lined with restaurants, retains the form it had as the ancient PORT OF MUNYCHIA. This also was protected by two long moles, each ending in a lighthouse tower, leaving an entrance between them only 36·5m wide. The *N Mole* affords a good example of ancient marine fortification and bears lower courses of a massive structure of unknown purpose. The harbour had slips for 82 triremes, of which some foundations can be seen under water to the N and S. The buildings themselves, apparently of wood, have long since vanished and traces only of the surrounding wall exist. The name Tourkolímano seems unlikely to survive a chauvinist campaign to change it to *Mikrolímano* or *Mikró Limáni*.

The return to either Pashalimáni or the Great Harbour can be accomplished by bus No. 904/905 (circular route).

The rocky and usually deserted S coast of the **Akte Peninsula** affords a delightful *Walk, especially in the late afternoon when Salamis and the islands of the Saronic Gulf are thrown into relief by the setting sun, which falls full on Hymettos and the coast to the E.

The tour is best made in an anticlockwise direction; the uninteresting popular quarter on the N side of the peninsula may be avoided by taking bus No. 904/905 (circular route from Plateía Koraí) to the point S of the Naval School where it emerges on the shore. Then Pashalimáni can be reached on foot in 1 hour.

The W extremity of the peninsula, once a royal park, is now a restricted naval area whose points of interest can be seen only from offshore. On the most northerly point, the ancient promontory of *Alkimos* (Pl. 1), once stood the great *Marble Lion* (probably from Delos) that was inscribed in runes by Harald Hardrada and gave to Piraeus its alternative names of *Porto Leone* and *Porto Draco*. The lion was removed to Venice by Morosini in 1687. About 275m W of Alkimos are some graves of English soldiers and a *Monument to Andreas Miaoulis* (1769–1835), the admiral. Behind are quarries from which comes the bluish-grey Piraeic stone, and farther on, to seaward of the lighthouse, a rock-hewn grave traditionally known as the Tomb of Themistocles and a poros *Column*, re-erected in 1952, that marked the S entrance to the harbour.

Leofóros Iróön Polytekhníou is continued to the W by Leofóros Kiriákou to the *Naval School* (Pl. 5), where Akti Themistokléous follows the indented S shore of the peninsula. The **Wall of Konon** is visible in its lower courses for most of the way. Built of local stone (c 394–391 BC) just beyond the reach of the waves and often of blocks cut from the rocks above which it is built, it is closely followed by the road, which is sometimes supported by it. The curtain, 3–3·5m thick, is reinforced at intervals of 46–55m by square *Towers*. The bases of many of these now support little wayside tavernas. A short section of the *Wall of Themistocles* survives to the SE of the *Signal Station* (56m) that crowns the highest point of the peninsula. Beyond the *Villa Skouloudhis* (Pl. 10), now the Institute of Hydrology, polygonal masonry at the base of Konon's wall shows where the earlier wall was at first carried some way to the SW of the point where it turned across the peninsula.

Cape Soúnion at sunset, see p. 195
Photo by Bernard McDonagh

II ATTICA

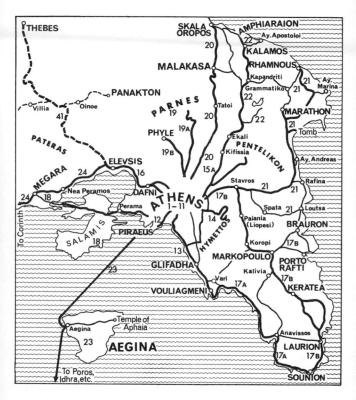

The name of **ATTICA** (Αττική; Attikí), the region which surrounds
Athens, is probably derived from the word ἀκτή (akte), 'promontory'
or 'peninsula', literally 'the place where the waves break'. It became
an entity with the amalgamation of the old Mycenaean centres
during the late-Geometric period. Geographically the region forms a
roughly triangular peninsula terminating in Cape Sounion; its base,
c 50km wide, is the almost continuous mountain barrier that runs
from the bay of Aigosthena, in the W, to the channel of Euboea, in the
E. This consists of the ranges of Pateras, Kithairon, and Parnes and
the coastal hills of Mavrovouni. The ancient boundary between
Attica and Boeotia lay along this barrier, with disputed areas around
the three passes: the Megarid, Eleutherai, and Diakria. Possession of
Salamis and the Megarid secured the W approaches, which are
effectively cut off from the Peloponnese by the great Yerania range.
Athens itself, protected by the inner ring of Aigaleos, Pentelikon, and
Hymettos, but connected by easy roads with the plains beyond, is the
natural centre of the region. Many of the Attic mountains, in the time
of Pausanias crowned with images of the gods, are now surmounted by
ugly radar stations, which inhibit access to their summits.

Modern Attica became a separate administrative entity in 1899 when it was detached from Boeotia. The boundaries have been altered several times since. There are now two nomes: Attikís and Piraiós. Attikis consists of two eparchies: Attica proper and the Megarid. Piraios has five: Piraeus itself (which, however, includes Salamis and Spetsai); Aegina; Idhra; Kithira; and Troezenia. Greater Athens, comprising part of the eparchy of Attica and part of the eparchy of Piraeus, enjoys special administrative status within its territory.

Among features of interest are the coastal resorts SE of Athens; the hill resorts to the N; Mt Hymettos; the monasteries of Kaisariani and Daphni; the Mesogeia with the remains of Brauron; and Sounion. Archaeologically rewarding in addition are Eleusis and Aegina, the new discoveries in the plain of Marathon, and farther away the Amphiaraion at Oropos, and Rhamnous. Many new roads have been built and old ones improved, and with a car it is possible to combine two or three places in one day. Bus services are steadily becoming more extensive and frequent to outlying places, though they radiate from central Athens and are of little help to those in seaside hotels. In the season there are coach excursions to the main sites. Walkers will find much of Attica within their reach, though expanding towns, military zones, and spreading villa development are ever-increasing obstacles. The countryside is carpeted with flowers in spring, when also the crisp air and clear Attic light are best enjoyed.

Rtes 13–16 are in the nature of excursions which can be made by public transport leaving every few minutes from Central Athens; they can be accomplished at any time of day without advance planning. The later routes demand a little organisation but can each be made in a single day from Athens. In Rtes 19, 20, and 22 the old roads out to the N are described, in order to indicate what remains of historical interest, every day more hidden in suburbia, a speedier arrival can be gained at the expense of intermediate interest by using the Athens–Salonika Highway.

13   The Attic Coast to Vouliagméni

ROAD, dual carriageway, 25km (15½ miles). BUSES (Prefix 1) every few minutes from Síndagma Sq. to Edhém; from the Academy, Omónia Sq., Leofóros Olgas, etc. (meeting at the Olympieion) to Glifádha and Vouliagméni, see under Athens. The distances below are measured from Síndagma Sq.

The WEST COAST OF ATTICA, in classical times a flourishing region with many demes, degenerated into insignificance at an early date, and for centuries lay neglected and difficult of access. The discovery of medicinal springs near Glifádha and Vouliagméni after the First World War led to the foundation of bathing resorts, and in recent years the coast has been developed as the summer playground of Attica. The hinterland, a bare stony tract, is little developed beyond the airport, and still studded with ancient graves, but the coast is very crowded in July–August.

From the Olympieion to (6km) the *Racecourse*, see Rte 12. Turn left. The rocky headland that closes Phaleron Bay to the E, once identified with Cape Kolias (see below), is more likely the site of ancient Phaleron itself, which is usually placed near the Chapel of St George. At the bus-stop called Trocadero below the road is the *Marine Biological Institute*.

The ancient deme of *Phaleron*, which was the original port of Athens, was

connected with the capital by the Phaleric Long Wall. Scanty remains of this
have been found on the hill, and the foundations of a mole have been detected
in the sea. In the neighbouring plain were defeated the Spartans who had been
tricked by the exiled Alkmaeonids into invading Peisistratid Athens.

7km **Palaión Fáliron** (Παλαιόν Φάληρον: Hotels B, C; Restaurants), or
Old Pháleron, a pleasant seaside resort (53,273 inhab.) with a water-
sports stadium and swimming pool, extends E along the shore, here
broken into tiny creeks. The *Pumping Station* of the Ulen Company
on the shore supplies salt water for the Athens fire brigade. You cross
the stream of Pikrodaphne. The *Edem Restaurant*, on a small headland, is the terminus of the Edhém bus. To the left in the *Phaleron
War Cemetery*, stands the Athens memorial, dedicated in May 1961,
to 2800 British dead of 1939–45, who have no known grave in Greece
or Yugoslavia.—9·5km **Kalamáki** (Hotels A, B, C) with a small yacht
basin and good tavernas, affords views of Hymettos.—11km *Alimós*
(Hotel B) corresponds to the ancient *Halimous*, birthplace of
Thucydides (471–c 400 BC), whom Macaulay called 'the greatest
historian that ever lived'. The clay in this area was highly valued by
Athenian potters.—13km. A turning (left; signs to Mesogeíon Avenue and Olympic Stadium) skirts the airport and joins a major new
bypass of Athens which leads through the S suburbs on the foothills
of Mt Hymettos, to debouch in Od. Mesogeíon, on the NE side of the
city (Rte 17B). Trees partly hide a wireless station, beyond which
extends the promontory of **Ayios Kosmás**, named after a 19C chapel,
whose conventual buildings are now a taverna. The headland
probably represents the ancient *Kolias Akra*, where many wrecked
Persian ships were washed ashore after the Battle of Salamis.

Excavations by Prof. G. Mylonas in 1930–31 revealed no evidence of ships but
proved that the coast has sunk since Classical times. On the E side of the
headland and in the sea below were found remains of two separate occupations,
one Early Helladic, the other Late Helladic. Stone walls of houses may be seen.
The necropolis along the E shore, which provided many finds, belongs to the
early Bronze Age. The graves show affinities with Cycladic types, suggesting
that this was a trading-post to which mariners from the Cyclades brought
Melian obsidian. It came to a violent end c 1900 BC. In Mycenaean times the
site was a fortified village, which was abandoned in the 12C BC. The Classical
sanctuary of Aphrodite seen by Pausanias may lie beneath the chapel.

To the right of the road is the *National Athletic Centre*; to the left
extends *Athens Airport*, named after (12km) *Ellenikó*. The terminal
building, begun in 1961, was one of Eero Saarinen's last works.
17km **Glifádha** (Γλυφάδα; Hotels L, A, B, C, D, Restaurants), a
flourishing seaside resort (44,018 inhab.) with sandy beaches and an
18-hole golf course, owes its foundation in 1920 to the discovery of
medicinal springs. Prospective visitors should be aware that the flight
path to the airport lies over the town. Near the Antonopoulos Hotel
are the ruins of an early Christian basilica said to commemorate St
Paul's supposed first landing in S Greece at this spot. You join the old
road from Athens.

The old inland road, a trifle shorter, passes S of the Olympieion, crosses the
Ilissos near the Kallirrhoë (8, 5) and turns S. Beyond (3km) *Ayios Dhimítrios*, a
pleasant modern church; Mt Hymettos, previously hidden by suburbs, is well
seen to the left.—5m (turn right into Od. Arkhaíou Theátrou at lights) *Trákhones*
(the ancient deme Euonymon) has a theatre of the mid-4C BC with an unusual
rectangular orchestra (cf. Thorikos) suggesting an earlier origin.
  A turning to the West Terminal (Olympic Airways) follows immediately
(further lights) and access roads to the new bypass (cf. above) lead off to the left.
You pass the airport itself and, farther on, entrances to the Greek and U.S. Air

Force bases, followed immediately by the access road to the East Terminal (foreign airlines).

A right fork serves Glifádha, joining the coast by Astir Beach.—At the S end of Hymettos lay ancient *Aixone*, where the Thesmophoria, celebrated by women in the Temple of Demeter, provided Aristophanes with the theme for a play; Aixone has been identified with Glifádha.

Beyond the airport (c3km) the little church of Ayios Nikólaos is a landmark (right) by traffic lights. A left turn at the following lights allows us to bear right and join Od. Proódhou to begin an excursion to the remarkable stalactite GROTTO OF PAN, APOLLO, AND THE NYMPHS (the Vari Cave, overlooking Vari. You continue along Od. Imittoú (extension of Proódhou) and climb into the hills. Beyond the cemetery of Ano Voula (c 4·5kms from the main road) you pass through a disused metal gateway and 200m further, a dirt road diverges (right) on a corner. The track leads to a hill (c 10 minutes) where it divides (keep right) and you soon reach the cave, visible just below the road to the right, its mouth covered by a metal grill. The descent needs non-slip shoes and care. A rope would give added confidence. A wall of rock divides the grotto into two chambers. The large chamber, in which is a spring of clear water, contains the curious *Relief of Archidamos*, by whom the grotto appears to have been decorated. The figure holds a hammer and chisel, with which it is working at some indefinite object cut in the rock. Likewise cut in the rock are a primitive altar of Apollo Hersos, a headless seated goddess, and a much defaced head of a lion. The cave was excavated by the American School in 1903, when votive reliefs representing Hermes and the Nymphs, Pan playing the syrinx, etc., of the 4–3C BC were found as well as coins and deposits proving occupation from c 600 to 150 BC and in the 4C AD.

At the S foot of the hill, below and visible from the cave (15 minutes scramble), a classical farmhouse was explored by the British School in 1966. The lower courses of the walls survive and the plan can be easily made out. This is the so-called 'Vari house'.

Prominently visible from the cave, and dominating the plain beyond the farmhouse is the *Military Academy* at Vari (see Rte 17).

The main road continues to join the coastal route at Voula (see below).

Vari. Reconstruction of the Classical farmhouse

On the promontory of *Alikí* (right) late-Mycenaean chamber-tombs have been explored.—At (19km) **Voúla** (Hotels A, B, C, D; Restaurants), a garden city (10,539 inhab.) of summer villas, the beach and camping site are controlled by the NTOG. In Ano Voula, to the E and to be identified with the ancient deme of Halae Aixonidae, a variety of ancient structures have been excavated, including farm and country houses, terrace and boundary walls and roads with kerbs. The little church of *Ayios Nikólaos ton Pálon* stands just beyond the junction of the Vari road (cf. above), beyond which the main road passes behind (22·5km) *Kavoúri* (Hotels A, B, C), crossing the peninsula of *Kaminia* to Vouliagméni. Two wine-trading galleys (of the 4C BC) were found in 1960 lying in five fathoms off the islet of *Katramonisi*.

The three-tongued promontory, which forms the seaward end of the Hymettos range, was famous in antiquity as CAPE ZOSTER ('girdle'), strictly the name of the central tongue (now *Cape Lomvárdha*). Here Leto unloosed her girdle before the birth of Apollo and Artemis (see Paus. I, 31, 1). The 6C *Sanctuary of Apollo Zoster*, unearthed in 1925–26 at the neck of the central tongue, has been absorbed by a hotel garden; the attendant building of the same period, later enlarged, discovered in 1936, may be the priests' house or a pilgrims' hostel. Herodotus (VIII, 107) tells us that, after the battle of Salamis, the Persians mistook the rocks of the headland for Greek ships. The uninhabited island of *Fléves* (the ancient *Phabra*) lies 1·5km off the cape.

25km **Vouliagméni** (Βουλιαγμένη; Hotels L, A, B; inc. luxury flats; Restaurants), the most fashionable seaside resort in Attica (2743 inhab.; no hotels below class B), has a large yacht marina. It takes its name from a picturesque *Lake* (bathing establishment) of warm, green water enclosed by the sheer limestone rocks of the E cape of Kaminia. Its brackish, sulphurous waters are beneficial in cases of rheumatism, neuritis, arthritis, and skin diseases. The overflow from the lake runs underground to the sea and bubbles up from the sea bottom, raising its temperature for some distance. The fine sandy beaches (open all year) enclosed by the three headlands have been efficiently equipped by the NTOG in the international style with good restaurants.

From Vouliagméni to *Soúnion*, see Rte 17.

14   Kaisarianí and Hymettos

ROAD, 15·5km via Kaisarianí, to the Prohibited Area, c 3km before the summit of Hymettos. BUS (No. 224/234 from the University) in 20 minutes to the suburb; the monastery is 30 minutes on foot.

Hymettos (Υμηττός, in modern Greek *Imittós*), famous for its sunset glow, its honey, and its marble, is the range of hills, 16km long, that shuts in the Attic plain on the SE, almost reaching the sea at Cape Zoster. It is divided by the Pirnari Glen into the *Great Hymettos* (Μεγάλος Υμηττός; 1027m) and the *Lesser* or *Waterless Hymettos* (Ανυδρος Υμηττός), of which the highest point is *Mavro Vouni* (804m). The W slopes reach almost to Athens, the *Kakórrhevma Gorge* extending from below the summit to Zoödhókhos Piyí and Pankráti; the abrupter W side dominates Liópesi. The mountain is almost treeless and the aromatic plants and shrubs which produced the best food for bees are less widespread than in classical times, though terebinth, juniper, thyme, sage, mint, lavender, etc., are still to be found.

The Hymettian bee has migrated to Pentelikon and Tourkovouni. The violet colour which now, as in antiquity, suffuses the mountain at sunset is peculiar to Hymettos (cf. the 'purpureos colles' of Ovid, below). Hymettian marble (so-called Kara marble) was anciently quarried on the W side of the mountain, close to the Kakorrhevma Gorge and approximately on the site of the ruined *Convent of Karyaes*.—Near the Convent of St John the Hunter (Rte 17B), at the N end of the ridge, are some modern quarries.

From a little E of the Hilton Hotel (5, 8) a shrinking pine copse marks the defile of the Ilissos between the suburbs of Zográfou and Kaisarianí. Leofóros Vasiléos Alexándrou to the S of the wood is the main approach road to the suburb of *Kaisarianí*. Beyond, you cross the city bypass and climb to (5·5km) **'Moní Kaisarianís** (341m), an 11C monastery, closely confined at the end of the ravine amid the welcome shade of cypress, pine, and plane trees. Here since pagan times shrines have marked the source of the Ilissos.

On the brow of the hill just above the monastery is a famous fountain, known in ancient times as *Kyllou Pera*; its waters were supposed to cure sterility. A temple of Aphrodite was adjacent and the spot was made famous by Ovid in the well-known lines of the Ars Amatoria (III, 987) describing the sad legend of Cephalus and Procris. The spring supplied Athens with drinking water before the construction of the Marathon Dam. It feeds a fountain on the outside E wall of the monastery where the water gushes from a ram's head (cast; the original is now in the Acropolis Museum). Fragments built into the walls belong to an earlier Christian basilica, probably of the 5C.

The present structure is first mentioned in the 12C. It has been conjectured that the name derives from Caesarea, from which, perhaps, came its original ikon. In 1458 when the Sultan Mehmed II visited newly conquered Athens, the Abbot of Kaisarianí was chosen to deliver up to him the keys of the city, in recognition of which the convent was exempted from taxation by the Turks. Until 1716 it was independent of the Metropolitan and had a school and a celebrated library (moved to Athens and destroyed in the War of 1821). It was noted also for its honey. Deserted in the 18C, it is now a national monument. During the Second World War the secluded ravine was used by the Germans for the execution of hostages. The monastery was restored in 1956–57; the church is still a goal of pilgrimage on Ascension Day.

The CONVENTUAL BUILDINGS (entered from the far side), grouped round a pretty court, include a *Mill* and *Bakery*, and a *Bath-House*, now restored after use as an oil-press. The *Refectory* has a finely moulded Roman lintel over the door and a domed kitchen. The *Church*, built of stone with brick courses, takes the form of a Greek cross. The dome is supported on Roman columns. The parecclesion (dedicated to *St. Anthony*) was added in the 16C, the narthex in the 17C, and the belfry in the 19C. The frescoes, save for those by Ioannis Ipatos (Peloponnesian, 1682) in the narthex, are in a 17–18C Cretan style. A tomb in the crypt was explored in 1950.

The area round the monastery has been discretely provided with picnic tables, and some paths laid out among the trees.

The road crosses a bridge over a gully, then swings left to a saddle below an outcrop of rock that affords a sudden view of the whole of Athens. It then climbs to (9km) the pretty *Moní Asteríou* (548m), another 11C monastery, restored in 1961. A path descends in c 1·5km to *Ayios Ioánnis Theológos*, another Byzantine church above the suburb of Goudhí (Rte 17B).—You reach (10km) *Mávra Vrákhia* (646m) a col 3km N of the summit. The col is marred by a radar station, but now that the summit is prohibited, affords the best vantage point on Hymettos, with a wide view over the Mesogeia and to the plain of Marathon. The road climbs S but the view, though more extensive toward the W, looking across Salamis to the Peloponnese, does not include the E.—At 15km are Stop signs, with a place for turning.

The summit (1027m) was crowned in Classical times with a statue of Zeus. Vestiges of an altar were found in 1939, and a cave has yielded Geometric pottery.

15 Kifissiá and Pentelikon (Pendéli)

A. From Athens to Kifissiá and Ekáli

ROAD. 14km (9 miles). Bus 525, 538/539 from Plateía Kánningos every few minutes to Kifissiá; 513 (Ayios Stéphanos) and others from same terminal, to Ekáli.The nearer suburbs are served by many local routes.

RAILWAY, 16km, by Piraeus Electric Railway (EHΣ) from Omonia Square.

Leofóros Vasilíssis Sofías (Rte 10) from Sindagma Sq. and Leofóros Alexándras from Omonia Square meet at *Ambelókipoi*, 2km from Sindagma Square. You take the left fork and follow LEOFÓROS KIFISSÍAS. To the left rises *Tourkovoúni* (338m), the ancient *Anchesmos*, with a reservoir and purification plant of Athens Waterworks. On the E slope is (6km) **Psikhikó** (Ψυχικό), a garden suburb. Here at Benaki Hall is *Athens College*, a co-educational boarding school on an American pattern, founded in 1925; its Greek pupils, many from overseas, are taught bilingually in Greek and English. It has a modern theatre, where productions (including visiting artists) are often open to the public. Next to it is the *Arsakeion*, a progressive girls' school removed c 1930 from a site near the University.—6·5km. Turning (right) to Néa Pendéli, see below.—8km. *Filothéi* (Φιλοθέη), a model suburb erected by the National Bank of Greece in 1930–35, with film studios, is favoured by foreign residents. Roads lead W to Néa Ionía and E to Ayía Paraskeví (Rte 17B).—9km. There is a turning (right) for the *Olympic Stadium*. Completed in 1982, the stadium, which is set in 250 acres, seats 80,000 spectators. It has an indoor sports hall, training fields, tennis courts, an Olympic training centre and accommodation for 320 competitors. The 1996 Olympic games, for which it was designed, were not awarded to Greece. For visitors without cars, access is either by the electric railway from central Athens (Omonia, etc.) to the new station of Eirene (Iríni) or by any Kifissiá bus (and 500m walk).—The main highway passes to the right of (12km) **Amaroúsion** (Hotel D), or *Maroússi*, the ancient *Athmonia*, which derives its name from a temple of Artemis Amarousia. It is celebrated for its bright glazed pottery. Off the old road, *Anávryta College* (originally a boarding school), started in 1947 by Jocelyn Winthrop Young after the model of Gordonstoun, occupies the former Singros estate.

In the main square is a bust, by Tombros (1961), of Spiros Louis, the local shepherd who won the first modern marathon race at the Olympic Games of 1896.

The small church of Ayios Dhimítrios has 17C frescoes by the painter-priest Dhimítrios.

The Tsaroúkhis Foundation (signs; closed at the time of writing) has a collection of works of the famous modern artist (1910–89).

You pass (left) the large KAT (Kéntron Atikhimáton or Accident Centre) hospital.

14·5km **KIFISSIÁ** (Κηφισσά; 268m) is an attractive and popular 'garden city' (31,876 inhab.) on the SW slopes of Pentelikon. The summer temperature averages 10° lower than in the city, and the shade of its pine trees affords a welcome relief from the glare of Athens. Menander was a native of Kifissiá, and here Herodes Atticus had a villa, a visit to which inspired Aulus Gellius to write his rambling 'Noctes Atticae'. Now, as in Roman times, the town is a favourite retreat of the Athenians in summer. It is the seat of the Metropolitan of Attica and Megaris.

The suburb has many *hotels*, mostly in the higher categories, and mainly in the Kefalári area. There are also excellent *rakhaiouplasteia* and numerous *restaurants*. Kifissiá and the Northern suburbs generally are pleasant places to eat, especially in summer, when there are also direct buses to bathing resorts. In Kifissiá also is the *Goulandris Natural History Museum*, at Od. Levídhou 12.

In December 1944 Tatoï aerodrome (occupied by the RAF in October) was evacuated in face of the ELAS rising and British air headquarters set up in the Pentelikon and Cecil hotels in Kifissiá, already cut off from Athens. ELAS attacked on 18 December and forced the garrison to capitulate. On the 20th the survivors (c 600 officers and men) were subjected to begin a forced march, in company with civilian hostages, largely on foot through Central Greece. RAF aircraft tracked their progress through Thebes, Levadhia, Lamia, and Larissa to Trikkala, dropping supplies wherever possible. At Lazarina in the Pindos on 23 January an exchange of prisoners was effected and the airmen repatriated from Volos.

The road enters Plateía Platánou. On the left gardens descend to the station; the road to Kefalári forks right. On this corner (right) a shelter covers four *Roman Sarcophagi*, with reliefs, perhaps from the family vault of Herodes (busts of Herodes and of Polydeukion, his pupil and cousin, were found in 1961 in a garden near the church of Panayia tis Xidhou, a short way N of the Plateia. Subsequent discoveries, 1972–74, have revealed more sculpture and a probable bath building. All may be from the villa of Herodes Atticus; cf. above). *Kefalári*, a district of villas, gardens, and hotels, takes its name from a small and usually dried up stream, which, after rain, is a source of the Kifissos. The place is fast expanding into the foothills of Pentelikon, and it is possible to walk to Moní Pendéli and the ridge of the mountain.

From the N end of Kifissiá a road branches to the left towards Tatoï and Dhekélia (cf. Rte 20).

The main road continues NE to *Kastrí* (Hotel C), above which (right) an ancient fort crowns the NW spur of Pentelikon, and (20km) **Ekáli** (Hotel C), a pleasant summer resort amid pine woods, which has adopted the name of an ancient deme situated farther NE.

Immediately N of Ekáli a road diverges (right) to (3km) **Dhiónisos** (Hotel C), ancient *Ikaria*, where Dionysos is alleged to have been entertained by Ikarios, and the grateful god of wine instructed his host in the cultivation of the grape.— At 5km a turning to the left leads (550m) to the Sanctuary of Dionysos (left) discovered by the American School in 1888.—At 10·5km *Ayios Petros* (café), fine view over Marathon Bay.—The road descends to Néa Mákri (Rte 21).

B.   From Athens to Moní Pendéli

ROAD, 16km (10 miles). Bus 415 from Od. Vasiléos Iraklíou (behind
National Archaeological Museum).

From Athens to (6km) *Psikhikó*, see above. Shortly beyond you take
the right fork to (10km) **Khalándri** (Χαλάνδρι; Hotels B, C on the road
to the N), a pleasant suburb occupying the site of *Phyla*, birthplace of
Euripides (480–406 BC). The ancient orgies of the 'Great Goddess'
(probably Mother-Earth) at Phyla antedated the mysteries at Eleusis.
About 1km S the chapel of *Panayía Marmariótissa* covers the remains
of a Roman tomb.—At 14·5km, near a rustic villa (now a taverna) built
by the Duchesse de Plaisance, there is a by-road from Amarousion
(4km, via *Melíssia*, with film studios).

16km *Moní Pendéli*, a monastery founded in 1578 and now one of
the richest in Greece, is shaded by a cluster of lofty white poplars.
The buildings are modern, but the chapel contains 17C paintings.
The main church has important modern fresoes by Rallis Kopsídis in
the narthex. In the basement of the monastery are displays illustrating the history of education in Greece under Turkish rule, in which
the church played a leading role. The road curves round the monastery grounds and ends at a large open space (bus terminus; Hotel D;
tavernas); in the centre is the chapel of *Ayía Triádha*, near which
traces of terraces mark the site of *Palaia Pendeli*, the ancient deme of
Pentele. A little to the S of the convent (on a by-road towards Stavrós)
stands the *Palace of Rodhodhafnis*, built in a Gothic style for the
Duchesse de Plaisance by Kleanthes. Here she died (1854) and is
buried. It was restored in 1961 as a royal residence, and is now the
setting for concerts on some evenings in the summer.

PENTELIKON (Τὸ Πεντελικόν; modern Pendéli), the mountainous
range enclosing the Attic plain on the NE, extends for 7km from NW
to SE. Its ancient name was *Brilessos* (Βριλησσός), but by Classical
times it had come to be called Pentelikon after the township of
Pentele where the famous marble quarries lay. The principal summit
(*Kokkinarás*; 1110m), to the NW, is, like that of Hymettos, inaccessible since it was crowned by an ugly radar station. *Vayati* (1007m),
the secondary summit, 500m SE, can still be attained on foot, as can
the little platform between them, the site of the statue of Athena
mentioned by Pausanias.

The area beyond the monastery is largely blocked by quarrying, a
military hospital, and villa development. However it is still possible to
find a way through to the slopes of Pentelikon and the ANCIENT
QUARRIES which lie SE of the summit.

No less than 25 of them can be made out, one above the other, at a height of
700–1000m. Their exploitation, though begun c 570 BC, was unimportant
before the 5C BC, and became general in Pericles' day. The crystalline rock of
Pentelikon yielded the fine white marble which was used for the most important
buildings and even in sculpture. It superseded Hymettian marble and poros for
architectural purposes, though it never quite ousted Parian marble, which is
easier to chisel, for sculpture. The rich golden tint that age gives to Pentelic
marble is due to the presence of iron oxide. The stone yielded by the modern
quarries at Dhiónisos, on the N slope of Pentelikon, is less white.

You come first to an ancient *Paved Way*, down which the cut blocks
were transported on wooden sledges. The holes on either side held
bollards round which steadying ropes were wound. The *Quarry of
Spiliá* (700m) was worked out by the ancients. In the NW corner

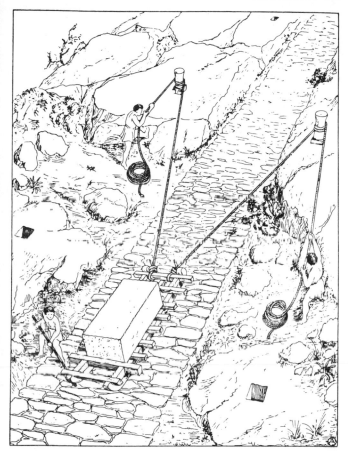

Representation of the way blocks of Pentelic marble were brought down from the mountain

opens a large *Stalactite Grotto* containing twin chapels. The S unit contains some relief decoration with crosses, angels, eagles and an inscription, indicating that it probably was a place of worship in the pre-Iconoclastic period. To the N a domed chapel of the abbreviated cross type was subsequently added. The S chapel retains frescoes from c 1225, including a representation of the *Melismos* in the apse and a portrait of Michael Choniates, bishop of Athens between 1182 and 1204. The N chapel also retains fresco decoration. Remains of walls and inscriptions at the entrance mark a monastery of Byzantine date that survived the Frankish period.—From the grotto the climb to the ridge takes c 75 minutes.

The *View, one of the most extensive in Attica, is remarkable for its vast expanse of water, visible in all directions save on the NW. To the N rises the pyramidal Dhirfis, while on the E lie Euboea,—Andros, and Tinos. The Plain of Marathon is partly hidden by an intervening spur. To the SE the sea is studded with innumerable islands; across the valley to the S the ridge of Hymettos runs down to the sea; on the SW Athens spreads itself over the plain. Far to the S are the mountains of Milos, 150km distant.

16 From Athens to Eleusis

ROAD, 22km (14 miles), by the Ierá Odos to *Eléfsis (Elefsína)*, via (11km) *Dhafní*. Buses: No. 864, every 15 minutes, from Plateía Koumoundhoúrou (Eleftherías) (2, 6) for Dhafní (20 minutes) and beyond to Elefsis (45 minutes); No. 026 from Sindagma Sq., etc. to Plateía Koumoundhoúrou and Votanikós; buses also from Piraeus.

The first 5 or 6km are heavily industrialised and tedious to the pedestrian.

The faster but unrewarding LEOFÓROS ATHINÓN (taken by all long-distance buses), which forms the initial section of the highway to Corinth, runs almost parallel, c 1km to the N. It is reached from Omonia Sq. by Ayíou Konstandínou and Akhilléos streets (2, 5) and, after crossing Leofóros Kifissoú by a new flyover near the Peloponnesian bus station, it joins the Sacred Way just beyond the conspicuous mental hospital (right) at Dhafní.—Beyond Asprópirgos you must take the old road (right); the Corinth highway now by-passes Eleusis.

By RAIL TO ELEUSIS (S P A P), 27km in 35–45 minutes. The line strikes N through haphazard suburban settlements to (10km) *Ano Liósia*, where it curves SW. Beyond a large army transport depot it threads a low defile, passing through a gap in the DEMA (τὸ Δέμα; 'the Link'), or *Aigaleos-Parnes Wall*, a westward-facing rampart that follows an undulating course for 4·5km along the watershed. The S two-thirds are built in various styles of masonry (cf. B S A, v. 52, 1957) in 53 short sections separated by 50 sally-ports and two gateways. Farther N the wall is crude and continuous. Two signal (?) towers command the wall, which is apparently military and may date from the Lycurgan period. A *House*, of the late 5C BC (the Dema House), disposed round a court, was excavated in 1960 just N of the railway.—The uninhabited valley between the Aigaleos ridge and the foothills of Parnes is dotted with beehives. Emerging into the Thriasian Plain (see below) at (23km) *Asprópirgos*, with a huge oil refinery, the line joins the road on the outskirts of (27km) *Eleusis*.

From Omonia Square (3, 3) Od. Piraiós leads to (1km) the Kerameikos (Rte 4). The Ierá Odos preserves both the name and very largely the original course of the SACRED WAY (Ἱερά Ὁδος) traversed by initiates from Athens to Eleusis, though nowadays few indications remain of the tombs and shrines described at length by Pausanias. Sections of the road itself have been regularly uncovered in excavations: in 1984, roadworks over a distance of 5km led to such discoveries and to the location of many tombs which lay beside. From the Kerameikos the narrow road threads through the noisy industrial area of *Votanikós*. You pass (2km; left) the *Botanic Gardens* (Βοτανικός Κῆπος), with its tall poplars, and the Agricultural School of Athens University. A little farther on, *Plato's Olive-tree* (so called) is one of very few survivors from the famous grove that once bordered the Kifissos from Kolonos to the sea.—3km *Ayios Sávas* (right), a medieval church near the conspicuous naval signal station, stands on the site of a Temple of Demeter supposed to commemorate the spot where she rewarded the hospitality of Phytalos by giving him the first fig-tree. Classical and Byzantine marbles are visible in the walls. Farther on, a by-road to the right passes the *Hydrographic Office* of the Greek navy, and joins Leofóros Athinón. You cross Leofóros Kifissoú, the extension to Piraeus of the National Highway, with the

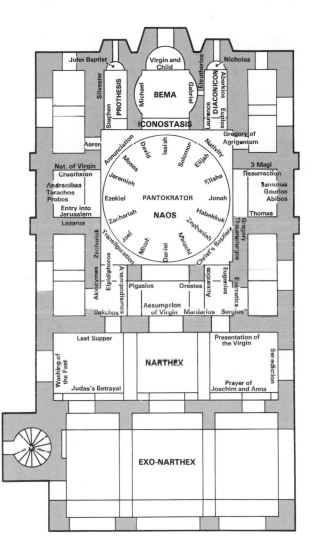

DAPHNI

0 _____ 3 metres

canalised Kifissos, some way W of its ancient bed. The country opens out amid sparse olives as you approach the comparatively low ridge of *Aigaleos* (Αιγάλεως), the W horn of the natural amphitheatre that surrounds Athens. On the right is the conical hill of *Profitis Ilias* (189m), surmounted by a chapel. From this point the traveller from the W gets the first sudden view of Athens, especially striking at sunset. The new highway (see above) joins the ancient road at *Dhafní*.

The **Monastery of Daphní** (or *Dhafní*; camping site), surrounded by a high battlemented wall, stands to the S of the junction. Both church and walls incorporate ancient materials from a *Sanctuary of Apollo*, on the same site, mentioned by Pausanias but destroyed c AD 395. The convent owes its name to the laurels (δάφναι) sacred to Apollo, which once flourished in the neighbourhood.

History. The monastery, founded in the 5C or 6C, was dedicated to the Virgin Mary. It was rebuilt at the end of the 11C, but sacked by Crusaders in 1205. In 1211 Otho de la Roche gave it to the Cistercians, who held it until 1458. Two Dukes of Athens, Otho himself and Walter de Brienne, were buried here. The convent was reoccupied in the 16C by Orthodox monks until its abandonment in the War of Independence. Restorations were made in 1893 after the building had been used in turn as barracks and lunatic asylum. The structure was strengthened in 1920, and a more elaborate restoration was undertaken after the Second World War.

The fortified enceinte and a few foundations inside near the NE corner survive from its earliest Christian period. Of the 11C monastic buildings only some foundations of the great *Refectory* can be seen on the N side. The pretty *Cloister* (restored), S of the church, dates from the Cistercian period, with the addition of 16C cells. Round it are displayed sculptural fragments, Classical and Byzantine, but the two sarcophagi, ornamented with fleurs-de-lys and Latin crosses, are doubtfully those of the Frankish dukes.

The *CHURCH is a fine example of Byzantine architecture of c 1080, with an added exo-narthex, which was restored in 1961 to the later form given it by the Cistercians. The pointed arches and crenellations contrast not unpleasingly with the reused classical pillars. The truncated W tower on the N side bore a Gothic belfry. The three-light windows of the church are separated by mullions and surrounded by three orders of brickwork. The lights are closed by perforated alabaster slabs. The drum of the dome has round engaged buttresses between each of its sixteen windows. You enter from the cloister by the S door. The interior is noted for its *Mosaics, which, though fragmentary in comparison with their original extent, have no rivals in S Greece; indeed none nearer than Salonika save for those of Osios Loukas in Phocis. Most complete are those on the S side of the narthex, portraying the Presentation of the Virgin and the Prayer of Joachim and Anna. On the vault of the dome is a celebrated representation, uncompromisingly stern, of Christos Pantokrator, on a gold ground. The frieze, round the drum below, depicts saints and prophets. Finely preserved on the pendentives are the Annunciation, Nativity, Baptism, and Transfiguration. On the W side of the N choros, the Entry into Jerusalem shows interesting perspective effects (note the little boys' foreshortened feet). In the bema, or sanctuary, though the Virgin above the apse is fragmentary and the vault is empty, the flanking Archangels are well-preserved. Of the frescoes that once adorned the lower walls of the church, four are still comparatively clear.—The *Crypt* has recently been cleared.

WINE FESTIVAL (September–October, daily in the evening; sometimes rather rowdy) in grounds and pine woods. Entrance fee covers *ad lib*. tasting of 60 or more wines, folk dancing, etc.

Beyond Dhafní the highway has been straightened and nearly trebled in width by blasting away the rock, so that the now intermittent traces of the Sacred Way must be sought first to the left then to the right. A mile beyond the monastery (right) are the scanty foundations of a *Temple of Aphrodite*.

In the face of the wall of rock behind are several niches for votive statuettes with mutilated inscriptions below them. Remains are visible also of 'the wall of unwrought stones that is worth seeing' (Pausanias, I, 37, 7). This wall, which was outside the precinct of Aphrodite, at its SE corner, was built of rude blocks of stone and was over 9m thick; it may have been part of an ancient fort. The Sacred Way, laid bare here during the excavation of the temple in 1891–92, ran between the temple and the wall.

You descend towards the Bay of Eleusis, landlocked by the island of Salamis and horribly industrialised. At 14·5km the road reaches the shore, and turns abruptly to the right (N).

To the left a road leads in 1·5km to **Skaramángas** (Hotels C), with the *Hellenic Shipyards*, founded in 1956 by Stavros Niarchos, on the site of naval yards destroyed during the Second World War and taken over by the State in 1985. The first ship to be built here, a 25,000-ton tanker, was launched in 1960. The graving dock, opened in 1970, can accommodate vessels up to 250,000 d.w. tons, and is the largest in the Mediterranean. At the *Naval Training Headquarters* conscripts of the Royal Hellenic Navy receive instruction. The recent reconstruction of an ancient Greek trireme is normally kept here (access by special permission only; occasional summer 'open days' on the island of Poros).—A coastal road continues round the Skaramángas Hills (270m; a spur of Aigaleos) to *Pérama* (8km; see Rte 18), the starting-point of the ferry to Salamis.

The modern road along the *Paralía Aspropírgou* or Asprópirgos shore, which for a long time occupied the ancient causeway of the Sacred Way, has been widened by land reclamation. On the right are the *Limnes Koumoundhourou*, now salt marshes and ponds but anciently the *Rheitoi* streams, which formed the fish preserves of the Eleusinian priesthood, and marked the boundary between Athens and Eleusis. You are now skirting the Thriasian Plain, so called from the ancient deme of Thria.

The **Thriasian Plain**, extending for c 14·5km along the Eleusinian Gulf, is usually identified with the Rarian or Rharian Plain, in Greek myth supposedly the first to be sown and the first to bear crops, here Demeter made the ground lie fallow while her daughter remained in the underworld. The plain is now one of the most highly industrialised areas in Greece; its oil tanks, chimneys, and the installation of cargo quays combine with the heavy motor traffic to make the last 6·5km of the Sacred Way the least romantic road in Greece. Salamis is usually obscured by dust and sulphur fumes.

18km. The *Government Nautical College* (500m left) trains captains of the merchant navy.—18·5km. Turning (right) to Asprópirgos (1·5km; see above).—At 21km you fork right (signposted 'No toll road') from (and pass under) the main highway. To the left of the old road, c 200m beyond a group of cypresses, by a well ('Kaló Pigádhi'), are four complete arches of a *Roman Bridge*, which carried the Sacred Way across the Eleusinian Kifissos. The bridge, 5·5m wide and c 46m long, built of poros, probably dates from AD 124 when Hadrian was initiated into the Eleusinian mysteries. A hundred feet of the Sacred Way have been uncovered to the W. At the entrance to Eleusis is the desecrated chapel of *Ayios Zakharias*, where the famous relief of Demeter and Kore was found.

22km (14 miles) **ELEUSIS** (Ἐλευσίς, usually accusative, Elefsína; Hotels C), an expanding industrial town (20,320 inhab.) with cement, petro-chemical, and steel works, is occupied also with shipbuilding and the manufacture of soap and olive oil. The ancient city of **Eleusis**, birthplace of Aeschylus (525–456 BC) and home of the Sanctuary of Demeter and of the Eleusinian Mysteries, was situated on the E slopes of a low rocky hill (63m) which runs parallel and close to the shore. The *Sacred Way*, of which large sections (paved and with kerbs) have been traced, led direct to the sanctuary. It lies left of the modern road at the entrance to the town, but the modern approach to the site is signposted from the centre. The extensive excavations of the sanctuary, which had a continuous history from Mycenaean to Roman times, are of the greatest interest to antiquaries, but their appreciation is demanding to the lay imagination.

History. The legendary foundation of a city at Eleusis by Eleusis, a son of Ogygos of Thebes, before the 15C is substantiated in date at least by existing remains of houses (Middle Helladic II), dated to the 18–17C BC. Tradition tells of wars between the Athenians and Eleusinians in heroic times, resulting in the deaths of Erechtheus and of Immarados, son of Eumolpos. Eumolpos was reputed to be the first celebrant of the mysteries of Eleusis. The introduction of the cult of Demeter is ascribed by the Parian Chronicle to the reign of Erechtheus (c 1409 BC) and by Apollodoros to that of Pandion, son of Erichthonios (c 1462–1423). The first shrine on the sanctuary site is dated by sherds to the Late Helladic II period, though there is nothing concrete to connect it with Demeter. The 'Homeric' Hymn to Demeter (late 7C BC) gives the orthodox version of the institution of the mysteries by Demeter herself (cf. below). The city seems to have been a rival of Athens until it came under firm Athenian sway about the time of Solon. From then on its cult grew and the sanctuary was constantly enlarged. Its reputation became panhellenic and initiation was opened to non-Athenian Greeks. Peisistratos rebuilt it, enclosing it with a strong wall and doubling its area; but his work fell victim to the Persian invasion. Kimon initiated the reconstruction which was completed under Pericles. His Telesterion was to survive with modifications to the end. Eleusis suffered heavily under the Thirty Tyrants, who here established a fortified base against Thrasyboulos, massacring those who opposed them. The sanctuary was extended again in the 4C BC. The town remained a stronghold throughout the Macedonian period. Under the *pax Romana* the sanctuary was adorned with a new gate. The Imperial transformation of Eleusis probably began under Hadrian. In AD 170 the sanctuary was sacked by the Sarmatians, but was immediately restored at the expense of Marcus Aurelius. At his initiation in 176 the Emperor was allowed to enter the anaktoron, the only lay person so honoured in the whole history of Eleusis. The Emperor Julian was initiated, completing his sanctification (according to Gibbon) in Gaul; Valerian (253–60) reorganised the defences of the site in the face of threats from Barbarian tribes (Goths and Herulians); Valentinian permitted the continuance of the Mysteries, but Theodosius' decrees and Alaric's sack were jointly responsible (c 395) for their end. The town was abandoned after the Byzantine era and not reoccupied till the 18C.

The Homeric *Hymn to Demeter* sets down the anciently accepted mystique of the cult's divine foundation. While gathering flowers, Persephone (Kore, or the Maiden), Demeter's daughter, was carried off by Hades (Pluto) to the nether regions. Demeter, during her quest for Persephone, came to Eleusis, where she was found resting, disguised as an old woman, by Metaneira, consort of King Keleos. After her first disastrous attempt to reward the king's hospitality by immortalising his son Demophon, Demeter revealed her identity and commanded Keleos to build a megaron in her honour. To this she retired, vowing that she would neither return to Olympos nor allow crops to grow on earth until Kore was delivered up. Finally Zeus commanded Pluto to return Persephone, but because she had eaten pomegranate seeds while in the underworld she was bound to return there for part of every year. Before leaving Eleusis, Demeter broke the famine and gave to Triptolemos, second son of Keleos, seeds of wheat and a winged chariot, in which he rode over the earth, teaching mankind the use of the plough and the blessings of agriculture.

Candidates for initiation were first admitted to the *Lesser Eleusinia* which were held in the month of Anthesterion (February–March) at Agrai, in Athens, on the banks of the Ilissos. Being accepted as Mystai (initiates), they were allowed to attend the GREATER ELEUSINIA, which took place in Boëdromion (September), and lasted nine days, beginning and ending in Athens. For them a truce was declared throughout Hellas. During the seventh night the qualified Mystai became Epoptai. These annual celebrations (*teletai*) consisted of a public secular display and a secret religious rite. The former, the responsibility of the Archon Basileus and his staff, took the form mainly of a *Procession* (*pompe*) from Athens to Eleusis. The religious rite was entirely in the hands of the Hierophant and priesthood of Eleusis, hereditary offices of the Eumolpids and the Kerykes. The most important officials included the Dadouchos (torchbearer) and the Hierokeryx (herald). The procession, which took place on the fifth day, was headed by a statue of Iacchos, god associated with the cult, and bore with it the Hiera, or sacred objects, in baskets (*kistai*). During the Peloponnesian War, when no truce was declared, the procession was reduced; for some years after the Spartan occupation of Dekelia the pompe went by sea. In 336 BC the news of the destruction of Thebes by Alexander the Great caused the only recorded instance of the procession's cancellation after it had set out.

The fundamental substance of the **Mysteries**, the character of the sacred objects displayed, and the nature of the revelation experienced were never divulged. Alcibiades was condemned to death in absentia for parodying part of the mysteries (though later reprieved); Aeschylus was almost lynched on suspicion of revealing their substance on the stage. It is thought probable that a pageant (dromena) was performed representing the action of the Hymn of Demeter. Initiation carried with it no further obligation, but seems to have afforded spiritual pleasure. Cicero derived great comfort from the experience.

Eleusis attracted the attention of western travellers from Wheler (1676) onwards. E.D. Clarke bore away a statue to Cambridge in 1801. The Propylaea were laid bare in 1812 by the Society of the Dilettanti. Systematic excavations, started by the Greek Archaeological Society in 1882, were greatly extended by Konstantinos Kourouniotes in 1917–45, especially after the Rockefeller Institution had provided a grant in 1930. Both the earlier work and that done since the war by G.E. Mylonas, A. K. Orlandos, and John Travlos are admirably summarised in Mylonas: 'Eleusis and the Eleusinian Mysteries' (1962).

A good idea of the layout and complexity of the excavations can be gained from the terrace in front of the prominent 19C chapel. Visitors who are pressed for time can then confine themselves to the forecourt, the two propylaea, the Telesterion, the SE walls, and the Museum. A full exploration of the remains takes all day and necessitates a certain amount of scrambling. Care should be taken on the Acropolis, where there are unfenced cisterns.

The EXCAVATIONS lie at the foot and on the E slopes of the Acropolis and comprise the greater part of the **Sanctuary of Demeter and Kore** and its dependencies. This was protected on three sides by the main city wall and separated from the city on the fourth side by a dividing wall. As you pass the entrance gate the *Sacred Way* changes from a modern to an ancient paved road, which ends on the **Great Forecourt** before the city walls. This spacious square formed part of the new monumental entrance planned probably in the reign of Antoninus Pius. Here the mystai gathered in order to perform the necessary acts of purification before entering the sanctuary. From the square the Great Propylaea led directly to the sanctuary; to left and right triumphal arches led towards the main gate of the town and to the visitors' quarter of baths, hotels, and recreation centres.

Numerous marble blocks on the square came from the buildings that defined its limits. To the left are the remains of a *Fountain*. Beyond it stood a *Triumphal Arch*, one of two (cf. above) faithfully copied from the Arch of Hadrian at Athens. The foundations remain; its gable has been reassembled in front; and its inscription (replaced near by) reads 'All the Greeks to the Goddesses and the Emperor'. Close to the NE corner of the Great Propylaea is the sacred well that passed throughout classical times for the **Kallichoron**, or *Well of the Fair Dances*. The well-head, beautifully fashioned in polygonal masonry with clamps, probably dates from the time of Peisistratos. Mylonas has suggested that this is, in fact, the *Parthenion*, or Well of the Maidens, mentioned in the Hymn as the place where Demeter sat to rest. The name Kallichoron may have been transferred to it from the well near the Telesterion after the importance of the Parthenion had been centred on the 'Mirthless Stone' on which she sat (cf. below).

In the centre of the court are the scanty remains of the *Temple of Artemis Propylaia and of Poseidon*, amphiprostyle in form and constructed in marble. It must have been quite new when described by Pausanias. The *Altar* to the E was presumably dedicated to Artemis, that to the N probably to Poseidon, while at the NW corner is an *Eschara*, constructed in Roman times, on remains proving that the sacred nature of the spot goes back to the 6C BC. The rectangular area that interrupts the pavement beyond the eschara has been identified with the *Temenos of the Hero Dolichos*; beneath the houses outside the enclosure are extensive remains conjectured to be of a *Pompeion*.

The **Great Propylaea**, built in Pentelic marble on a concrete core by Marcus Aurelius or his predecessor, is a close copy of the Propylaea at Athens, both in plan and dimensions. It is approached by six marble steps and faces NE. Reassembled on the pavement in front are two of the six Doric *Columns* of the façade and the *Pediment* with its central medallion bust of (?) Marcus Aurelius. Parts of the entablature are assembled to the right of the steps. The bases of the six Ionic columns that flanked the central passage are *in situ*. The transverse wall was pierced by five doorways: the threshold of the small one to the left shows the greatest wear. At some time of danger (? under Valerian) the Doric colonnade was closed by a thick wall; the single door that then gave entrance has left a roller groove in the pavement. Crosses scored on the pavement probably derive from Christian fears of pagan spirits.

The gateway covers a corner tower of the Peisistratid enceinte. To the W this remained the city's fortification in later times; to the E a later wall enclosed a Classical extension to the city, while the Peisistratid circuit continued to serve as the peribolos of the sanctuary. Between the two walls are numerous small buildings dating mainly from the time of Kimon. The area between the two propylaea seems to have been a level forecourt in Roman times.

The **Lesser Propylaea** which face N and form the entrance to the innermost court, were vowed to the Goddesses by Cicero's friend Appius Claudius Pulcher in his consulship (54 BC) and completed after his death by two nephews. The structure consisted of two parallel walls, each 15m long, with Ionic attached columns, which enclosed a passage 10m wide. This is divided into three at its inner end by two short inner walls (parastadia) parallel to the exterior walls. Forward of the doors, whose supporting rollers have left prominent grooves, extended antae; the bases in front of them supported two Corinthian columns. The inner façade had caryatids instead of columns. Portions of the inscribed architrave and frieze are recomposed at the side. The frieze is composed of triglyphs and metopes, both carved with emblems of the cult.

You now enter the inner **Precinct of Demeter**, for two thousand years an area forbidden to the uninitiated on penalty of death. To the right is the *Plutonion*, a triangular precinct of the 4C BC, enclosing a cavern sacred to Pluto. A shrine was built at its mouth in the Peisistratid era; the surviving foundations are of a temple completed in 328 BC (a dated inscription has been found referring to the purchase of its wooden doors). Following the *Processional Road*, you come next to a rock-cut *Stepped Platform* (Pl. A) which adjoined a small building, perhaps a *Treasury* (Pl. B). The platform may have served as a stand from which the start of a sacred pageant was watched; Mylonas suggests that the *'Mirthless Stone'* (Agelastos Petra) may be identified with the worked piece of rock that here projects above the pavement of the Roman sacred way. The levelled terrace beyond the treasury supported a *Temple* (Pl. C) possibly dedicated to Sabina, wife of Hadrian, on whom the Greeks had conferred the title of New Demeter. Between this and the treasury is a *Thesauros* (offertory box) hewn from a boulder. You ascend to the large square platform on which stood the Hall of the Mysteries.

The first shrine decreed by Demeter 'beneath the citadel and its sheer wall upon a rising hillock above the Kallichoron' occupied a limited site on ground which sloped steeply away. As each enlargement of the sanctuary was undertaken, it became necessary to extend the artificial terrace on which it stood. In consequence each shrine in turn escaped complete destruction by being buried under the next. The result is an archaeological palimpsest of rare completeness but, to the layman, of baffling complexity.

The great **Telesterion**, or TEMPLE OF DEMETER, the Hall of Initiation and the Mysteries, is an almost square chamber 53m by 52m, partly cut out of the rock of the Acropolis and partly built on a terrace. The existing remains appear to be those of the Periclean rebuilding (with the addition of the Portico of Philo), as finally remodelled by Marcus Aurelius. On each of the four sides were eight tiers of seats, partly hewn from the rock and partly built up; these were interrupted at six points only, where two doors on each of the disengaged sides afforded entrance. The hall accommodated 3000. Six rows of seven columns each supported the (? wooden) roof; they were in two tiers separated by an epistyle (possibly with a frieze). The bases of most remain; one of them has as its top course a reused block of the 1C AD, showing the extent of the Roman restoration. In the centre, on a site it had occupied from the first, was the *Anaktoron*, or holy of holies, a small rectangular room roofed somehow by Xenokles with an *Opaion*, or lantern, of which no vestige has survived. By the side of the anaktoron stood the throne of the Hierophant. Externally the solid walls, broken only by doorways, must have enhanced the air of mystery. Later the SE front was adorned along its whole length by the PORTICO OF PHILO, whose pavement and massive supporting wall (18 courses of masonry) form one of the most prominent features of the site. It was completed, according to Vitruvius, in the reign of Demetrios of Phaleron. The huge prostoön had a colonnade of twelve Doric columns by two, which were left unfluted. An ancient *Well* cut into the rock below may be the original Kallichoron (cf. above).

Excavations have revealed traces of at least six earlier structures on the same site. The *Mycenaean Megaron*, traceable in the remains of two walls in the NE half of the hall, was a chamber c 17m square. This was replaced by a Geometric edifice, a Solonian Telesterion, and again by the *Telesterion of Peisistratos*, which occupied the NE corner of the final structure. This hall had five rows of five columns each, with a portico on the NE front, and was destroyed by the Persians. Kimon incorporated the ruins into a rectangular hall, designed round the old Anaktoron, and having seven rows of three columns each. It was apparently not finished. Pericles probably instigated a grander design by which the building again became square, doubling that of Kimon. This was first entrusted to Iktinos, whose plan to support the roof on only 20 columns (foundations visible) had to be abandoned for technical reasons. The design was replaced by another by Koroibos, which was completed after his death by Metagenes and Xenokles. Lycurgus may have ordered the Portico of Philo. The L-shaped foundations that extend beyond the E and S corners show that earlier plans for building a peristyle were started. After the Sarmatian sack, the Romans restored the interior with somewhat makeshift columns and extended the NW side another six feet into the rock.

From the Portico of Philo the *Court* of the sanctuary, a level artificial terrace, extended to the E and S. This had been built up and enlarged with each successive reconstruction, generally using the fortification wall of the previous sanctuary as a retaining wall for the new. The greater part of the late-Classical fill has been removed to show the successive stages, making apparent the steepness of the natural contour. Sections of the *Wall of Peisistratos* are roofed with corrugated iron to preserve their upper part constructed in unbaked bricks. A stretch immediately below the centre of the Portico of Philo shows where Kimon filled the Persian breach in the mud-brick wall with limestone masonry in alternately large and small courses (pseudo-isodomic), based directly on the Peisistratean socle. The inner face is rough and evidently retained a fill of earth. Within this wall parts of an Archaic polygonal terrace wall may be seen. Beyond the Peisistratean corner-tower are the remains of a Kimonian *Gate*. This was later blocked by the Periclean *Siroi*, where the first-fruit offerings were stored; five of its piers are very prominent.

The S side of the court was bounded in the 5C by the *Periclean Wall*, the function of which was minimised in the following century when the sanctuary was extended to the new *South Wall* of Lycurgus. Against the inside face of this are some remains identified with successive rebuildings in Hellenistic and late-Roman times of a *Bouleuterion*, or chamber of the city council. Outside the Lycurgan *South Gate* is a trapezoidal precinct surrounded by a wall (see below). Within this wall are the foundations of a *Hiera Oikia*, a Geometric house sacred to the memory of a hero; the building was destroyed early in the 7C, but remained a scene of religious rites into the Archaic period. Beyond are some vestiges of a *Mithraeum*. From outside the extreme S corner of the precinct you get an instructive panorama of contrasted types of ancient wall building.

Looking towards the museum you see the perfectly fitted polygonal masonry (6C) of the peribolos of the Sacred House. To the right is the 'Lycurgan' Wall (? 370–360 BC), one of the best preserved examples of ancient fortification, with both a square and a round *Tower*. On four slightly receding courses in pecked Eleusinian stone are set tooled courses in yellow poros; this is probably a conscious matching of the Periclean style. Beyond the corner the wall is masked by ruined Hadrianic cisterns. Farther on, the *Periclean East Wall*, like the Lycurgan, has a separate socle, here rusticated, while the upper part shows traces of bevelling.

On either side of the Telesterion a flight of steps was hewn in Roman times to give access to a wide *Terrace*, 6m above the hall floor. You mount the S steps to the **Museum**, which houses the important but relatively few works of art found in the ruins. Outside the entrance are a Roman sarcophagus (c AD 190) in marble with a well-carved representation of the Kalydonian boar-hunt (the lid does not belong to it); two representations in white marble of torches, c 2·5m high; a capital from the Lesser Propylaea; and a fine head of a horse.—ROOM I (to the right). Copy of the 'Niinnion Tablet', a red-figured votive pinax now in the Athens museum; the figures are believed to be performing rites from the Mysteries, the only known representation. Reconstruction of one corner of the geison of the Peisistratid Telesterion; Archaic kouros (c 540 BC); running girl from a pediment of c 485 BC. In the centre, huge Protoattic *Amphora (7C BC), depicting Odysseus blinding Polyphemos and Perseus slaying Medusa. Dedication reliefs: marble stele, Demeter seated with (probably) Hekate (c 475 BC); stele (411 BC) depicting a fight between Athenian cavalry and Spartan hoplites. Decree of 421 BC concerning the construction of a bridge over the Rheitoi (cf. above), with relief.

ROOM II (entrance-hall) contains a cast of the most famous Eleusinian Relief, now in the Athens museum. Facing the door is a *Statue of Demeter (headless and armless), perhaps by Agorakritos of Paros, pupil of Pheidias (420 BC); behind is the fragmentary Relief of Lakratides (1C BC), showing Triptolemos setting out in his chariot; the statue of Persephone is of Roman date. Relief: Demeter as the 'Mirthless Stone' approached by votaries.—ROOM III. Heads and statues, including Asklepios, dedicated by Epikrates (320 BC), found in a field.—ROOM IV displays a model of the site at two stages of its development (Peisistratid and Roman). Roman statuary: *Antinoos, represented as a youthful Dionysos standing by the Delphic omphalos; Tiberius as pontifex maximus; small and delicate Herakles.

ROOM V. Caryatid in the form of a kistephore (basket-carrier) from the inner parastade of the Lesser Propylaea (its fellow is in the Fitzwilliam Museum, Cambridge); green stole, in a good state of preservation, from a burial of the 5C BC (the only linen cloth surviving from the Classical era); Amphora of c 610 BC from Megara by the Chimaera painter; inhumation burials, including that of a boy in a larnax (terracotta coffin); decree reliefs.—ROOM VI. Vases of all periods from 1900 BC to AD 450, including a plain Mycenaean vase with a Linear B inscription (? an unidentified Cretan place-name) which recurs on the Knossos tablets; kernoi, the characteristic sacred vessels of the cult.

The tourist may well conclude his visit with the museum. The student of antiquities should continue to visit the Mycenaean complex beyond, the Acropolis, and the sectors of the town adjoining the forecourt.

Beyond the museum are some remains of a settlement of Middle Helladic date (18C–17C BC). Many Late Helladic vestiges have been discovered on the ACROPOLIS, from which there is a pleasant view towards Salamis. On the plateau beyond are Hellenistic remains. The Frankish tower that formerly crowned the W height fell victim to the quarrying activities of the cement factory. At the E point of the acropolis a *Chapel* (Panayia) with a detached belfry occupies part of a platform on which, in Roman times, stood a *Temple* (Pl. 1), probably dedicated to Faustina, wife of Antoninus Pius. You descend from here to the Lesser Propylaea. To the NW are some ruins of a Roman house conjectured to have belonged to the Kerykes, one of the hereditary priestly families. Farther off is the *Asty Gate* of the Peisistratid enceinte; its plan, uncovered by Travlos in 1960, is well preserved; still further W lay the *Megarian Gate*. The wall is not preserved but part of the ancient road from *Eleusis to Megara* has been found there. The *Roman Quarter* to the E of the Great Forecourt is interesting for its bathing establishments with piped water and a great drain having brick vaults and manholes at regular intervals.—In the town, near the church of Ayios Yeoryios, another *Roman Bath*, partially excavated in 1959, proved to be one of the largest discovered in Greece (time of Hadrian).

Many discoveries of all periods are continually made in excavations in building plots in the town. In 1977 parts of Roman (?) harbour installations were identified and what may be a terrace wall of the 'dolicho' (3C–2C BC racecourse).

17 From Athens to Soúnion

The excursion to Soúnion, seldom omitted by any visitor to Athens, is generally made by the coast road. The old inland road, less obviously attractive, nevertheless abounds with interest, especially for the unhurried visitor who can make diversions at will. Much of the E coast of Attica, c 8km from the road and easily accessible from it by track or footpath, is yet largely unspoilt, though a coastal road from Lavrion to Marathon, already approved, will ensure its rapid spoliation.

A.   By the Coast Road

ROAD, 70km (43½ miles). Buses from Od. Mavrommatéon c hourly take passengers for destinations beyond Várkiza. Half-day excursions by coach (CHAT., etc.). Buses (No. 145 etc.) for Várkiza depart from Leofóros Olgas.

To (25km) **Vouliagméni**, see Rte 13. The road continues 'en corniche' winding along a rocky *Coast, though the pine-clad slopes, once renowned for game, are fast being interspersed with hotels and bungalows.—31km *Várkiza* (Hotels A, B, C), with camping sites, a sandy beach (NTOG), a marina, and water-sports. The place gave name to the Agreement of 1945, whereby the organisations ELAS and EAM were demobilised and disarmed, bringing the first Communist rising to an end.

A little farther on a road leads inland to *Vári* (1·5km), a village amid pines (for the Vari Cave and House cf. Rte 13). Leaving Vari in the direction of Koropí (Rte 17B), the road crosses a flat plain, dominated (left) by the MILITARY ACADEMY, or *Officer Cadets' School*, the Sandhurst of Greece. In addition to military leaders, it trained naval cadets until 1846 and civil engineers in 1870–87. Founded at Nauplia in 1828 by Capodistrias, the academy was transferred first

Sounion. Restored view of the Sanctuary of Athena

to Aegina, then in 1837 to Piraeus. In 1894 it moved to the *Evelpidhon* building (now lawcourts) in central Athens. It has been in its present location since 1981. Cadets wear a dark blue uniform, with yellow collar and bands and white gloves.

About 700m beyond the further limits of the Academy, opposite the first of two boat yards, a road climbs straight towards the summit of Kiáfa Thíti above the village of Thítsi. On the top are the recently excavated remains of a fortified prehistoric stronghold of the early Mycenaean period, with a later church on the same site.

35km. The *Bay of Lomvardha* may represent the harbour of the Attic deme of *Lamptrai*, sited due N on the slope of Hymettos. Churches mark the seaward ends of roads from Koropí (Rte 17B).—42km *Luyonísi* (Hotels L, B) is a bungalow resort. Mt Panion, to the NE, is lost behind the Attic *Olimbos* (Olympus; 486m), a pyramidal hill which you skirt. Beyond (46km) *Saronís* (usually Saronídha, Hotel B) are the large Eden Beach and Alexander Beach hotels.—The little island of *Arsidha* lies close to the coast off the Bay of *Anávissos* (Hotels A, B, C). A by-road leads left to the hamlet (1·5km), where the celebrated kouros was found and an important Geometric cemetery has been excavated, then passes between Olimbos and Panion to Kalívia (16km).—Off (60km) *Cape Katafíyi*, which affords a fine panorama of the Saronic Gulf, lies the uninhabited *Gaidhouronisi*, known to Strabo as *Putroklou Charax*, the palisade of Patroclus.

Remains may be seen of the 3C fortifications built here by Patroclus, admiral of Ptolemy II, who commanded the Egyptian fleet sent to help the Athenians against Antigonus Gonatas in the Chremonidean War.—64·5km *Legrená* (Hotels B).

70km (43¹/₂ miles) **Cape Soúnion**, known also as *Cape Kolónes* (Κάβο Κολώνες), is a precipitous rocky headland rising 60m from the sea. The low isthmus which joins it to the mainland separates the sandy and exposed *Bay of Soúnion* (Hotels A, B, C), a developing resort, from the rocky but sheltered haven to the E, which provides a welcome refuge for mariners unable to weather the cape. On the highest point of the headland, at its end, are the columns of the ruined Temple of Poseidon (see below), which give the headland its alternative name. The visitor wishing to share Byron's experience of 'Sunium's marbled steep, Where nothing save the waves and I may hear our mutual murmurs sweep' should visit the site out of season and in the morning. On Sundays and towards sunset it is overrun by coach trippers.

The township of *Soúnion* (Σούνιον; Lat. *Sunium*), whose wealth was proverbial in classical times, stood at the head of the bay of the same name, where regattas were held in honour of Poseidon. After the battle of Salamis the Athenians here dedicated a captured Phoenician ship (one of three; Hdt. VIII, 121). Some years before, the Aeginetans had seized the sacred Athenian *Theoris*, the ship that conveyed the sacred envoys (Θεωροί) to Delos, while it lay at Sounion (Hdt. VI, 87). The town was a port of call of the corn ships from Euboea to Piraeus. The Athenians fortified it during the Peloponnesian War and, in 413 BC (Thuc. VIII, 14), the entire headland was enclosed, the promontory forming the citadel. The inhabitants were noted for harbouring runaway slaves whom they often enfranchised without question. On one occasion a strong gang of slaves seized the fortress and devastated the neighbourhood. Terence mentions Sunium as a haunt of pirates. It was a favourite resort of the corsairs, one of whom, Jaffer Bey, is supposed to have destroyed some of the columns of the temple. One of three of the crew who escaped the foundering of a Levantine trader here was the second mate and poet, William Falconer, who immortalised the incident in 'The Shipwreck' (1762).

The remains of the W half of the promontory now form an archaeological precinct. The Temple of Poseidon was measured by Revett in 1765 and by the Dilettanti Society in 1812. Byron carved his name on a pillar. The site was excavated by Dörpfeld in 1884 and by the Greek Archaeological Society in 1899–1915. In 1906 two colossal kouroi were found in the debris to the E of the temple. Since 1958 some columns have been re-erected.

The whole Acropolis was enclosed by a double *Fortification Wall*, c 500m long and strengthened at intervals by square towers. It formed a semicircle from the Bay of Soúnion on the NW, where some remains are well preserved, to the S cliff edge. Its SE angle enclosed the TEMENOS OF POSEIDON, a precinct supported on the N and W by a terrace wall. This was entered on the N side by Doric *Propylaea*, built of poros and marble in the 5C, the axis of which is aligned with the E front of the temple.

A square room to the W of the gate separated it from a *Stoa*, which extended along the peribolos wall. Its foundations have collapsed in the far corner, but five bases remain of six interior columns that divided it lengthwise. A second stoa, running N–S, abuts on the first at the W.

The ***Temple of Poseidon**, near the edge of the cliff, forms a conspicuous landmark from the sea. From a distance it presents a dazzlingly white appearance that proves illusory at closer view: the columns are of grey-veined marble quarried at *Agriléza* (5km N by an ancient road), where bases of columns of the same dimension can still be seen. The attribution to Poseidon was confirmed by an inscription. On stylistic grounds Prof. Dinsmoor ascribes the design of the temple to the architect of the Hephaisteion at Athens, placing it c 444 BC. It stands on the foundations of an earlier edifice in poros stone, founded shortly before 490 BC and unfinished at the time of the Persian invasion. The Doric peristyle had 34 columns (6 by 13), that stood on a stylobate measuring 31·1m by 13·4m. Nine columns remain on the S side and six (four re-erected in 1958–59) on the N side, with their architraves. The columns are unusual in having only sixteen instead of the normal twenty flutes. The sculptural arrangement also departed from the normal custom, an Ionic frieze (see below) lining all four sides of the interior space in front of the pronaos (cf. the Hephaisteion), and the external metopes being left blank (perhaps because of the exposed nature of the site); the pediments, which were sculptured, had a raking cornice with a pitch of 12½° instead of the more usual 15°.

The INTERIOR had the usual arrangement of pronaos, cella, and opisthodomos. Both pronaos and opisthodomos were distyle in antis. There survive only the N anta of the pronaos, with its adjacent column, and the S anta, which was reconstructed in 1908.

Thirteen slabs of the frieze, in Parian marble, stand to the E of the approach path. The sculpture, much corroded, is believed to illustrate a contest of Lapiths and Centaurs, the Gigantomachia, and exploits of Theseus (cf. the *Hephaisteion*).

The *View from the temple over the sea is most striking. To the E lies Makronisos. About 11km S lies the rocky island of Ay. Yeoryios, the ancient *Belbina*. The nearest islands to the SE are *Keos*, *Kithnos*, and *Seriphos*, to the S of which, on a clear day, even *Melos* can be made out. To the W is *Aegina*, in the centre of the Saronic Gulf, with the E coast of the Peloponnese behind it.

Beyond the Tourist Pavilion on a low hill commanding the isthmus on the N, are the remains of a small *Temple of Athena Sounias*, noted by Vitruvius for the irregularity of its plan with an Ionic colonnade along the E and S sides of the structure of c 450 BC. The cella was 5·9m by 3·8m, with four columns in the middle arranged in a square. The cult statue stood at the back. A little to the N are the remains of a small Doric temple, distyle prostyle, probably dedicated to the hero Phrontis.

B.   Via the Mesogeia

ROAD, 64·5km (40 miles). 12km *Stavrós*.—18km *Paianía* (*Liópesi*).—24km *Koropí*.—30km **Markópoulo**.—40km *Keratéa*.—55km **Lávrion**.—64·5km **Soúnion**. Buses from Od. Mavrommatéon every hour (more frequently on Sundays and holidays) to *Lavrion* (in 1½ hours (taking passengers for Keratéa and beyond only); usually continuing after an interval to *Soúnion*); also to *Markópoulo* and *Pórto Ráfti*. To *Paianía* (=Liópesi; Nos 125, 310) and to *Koropí* (Nos 307, 308), every 20 minutes from Thissíon.

From the centre of the city to (2·5km) *Ambelókipoi*, see Rte 11.—You take the right fork (Od. Mesogeíon). The N foothills of Hymettos appear intermittently above the suburban development. In trees (right) stands the *Police College*. The S bypass (Rte 13) joins Mesogeíon by an underpass.—At (4km) *Goudhí* the University of Athens has its Ilissia precinct. Above stands Ay. Ioannis Theologos (Rte 14).—At (6·5km) *Kholargós*, which bears the name of the native deme of Pericles (c 490–429 BC), you pass (left) the huge administrative HQ of the Greek army. Mt Pentelikon rises behind.—6m. *Ayía Paraskeví*. The Nuclear Research Centre (which includes amongst its activities the analysis of archaeological artefacts), designed by a British company and opened in 1961 by King Paul, bears the name of Democritus, the first scientist to propound an atomic theory. The headquarters of the Greek broadcasting services (EPA and ET) are also here. A by-road leads (right; 2km) to *Moní Ayios Ioánnis Kynigós*, the monastery of St. John the Hunter (view); its 12C church has a strangely supported dome and a 17C narthex (festival, 26 July).—At (12km) *Stavrós*, by a radio-telephone station, you round the N spur of Hymettos, leave the Marathon road (flyover), and turn S into the Mesogeía.

The *Mesogeía* (τὰ, anciently ή, Μεσόγεια, 'the inland'), which lies between Hymettos and the Petalion Gulf, is watered by two seasonal rivers: the Valanaris entering the sea S of Rafína and the Erasinos near Vráona. Its red clay is the most fertile soil in Attica, producing good wine, much of which is flavoured with pine resin to produce the retsina favoured by Athenians. Anciently Brauron was of importance; the modern capital is Koropí. Many of the attractive little churches have frescoes by Yeoryios Markos and his school.

18km **Paianía** (also Liópesi; *Kanakis Taverna* in a lemon-grove at the N end), a straggling village (7278 inhab.) in pleasantly wooded country, has readopted the name of the birthplace of Demosthenes (c 384–322 BC), identified with some remains to the E. Here is the *Vorrés Museum* (open weekend mornings only), a seven-acre complex which combines modern with traditional architecture and gardens. The buildings contain traditional artefacts, prints and pictures relating to modern Greek history and (in a specially designed gallery) a collection of modern painting and sculpture. To the S of the village is the church of *Ayios Nikólaos Chalídhou* which has unusual decoration in the dome (12C). A by-road (signposted) leads to the *Koutouki Cave* (open daily). You bear right off the new road which leads direct to Markopoulo for—24km **Koropí**, the liveliest village (11,214 inhab.) in the Mesogeia, which is surrounded by vineyards; the retsina vats are prominent. By-roads lead (right) to the coast. SE of the village is the church of *Metamórphosis Sotíras*, decorated with late 10C/early 11C frescoes. Interesting is the dome decoration which includes the Pantocrator, the symbols of the Evangelists, Seraphim and Cherubim.—30km (18½ miles) **Markópoulo**, a busy and prosperous centre (6116 inhab.) is noted for its bread. By its conspicuous *Church*, the interior of which is enlivened with encaustic illustrations of the lives of various saints, diverges the road to Brauron and Pórto Ráfti.

FROM MARKÓPOULO TO PÓRTO RÁFTI, 8km (through bus from Athens). 2·5km. By-road to Vráona (see below). About 5km S rises *Mt Mirenda* (613m). Between our road and the mountain near a medieval watch-tower, lay the ancient deme of *Myrrhinous*, where Artemis Kolainis, the Bird Goddess, was worshipped. Inscriptions to Artemis were found on the site in 1960–61, after the Greek Archaeological Service had explored 26 tombs, mostly of the 8C BC, uncovered a section of prehistoric road, and confirmed the existence of a Shrine of Pythian Apollo. From this area in 1972 came also a superb kouros and kore now in Athens Museum.—6km. Track (right) to Prasiai (Hotels A, C, D, E), see below.

6·5km. **Pórto Ráfti** has one of the best natural harbours in Greece, of which little use is made. The beautiful bay is unequally divided by the narrow rocky spit of *Ayios Nikólaos* (Tavernas), off which lies the islet of *Prasonísi*. It is protected on the seaward side by the islets of *Ráfti* and *Raftopoúla*. On Ráfti is a colossal seated marble statue of the Roman period, popularly known as the 'tailor' (ράφτης), whence the modern name of the harbour. The statue, which is female, is conjectured to represent Oikoumene and to have served as a beacon-light. Helladic and Byzantine sherds have been noted on the steep slopes of both islets. From the beach, the last in Attica to remain in Allied hands, 6000 New Zealand troops were evacuated in April 1941. Scholars locate ancient *Prasiai* on the S slopes of the bay, where 22 Mycenaean tombs were found in 1894–95.

From **Prasiai** the annual Theoria, or sacred embassy, set out to Delos in the ship believed to be that in which Theseus returned triumphant from Knossos. Here Erysichthon, an envoy of Delos, who died on his return journey, was buried, and here came the mysterious first-fruits of the Hyperboreans on their way from central Europe to Delos.

The bay is closed on the S by the peninsular headland of *Koróni*, anciently *Koroneia*. Its Acropolis and an unbroken Long Wall with nine towers within the Isthmus formed a *Fortress*. Excavated in 1960 by the American School, this is proved by coins of Ptolemy II Philadelphus to be an Egyptian encampment of the Chremonidean War (? 265–261 BC). In this war the Athenians threw in their lot with Egypt and Sparta in an unsuccessful bid to free themselves from Macedonian domination.—On the N side of the bay at Dhrívlia (in a grove c 200m inland from a prominent sea-side kiosk) are the remains of a 3-aisled Early Christian basilica of the 5C. This area is dominated by the precipitous *Peratí* (307m), with unexplored caves. The road continues beneath the hill past two tavernas to *Ayios Spíridhon* (the bus terminus, 2km from Ayios Nikolaos; Hotel C), 10 minutes beyond which, above the banks of a stream, has been discovered a huge *Necropolis* of chamber tombs (Late Helladic III c). You can continue round the shoreward side of Perati (taverna) to Brauron (c 8km; see below).

From Ay. Spiridon a boat may be hired for the visit to Ráfti (see above; rocky disembarkation and stiff climb).

THE BY-ROAD TO VRÁONA (Brauron), 6km from Markópoulo, diverges from the Pórto Ráfti road (cf. above). A square *Tower* (left; c 1km from the road), beyond the fork, is of Frankish date. Farther on (left) are the interesting remains of an Early Christian *Basilica*. You pass a by-road (left) which ascends to the prominent Hotel Vraon and continues to Loútsa and Rafína.

The name Vráona (Βραώνα) is a medieval corruption of Βραύρων, but the ancient name is being readopted as Vravróna.

Brauron, one of the twelve ancient communities antedating the Attic confederation, is situated in the broad and marshy valley of the subterranean Erasínos c 1·5km from the sea. The district apparently comprised the townships of *Halai Araphenides* (now Loútsa, a little to the N) and *Philiadai*. Peisistratos had estates in the neighbourhood. The attractive SANCTUARY OF ARTEMIS BRAURONIA (not open regularly but visible from road) lies just beyond the Loutsa fork at the foot of a low hill, immediately below the little late-Byzantine chapel of *Ayios Yeoryios*.

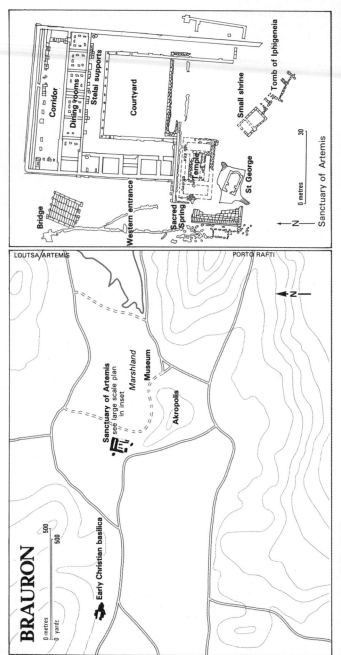

The site may be reached by bus (for Hamólia) twice daily from Markopoulo which has a regular service from Athens. Alternatively the 304 service from Thissíon to Artemis or Néa Loútsa terminates at the Hotel Vraon (above), c 30 minutes walk away (less if the intervening valley is dry).

Beyond the chapel a small *Shrine* marked the entrance to a cavern, the roof of which fell in the 5C BC. This seems to have been venerated in Archaic times as the *Tomb of Iphigeneia*. Other tombs probably belong to priestesses of Artemis.

Tradition relates that Iphigeneia brought to Brauron the image of Artemis which she and Orestes stole from Tauris (Euripides, 'Iphigeneia in Tauris', 1446–67). In one version she is virtually identified with the goddess and performs the ritual sacrifice of her brother; in another she herself dies at Brauron. A wooden image was taken by the Persians from Brauron to Susa. In Classical times the savage rites had been moderated, and Artemis was worshipped in her function as protectress of childbirth. The Brauronia was a ceremony held every four years, in which Attic girls between the ages of five and ten, clad in saffron robes, performed rites which included a dance where they were dressed as bears (cf. Aristophanes, 'Lysistrata', 645.) The connection between bears, childbirth, and Artemis recalls the legend of Callisto, but the purpose of the ritual remains mysterious. In the late 4C BC the site suffered from inundations and by the time of Claudius it was deserted, for Pomponius Mela (De situ Orbis, II, 3) exclaims that Thorikos and Brauron, formerly cities, are now but names. Excavations, carried out with difficulty in the waterlogged valley by the Greek Archaeological Society under John Papadhimitriou in 1946–52 and in 1956–63, show occupation since Middle Helladic times (earliest on hill above).

At a lower level, discovered in 1958, are the remains of a Doric *Temple* of the 5C BC, measuring c 20m by 10m, the foundations of which stand on rock-hewn steps (? the 'holy stairs' of Euripides). Here were discovered dedicatory reliefs in coloured terracotta, bronze mirrors, and votive jewellery. Many of these were found in a sacred pool (now dry) below the temple. Adjoining the temple is a huge Π-shaped *Stoa*, built before 416 BC, in which have been found inscriptions recording it to be the 'parthenon' of the arktoi, or 'bears'. It had nine dining-rooms. Part of the colonnade and entablature was re-erected in 1962. Just to the W is a remarkable stone *Bridge* of the same period. Inscriptions (see also Athens, Acropolis, Sanctuary of Brauronian Artemis) record other buildings (gymnasium, palaistra, stables etc) which have not been found.

The large well-arranged site MUSEUM (round the next bend of the road) displays marble statues and heads of little girls and of boys, and beautiful 4C marble reliefs. There are numerous dedicatory offerings from the sanctuary-vases, figurines, mirrors, jewellery, etc. Models reconstruct the appearance of the site. Here also are Geometric finds from Anavyssos and splendid Late Helladic III c *Pottery from Perati.

Past (2km) the museum is a right fork to Porto Rafti (7km from Brauron), while the left branch terminates at Hamólia (3km, Camping).

The main road by-passes (34km) **Kalívia** (2577 inhab.), with attractive churches. Inscriptions suggest that the ancient deme of *Prospalta* was in the vicinity. In the village is the church of *Ayios Petros*, which has a portrait of Michaelis Choniates, bishop of Athens. The halo shows that the picture was executed after his death and the frescoes must therefore date to after 1220. About 1·5km SW, on a by-road to Anávissos (16km; Rte 17A), is the pretty *Taxiarkhis*, a deserted monastic church. At the 36th kilometre post a track leads (left) to *Ayios Yeoryios*, a Byzantine church with reused Ionic capitals. The countryside becomes more hilly. To the left rises Mt Mirenda (see

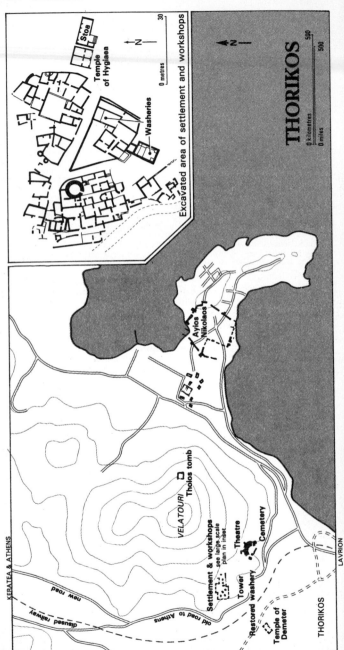

above), to the right the double crest of *Paneion* (651m), known locally as Keratovouni (the horned mountain). Its steep E summit dominates (40km) **Keratéa** (Hotel A), a prosperous village (5600 inhab.), with orchards, vineyards, and good water, where Chateaubriand suffered from sunstroke. Here a track descends to the *Convent of the Palaioimerologítai* (Adherents of the Old Calendar), 8km E, above the exposed beach of Kakí Thálassa. The new main road to Lavrion swings left, you keep to the old (right).—The little mining hamlet of (50km) *Pláka* lies below the top of the next ridge (168m), from which you look down towards the *Bay of Thorikós*, reached by a zigzag descent. The new road joins our route.

Dominating the bay (1·5km NE of the road), is the conical hill of *Velatouri*, the acropolis of ancient **Thorikos**. Towards the sea is the promontory of Ayios Nikolaos, which divides Portomandri, to the S, from Frankolimani, a smaller bay to the N, protected by Cape Vrisaki. This deep refuge is half-way between Piraeus and Rhamnous.

The mines of Thorikos are now known to have been exploited in the third millennium BC. In the Mycenaean period legend (its king, Kephalos, married Prokris, daughter of Erechtheus) suggests dynastic ties with Athens. Thorikos was fortified in 41? BC as a defensive outpost of the Laurion mines (cf. Xenophon Hell. i. 2, 1) It was deserted after the Classical period but there are signs of renewed settlement in late antiquity (4–6C AD).

The site is reached from the main road by turning left at a prominent sign (PPC Public Power Corporation) and again at a smaller sign to— Ancient Theatre of Thorikos. The most significant remains lie at the S foot of the hill. There is a stretch of fortification wall, with one *Tower* standing to a height of c 3·5m. Higher up is the *Theatre*, unique in its irregular plan, which clumsily follows the contour of a natural declivity. The first orchestra was laid out with a retaining wall in the Archaic period. In the mid 5C the theatre had 21 rows of seats; a century later it was extended to provide room for a further 12 rows, some of which may have had temporary seats. At that point the theatre would have accommodated about 6000 spectators. The *Cavea* forms an irregular ellipse and is divided by two stairways, almost parallel, into three sections, the central one nearly rectangular, those at either end sharply curved. The seats are roughly hewn. The lower rows were approached from below; the upper via two ramps set against the marble retaining wall of the structure. The W ramp is pierced by a corbelled passage. The narrow W parodos is bounded by a small *Temple of Dionysos* in antis, which faces across the rectangular orchestra towards a large *Altar*. Below the theatre has been recently excavated an Archaic and Classical cemetery whose tombs are grouped round small funerary monuments. To the W of this the hillside was quarried for construction of the theatre. Above the quarry is a restored ore washery.

Many such washeries have been found in the Lavrion area. They were used for grading the crushed ore–bearing rock from the local mines. A rectangular water tank (often with a cistern behind) has small perforations in its front wall to release jets of water into long sloping wooden troughs with cross partitions (none of these have survived). The heaviest (richest) fragments were retained in the highest partitions, while the remainder were caught lower down or (if light and valueless) swept away by the water. A broad 'table' in front of the tank and troughs was used for drying the material. Round the table ran a water channel with settling tanks at the corners. The water used in the washing process escaped into this, was purified and could be reloaded into the main tank when it reached the end of the circuit.

A good deal of excavation has been undertaken in an area c 100m NW of the theatre, where 7C houses were converted into workshops (including washeries) for processing the metal ores mined close by in the late 5C or early 4C. A late Archaic double *Temple of Hygiaea* and small adjacent stoa can also be seen here.

On the top of the hill, Mycenaean and earlier remains have been excavated by the Greek Archaeological Society in 1890 and 1893; and recently by the Belgian Mission. On the NE side of the hill are Mycenaean chamber and tholos tombs. There is an unusual oblong tomb and, nearby, a Middle Helladic tumulus in some respects resembling those found at Marathon. The maritime fortress of 412 BC occupies the isthmus between the two harbours to the W of the church.

A hoard of 4–3C tetradrachms was found in 1969.—The remains of a peripteral Doric *Temple of Demeter and Kore* of unusual design, with 7 columns on the fronts and 14 at the sides, unearthed in 1812 c 1km W of the theatre, have been covered again. Much of its materials were transported to Athens in Augustan times and re-erected in the SE corner of the Agora.

About 5km offshore lies the island of *Makrónisos*, anciently called *Helena*, from a tradition that Helen rested here on her flight with Paris. Used after the civil war of 1946 as a detention centre, it is now uninhabited save by shepherds in summer. Traces of prehistoric settlement have been located.

54km (34 miles) **Lávrion** (Λαύριον), known in the 19C as *Ergasteria* because of its workshops, is a scattered industrial town of 8921 inhab., which owes its existence to the neighbouring mines and its name to the ancient district of *Laurion*. Its chimneys, placed on the surrounding hills to render the fumes less unpleasant, are conspicuous from afar. To the possession of the silver mines of Laurion the Athenians owed, in great measure, their commercial and political greatness; the Athenian silver coinage ('Laureot owls') had prestige all over the world.

The mines were exploited in prehistoric times; Aeschylus alludes in the 'Persae' (235) to the Θησαυρὸς Χθόνος. The decision of the Athenians in 483 BC to finance the building of a fleet with the surplus yield of the mines laid the foundations of their naval supremacy, and by the time of Pericles the industry had reached the peak of its prosperity. As a result of the incursion of the Spartans in 413, the mines were closed. Though they were reopened c 355 thanks to Xenophon's treatise on mines as a neglected source of revenue and lasted another four centuries, they were never again as important. Pausanias refers to them in the past tense and for centuries they lay neglected. Modern exploitation, very largely the result of French initiative, is in the hands of three companies: one French (reconstituted after disputes about government royalties in 1873), one Greek (1860), and one American. The modern mines are concerned principally with the extraction of cadmium and manganese, and, to a lesser degree, with reworking the ancient slag-heaps for lead. The synthetic textile mills are important.

The best preserved ANCIENT MINES are situated in the Berzeko valley, which runs S from *Ayios Konstandínos* (Kamárisa), about 5km to the W of Lavrion (sign on N outskirts). A car can be taken (3km; sign in Ayios Konstandínos) to the church of Ayía Triádha beyond a huge ruined 19C installation above the valley. (This road continues to the coast (c 8km from Lávrion).

Beyond Ayios Konstandínos the road continues to the W coast at Anávissos (14km from Lavrion).

The mines anciently belonged to the State, which granted them on perpetual leases to contractors. They were worked by slave labour. Over 2000 ancient shafts have been found, some perpendicular (18–122m deep) and some sloping. Some are visible, protected by low walls, by the roadside, e.g. c 1km past Ayia Triadha. The roofs of the galleries (24–46m deep) were supported either by artificial piers or by natural ore-bearing pillars left in the rock. The removal of these pillars, which was dangerous, was punishable by death. Ventilation shafts carried off the bad air. Some miners' lamps and other relics have been found. In various places chains of huge *Cisterns* and ore-washeries and furnaces are to be seen. A washery in the Agriléza valley (6km SW of Lavrion) was excavated by the British School in 1977–78.

From Lavrion a boat plies to the island of *Kea* daily in summer (pm); sometimes continuing to Kíthnos.

The road continues S at some distance from the sea. On the W are moderate wooded hills. Above the coast (Hotel B) are dotted many summer villas of the Athenians.

At (59km) Pashalimáni on the coast below can be seen some remains of a Greek and Roman harbour town with an agora and metal working establishments.

The columns of the Temple of Poseidon are seen on the skyline as you join the coast road at the approach to (64·5km) *Soúnion*.

18 Sálamis

The crescent-shaped island of **Sálamis** (ΣΑΛΑΜΙΣ; usually accusative Salamína; 93 sq. km) lies in the N of the Saronic Gulf close inshore. Its NW coast is less than 1km from the coast of Megaris, and its NE coast is separated from the mainland of Attica by the Strait of Salamis, scene of the famous battle. The island thus gives to the Bay of Eleusis the character of a lagoon. Salamis with 20,407 inhabitants, mainly of Albanian descent, forms part of the eparchy of Piraeus. Its soil is dry and rocky and, though a few vineyards and cornfields are found in the plains, the climate is unhealthy. The highest point is *Mavrovouni* (404m). According to Strabo the ancient capital originally lay on the S coast opposite Aegina; this was moved before Classical times to the E coast; the modern capital is on the W side of the island at the head of the Bay of Koulouris. Salamis is famous for its battle and important as a naval base, but it is of run-down appearance and archaeological remains are meagre. Military establishments impede a close study of the scene of the battle, the best general view of which is still obtained from Xerxes' vantage-point behind Perama.

History. In Mycenaean times *Salamis* seems to have had dynastic connections with both Aegina and Cyprus. The Homeric catalogue records a contribution of twelve ships led by Telamonian Ajax. In the 7C the island was disputed between Athens and Megara. It was annexed to Athens as a cleruchy by Solon, the Athenians going so far as to forge an extra line of Homer in support of their claim. In 480 BC the Athenians evacuated Athens and, with Salamis as base, entrusted themselves to their 'wooden walls'. After 318 BC Salamis surrendered to the Macedonian Cassander, but in 229 BC it was recovered for Athens by Aratos, when the Salaminians were expelled in favour of new colonists.

Approaches. FROM ATHENS in 35 minutes by frequent bus Nos 841, 842 from Plateía Koumoundhoúrou (Eleftherías) (or from Piraeus by frequent bus, No. 843) to Pérama on the S coast of the Skaramangas peninsula. The road traverses the sprawling industrial town of *Nikaia* (90368 inhab.), which extends NW of Piraeus to the Aigaleos hills, and passes below the supposed vantage-point from which Xerxes watched the Battle of Salamis.—15km **Pérama** has shipyards where trawlers, tugs, and coastal steamers are built. The buses terminate at the quay, where ferries (c ½ hourly) cross the Strait of Salamis to the island; to *Paloúkia* (cars taken), via the N side of the island of Ayios Yeoryios, for the town of *Sálamis* (2km; bus every 10 minutes); to *Kameteró*; and to a landing-stage E of Ambelákia for Selínia. The crossings take c 15 minutes. Buses serve all main points on the island.

The **Battle of Salamis** was fought about 22 September 480 BC. The tactics of the battle and the fundamental identification of the island of Psyttaleia (Ψυττάλεια) are still the subject of scholarly disagreement. Most commentators identify Psyttaleia with Lipsokoutáli, a view excellently argued by A.R. Burn ('Persia and the Greeks', 1962) and by Paul W. Wallace (A J A, 1969). N.G.L. Hammond (J H S, 1956) identified Psyttaleia with Ayios Yeóryios and Lipsokoutáli with Atalante. This may be thought to accord better with the accounts of Herodotus (VIII, 70–94) and of Aeschylus who fought in the battle and describes it in the 'Persae' performed eight years later. The general strategy of the battle is not in doubt though Athenian tradition seems as usual to have exaggerated the disparity between the opposing forces.

Salamis was a key point in Themistocles' plan of defence against the Persians and in the event a decisive one. While all Athenian women and children were evacuated to Troezen, Salamis was to receive the old men and exiles (who were ordered to return). An attempt to stem the Persian advance was to be made with half the allied fleet at Artemision while the remaining Athenian triremes with the reserves of the fleets of Sparta, Corinth, and Aegina were to lie off Salamis. Before the action the Persians were in Phaleron Bay. The news that they had despatched an army by land towards the Isthmus alarmed the Peloponnesians who had to be persuaded against retiring on Corinth. Xerxes' first plan to bottle the Athenians in the Skaramangas strait or force them into open water to the E by building a pontoon boom across the strait itself was foiled by Cretan archers. Themistocles, hoping to force an immediate battle in the narrows, where he would have the advantage, organised a leak of information to Xerxes that the Peloponnesians intended to retreat. Under cover of darkness the Persians put into operation a new plan to encircle the supposedly disunited Greeks; Psyttaleia was occupied; a squadron of 200 Egyptian ships was despatched to block the W strait between Salamis and Megara; and the remaining ships were drawn up in a line right across the E exit. The Persian plan seems to have been to surprise the Greeks, while they were still drawn up on the beaches at dawn, and capture their base. Xerxes himself set up a silver throne on Aigaleos, 'the rocky brow that looks o'er sea-born Salamis', where he could watch the battle. Aristides, the exiled rival of Themistocles, who succeeded in slipping through to the Greek fleet from Aegina, was the first to bring the news of the investment. His statement was confirmed by a Tenean deserter. The forewarned Greeks, who now had no alternative but to fight, embarked before dawn, retired apparently in flight before the advancing enemy and formed up in hiding behind a promontory. When they emerged in battle order the advantage of surprise was with them. With their more manoeuverable ships, lower in the water, they made deadly use of the technique of ramming. As Themistocles had foreseen, the Persians became hopelessly confused, Artemisia, queen of Halicarnassos, being noticed to sink one of her allies' ships. 'Their multitude became their ruin' (Aeschylus). The Corinthian contingent (70 ships) under Adeimantos was later said by Athenian gossip to have taken no part in the battle, perhaps because executing a feint withdrawal or shadowing the Egyptian squadron.

At the critical moment a force under Aristides captured Psyttaleia, making the victory complete. The fleet of Aegina is said to have distinguished itself most, and next the Athenians. Although the battle did not become such a legend to the Athenians as Marathon, it is much more entitled to rank as one of the 'decisive battles' of the world. To the Persians Marathon was merely the defeat of a punitive expedition, Salamis the overthrow of a royal scheme of conquest.

To the N of *Paloúkia* the *Arsenal*, the most important naval station in Greece, extends round the Bay of Arapi, cutting off access to the NE part of the island. From Paloúkia one road leads S to *Ambelákia*, near which (1. 5 km; at Palaiomagoúla on the Kynosoura promontory) a stone mound 20m in diameter has been identified as the *Tomb of the Fallen* of the great battle, and crosses the base of the *Kamateró peninsula on which stood classical Salamis (few traces) to Selínia*, a villa resort. Alternatively you can travel W to **Sálamis**, or *Kouloúri*, the chief town (20437 inhab.) of the island, at the head of a deep bay on the W coast. Much of the bay is a rash of bungalows. In the bay, since the laying up in 1959 of ships from Far Eastern waters, the Japanese pearl oyster has been found: attempts to cultivate it are being made at Megálo Péfko.—A road skirts the bay to the straggling village of *Aiándeion*; at the entrance to the village roads lead E to

Kakí Vígla, a hamlet on the coast, and S over the mountain to (6·5km) *Ayios Nikólaos* and then down to the coast.

Beyond Sálamis the road traverses the island's NW peninsula.—8km. The *Moní Faneroméni*, or Convent of the Apparition of the Virgin (Φανερωμένη), has a remarkable fresco of the Last Judgment. Nine glazed bowls built into the exterior fabric are 13C–16C AD and include two Corinthian and two Italian pieces. The monastery is crowded with pilgrims on 4 September and there are traditional processions in Passion week. Néa Péramos is seen across Vasiliká Bay.—The road ends at (10km) the landing-stage of the Megaris ferry (see above).

To the S of the road, overlooking St. George's Bay just below the ridge, is a long fortification-wall, identified in 1960 by the American School with the fort of *Boudoron*, built by the Athenians in the 5C to keep watch over Megara, and ravaged in 429 BC by the Peloponnesian fleet.

19 Mount Párnes

Mount Párnes, in Greek *Párnis Oros* (Πάρνης Όρος), the rugged mountain range to the NW of Athens, forms the central part of the massif dividing Attica from Boeotia. It is limited at the E end by the Diakria, or 'Upland', the lowest exit from the Attic plains, and on the W by the pass between Mt Pastra, its W extension, and Kithairon. Parnes thus extends some 40km from E to W. Its wildness is well appreciated from the air. Though the disfigurement of radar has come to its summits, it remains sparsely populated, scored by ravines, and, except where its slopes are clothed in forests of pine or oak, exposed to the elements. Wolves and bears, seen in Roman times, are no longer found, but sheepdogs may be encountered. The mountain is crossed by only one road suitable for wheeled traffic (via Dekelia; see Rte 20), though the ancient route to Thebes by way of Phyle and Pyli is still practicable on foot. Walkers intending to make expeditions should take provisions and a compass; prudent travellers will also take a tent, since to the W of Phyle there is no hotel nearer than Thebes, and, except on the two approaches described below, public transport can be reached only on the Salonika highway or at Avlon Station to the N, or on the Thebes road to the S. The SE slopes have been made easily accessible since 1960 and are being developed for winter sports. The W forts (Panakton etc.) are more readily visited from the Thebes road.

By car the two routes below may be combined without returning to Athens by using the link road through Akhárnai to Ano Liósia.

A.   To Ayía Trías and the Summit

ROAD to *Grand Hotel Parnes*, 35km (22 miles); bus No. 714 to Ayía Trías (twice daily) from Od. Sourmelí, 736 (Sundays only; hourly, 0900–2100) to terminus (then by telepherique) from Od. Sourmelí (Plateía Váthis, below Archaeological Museum; 2, 4). ('Parnis' is signposted via Od. Akharnón and the National Highway, quitted after 10km to join the road described below c 1·5km N of Akhárnai.)

From Plateía Váthis, NW of Omonia Sq., Od. Liossíon (*Railway Museum* at No. 301; open Wednesday 17.00–20.00, Friday 10.30–13.30) passes under the National Highway at (5·5km) *Tris Yéfires* ('Three Bridges'), in the natural 'gap' where the road and two railways cross the Kefissos.—At (6km) *Ayioi Anáryiroi* the Fíli road diverges left (see below). You bear right and after c 2km pass a knoll (left) marked by some medieval remains; this is possibly the hill occupied by the Peloponnesian army under King Archidamos in 431 BC, when it ravaged the Athenian Plain. The frustrated Acharnians, prevented by Pericles from defending their lands, were later prominent in opposing the peace party in their desire for revenge (cf. Aristophanes).—12km **Akhárnai** (Αχάρναι, Hotels C, D), or *Menídhi*, in modern as in ancient times is a large deme surrounded by vineyards. Its classical inhabitants engaged in charcoal-burning on Parnes. Here in 1932 was found a marble stele of the 4C engraved with the 'Oath of Plataia'. For Menidhi Tomb, see p. 208. The road climbs gradually at first, then in steep turns, offering wider and wider views over the plain of Attica. At (33km) *Ayía Trías*, a little mountain resort amid pine woods, the bus terminates. The road divides: to the right on a spur with a superb *Panorama is (2·5km farther) the Grand Hotel Mont Parnes (L; cable-car, casino, swimming pool, tennis courts, cinema, etc.); to the left you reach (3km) the *Refuge* of the Greek Alpine Club (1165m) and the entrance to the radar station (no adm.) that crowns (7km) *Karábola* (1413m), the summit of Párnes.

Within a few yards of the top a sacrificial pyre, explored in 1959–60, yielded pottery and 3000 knives of the period 1000–600 BC. This discovery probably locates one of the two altars to Zeus mentioned by Pausanias.

From the left fork (see above) a track branches (left) towards the W, then divides. Bearing right, a winding descent may be followed towards the gorge which runs SW to the Moní Klistón (see below). At a conspicuous pine tree, a path leads SW into the gorge to a spring gushing from a column. Immediately below (easy scramble) is the *Cave of Pan* which forms the locale of Menander's 'Dyskolos'. Across the gorge (SW) rises the wooded spur of *Kalamara*, a hump with sheer sides anciently called *Harma* because, when seen from Athens, it resembled a chariot. The Pythiasts watched for lightning to play on its summit as a signal for the departure of the sacred mission to Delphi. A covering of cloud is today taken as a sign of rain.

B. To Phyle

ROAD. 31km (19½ miles) through the village of Filí (bus No. 737 from Plateía Váthis (Od. Sourmelí); 2, 4) and on to Moní Klistón and the fortress of Phyle.

To (8km) *Ayioi Anáryiroi*, see above. You bear left in company with the Peloponnese railway, beyond which can be seen a castellated mansion (Pirgos tis Vasilissis), once a model farm of Queen Amalia. Its wine ('Tour la Reine') is celebrated, but the house is now a school for officers of the Boy Scout movement.—12km. *Ano Liósia* (railway station; see Rte 16) stands in the gap between Aigaleos and Párnes. You ascend through a defile to (18·5km) *Filí* (Φυλή), a village (formerly Khasiá) in a hollow, which has readopted the ancient name. The road enters the gorge of *Potámi Goúras* and then climbs to (22·5km) **Moní Klistón**, correctly Panayia ton Kleiston (Our Lady of the Gorges), an old convent with a 14C church rebuilt in the 17C.

There is a school and a terrace with a fine view down into the gorge. A fountain in the court bears the date 1677.

For **Phyle** you ignore the turning to Moní Kleistón and continue upwards to (31km) the fortress which lies (left) on a prominent flat-topped hill. It can also be reached on foot (c 2 hours) by leaving the main road (left) at the entrance to the gorge and, after c 15 minutes, ascending to the right up a ravine; but the route is difficult to find.

The fortress (649m) crowns a precipitous triangular platform extending forward from a summit some 5m higher. It dominated alternative defiles of the ancient direct route from Thebes to Athens (of strategic value only for a comparatively small force) and looks out over the whole Athenian plain. It apparently replaced an earlier fort (see below) in the 4C BC; it was garrisoned by Kassander and subsequently dismantled and ceded to the Athenians by Demetrios Pollorketes.

The main entrance is on the E side. The enclosure has a pentagonal plan. To the W and SW the defences have crumbled, but elsewhere the well-preserved walls stand to the sixth course of squared blocks. Of five towers, four were square and one round. Like Eleutherai and Rhamnous, the fort had no water supply within the walls; in the neighbourhood and also near a spring, 20 minutes NE, are vestiges of houses.

A track continues along an ancient course to the Plateau of Skourta, in which stand *Pili* (24km from Fili) and *Pánakton*. Many ancient sites, including watchtowers presumably belonging to the Attica-Boeotia frontier of classical times have been located in a recent survey (1986-). From Pili the Skhimatári–Thebes road can be joined at various points. Thebes is at least 12 hours walk further.

About 1·5km to the NE of Phyle is another summit, on which are considerable remains of polygonal masonry. These are sometimes thought (Chandler JIIS 46 1926) to mark the post which Thrasyboulos captured in 403 BC after his expulsion from Athens by the Thirty Tyrants and defended with 70 men against 3000. From here he proceeded to the capture of Piraeus.

20 From Athens to Tatóï and Skála Oropoú

ROAD, 50km (31 miles). Local buses (No. 505 etc. from Plateía Kánningos) to Tatóï and Varibóbi; buses to Skála Oropoú (twice daily), and for Euboea via the ferry, start from Od. Mavrommatéon, but follow the Kifissia road (Rte 15), joining this route at Malakássa. (Skála Oropoú can be reached more directly and frequently by the National Highway and a new road diverging at 34km).

You quit central Athens by the Patissia road (Rte 8), passing the National Archaeological Museum.—5km **Patíssia** (Πατήσια) is a favourite suburban resort of the Athenians. It is said to derive its name (*padishah*, Sultan) from the fact that under the Turks the land was crown property.—6km *Alissídha*.

Above *Perissós*, 2·5km NE, on the NW slope of Tourkovouni, is the *Omorphi Ekklesia*, or 'beautiful church', dedicated to St. George in the 12C. It has mural paintings by a Salonican artist of the 14C, when the S chapel was added; the narthex is more recent.

You cross the Piraeus Electric Railway, then pass through (7km) *Néa Filadélfia*, a planned refugee suburb. The road divides by the football stadium.

The left fork leads to Akharnai (5km; Rte 19), crossing in turn the old Lavrion railway, the National Highway, and the Kifissos. In *Likótripa* (2·5km), up the hill beyond the cemetery, to the right of the road, is the tumulus covering the so-called *Menidhi Tomb*, a Mycenaean tholos tomb dug by the German School in 1879. Its yield is in the National Museum.

You continue NE. On the hill of Nemesis (left of road) was the Mycenaean settlement to which the Menidhi tomb belonged.— Beyond (10·5km) *Koukouváounes*, you cross the National Highway, then the Kifissos.—Near (14·5km) *Dekélia Station*, on the State Railway, is *Tatóï Airfield*, a Hellenic Air Force base and flying school.—19km. *Varibóbi* (Βαρυμπόμπη; Hotels L, B, C; restaurants) where you join a road from Kifissia, is noted for its golf course. About 1·5km NW are the ruins of the so-called *Tomb of Sophocles*. You ascend towards the pass.

24km Tatóï, known also by its ancient name of *Dekelia* (mod. Dhekélia), is beautifully situated amidst oak-woods in the entrance to the pass of Klidhí ('key'). To the right the former *Summer Palace* stands in a fine park, a good example of scientific afforestation on uncongenial soil. Local antiquities from the royal estate were gathered together into a small museum by George I; this was destroyed by fire in 1916 but its surviving objects, together with later finds from the area, have been described by the Princesses Sophia and Irene (1959–60). George II (1890) and King Alexander (1893) were born at Tatóï. The *Mausoleum* of George I and Alexander (died 1920) stands on the hill called *Palaiokastro* above the village (left), where are also the ruins of a Spartan fortress constructed in 413 BC. George II and King Paul are also buried at Tatóï.

Ancient *Dekelia* (Δεκέλεια) guarded the easternmost of the three passes over Parnes, the vital route by which food from Euboea reached Athens. By this pass Mardonius retreated into Boeotia before the battle of Plataia. On the advice of the renegade Alcibiades, the Spartans captured the pass in 413 BC and built a fortress (see above), initiating the blockade by land which, after the naval victory of Lysander at Aegospotami, led to the surrender of Athens.—*Hadrian's Aqueduct*, lengthened and restored by the Ulen company, runs S from Tatóï to a reservoir below Lykabettos.

The defile passes between the two hills of *Strongyle* (right) and *Katsimidhi* (850m). On the latter are vestiges of an Athenian fort, built in the 4C to guard the pass. The wooded uplands resound to the clonking of sheep bells.—Beyond (32km) *Ayios Merkourios*, a chapel with a spring, the steep zigzag descent commands a superb *View across the Euripos to Euboea. In the foreground are the railway and the highway to the north, which you cross at (37km) *Malakássa*. The road winds through upland scrub, then descends in more wooded country, with good views of the Strait of Euboea, to (50km) **Skála Oropós** (Hotels C; Tavernas), or more correctly *Skála Oropoú* (Σκάλα Ωρωπού), on the site of the ancient Oropos. From its shallow bay a ferry provides the shortest connection between Athens and Euboea. From the beach King Constantine I embarked in 1917 for Messina on his way to exile in Switzerland.

Ancient *Oropos* was important to Athens as the nearest accessible place of embarkation affording a short sea passage to Euboea. To it came ships bringing vital corn supplies and cattle for the capital. According to Dikaiarchos, the Oropians were rapacious and ill-mannered; their customs officers were especially notorious. The town fell alternately under Thebes and Athens, with intervals of independence.

Many finds of ancient buildings (including an Early Christian basilica) have been made in recent years in the town and its suburbs (Lagovouni, Nea Palatia)—parts of the city wall, cemeteries, a stoa—but no full discussion has yet

been published. A building in the town has been assigned for a new Archaeological Museum.

Diodoros records that in 402 BC the Thebans moved the Oropians 7 stades
inland, presumably from Skala to the site of modern Oropós.

The modern village of *Oropós*, 5km inland to the SW, has a 17C church.
Lignite mines are worked in the neighbourhood.

Road from Skala to the *Amphiaraion*, see Rte 22. Car Ferry (frequent) to
Eretria.

21 From Athens to Marathon. Rhámnous

ROAD to Marathon (Marathóna), 42km (26 miles). 12km *Stavrós.*—
27km. Turning for *Rafína* (3km right).—30km. Turning for *Ayios
Andréas* (2km right).—38km. *Marathon Tomb.*—42km. *Marathón.*—
47km *Káto Soúli.*—51·5km. Turning (right) to *Ayía Marína*
(2·5km).—58km *Rhámnous* (Rhamnoúnda).

BUS to *Marathón* from Od. Mavromatéon (frequently) in c 1 hour,
continuing (regularly) to *Grammatikó* (cf. below) or to *Káto Soúli*
(1/2 hour more); also several times daily to Ayía Marína (best for
Rhámnous; ferry to Néa Stíra); also to *Rafína* and to *Spáta*.

From Athens to *Stavrós*, see Rte 17B. You leave the Mesogeion road
to the right at a flyover, cross the old Lavrion railway, and pass a
modern church surrounded by cypresses and a cemetery. *Gargetos*,
birthplace of Epicurus (341–270 BC) lay hereabouts.

(13km) Turn for *Spáta*, a large village, c 6·5km SE, in a wine-producing district,
which has enriched the National Museum with Mycenaean finds from
chamber-tombs excavated by Stamatakis in 1877. It has been designated the
site of a second airport for Athens. Beyond Spáta, on the coast, is the frequented
beach of *Loútsa*, now often known as *Artemis* (or Artemídha; Hotel D;
Tavernas), identified by an inscription as *Halai Araphenides*. Here in 1956
remains were discovered of a Dionysion and a temple of Artemis Tauropolos
and (1975–76) a possible *propylon* (originally 5C BC) to the sanctuary.

—15km *Pallíni*, formerly Kharvati and now marked by a radio station,
has readopted the name of classical *Pallene*, which had a noted
temple of Athena. It was associated with the legendary victory of the
Heraklids over Eurystheus and with Theseus' defeat of the Pallan-
tids. Here c 545 BC Peisistratos, returning from exile in Macedonia,
defeated an Athenian force to make himself finally master of Athens.
The local white wine is noted. You pass (right) a tomb of partisans
executed in 1942.—22km *Pikérmi* (Hotel C; Restaurants) is noted for
the discovery of fossil remains of the neo-Tertiary period, brought to
light by the action of a local torrent; the finds, which include the
dinotherium, largest fossil known, are now in the natural history
museum of Athens University. The 16C nunnery of Ayía Filothei is
now a private house. You now pass through a district rich in
vineyards and olive-groves, and the scenery is most attractive. The
summit of Pentelikon, which you have been skirting, is hidden
behind an intervening spur. Along the road here in April 1941 British
troops abandoned their transport before embarking.—Near (24km)
Drasesa Bridge, where the road crosses the Megalo Rhevma, some
English tourists, including Lord Muncaster, were captured by brig-
ands in 1870. The scandal attending the subsequent murder of four of
them at Dílessi in Boeotia caused energetic steps to be taken to
suppress brigandage.—27km. Turning (right) for Rafína.

Rafína (Hotels C, D, E), site of the ancient deme of *Araphen*, is 3km away on the
sea (bathing). Its small harbour is connected by steamer with Karystos (Euboea)

and with Andros, Tinos, Syros, Paros and Naxos. A heavy swell hampered evacuation here in 1941. On the height of *Askitarió* (2km S) are the remains of an Early Helladic town (explored in 1955).

On the outskirts of Rafína there is a turn (right) for (8km) *Artemis (Loutsa)* (15km), *Brauron* and *Porto Rafti* (23km from Rafína).

On the wooded SE slope of Pentelikon, sharp left opposite the junction for Rafína, stands the conspicuous sanatorium of the *Moní Dáou Pendéli*. The convent, founded in the 10C, was refounded in 1963 after being deserted since 1690. A huge dome, borne on six columns, crowns the church, which shows many Eastern features. The 13C narthex dates from its Frankish period which ended in 1456. The woods are scored by fire lanes. Here, in a *German Military Cemetery* approved in 1962, have been concentrated the German dead of the campaign in Greece (1941–44).

The road approaches within a mile of the shore to cross the ridge where *Xilokeratiá* (268m), the last spur of Pentelikon, descends to the sea. As you descend behind the attractive shore of *Máti* (Hotels A, B), the whole Bay of Marathon is seen across the woods that back *Ayios Andréas* (2km right), a popular bathing place with tavernas.—32km **Néa Mákri** (Hotels B, C, E), frequented for bathing, stands at the seaward end of a road that follows the N slope of Pentelikon from Ekáli (Rte 15A). It has an extensive Neolithic settlement and may be the site of *Probalinthos*, whose name betrays a prehistoric origin. The road passes between *Mt Agriliki* and the small marsh of *Brexisa* (cf. below) into the Plain of Marathon.

The PLAIN OF MARATHON claims attention both because of the battle and because of archaeological discoveries, particularly those made in 1969–70. Geographically the plain, 10km long and 2·5–5km wide, extends in crescent form round the Bay of Marathon from the *Kynosura Promontory* (with an unidentified acropolis) in the N to Cape Kavo in the S. On the landward side it is shut in by the stony mountains that 'look on Marathon', making up for their moderate height by rising abruptly from the plain. *Stavrokoráki* (310m), the northernmost of these, is separated from *Kotróni* (235m) by the torrent bed of the *Kharadra*, which descends from the Marathon Lake past the modern village of Marathon to the sea. Geologists suggest that in the plain it would have been a negligible obstacle in Classical times. Between Kotroni and *Aforismós* (573m) runs the *Valley of Avlona*. The valley is joined at the village of VRANÁ (possibly the ancient Marathon) by the Rapentosa Gorge. This defile runs NNE from the hamlet of Rapentosa between Aforismos and *Agrilikí* (556m), the mountain forming the southern barrier of the plain. Agriliki has rubble walls that may date from the Mycenaean period.

In the N of the plain the *Great Marsh* (Μεγάλος Βάλτος; nowadays criss-crossed by drainage canals) stretches from Stavrokoraki to the base of the Kynosura Promontory, where it ends in the small salt-water lake of *Drakonera*. The *Little Marsh* (*Brexisa*) at the S end is probably a post-Classical formation; it is now partially drained and occupied by a United States forces radio station and the Golden Coast Hotel.

Battle of Marathon. After the easy destruction of Eretria the Persians crossed to Attica. Datis, their general, was probably influenced in his choice of the Bay of Marathon by Hippias, whose father had landed here successfully fifty years before. Meanwhile the Athenians, after despatching Pheidippides post haste for Spartan aid, marched to Marathon and encamped in the Sanctuary of Herakles, a strong position astride the mountain track from Athens and commanding the only road. The Persian numbers, not stated by Heredotus and grossly

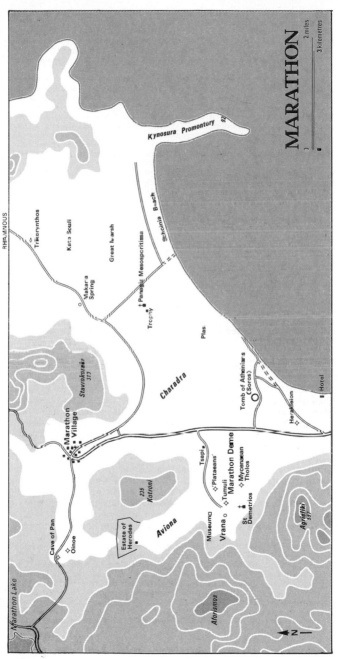

MARATHON

0   2 miles

0   3 kilometres

RHAMNOUS

Kynosura Promontory 92

Trikorynthos

Kato Souli

Great Marsh

Makaria Spring

Schoinia Beach

Panagia Mesosporitissa

Trophy

Plas

Stavrokoraki 317

Charadra

Marathon Village

Tomb of Athenians (Soros)

Hotel

Heraklion

Kotroni 235

Tsepi

'Plataeans'

Tumuli Marathon Deme

Museum

Vrana

Mycenaean Tholos

St Demetrios

Aviona

Cave of Pan

Oinoe

Estate of Herodes

Agrieliki 557

Aforismos

Marathon Lake

N

exaggerated by later Athenian tradition, are now thought not to have exceeded two divisions of infantry (? 24,000 men) and a small force of cavalry. The Athenians received unexpected aid from Plataia, which sent its whole available force, perhaps 1000 strong to join the 8000–9000 men of Athens. The command was vested in the Polemarch, Kallimachos, whose staff of ten generals included Miltiades (the traditional architect of the victory), and perhaps Themistocles and Aristides.

Four days passed, the Persians being unwilling to attack the strong Athenian position, the Athenians loth to leave it without the expected Spartan reinforcements. Believing he had failed to lure the Athenian army down into the plain, Datis re-embarked his cavalry to move on Athens by sea, sending a land force forward to cover the operation. Seeing them within striking distance, probably soon after dawn on 12 September 490 BC, Miltiades gave the word for action. He had left his centre weak and strengthened his wings to the utmost: the right wing, the place of honour, was led by Kallimachos; on the left wing were the Plataians. The Greek hoplites advanced rapidly across the mile of No Man's Land before the surprised Persians could get their archers properly into action, aided possibly by tree cover (Prof. Burn has pointed out the similarity of tactics used at Bannockburn). The Athenian wings were successful, while their weak centre was pierced by the Persians. The wings then enveloped the Persian centre which broke. In the ensuing rout the Persians fled to their ships. Many of them were caught in the Great Marsh. They lost 6400 men, while the Athenian dead numbered only 192, including Kallimachos. All were buried on the spot. A runner is said to have been sent to Athens, where he died of exhaustion after announcing the victory.

The Persian fleet, having lost only seven ships, put out to sea in an attempt to surprise Athens; but Miltiades, by a rapid march, reached Athens first, and the Persians sailed back to Asia. The battle proved that the long-dreaded Persians were vulnerable and was 'the victory of which the Athenians were proudest'. The Spartan army arrived in time to view the battlefield on the following day. Of the many legends that accrued to Marathon perhaps the best known are those of the ghostly assistance of Theseus and of Pan. The impressive silence of the plain is said to resound at night to the clash of arms and the neigh of steeds (though it is almost certain that no cavalry took part). Unsolved mysteries connected with the battle include the flashing of a shield on Pentelikon (Hdt. VI, 115). The most detailed modern appraisals are by Burn ('Persia and the Greeks') and in 'Journal of Hellenic Studies' (vol. 52, 1932), but these and even Kendrick Pritchett's 'Studies in Ancient Topography' II (1969) need to be considered in the light of continuing finds.

THE ARCHAEOLOGICAL SITES. As you enter the plain, there is first a road (right) across the Brexisa Marsh to the Golden Coast hotel (cf. above), just to the S of which, on an island of solid ground are vestiges of Roman masonry, commonly supposed to be the family mausoleum of Herodes Atticus (AD 101–177, a native of Marathon), and earlier remains have been located in the area. A little farther along, a second road (right) is signposted 'Marathon Tomb' (350m; large car park; café). This **Sorós**, 10m high and c 180m round, marks the graves of the 192 Athenians who fell in the battle. The top of the mound commands a view of the battlefield. At the foot is a marble bas-relief, copied from the 'Warrior of Marathon'. The 'tombstones with the names of the fallen arranged according to tribes', which Pausanias (I, 32, 3) tells us were set over the Sorós, have disappeared.

Contrary to usual practice, the fallen at Marathon were buried where they fell in token of their signal valour. Excavations undertaken in 1890 confirmed the ancient tradition attaching to the Sorós: ashes and calcined bones, as well as small black-figured lekythoi of the early 5C, were discovered. Obsidian arrowheads found on the surface by Schliemann six years earlier, which led him to attribute a much earlier date to the mound, may have been used by the Ethiopian archers (Hdt. VII, 69). No graves have been located of the slaves, who are said to have fought for the first time at Marathon. It is probable that Pausanias was right that the Persian dead were merely flung into an open trench.

The Soros road continues to the shore (Hotels A, C; cafés) where a road leads N along the beach for c 1km to the site of *Plasí*, a slight rise 100m inland, excavated in 1969–70 and again in 1979. Here are an Archaic peribolos of polygonal stones, possibly belonging to a shrine, and, near by, a settlement with chiefly prehistoric and early Iron Age finds. This may be the site of the ancient deme.

You return to the main road, where c 1·5km farther on, a road forks back to the hamlet of Vraná (3km; signs to Mouseion Marathona). About 100m down this road (right), largely covered by a hangar is the *Tsépi Vraná* site, a large Early Helladic cemetery containing carefully arranged and well-built cist graves. Vases found, as well as the graves themselves, are of Cycladic type. Between here and Vrana extends NW the Avlona valley, where (2·5km) a huge walled enclosure is known from an inscription on the ruined gateway to have belonged to Herodes Atticus. At the entrance to Vrana is (left) a large tumulus, excavated in 1969–70 and probably the TOMB OF THE PLATAIANS who fell at Marathon, which Pausanias records as a separate memorial. The identification is not certain. The mound, constructed entirely of stones, contains two circles of pit graves; skeletons found were mostly of young men, and the pottery in the graves is contemporary with that in the Athenian Soros.—At the far end of Vrana, under a large shelter, are groups of grave circles consisting of paved slabs, each circle containing stone tombs of Mid–Late Helladic date. The skeleton of a Przewalski-type horse occupies a separate tomb but this is probably a later intrusion. Another circle stands in the open.

The **Museum** has five rooms. You turn right. Room A, Neolithic pottery from the Cave of Pan (cf. below). Room B, case 5, finds from the Early Cycladic cemetery (Tsepi); case 6, from Middle Helladic tumuli (Vrana); case 8, from Geometric graves. Room Γ, vases etc. from the Tombs of the Athenians (case 13) and Plataians (case 10); bronze cinerary urn; boundary stones and inscribed stelai. Room Δ, Classical grave stelai and furnishings; rare bronze mirror with wooden covers; objects from various cemeteries; Panathenaic amphorae. Room E, Hellenistic and Roman finds, including an inscription concerning Herodes Atticus, and an Egyptianising 'kouros' of 2C AD.

About 1km SE of the museum, the small chapel of *Ayios Dhimítrios* stands alone just above the foot of Agriliki; close by are the remains of an open-air precinct, c 140m square, identified in 1954 by Prof. Sotiriades with the celebrated sanctuary of Herakles (cf. above).—On the plain, 1km from the chapel, in a small grove of low trees, is a Tholos Tomb (Mycenean II; locked): it yielded a gold cup, and the complete skeletons of two horses were buried beneath the dromos. Also in the vicinity of the church are the foundations of the funerary peribolos of Gyles of Probalinthos and his family.

The main road continues N past the Rhamnous turn.—42km **Marathón** (commonly Marathóna), a sprawling agricultural village. At the entrance is a marble platform with flag poles, the starting-point for annual marathon races.

FROM MARATHON TO KAPANDRÍTI, 20km (12½ miles), occasional buses to Grammatikó. Beyond Marathon the road climbs via (5km) *Ano Soúli* to (8km) *Grammatikó*.—14km. *Varnávas*, on the slope of Mavrovouni, with a Frankish tower.—20km *Kapandríti*, see Rte 22.

A road leads W from Marathon to (8km) Marathon Lake (Rte 22), passing below the site of ancient *Oinoe*. Here in 1957 Papadimtriou discovered the *Cave of Pan and the Nymphs* of Marathon, described by Pausanias and identified by an inscription of 60 BC found in situ. The cave (no adm.) seems to have been a place of cult from Neolithic times to the end of the Bronze Age, after which it was deserted until the 5C BC. Herodotus tells of the resurgence of the worship of Pan following his aid to Pheidippides before the Battle of Marathon.

To reach Rhamnous you take the *Káto Soúli* road (right) at the entrance to the village, following the foot of the hills. At 46km there is a turn (right) to *Skhoiniá*, the narrow strip of solid ground between the marsh and the sea chosen as the venue of the Boy Scouts' 11th World Jamboree in 1963. It is being developed as a bungalow resort.—47km *Káto Soúli*, where (left) are vestiges of the walls (3C AD) of ancient *Trikorythos*. You cross a lonely upland valley with barren hills on either side.—51·5km Fork; to the right lies the little seaside hamlet of *Ayía Marína* (regular ferries to Néa Stíra in Euboea). You bear left and rise gradually to (58km) *Rhamnous*.

Rhámnous (commonly Rhamnoúnda), uninhabited save for the phylax and a few shepherds, is one of the least spoilt sites in Attica, worth visiting as much for its romantic isolation and the beauty of its setting as for its archaeological interest.

The headland was famous as early as the 6C BC for the worship of Nemesis. Its small cove provided shelter on an otherwise inhospitable coast for ships about to pass the dangerous narrows of Ayía Marína. Later a fortress was built to watch over navigation in the Euripos. This achieved importance in 412 BC after the Athenian loss of Dekelia, when Rhamnous became the port of entry for food from Euboea, since it offered the only route wholly on Attic soil that did not involve passing the narrows. The name of the city was derived from the prickly shrub (ῥάμνος) which still grows in the neighbourhood. In more recent times it was known as *Ovriokastro*, a corruption of Εβραιὸν κάστρον (Jews' Castle). It was the birthplace of the orator Antiphon (b. 480 BC), whose school of rhetoric was attended by Thucydides.—The sanctuary was first described by the Dilettanti Society in 1817; partially excavated by Staïs in 1890–94; and re-examined by Orlandos in 1922–23 (B C H, 1924). The fortress was described by J. Pouilloux 'Le fortresse de Rhamnonte' (1954). Since 1975 extensive reinvestigation has been directed by V. Petrakos (author of *Rhamnous; a concise guide*, Athens, 1983).

Nemesis was the compensating goddess, measuring out happiness and misery. She took especial care of the presumptuous, punishing 'hubris', the crime of considering oneself master of one's destiny. She was known also by the surnames of 'Adrastia' ('inescapable') and of Rhamnousia, from her sanctuary at Rhamnous. Associated with the worship of Nemesis was Themis, the goddess who personified law, equity, and custom.

Note: Most of the site apart from the temples has been closed to the public for some years. The full description is here retained in the hope that public access will soon be restored.

At the head of a glen is an artificial platform, 45m wide, constructed, in the 5C BC, of large blocks of local marble laid horizontally. Nine courses are exposed at the NE corner. The sacred precinct thus formed contains the remains of two temples, an altar, a stoa and a small fountain house. Although none of the visible remains are earlier than the 5C, both votive offerings and rooftiles of the early 6C show that there was ritual activity from that time.

The smaller TEMPLE (of Themis?) was built on a virgin site in the early 5C. It measures 10·7m by 6·5m and consists merely of a cella in antis with a Doric portico of two columns. The walls which stand to c 1·8m are built of large polygonal blocks of white marble. Two marble seats (casts *in situ*) dedicated to Themis and Nemesis and three statues from the cella with inscribed pedestals (found in 1890) are in Athens. The building continued in use (as a treasury/storeroom) into the 4C AD.

The first TEMPLE OF NEMESIS, nearer the sea, was constructed at the end of the 6C BC in poros limestone as a Doric building, distyle in

The Sanctuary of Nemesis. Left to right: the little temple; the large temple; altar; fountain house; stoa

antis. This temple was probably destroyed by the Persians and replaced by that whose remains are still visible. This successor is a Doric peripteral building with six columns by twelve, the last of four sometimes ascribed to the so-called 'Theseum architect'. According to Dinsmoor, it was probably begun on the Festival Day of the Nemesiera (Boëdromion 5; i.e. 30 September) 436 BC, and it is known by an inscription to have been rededicated to the Empress Livia, probably by Claudius in AD 45. The interior had the usual arrangement of cella, pronaos and opisthodomos in antis. The unfinished fluting on the remaining drums of six columns (S side) suggests that the building was never completed.

Fragments both of the cult statue of Nemesis (including a colossal head, now in the British Museum) and of its base have been found. The statue (c 421 BC) was in Parian marble and the work of Agorakritos. Pausanias believed it to have been made from the very marble brought by the Persians for use as a victory monument and incorrectly attributed it to Pheidias. The base (partly reconstructed but not accessible) had carved decoration on three sides, showing Leda introducing Helen to her real mother, Nemesis.

Still within the precinct are, to the E of the temple, the foundations of an altar; to the N the scanty remains of a stoa of the 5C (34m long) which originally had wooden columns in its façade. In front of the stoa was a small fountain house, with a two-columned porch. Opposite the precinct, on the other side of the road, are the foundations of a large Hellenistic structure.

Descending the rocky glen N towards the sea (*access not permitted at present*) you reach in 10 minutes an isolated hill girdled with the picturesque but overgrown enceinte (c 1km in circuit) of the ANCIENT TOWN. The lower part of the South Gateway is well preserved, as are short portions (3·7m high in places) of the walls, in ashlar masonry of grey limestone. Nine towers of the fortress can be made out. Within are some remains of a small *Temple*, a *Gymnasium*, and an inner citadel. A small sanctuary of Amphiaraos lies outside, to the NW.

Visible beside the road below the temples are the substantial remains of some of the funerary enclosures (*periboloi*; see R. Garland in BSA 77 1982 and illustration above under Athens, Kerameikos), with which it was lined. These were topped with sculptured stelai etc. and inscriptions commemorating the dead. The line of the road can be traced back towards the entrance beyond the custodian's hut and the remains of other enclosures, less well preserved, made out.

A rough track (passable with a tough car) continues the line of the road by which you approached the site and leads (after 3km) to a wider but indifferent unsurfaced road which, partly utilising an abandoned mineral railway, comes up from Grammatikó (8km; 1¹/₂ hours on foot).

22   From Athens to Marathon Lake, Kálamos, and the Amphiaraion

ROAD to the *Amphiáraion*, 49km (30¹/₂ miles); to *Marathon Lake*, 31km (20¹/₄ miles). Buses to *Kálamos* (45km; for the Amphiáraion) from Od. Mavromatéon; to *Marathon Lake* (infrequent) from Plateía Kánningos; to Stamáta (bus 507) from Plateía Kánningos.

From central Athens to (20km) *Ekáli*, see Rte 15. You continue N passing the road to Dhiónisos (Rte 15). 1km beyond the Dhiónisos turn, another road leads (right) in 2km to Stamáta where, on the hill of *Mygdhaleza* (2km to the N) an Early Christian basilica and associated buildings were excavated in 1977. The complex, probably built in the 5C AD, like the nearby settlement, incorporated Classical masonry and inscriptions and may be on the site of the ancient deme of Hekale, where Theseus instituted a festival to Zeus in memory of the priestess who sheltered him on his way to fight the Bull of Marathon. *Plotheia* was also hereabouts.—(22·5km) *Dhrosiá* (Dionysos, Hotel C, D) is another upland resort.

At (24km) *Ayios Stéfanos* a road (right) leads in 9km to Marathon Lake (Tourist Pavilion) and on to Marathon (Rte 21).

Marathon Lake (in Greek *Límni Marathónos*) is an irregular sheet of water (c 243 hectares) formed by impounding the Charadra and Varnava torrents. It supplies some of the needs of Greater Athens, though since the Second World War its capacity has had to be augmented by artificial inflows from Parnes and the Boeotian lakes and further north. The *Dam*, built by the Ulen company of New York in 1925–31, at the SE end of the lake, consists of a curved concrete wall 285m long, 47m wide at the base, and 4m wide at the top. It is claimed to be the only dam in the world faced with marble. A roadway runs across it. It rises 54m above the river bed to an elevation of 227m above sea-level. At the downstream side is a marble replica of the Athenian Treasury at Delphi, which serves as an entrance to the inspection galleries.

At Ayios Stéfanos you can, after 1km, join the Athens–Salonika highway, leaving it again at the Kapandríti exit. Alternatively you can take the Marathon Lake turning, then bear left almost immediately in Ayios Stéfanos, rounding the station (*Oion*) on the left and crossing the line, to continue by the old road running parallel with the highway. Seen to the left is modern *Kioúrka*, formerly *Aphidnai*; to the right, at the N end of Marathon Lake, beyond the new works which control the entry of waters piped from N Parnes, is a hill (Kotroni) with some ancient walls to be identified either with classical Aphidna or with Oion.

Theseus hid Helen at Aphidna after carrying her off from Sparta. Her whereabouts were divulged by the inhabitants of Dekelia to her brothers, Castor and

Pollux, who laid siege to Aphidna and rescued her. Aphidna was the home of Kallimachos, polemarch at Marathon.

After (36km) *Kapandríti*, where you join a road from Grammatikó (Rte 21), the pleasant road winds over tree-clothed hills to (45km) **Kálamos**, the small centre (329m) of a well-watered and wooded region above the Gulf of Euboea.

The road continues to (5km farther) *Ayioi Apóstoloi* (Hotels B, C; restaurants), originally a fishing village, now a seaside resort.

From Kálamos a road descends in loops to the *Amphiaraion* (4km) in the Mavrodhílisi ravine. On foot the site can be reached in 25 minutes by the old path (difficult not to lose), shaded by pines, which crosses the road several times. The road must be followed for the last 100m as the entrance lies beyond the bridge that crosses the stream. Approach by the road is less uncertain and not unpleasant.

The ***Amphiaraion**, or *Sanctuary of Amphiaraos*, founded in honour of the healing god, was at once an oracle and a spa. It occupies a sheltered and sunny situation, well suited to a resort of invalids, on the left bank of a wooded glen, watered by a mountain torrent. In spring anemones carpet the site.

The sanctuary commemorated the elevation to divinity of Amphiaraos, the great seer and warrior of Argos, who fought as one of the seven against Thebes. On the defeat of this expedition he fled, pursued by Periklymenos, but the earth opened and swallowed him up, together with his chariot, near Thebes. His cult was adopted by the Oropians and concentrated here near a spring famed for its healing properties. Mardonius came to consult the oracle before the battle of Plataia. Whoever wished to consult the god sacrificed a ram and lay down for the night, wrapped in its skin, in the portico allotted for the purpose, and there awaited the revelations to be made to him in his dreams. The process of incubation ('Εγκοίμησις) was very similar to that practised in the Asklepieion. The cure did not, however, wholly depend on these miraculous communications, for there were medical baths in the precinct. After his cure, the patient had to throw gold or silver coins into the sacred spring.—The excavations (1927–30) of the Greek Archaeological Service were interrupted by the death of Leonardos, the excavator. Restorations have been effected since 1960.

Descending the path parallel to the stream, you see (right) the little *Temple of Amphiaraos*, a Doric building of the 4C, with a pronaos and a cella divided into three by parallel colonnades. The foundations, partly eroded by the stream, have been restored. The base of the cult statue is still in position. The back wall was joined by a porch (door marks in the threshold) to the priests' lodging. Ten yards from the temple is the *Altar*, on which the ram was sacrificed; and below the altar the *Sacred Spring*, into which the coins were thrown. Its waters were drunk from shells, many of which have come to light. Above the altar is a terrace with a line of over 30 inscribed *Pedestals* of statues, mostly Roman. On a line with these are the remains of a long bench. In front is the *Museum* (rarely open; enquire at entrance to site), containing numerous inscriptions, a curious early Herm, torsos, and, in the back court, reassembled architectural members of the temple and stoa. Beyond are the remains of the *Enkoimeterion*, a long stoa, erected c 387 BC, having 41 Doric columns on the façade and divided internally into two long galleries by 17 Ionic columns. It had a small room at either end, possibly reserved for women patients. Along the walls ran marble benches, resting on claw feet, on which the patients submitted to the process of incubation. Behind the stoa is a small THEATRE, having a circular orchestra and seating for 300 spectators. Five marble *Thrones* with scroll ornaments are preserved. The *Proskenion* (restored) has 8 Doric columns surmounted by an epistyle with a dedicatory inscription. Beyond the stoa were the *Baths*. On the opposite bank of the stream are some confused remains of the accommodation provided for patients and part of a *Klepsydra*, or water-clock, its bronze plug mechanism visible.

A new road continues to *Skála Oropoú* (Rte 20), c 13km NW.

23 From Piraeus to Aegina (Aíyina)

Motor Vessels of the Argosaronikós Lines from Piraeus (opposite the Dhimarkhíon) ply several times per hour to *Aégina* in 1¼ hours. Some continue to further destinations—*Méthana* (2 hours), *Póros* (2½ hours), *Hydra* (3¼ hours), *Ermióni* (4¼ hours) and *Spétsai* (4–5 hours). Not every boat calls at every port. Also (by launch) to Ayía Marína (Aegina) direct.

EXPRESS SERVICE ('*Flying Dolphin*' *Hydroplanes*) from Piraeus (Plateía Karaïskáki; Pl. 3), 10 times daily to *Aégina* in 35 minutes. Hydroplanes for other Saronic islands and the Peloponnese leave from Pashalimáni (Zéa; Pl. 7/11). Bookings may be made at Wagons-Lit Cooks at 2 Karageórghi Servías (Síndagma).

Some organised day trips (C.H.A.T., etc.) briefly visit Aégina, Póros, and Hydra (Idhra).

The steamer passes down the centre of the *Great Harbour* of Piraeus with liner berths to the left and commercial wharves to the right. The prominent square building on the Akte peninsula is the Hadjikiriakou Orphanage. You pass between the remains of the ancient moles; from the *Outer Harbour* the W landmarks of the Akte peninsula (cf. Rte 12) are clearly visible. The channel opens out into the **Saronic Gulf** (*Saronikós Kólpos*), the skyline of which, on a clear day, seems filled with mountains. The long islet of *Lipsokoutali*, with naval installations, is usually taken to be the ancient *Psyttaleia*, though some recent theories about the Battle of Salamis have thrown doubt on this (cf. Rte 18). To the W rise the scrubby hills of *Salamis*, backed by the higher peaks beyond Megara. Astern the scars of Pentelikon are prominent and the Attic coastline is visible as far as Vouliagmeni and the islet of Fleves. As you draw level with the lighthouse on the S point of Salamis, you see the sugar-loaf of Acrocorinth backed by the frequently snowy cap of Killini filling the W end of the Saronic Gulf. Ahead rises Aegina; the temple of Aphaia can just be made out high up on the left. The steamer passes E of *Eleousa* and heads towards the low Akr. Plakakia, the NW cape of Aegina (lighthouse). Away to starboard appear the five *Dhiaporioi Nisoi*, the ancient Isles of Pelops. You turn S into the Strait of Metopi, the shallow channel that separates Aegina from *Angistri*. The jagged peaks of Methana rise ahead to the right of Moni. A solitary column (see below) marks the promontory guarding (27km) the port of Aegina.

AÉGINA or AIYINA (Αἴγινα; the stress is on the first syllable), a triangular island of 86 sq. km occupies the centre of the Saronic Gulf, being almost equidistant from Attica and from Argolis. With Angistri and the small attendant islets to the W it forms nowadays an eparchy (11,893 inhab.) of the nome of Piraios. The island is difficult of approach on account of the sunken rocks and reefs that surround it. It relies for its water on wells. Much of the W part consists of a plain which, though rich, is well cultivated with pistachio nuts and, farther S, with citrus fruits. The interior of the island is mountainous, pine-clad to the NE, and affords pleasing landscapes, while at the S corner rises the magnificent conical mountain, *Oros* (531m), the finest natural feature of the island. The climate is delightful and the island is fast developing as a holiday area. The local industries include sponge fishing and pottery. The two-handled porous water jars (*kanátia*), common in Athens, are made here. In addition to pistachio nuts, olives, vines, almonds, and figs are cultivated.

History. Notwithstanding its small size, the key position of Aegina in the Saronic Gulf ensured the early importance of the island. The name probably derives from a divinity (Hellenised as *Aigaios*) imported from Anatolia by Early Helladic invaders speaking a Lycian dialect, but Neolithic finds make it certain that the island was occupied as early as the end of the 4th millennium BC. About 2000 BC the inhabitants were supplanted by a Bronze Age people, probably of Indo-European race, speaking an Aeolian or Arcadian dialect and worshipping Poseidon. Their culture was brought to an end, c 1400, by an Achaean invasion and a period of Mycenaean occupation. Later legend tells of its only hero-king, Aiakos, son of Zeus and Aegina, who afterwards became one of the three judges of the Underworld. His sons Peleus and Telamon had to flee for the murder of their half-brother Phokos; Telamon afterwards became king of Salamis. A Dorian invasion brought the Thessalian cult of Zeus Hellanios. Aphaia seems to have been a variant of the Mother-Goddess from Crete, perhaps imported during the early Iron Age.

Perhaps abandoned for two centuries before 950 BC, the island was recolonised probably from Epidauros (Herod, VIII, 46). Its infertile soil combined with its geographical situation spurred the inhabitants to maritime enterprise. At the end of the 8C it enjoyed parity with fellow members of the Kalaurian League, and was apparently no longer subject to Argos. By the 7C the Aeginetan marine held first place in the Hellenic world. The island was noted for pottery and especially for the quality of its bronze-founding. The system of coinage introduced in Argos by Pheidon (c 656 BC) was probably borrowed from Aegina (rather than the other way about); indeed coinage very likely first reached Europe by way of the island. Its silver coins became the standard in most of the Dorian states, and in the 6C Aegina was a major centre of Greek art. Aeginetan merchants set up a temple to Zeus at the founding of Naukratis on the Nile; one, Sostratos, according to Herodotus (IV, 152) had also sailed to Spain. Their harbour was crowded with merchant ships (Thuc., V, 53) and the Aeginetan navy grew to a formidable size, exciting the jealousy of Athens. Solon's laws prohibiting the export of corn from Attica were probably directed mainly against Aegina, which henceforward, whatever its alliance, was always anti-Athenian. Aristotle calls it 'the eyesore of Piraeus' ('Rhet.', III, 10, 7); Herodotus (V, 82) adduces a mythical feud, and may be historically unreliable about the war between Athens and Aegina (? 488–481) in which the Athenians were worsted.

At Salamis (480 BC) the Aeginetans atoned for any previous homage to Persia by distinguishing themselves above all other Greeks, and the battle marked the zenith of their power. As a member of the Spartan League, Aegina was protected from attack until the reversal of Kimon's policy, when the Aeginetans were quickly defeated by the Athenians in two naval battles. In 457 BC the city was humiliated after a siege (Thuc., I, 108). At the beginning of the Peloponnesian War the Athenians expelled the inhabitants and established a cleruchy. The scattered remnants were allowed to return in 404 from their exile in Thyrea (where the Spartans had accommodated them), but Aegina never rallied from this blow. It passed with the rest of Greece to Macedon and afterwards to Attalos of Pergamon. In Byzantine times it constituted a joint bishopric with Keos. Paul of Aegina, celebrated for a treatise on medicine and surgery was born here in the 7C AD. Saracen raids caused the inhabitants to shift the capital inland (cf. below) where it remained until the 19C. After 1204 the island was a personal fief of Venetian and Catalan families until, in 1451 it passed to Venice. Captured and laid waste in 1537 by Khair-ed-Din (Barbarossa), it was repopulated with Albanians. Morosini recaptured it for Venice in 1654, and it became one of the last Venetian strongholds in the E, being ceded to Turkey in 1718. In 1826–28 the city was the temporary capital of partly liberated Greece, and here the first modern Greek coins were minted. Many of the present inhabitants are descended from families who came at this time from the Peloponnese, or from refugees who fled here from Chios and Psara.

The modern town of **Aíyina** (6333 inhab.; Hotels B, C, D; Restaurants on the quay), near the NW corner of the island, occupies part of the site of the ancient city, which extended much farther to the N. It still preserves buildings erected during the presidency of Capodistrias, to whose memory a statue stands in the main square. From the sea the most conspicuous features are two churches: Ayios Nikólaos, and the Cathedral on the quay. The modern HARBOUR, oval in shape and crowded with picturesque caïques, corresponds with the ancient *Commercial Harbour*. Its moles were rebuilt by Capodistrias on the ancient foundations. The S mole marked the S limit of the ancient city, forming an extension of its walls. The N mole bears a tiny white chapel of typical Aegean design. Beyond the N mole remains of rectangular quays of the ancient *Military Harbour* (Κρύπτος Λιμῆν) can be seen beneath the surface of a smooth sea.

It was protected on the N by a low promontory (Kolonna; 10 minutes from the quay), which formed the citadel, fortified from Neolithic to Christian times. In the Classical period at least it was within the enceinte which was continued seaward from farther N by a breakwater. The *Museum* is to the right on entry to the archaeological site: ROOM 1. Models of the prehistoric 'white house' on the Kolonna site and of a prehistoric furnace; ROOM 2. Early and Middle Bronze Age pottery, much of it resembling Cycladic; some Anatolian forms; sword and gold from an MBA grave; ROOM 3. Mycenaean pottery and figurines; ROOM 4. Marble and poros architectural fragments, sculpture and inscriptions including a boundary stone from the temenos of Apollo and Poseidon and an inscription naming the goddess Aphaia; ROOM 5. Archaic and Classical reliefs and a 5C sphinx; ROOM 6. Geometric, Archaic and Classical pottery including (in case to right) the fine Orientalising Ram Jug (Odysseus and companions escaping from the Cyclops); ROOM 7. Relief with chariot; minor sculptures, bronzes, Roman lamps, altar; ROOM 8. Sculptural fragments; COURT. Various fragments of relief sculpture and architecture. Beyond the Museum are the main EXCAVATIONS.

German excavations by G. Welter in 1924 beneath the temple showed remains of a building about a century earlier, below which again were late-Mycenaean houses. Work has been greatly extended W and S of the temple since 1969, with the discovery of the substantial remains of an Early–Late Helladic fortified settlement, whose remains now dominate the area. Of the later *Temple of Apollo* (formerly attributed to Aphrodite), all that remains are a lone column, without its capital, from the opisthodomos, and some scanty poros foundations of polygonal masonry. The temple (Doric, 6 columns by 12), built c 520–500 BC, was superseded by a late-Roman fortress, fragments of which survive on the seaward side; the area was quarried during the rebuilding of the harbour.

To the SE a square edifice of Archaic date is possibly the *Aiakeion*. To the NW of the temple a circular structure is thought to accord with Pausanias' description of the *Tomb of Phokos*. On the extremity of the cape near the water, some scanty Pergamene remains are perhaps those of *Attaleion*.

The Quay has a Tourist Information Office (open only in the season). At its S end is the *Panayitsa* (1806), cathedral of the Metropolitan of Idhra, Spetsai, and Aegina. Inland from the quay is the Post Office and the former Museum which, although now closed, retains in its courtyard inscriptions, architectural fragments and reliefs.

Beyond the Post Office, you reach Od. Ayíou Nikoláou which leads past the medieval *Markelon Tower* to *Ayios Nikolaos*, a modern church. Behind this are some remains of an Early Christian basilica. A street running N leads shortly to *Kanaris's House*, once occupied by the hero of Chios. Many of the local houses are given over to the processing of sponges.—In the S part of the town (Od. Aféas) is the former *Orphanage*, built by Capodistrias for children orphaned by the War of Independence and, since 1854, used successively as barracks and prison and now a Folk Museum. Below the courtyard is an ancient catacomb. Further on (5 minutes) is the *Faneroméni* (18C), with the remains of a basilica over a crypt. On the coast road, opposite the cemetery is the *House of Triltoupis*, where both Chaillaos Triköupis (1832–96), the statesman, and Spyridion, his historian father, lived for a short period.—To the left of the main road to the Temple of Aphaia and Ayía Marína (see below; bus stop Assómatos on Ayia Marina route and 15 min. walk, or about 3/4 hour walk E of the town centre), is the *Omorfi Ekklesia*, a church of 1282 built of antique materials and dedicated to SS. Theodore. Its frescoes (somewhat later) are well preserved. Enquire at Archaeological Museum for key.

BUSES and taxis to the Temple of Aphaia and elsewhere, from beyond the W end of the quay.

THE PRINCIPAL EXCURSION is to the Temple of Aphaia (by Ayía Marína bus). The road runs through pistachio plantations, and vineyards dotted with olive and fig trees.—6·5km **Palaiokhóra** (left), capital of the island from the 9C until 1826. It was rebuilt twice after destruction by Barbarossa (1537) and by the Venetians (1654). Covering the bare hillside are the ruins of more than twenty churches and monasteries (contact phylax for access), survivors from the 13C and later, some with stone ikonostases and tolerably preserved frescoes. A ruined castle crowns the summit. Below this ghost town is a monastery containing the embalmed body of Ay. Nektários (Anastasios Kefalas; 1846–1920), Metropolitan of Pentapolis and the first saint to be canonised (1961) by the Orthodox Church in modern times.—8km *Mésagros*. From this village a road leads to the N coast and then through *Souvalá* (Hotels C, D), a pleasant fishing village with radioactive springs, back to Aiyina.—At 10·5km the road bears right and climbs.

12km. The *Temple of Aphaía stands on a pine-clad hill commanding a splendid view over the Saronic Gulf. Erected at the end of the 6C or in the early years of the 5C on the site of two earlier temples, it has been called 'the most perfectly developed of the late Archaic temples in European Hellas'. The appearance of its shattered peristyle was enhanced in 1956–60 by the re-erection of fallen columns and the restoration to position of their entablature, though lightning caused damage to the SW corner in 1969.

The temple was explored in 1811, when its sculptures were borne off to Munich (cf. below). Bavarian excavations undertaken in 1901–03 by Furtwängler in order to complete these groups proved the dedication to Aphaia, the Aeginetan equivalent of the Cretan goddess Britomartis. The shrine had previously been attributed first to Zeus Panhellenios and later to Athena. Numerous fragments were recovered (D. Öhly) in 1969 and subsequent years of the earlier Archaic temple's polychrome stonework.

You pass through the *Outer Peribolos Wall*. To the right are some remains of the living quarters of the priests; three stucco baths served for purification rites. The artificial *Terrace* on which the temple stands is approached by a *Propylon* of the 5C, having an unusual arrangement of pilasters on the façade. To the E are the foundations of the latest *Altar*, from the base of which a *Ramp* rises to the *Stereobate* of three steps on which the temple stands.

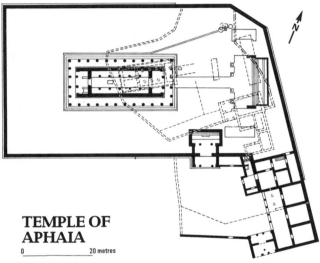

TEMPLE OF
APHAIA

0 _____ 20 metres

after Welter and others

The TEMPLE is now roped off to preserve the remaining traces of the red stucco which originally covered the floors of the pronaos and cella. It is Doric peripteral hexastyle, having twelve columns on the flanks. It was built in local limestone which was coated with a thin layer of stucco and painted. Of the original 32 columns, 24 now stand. They are 3 Doric feet in diameter at the base and axially spaced at 8 feet. The corner columns are thickened for optical effect. All the shafts are monolithic, save for three adjacent columns on the N flank which are built up of drums, presumably for the purpose of leaving a gap until the last moment to facilitate the erection of the interior. The architrave is extensively preserved and the whole entablature has been restored at the W end of the N side by the replacement of the triglyphs, metopes, and cornice. The sekos is divided into a cella with pronaos and opisthodomos in antis. Two columns survive of the *Pronaos*, which once housed figureheads of Samian triremes captured at Kydonia. Marks can be seen on the columns where the entrance was closed off with a high grille.

  The *Cella*, the walls of which have been partly rebuilt, was divided internally by two colonnades of five columns each; above an epistyle a second row of smaller superposed columns carried a flat ceiling. Seven of the interior columns have been restored to place with three of the upper shafts; their taper is continuous throughout. At a later date aisle floors were put in at triforium level, approached presumably by wooden stairs. The position of the cult statue (fragment of the acrolithic arm in the National Archaeological Museum in Athens) is shown by marks in the floor where a railing stood round it.—The doorway from the opisthodomos is not central and was pierced after a solid cross-wall was started.

The pedimental sculptures were of Parian marble. Seventeen statues found by Cockerell and von Hallerstein in 1811 were acquired by Ludwig I of Bavaria and, after restoration by Thorvaldsen in Rome, sent to Munich, where they remain. The scenes represented two combats before Troy in the presence of Athena. Parts of a third and a fourth group (now in Athens and Aegina museums) have since come to light; these are believed to have been deliberately removed but the reason is unknown.

At the NE corner of the terrace is a cistern which caught rainwater from the roof; it connects with a 'cave' which was built as a cistern for the Archaic temple.

To the W of the Temple is the excavation house, now an architectural museum (closed) with finds from recent excavations, in particular the (painted) façade of the archaic temple.

Beyond the temple the road descends to **Ayía Marína** (Hotels D, C, D, most closed in winter), a resort on an attractive bay, used by cruise ships to disembark passengers for Aphaia and served in summer by launches from Piraeus. The road is being extended S to join the W coast at Perdika.

FROM AIYINA TO OROS (3 hours). You take the Perdhika road (bus), which leaves the town by the S quay and skirts the shore, and follow it as far as (6km) *Marathon*. From here a path runs inland to *Pakheld Rákhi*, where a road (unfinished) leads to *Anitsaion*. 1·5km along the road, a track (right) leads to the church of *Taxiárchis*, on the site of substantial Hellenistic remains. These include a great stepped road (visible from the modern road below) which leads to a rectangular *Terrace* supported by stepped polygonal retaining walls. A staircase, 7m wide, gives onto a second area with a hypostyle structure. There are two connected cisterns higher up.

From the chapel an arduous path ascends the N slope of the pyramid to the summit. *Oros* (The Mountain), known also as *Ayios Ilias* and to the ancients as *Panhellenion*, is a conspicuous landmark (531m) from all over the Saronic Gulf. The gathering of clouds on its peak is a sure sign of rain, a phenomenon noted in antiquity. Near the summit was a settlement (13C BC) whose people may have introduced the cult of Zeus Hellanios (the rainbearer) from Thessaly and which came to the violent end suffered by so many Mycenaean sites. It was reoccupied in the Geometric period. The Oros commands a splendid *View; nearly the whole island is visible, rising apparently from the midst of a vast lake encircled by an almost continuous coastline.—The return may be made by descending to *Anitsaion* and following the road through *Pórtes* to *Ayia Marina* on the coast. Below Portes, a track (left) leads to the *Panayía Khrisoleóntissa*, an isolated monastery of 1600 whose church, enlarged in 1806, has a remarkable ikonostasis.

From Marathon the road continues to (9km) *Pérdhika* (Hotels B, D), where a track leads to the S point of the island. Here stands the monastery of *Ayía Triádha*, built by St Nectarius (cf. above). The islet of *Moní*, offshore from Pérdhika, is being developed for holiday use with a camp site and Tourist Pavilion. That of Anghístri, pleasant for bathing, can be reached by excursion launches in 20 minutes from Aegina town (summer only).

INDEX

Topographical names and names of most monuments are printed in Roman type; ancient place names and those of some major monuments in CAPITALS. Personal names—modern, ancient or mythological—are in *Italics*; subjects in **Bold**.

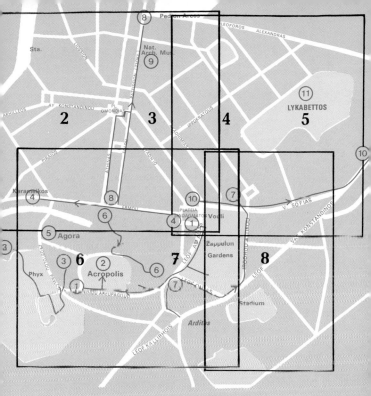

The numbers in circles refer to routes in the text.

Key page
to
Map numbers

| 0 | 100 | 200 | 300 | 400 yards |
| 0 | 100 | 200 | 300 | 400 metres |

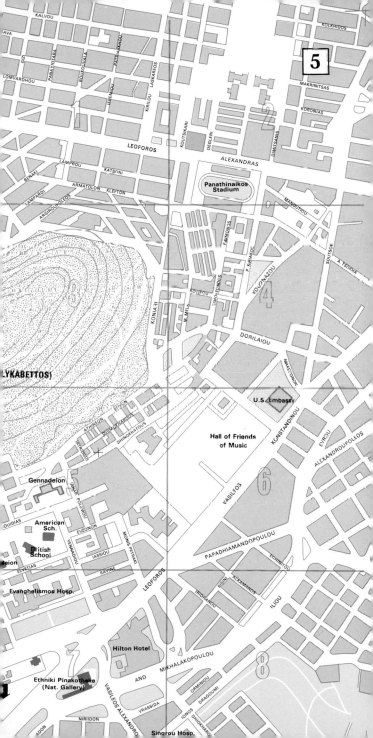

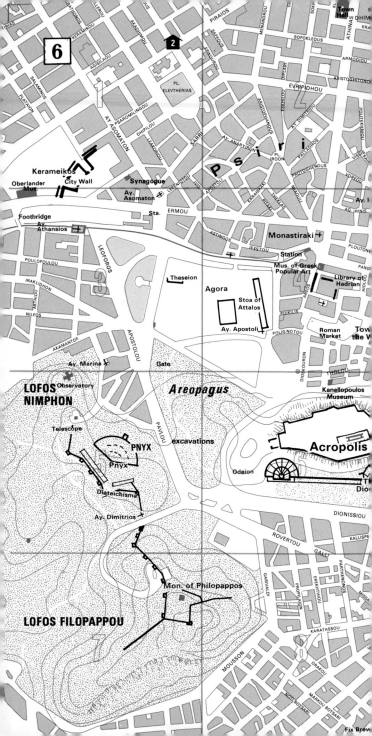

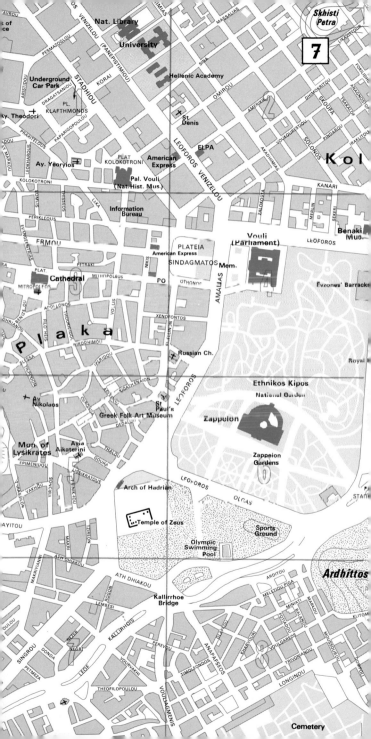

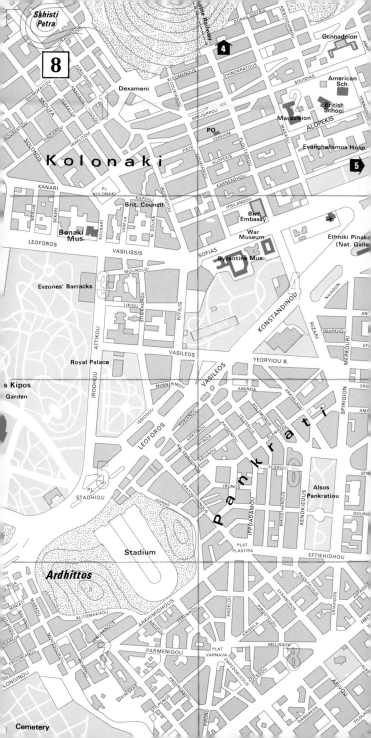

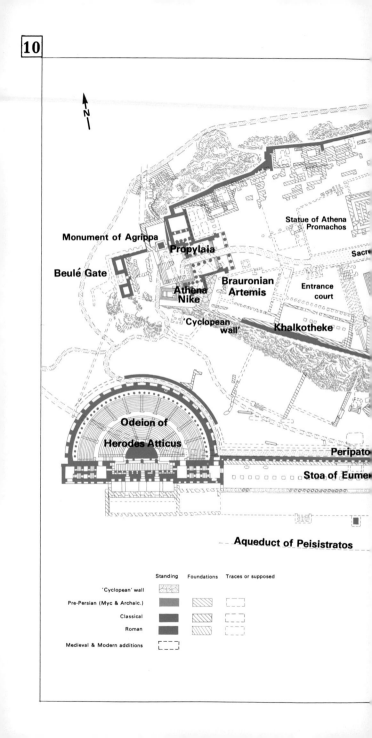

Monument of Agrippa

Beulé Gate

Propylaia

Athena
Nike

Brauronian
Artemis

Statue of Athena
Promachos

Sacr

Entrance
court

'Cyclopean
wall'

Khalkotheke

Odeion of

Herodes Atticus

Peripato

Stoa of Eume

Aqueduct of Peisistratos

	Standing	Foundations	Traces or supposed
'Cyclopean' wall			
Pre-Persian (Myc & Archaic.)			
Classical			
Roman			
Medieval & Modern additions			

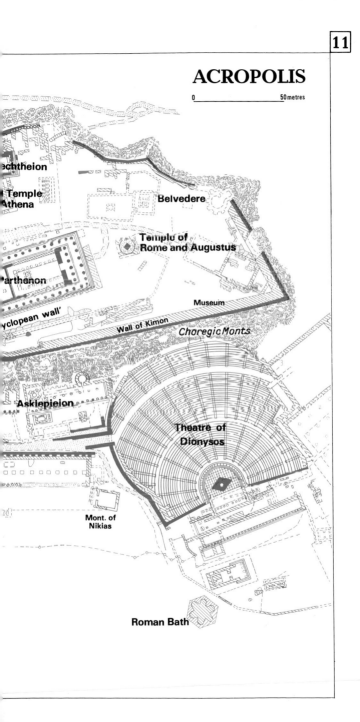

ACROPOLIS

0   50 metres

echtheion

Temple
Athena

Belvedere

Temple of
Rome and Augustus

Parthenon

Cyclopean wall'

Wall of Kimon

Museum

Choregic Monts

Asklepieion

Theatre of
Dionysos

Mont. of
Nikias

Roman Bath

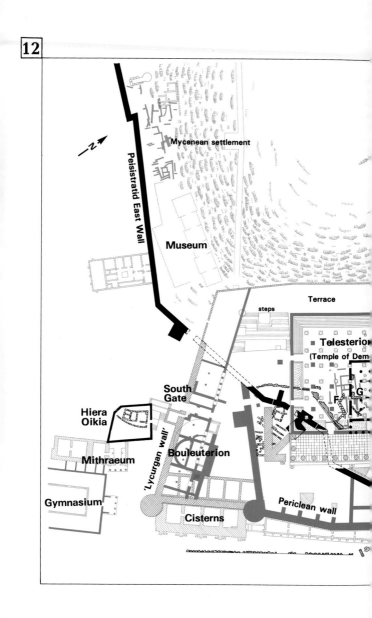

Mycenean settlement

Pelsistratid East Wall

_–z_

Museum

Terrace

steps

Telesterion

(Temple of Dem

South
Gate

G

F

Hiera
Oikia

Mithraeum

Lycurgan wall

Bouleuterion

Gymnasium

Periclean wall

Cisterns

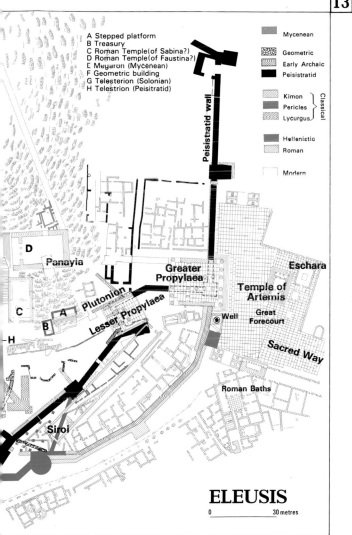

13

A Stepped platform
B Treasury
C Roman Temple (of Sabina?)
D Roman Temple (of Faustina?)
E Megaron (Mycenean)
F Geometric building
G Telesterion (Solonian)
H Telestrion (Peisistratid)

	Mycenean
	Geometric
	Early Archaic
	Peisistratid

Kimon ⎫
Pericles ⎬ Classical
Lycurgus ⎭

	Hellenistic
	Roman
	Modern

Peisistratid wall

D

Panayia

Plutonion

C

A

B

H

Lesser Propylaea

Siroi

Greater
Propylaea

Lesser Propylaea

Well

Eschara

Temple of
Artemis

Great
Forecourt

Sacred Way

Roman Baths

ELEUSIS

0 _____ 30 metres

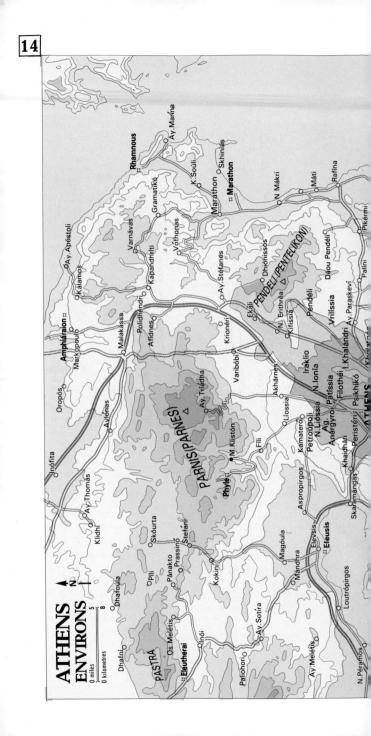